The Law of Treaties in Russia and other Member Countries of the Commonwealth of Independent States

Since the dissolution of the former USSR, twelve countries have, for the first time in modern history, been confronted with the task of defining their attitudes and policies towards the central means for law-making in the international community – the treaty. This is the first comparative commentary in any language on the law of treaties as reflected in the legislation of Russia and other member countries of the Commonwealth of Independent States (CIS), and in their international practice. Unusually, each has responded by enacting at least one law (sometimes more) on the procedures for treaty relations with other States and international organizations. The book is accompanied by original, authoritative translations of all the relevant laws, an extensive classified bibliography and an informed commentary on every article in the laws.

W. E. BUTLER is Chair of Comparative Law in the University of London, as well as founder and Director of the Vinogradoff Institute. He acts half-time as the Dean of the Faculty of Law (1993–8) and the M. M. Speranskii Professor of International and Comparative Law, Moscow Higher School of Social and Economic Sciences. His publications include *Soviet Law* (2nd edition, 1988), *Russian Civil Legislation* (3rd edition, 1999), *Constitutional Foundations of the CIS Countries* (1999), *Russian Law* (1999) and *Russian–English Legal Dictionary and Bibliographic Sources for Russian Law in English* (2001).

The Law of Treaties in Russia and the Commonwealth of Independent States

Text and Commentary

W. E. Butler

CAMBRIDGE
UNIVERSITY PRESS

PUBLISHED BY THE PRESS SYNDICATE OF THE UNIVERSITY OF CAMBRIDGE
The Pitt Building, Trumpington Street, Cambridge, United Kingdom

CAMBRIDGE UNIVERSITY PRESS
The Edinburgh Building, Cambridge CB2 2RU, UK
40 West 20th Street, New York, NY 10011-4211, USA
477 Williamstown Road, Port Melbourne, VIC 3207, Australia
Ruiz de Alarcón 13, 28014 Madrid, Spain
Dock House, The Waterfront, Cape Town 8001, South Africa

http://www.cambridge.org

First published 2002

Printed in the United Kingdom at the University Press, Cambridge

Typeface Plantin 10/12 pt   *System* LaTeX 2_ε [TB]

A catalogue record for this book is available from the British Library

Library of Congress Cataloguing in Publication data

The Law of treaties in Russia and the Commonwealth of Independent
states: text and commentary/[edited by] W.E. Butler.
p. cm.
Includes bibliographical references and index.
ISBN 0 521 81606 8
1. Russia (Federation)–Foreign relations–Law and legislation.
2. Russia (Federation)–Foreign relations–Treaties.
3. Treaty-making power–Russia (Federation)
4. Former Soviet republics–Foreign relations–Law and legislation.
5. Former Soviet republics–Foreign relations–Treaties.
6. Treaty-making power–Former Soviet republics.
I. Butler, William Elliott, 1939–

KLB2400.A28 2002 341.3′7′0947–dc21

2002073520

ISBN 0 521 81606 8 hardback

Contents

ANNEXES

UNION OF SOVIET SOCIALIST REPUBLICS

RUSSIA

Abbreviations

[Given in English alphabetical order as though the Russian was transliterated]

БМД	*Бюллетень международных договоров* [Bulletin of International Treaties] (1993–)
CIS	Commonwealth of Independent States
Commentary	V. P. Zvekov and B. I. Osminin (eds.), *Комментарий к Федеральному закону 'О международных договорах Российской Федерации'* [Commentary on the Federal Law on International Treaties of the Russian Federation] (1996)
EBRD	European Bank for Reconstruction and Development
ECSC	European Conference on Security and Cooperation
IBRD	International Bank for Reconstruction and Development
ILO	International Labour Organization
IMF	International Monetary Fund
M.	Moscow
MID	Ministry of Foreign Affairs
NATO	North Atlantic Treaty Organization
1969 Vienna Convention	Vienna Convention on the Law of Treaties of 23 May
1978 Law	Law of the USSR on the Procedure for the Conclusion, Execution, and Denunciation of International Treaties of the USSR
1993 Constitution RF	Constitution of the Russian Federation

1995 Law	Federal Law on International Treaties of the Russian Federation
OSCE	Organization for Security and Cooperation in Europe
РЕМП	*Российский ежегодник международного права* [Russian Yearbook of International Law] (1992–)
PRB	People's Republic of Bulgaria
RF	Russian Federation
РФ	Российская Федерация [Russian Federation]
RSFSR	Russian Soviet Federated Socialist Republics
САПП РФ	*Собрание актов Президента и Правительства Российской Федерации* [Collected Acts of the President and Government of the Russian Federation]
СЕМП	*Советский ежегодник международного права* [Soviet Yearbook of International Law]
SFSR	Soviet Federated Socialist Republic
Spb.	St. Petersburg
СУ РСФСР	*Собрание узаконений и распоряжений РСФСР* [Collection of Legislation and Regulations of the RSFSR]
СЗ РФ	*Собрание законодательства Российской Федерации* [Collection of Legislation of the Russian Federation]
СЗ СССР	*Собрание законов Союза Советской Социалистической Республикой* [Collection of Laws of the Union of Soviet Socialist Republics]
Talalaev	A. N. Talalaev, *Венская конвенция о праве международных договоров. Комментарий* [Vienna Convention on the Law of Treaties. Commentary] (1997)
TsIK SSSR	Central Executive Committee of the USSR
UN	United Nations
UNTS	*United Nations Treaty Series*
USSR	Union of Soviet Socialist Republics

Ведомости ВС РФ	*Ведомости Верховного Совета Российской Федерации* [Gazette of the Supreme Soviet of the Russian Federation]
Ведомости СНД и ВС РФ	*Ведомости Съезда народных депутатов и Верховного Совета Российской Федерации* [Gazette of the Congress of People's Deputies and Supreme Soviet of the Russian Federation]
Ведомости ФС РФ	*Ведомости Федерального Собрания Российской Федерации* [Gazette of the Federal Assembly of the Russian Federation]
Ведомости СССР	*Ведомости Верховного Совета СССР* [Gazette of the Supreme Soviet of the USSR]

Introduction

The Commentary is a traditional form of gloss widely employed in the pre-revolutionary Russian, Soviet, and post-Soviet legal traditions to guide and assist judges, arbitrators, advocates, jurisconsults, legal advisors, law teachers, law students, and other legal professionals in interpreting and applying a particular Law, Code, or other enactment. To many, it is the highest form of legal literature by virtue of the authoritativeness of its doctrinal propositions.

The present volume is a comparative commentary on the legislation of the twelve members of the Commonwealth of Independent States (CIS) regulating the procedure for the conclusion, ratification, performance, and termination of international treaties. It is believed to be the first article-by-article comparative Commentary in any language on CIS enactments from every single member.

The point of departure is the 1995 Federal Law on International Treaties of the Russian Federation. Although not the first to be enacted in the CIS after the dissolution of the former USSR, this Law is the most comprehensive and considered enactment on the subject and for Russia is the first dedicated Law on the subject in *Russian* history.

The former Soviet Union adopted the Decree on the Procedure for the Conclusion of International Treaties of the USSR in 1925[1] and in that same year a Decree on the Procedure for the Submission of International Treaties and Agreements Concluded in the Name of the USSR for Approval, Confirmation, and Ratification of the Government of the USSR.[2] On the basis of the 1936 Constitution of the USSR a brief Law on the Procedure for the Ratification and Denunciation of International Treaties of the USSR was enacted in 1938.[3] With the introduction of a new USSR

[1] *СЗ СССР* (1925), no. 35, item 258; transl. in *Soviet Statutes and Decisions*, III, no. 4 (1967), p. 53, and below as an annex.

[2] *СЗ СССР* (1925), no. 68, item 503; transl. in *Soviet Statutes and Decisions*, III, no. 4 (1967), pp. 54–6, and below as an annex.

[3] *Ведомости Верховного Совета СССР* (1938), no. 11; transl. in *Soviet Statutes and Decisions*, III, no. 4 (1967), pp. 56–7, and below as an annex.

Constitution in 1977, the 1938 Law was replaced by the 1978 Law on the Procedure for the Conclusion, Performance, and Denunciation of International Treaties of the USSR.[4]

The 1995 Law, based on the 1993 Constitution of the Russian Federation, also is the first to reflect fully the accession of the former Soviet Union to the 1969 Vienna Convention,[5] although the 1978 USSR Law also gave attention to that Convention notwithstanding the fact that the Soviet Union at the time had not ratified it. Some account also is taken in the 1995 Law of the 1986 Vienna Convention on the Law of Treaties Between States and International Organizations or Between International Organizations.[6] Russia is not a party to the 1978 Vienna Convention on the Legal Succession of States with Respect to Treaties.[7]

One may speculate why the former Soviet Union and the member countries of the CIS have found it necessary to not merely legislate on the procedure for the conclusion, performance, and termination of treaties, but to produce laws which amount to a veritable codification of the relevant rules. To be sure, the early Soviet decrees were minimalist and perhaps the product of good administrative housekeeping and an attempt to demarcate lines of administrative responsibility. In my view the Vienna Conference on the Law of Treaties made its own contribution to the Soviet approach to introducing comprehensive domestic legislation on the subject. There will have been those who wished to 'internationalize'

[4] *Ведомости Верховного Совета СССР* (1978), no. 28, item 439; transl. in *International Legal Materials*, XVII (1978), 1115–22; W. E. Butler, *Basic Documents on the Soviet Legal System* (Dobbs Ferry, Oceana Publications, 1983), pp. 285–92; and below as an annex.

[5] The 1969 Vienna Convention on the Law of Treaties was signed on 23 May 1969 and entered into force on 27 January 1980. The former Soviet Union acceded with effect from 29 April 1986. For the Russian text of the Convention, see K. A. Bekiashev and A. G. Khodakov (comps.), *Международное публичное право: Сборник документов* [Public International Law: Collection of Documents] (M., izd-vo BEK, 1996), I, pp. 67–87; Iu. M. Kolosov and E. S. Krivchikova (comps.), *Действующее международное право в трех томах* [Prevailing International Law in Three Volumes] (M., izd-vo Moskovskogo nezavisimovogo instituta mezhdunarodnogo prava, 1996), I, pp. 343–71; and A. N. Talalaev, *Венская конвенция о праве международных договоров. Комментарий* [Vienna Convention on the Law of Treaties. Commentary] (M., Iuridicheskaia literatura, 1997), who provides the Russian, English, French, and Spanish language texts.

[6] The Convention was signed on 21 March 1986 but has not entered into force. Russia has not ratified the Convention. For the Russian text, see K. A. Bekiashev and A. G. Khodakov (comps.), *Международное публичное право: Сборник документов* [Public International Law: Collection of Documents] (M., izd-vo BEK, 1996), I, pp. 87–113; Iu. M. Kolosov and E. S. Krivchikova (comps.), *Действующее международное право в трех томах* [Prevailing International Law in Three Volumes] (M., izd-vo Moskovskogo nezavisimogo instituta mezhdunarodnogo prava, 1996), I, pp. 372–408.

[7] See the Russian text in Iu. M. Kolosov and E. S. Krivchikova (comps.), *Действующее международное право в трех томах* [Prevailing International Law in Three Volumes] (M., izd-vo Moskovskogo nezavisimogo instituta mezhdunarodnogo prava, 1996), I, pp. 433–56.

Soviet legislation by codifying accepted international practices and those who wished to draw a ring around what the Soviet Union considered acceptable by way of international practice at the time. Whatever the answer may be, in the post-Soviet era the member countries of the CIS had either to repeal the 1978 USSR Law on treaties (which none of them did), or replace it with their own (which eventually all of them have done).

The present volume originated as part of the Lauterpacht Lectures delivered at Cambridge University in autumn 1991 on 'Russian Approaches to International Law', several short weeks before the Soviet Union disappeared forever. They have been in gestation ever since, waiting for Russian doctrine and State practice to accommodate the adjustments that have ensued. For time to prepare those lectures I am indebted to The Leverhulme Foundation for welcome support, and to Professor Sir Eli Lauterpacht for the invitation to deliver them.

Much of the material has been used in my LL.M. course on The Law of International Treaties offered (in the Russian language) at the Moscow Higher School of Social and Economic Sciences since 1995, where I have served on secondment from University College London as the M. M. Speranskii Professor of International and Comparative Law. It has benefited from the reflections, questions, and comments of postgraduates in this course, the more absorbing as the subject is taking new directions by reason of the 1995 Law and a particularly exciting era of Russian State practice. It is informed by such literature as has appeared, central place among which must be held by the admirable *Комментарий к федеральному закону 'О международных договорах Российской федераций'* [Commentary on the Federal Law on International Treaties of the Russian Federation] (M., izd-vo Spark, 1996) under the general editorship of V. P. Zvekov and B. I. Osminin. That Commentary has been cited frequently herein, most especially for data concerning Ministry of Foreign Affairs practices; in each case the name of the individual author who produced the particular observations is given. All have extensive experience in the practice of international law and diplomacy, and several took part in drafting the 1995 Law and in the negotiations leading to the 1969 Vienna Convention. Extensive use also has been made of A. N. Talalaev, *Венская конвенция о праве международных договоров. Комментарий* [Vienna Convention on the Law of Treaties. Commentary] (M., Iuridicheskaia literatura, 1997).

All translations have been made by myself from the Russian text published in the official gazettes concerned or in Russian texts supplied by the Ministry of Foreign Affairs of the country concerned (Armenia, Georgia). The names of parliaments have changed in most member countries of the CIS; the 'mejlis' in various spellings is used in Central Asia and the Caucasus, and for Ukraine I have used the Ukrainian term 'Rada' instead of 'Soviet', as that word would be expressed in the Russian language.

For the history of the development of the Law of Treaties in Russia, the incomparable source remains V. E. Grabar, *The History of the Development of International Law in Russia 1647–1917*, transl. W. E. Butler (Oxford, Clarendon Press, 1990). Other suggested sources are set out in the bibliography.

For the Soviet period the leading work is Jan F. Triska and Robert M. Slusser, *The Theory, Law, and Policy of Soviet Treaties* (Stanford, Stanford University Press, 1962).

So far as I can determine, this is the first comparative analysis of and commentary on the treaty laws of the Independent States other than the Russian Federation.[8] The annexes include my translations of the individual CIS treaty laws, including both generations of such laws where they exist, and the sequence of principal USSR enactments on the law of treaties. It should be borne in mind that the 1978 USSR Law on treaties remained in force on the territories of the CIS countries until they enacted their own treaty laws, for most of them served as the model for the first generation of treaty laws, and that many treaties still in force were ratified, confirmed, adopted, or acceded to at a time when one or another of the USSR enactments was in force.

Status juris: 1 April 2002, subject to the availability of amendments to Independent State legislation.

[8] For an early undertaking in this direction, see W. E. Butler, 'The Law of Treaties in Central Asia', in R. Mullerson, M. Fitzmaurice, and M. Andenas (eds.), *Constitutional Reform and International Law in Central and Eastern Europe* (The Hague, Kluwer Law International, 1998), pp. 287–94.

Federal Law of the Russian Federation on International Treaties of the Russian Federation

[Federal Law of 15 July 1995.
СЗ РФ (1995), no. 29, item 2757]

[Preamble]

International treaties form the legal foundation of inter-State relations and promote the maintenance of universal peace and security and the development of international cooperation in accordance with the purposes and principles of the United Nations. An important role belongs to international treaties in the defence of the basic rights and freedoms of man and in ensuring the legal interests of States.

International treaties of the Russian Federation, together with generally-recognized principles and norms of international law, are in accordance with the Constitution of the Russian Federation an integral part of its legal system. International treaties are a material element of the stability of the international legal order and relations of Russia with foreign countries and the functioning of a rule-of-law State.

The Russian Federation favours undeviating compliance with treaty and customary norms and affirms its adherence to the basic principle of international law – the principle of the good-faith fulfilment of international obligations.

Russia

The law of treaties has been defined as the 'aggregate of international legal norms, both treaty and customary, determining the procedure for the conclusion, conditions of validity, operation, and termination of international treaties'.[9] The Preamble, the most far-reaching of any of the CIS treaty laws, reflects a significant change in the traditional Soviet theory of international law, which emphasized the place of the treaty as the principal

[9] S. G. Kargopolov, in A. N. Sokolov (ed.), *Россия на рубеже веков* [Russia on the Borderline of Centuries] (Kaliningrad, Iantarnyi skaz, 2001), p. 712.

source of international law.[10] No such claim is made for the international treaty in this preambular formulation, although the undoubted significance of the treaty as a foundation stone of the international system is set out. The subordination of international treaties to the UN Charter has never previously been mentioned in Soviet or Russian legislation. The Commentary declares that in the event of a divergence between the UN Charter and an international treaty, the provisions of the Charter shall prevail (Article 103).[11]

The status of the Preamble, by analogy with the Preamble to the 1969 Vienna Convention, would be described by Talalaev as follows: 'The Preamble as a constituent integral part of the Vienna Convention must be taken into account when interpreting all of its Articles and Annexes thereto; that is, they must be interpreted by proceeding from the purposes and principles set out in the Preamble.'[12]

The place of international treaties in the Russian legal system is ambiguous. The formulation is based on Article 15 of the 1993 Constitution,[13] but in the Preamble acquires a different colouration. The 1993 Constitution speaks in Article 15(4) of 'generally-recognized principles and norms of international law and international treaties of the Russian Federation'; that is, mention is made first of generally-recognized principles and then of international treaties, which formulation reflects the widely accepted pre-eminent role of general principles. These are understood by most Russian international lawyers to refer to 'general, customary international law'.[14] The Preamble, in reversing the formulation set out in the Constitution, leaves a different impression when

[10] G. I. Tunkin, *Theory of International Law*, transl. W. E. Butler (Cambridge, Mass., Harvard University Press, 1974), p. 133: 'treaty norms presently occupy the principal place in international law as a result of the large growth in the number of international agreements'; confirmed in G. I. Tunkin, *Теория международного права* [Theory of International Law] (M., Zertsalo, 2000), p. 118. Also see G. V. Ignatenko, *Международное право* [International Law] (2nd edn. M., Mezhdunarodnye otnosheniia, 1995), p. 93, where Section 2 is entitled: 'International Treaty – The Principal Source of International Law'. Other writers, although they treat international treaties first and international custom second, no longer postulate a hierarchy between them. See P. N. Biriukov, *Международное право* [International Law] (M., Iurist, 1998), pp. 40–5; Iu. M. Kolosov and V. I. Kuznetsov (eds.), *Международное право* [International Law] (2nd edn.; M., Mezhdunarodnye otnosheniia, 1998), pp. 18–27; G. M. Melkov and M. V. Filimonova, in K. A. Bekiashev (ed.), *Международное публичное право* [Public International Law] (M., Prospekt, 1998), pp. 18–22.

[11] I. I. Lukashuk, Commentary, p. 6.

[12] Talalaev, p. 8.

[13] W. E. Butler (transl.), *Constitutional Foundations of the CIS Countries* (The Hague, Kluwer Law International, 1999), p. 426.

[14] Lukashuk, 'Конституция России и Международное право' [The Constitution of Russia and International Law], *РЕМП* 1995, p. 171.

read independently of the Constitutional formulation. The same reversal occurs in the last paragraph of the Preamble.

The reference to 'its legal system' is understood by most commentators to mean the legal system of the Russian Federation. However, one commentator believes the Constitution here refers to the 'Russian' [*Русская*, and not *Российская*] Legal System, by which he understands not merely the Russian Federation, but also Ukraine, Belarus, and the Slavs of southern Europe.[15] Another has called attention to the Russian concept of a 'legal system' as the 'entire aggregate of legal phenomena, including the realization of law, legal consciousness, legal culture, and others ... Article 15 of the Constitution of the Russian Federation is addressed not only to the legislator, but to any applier of law, above all the courts'.[16]

The Preamble links international treaties directly with the creation of a rule-of-law State, which likewise is a standard laid down in the 1993 Constitution.[17]

The final paragraph of the Preamble links treaties as one form of international obligation to customary norms of international law as another form of international obligation and restates the requirement of the Russian Federation to comply in good faith with the principle of the fulfilment of such obligations. This paraphrases to some extent the Preamble to the 1969 Vienna Convention.

The debates in the Assembly which prepared the draft 1993 Constitution and in the State Duma committees which prepared the 1995 Law disclose that 'Russia embraced the idea of direct incorporation of international law as part of a general policy of advancing the rule of law at the international and domestic levels. The 1993 Constitution represents a bold political commitment to the international community and its fundamental values expressed in principles and norms of international law.'[18]

[15] V. N. Siniukov, *Русская правовая система* [Russian Legal System] (M., 1994); also see Siniukov, in L. A. Morozova (ed.), 'Российская правовая система и международное право : современные проблемы взаимодействия' [Russian Legal System and International Law: Contemporary Problems of Interaction], *Государство и право*, no. 2 (1996), pp. 10–11.

[16] S. Polenina, in L. A. Morozova, 'Российская правовая система и международное право: современные проблемы взаимодействия' [Russian Legal System and International Law: Contemporary Problems of Interaction], *Государство и право*, no. 2 (1996), p. 4.

[17] Butler, *Constitutional Foundations of the CIS Countries* (The Hague, Kluwer Law International, 1999), p. 421: 'The Russian Federation – Russia is a democratic federated rule-of-law State with a republic form of Government' (Article 1[1]).

[18] G. Danilenko, 'The New Russian Constitution and International Law', American Journal of International Law, LXXXVIII (1994), 470.

CIS

The *Armenian, Azerbaidzhan, Georgian, Moldovan*, and *Uzbekistan* treaty laws do not contain a Preamble.

The Preamble of the *Belarus* treaty law places quite a different emphasis upon the role of treaties. Reference is first made to the Constitution and 'other legislation' of Belarus, which read literally places these ahead of treaties. The key term is 'perform', for presumably the reference to 'conclude' means the procedures within Belarus for concluding an international treaty. The word 'perform', however, raises the question of whether a treaty is to be performed in accordance with its conditions or to be read against Belarus legislation, in which case inconsistent Belarus legislation, possibly subordinate legislation as well, may prevail. It is an unhappy formulation and not consistent with other provisions establishing the primacy of the international treaty.

The Preamble secondarily mentions generally-recognized principles and norms of international law, of which the 1969 Vienna Convention is treated as an example. Belarus is a party to the 1969 Vienna Convention.

The primacy of Belarus domestic law is accentuated by the second paragraph of the Preamble of the Belarus treaty law, although the formulation is declaratory. To say that it is 'not permitted' to 'conclude' international treaties which are contrary to the Belarus Constitution does not address the question of who determines whether they are contrary or not and at what stage of the 'conclusion' process the issue must be addressed.

The *Kazakhstan* treaty law Preamble is concerned principally with procedural issues of Kazakhstan constitutional law. The document is styled an 'Edict of the President of Kazakhstan Having the Force of a Law', and the President in the Preamble cites his authority for issuing the Edict: a Law of 10 December 1993 which authorized the President to act when the Kazakhstan parliament was unable to do so. Second, the Preamble makes clear that the Kazakhstan Constitution calls for such a Law to unify the procedures for treaty-making. Third, the treaty law is viewed as part of the machinery of Kazakhstan foreign policy,[19] which is undoubtedly the case but rarely acknowledged explicitly in CIS treaty laws (*Turkmenistan* and *Ukraine* do the same in the Preamble to their treaty laws). It should be noted that the Edict was adopted in December 1995, that is, several months after the Kazakhstan Constitution of September 1995.

[19] Sarsembaev has declared that 'usually one-fourth of all treaties concluded by a State are political, one-half are economic and trade treaties, and one-quarter are devoted to everything else'. See M. A. Sarsembaev, *Международное право* [International Law] (Almaty, Zheti zhargy, 1996), p. 78.

The Preamble of the 1999 *Kyrgyzstan* treaty law is close in substance to that of the Russian Federation, although in a less elegant and more direct formulation. The first paragraph is programmatic, declaring that international treaties are the legal foundation of the international relations of Kyrgyzstan. A more ambitious statement might have reserved that position for international law itself.

The second paragraph of the Preamble of the Kyrgyzstan treaty law is based on Article 12(3) of the 1993 Constitution of the Kyrgyz Republic[20] but differs in two key respects. The Constitution refers to 'inter-State treaties ratified' by Kyrgyzstan, whereas the treaty law Preamble mentions 'international treaties' and omits the requirement of ratification. Thus, the Constitution excludes intergovernmental and interdepartmental treaties from being a part of Kyrgyz legislation, whereas the treaty law would include them. The legal status of intergovernmental and interdepartmental treaties must, therefore, be in doubt in Kyrgyzstan with respect to local law. The Constitution also mentions 'other norms of international law' as being part of Kyrgyz legislation, a formulation omitted from the Kyrgyz treaty law for no apparent reason.

Both the Kyrgyzstan Constitution and treaty law provide that the treaties within their respective purview are an 'integral and directly operating part of the legislation of the Kyrgyz Republic'. The term 'directly operating' here means 'direct effect'. 'Integral' indicates that treaties sit side-by-side with other legislation of Kyrgyzstan.

The third preambular paragraph, affirming the essence of the principle of *pacta sunt servanda*, is programmatic; it is replicated in the 1999 *Tadzhikistan* treaty law.

The 1999 *Tadzhikistan* treaty law replicates the first paragraph of the Kyrgyzstan treaty law and continues the programmatic thesis by accentuating the fact that treaties promote the maintenance of peace and security and the development of international cooperation in accordance with the principles and purposes of the United Nations. Tadzhikistan, having been the beneficiary of a UN presence throughout much of the civil strife that afflicted that Republic, understandably would make reference to the UN Charter. However, the second programmatic sentence of the first paragraph smacks of being patronizing in providing that international treaties have an 'important role in the defence of the basic rights and freedoms of man and in ensuring the legal interests of States'.

As noted above, the *Turkmenistan* treaty law mentions the foreign policy role of international treaties, but qualifies that role with the principles 'proclaimed and consolidated in the Constitution of Turkmenistan'.

20 Translated in W. E. Butler, *Constitutional Foundations of the CIS Countries* (The Hague, Kluwer Law International, 1999), p. 306.

This provision has particular reference to Article 1 of the Turkmenistan Constitution, which proclaims the country to be a permanently neutral State as confirmed by a Resolution of the UN General Assembly of 12 December 1995, and Article 6 of the Constitution, which elaborates the foreign policy obligations of Turkmenistan.[21]

In a laconic formulation *Ukraine* sees the purpose of its treaty law as ensuring the national interests of Ukraine, together with achieving the foreign policy objectives enshrined in the Ukrainian Constitution.

[21] Translated in W. E. Butler, *Constitutional Foundations of the CIS Countries* (The Hague, Kluwer Law International, 1999), pp. 558–559.

Section I

General Provisions

Article 1 Tasks and Sphere of Application of Present Federal Law

1. The present Federal Law determines the procedure for the conclusion, fulfilment, and termination of international treaties of the Russian Federation.

International treaties of the Russian Federation shall be concluded, fulfilled, and terminated in accordance with generally-recognized principles and norms of international law, the provisions of the treaty itself, the Constitution of the Russian Federation, and the present Federal Law.

2. The present Federal Law shall apply with respect to international treaties of the Russian Federation (inter-State treaties and treaties of an interdepartmental character) irrespective of the type and name thereof (treaty, agreement, convention, protocol, exchange of letters or notes, or other types and names of international treaties).

3. The present Federal Law shall extend to international treaties to which the Russian Federation is a party as the State-continuer of the USSR.

Russia

1 Although the first paragraph of point one read alone would appear to be exhaustive, the formulation of the second paragraph of point one is more accurate. The 1995 Law determines only part of the procedure for the conclusion, fulfilment, and termination of international treaties of the RF and is subject to being read against the provisions of customary international law, the 1969 Vienna Convention, the provisions of individual treaties, the 1993 Constitution, and the 1995 Law. The 1995 Law is itself elaborated by individual subordinate normative acts of the RF.

The Commentary observes that the reference to 'provisions of the treaty itself' and its placement ahead of the reference to the 1993 Constitution does not mean that the individual treaty enjoys supremacy over the 1993 Constitution, but rather that individual treaty provisions in this respect are a *lex specialis*.[22]

[22] Lukashuk, Commentary, pp. 7–8.

CIS

In the treaty laws of Turkmenistan and Ukraine the equivalent of this provision is found in the Preamble. The Moldovan treaty law does not address the matters regulated by this Article.

Russia

2 The Russian legal system, just as other CIS legal systems, distinguishes between the form (written or oral), type (inter-State, intergovernmental, or interdepartmental), and name (treaty, agreement, protocol, pact, etc.) of an international treaty. The terminology and classifications are not entirely satisfactory, especially with respect to the 'types' of treaties, which depend upon a mutuality based on the assumption that the parties share equivalent levels of types. That is not the case in a treaty between a State and an international organization. Insofar as the treaty laws of the CIS also regulate treaties with international organizations, they go beyond the 1969 Vienna Convention; however, since most of their provisions relate to internal procedures of treaty-making, this makes little difference.[23]

The classification of a treaty by 'type' can have important consequences for the role of the treaty within the Russian legal system. If one accepts that Article 15 of the 1993 Russian Constitution refers to 'ratified' international treaties, and not all international treaties of the RF, one observer has traced the relationship between a treaty and Russian normative legal acts as follows: (1) only a self-executing, officially published, ratified international treaty is applied in preference to a federal law; (2) a self-executing, officially published inter-State treaty, either ratified or not ratified, is applied in preference to an edict of the President of the RF of a normative character; (3) a self-executing, officially published, ratified or not ratified, inter-State or intergovernmental treaty is applied in preference to a decree of the Government of a normative character; and (4) any self-executing, officially published treaty is applied in preference to the normative act of a department.[24]

The 1995 Law applies to all treaties of the RF irrespective of the level of the State agency which represented the RF or the name or type of such treaty, even though intergovernmental treaties are not singled out

[23] Talalaev observes that 'all articles of the 1969 Vienna Convention were formulated by taking into account their application only to treaties between States'. See Talalaev, p. 9.

[24] A. V. Meleshnikov, 'Оговорки и отсылки международного права и российского законодательства' [Reservations and References of International Law and Russian Legislation], in V. M. Baranov (ed.), *Проблемы юридической техники* [Problems of Legal Technique] (Nizhnii Novgorod, Nizhegorodskaia pravovaia akademiia, 2000), pp. 439–40.

for mention here. This formulation is adapted from Article 2(1)(a) of the 1969 Vienna Convention, which incorporates the customary rule that the name of an international obligation does not affect its binding force. The 1995 Law is confined to treaties in written form (see Article 2, below), following the 1969 Vienna Convention; customary international law recognizes that a treaty could also be concluded orally between duly empowered representatives of States.

Although the position is not made expressly clear in this Article of the 1995 Federal Law, international treaties of the RF also include those concluded by the RF with international organizations (see Article 2, below).

CIS

The *Armenian* (Article 1), *Kazakhstan* (Article 1[1]),[25] *Kyrgyzstan* (Article 1[1]), *Ukrainian* (Article 1[1]), and *Uzbekistan* (Article 2) treaty laws make explicit that all three categories of international treaty are included irrespective of the form in which they may be concluded; that is, in written or oral form. The 1999 *Tadzhikistan* and the *Turkmenistan* treaty laws in effect reach this same result by allowing the expression of consent to a treaty 'by other means concerning which the parties have agreed' (Article 2, respectively).

The *Azerbaidzhan* (Article 1), *Georgian* (Articles 2 and 3), *Kazakhstan* (Articles 1[1] and 2)[26] treaty laws take the opposite view and expressly extend, as does the 1969 Vienna Convention, only to treaties in written form.

The *Belarus* treaty law (Article 1) applies only to inter-State and intergovernmental treaties, and those only in written form (Article 2). Interdepartmental treaties are expressly reserved to the jurisdiction of the President of Belarus.

In *Kazakhstan* (Article 1[2]) the treaty law is generally applicable to all types of international treaties of the Republic,[27] with the proviso that the

[25] A Kazakhstan international lawyer has called treaties concluded in oral form 'gentlemen's agreements'. See M. A. Sarsembaev, *Международное право* [International Law] (Almaty, Zheti zhargy, 1996), p. 97.

[26] In fact Articles 1(1) and 2 of the Kazakhstan treaty law are inconsistent on the point. Article 1(1) refers to treaties irrespective of 'form and name', whereas Article 2 refers only to the 'written form'. If Article 2 expresses the intention of the legislator correctly, the formulation of Article 1(1) should be 'type and name'. A Kazakhstan international lawyer wrote in 1996 that the '1995 Constitution of the Republic Kazakhstan determines for Kazakhstan the general procedure for the conclusion of international treaties'. See M. A. Sarsembaev, *Международное право* [International Law] (Almaty, Zheti zhargy, 1996), p. 77. No mention is made in the textbook of the Kazakhstan treaty law.

[27] Sarsembaev observes that 'there is a category of treaties which by structure consists of two or more separate documents. Such treaties are called an *exchange of notes*.

President may with respect to agencies subordinate and accountable to him introduce a different procedure other than that stipulated in the treaty law for the conclusion, performance, and denunciation of international treaties.

The *Kazakhstan* and *Turkmenistan* treaty laws expressly extend to international treaties concluded with international organizations.

Russia

3 The 1995 Law applies to international treaties of the RF concluded by the former USSR. In reality, however, the 1995 Law could not extend to the process of the conclusion of such treaties, merely to the fulfilment and termination thereof, and even in these respects would have regard to the individual provisions of such treaties of the USSR as *lex specialis*.

The expressions 'State-continuer' and 'legal-continuer' are new in international practice and reflect both the international legal and constitutional history of the RF during the twentieth century and the decision of the Government of the RF to assume the international obligations of the former USSR on a basis other than as legal successor. When the Russian Empire broke up in 1917 and thereafter into a number of independent States and other entities, the Russian Soviet Federated Socialist Republic (RSFSR) regarded itself as the legal successor of the Empire and to those of its international treaty obligations as it cared to assume. The USSR was formed on the basis of the Treaty of the Union concluded on 30 December 1922 and dissolved when the Treaty was denounced by its surviving initial participants on 12 December 1991.[28] With the demise of the USSR as an independent State, the RSFSR, later renamed the RF, regarded itself not as the legal successor of the USSR but rather as the 'legal-continuer' or 'State-continuer' of Russia, which had existed for more than ten centuries and never disappeared, and of the USSR. A diplomatic Note to this effect was circulated to the Heads of Diplomatic

In centuries past a treaty consisted of several interconnected letters, instruments, and other documents, which can be demonstrated by the example of the Treaty between the Young Zhous of Kazakhstan and Russia, which consisted of a message of Khan Abulkhair of 8 September 1730, a letter of 2 January 1731, and an instrument of Anna Ioannovna concerning the wish of Russia to take the lands of the Young Zhous under her protection of 19 February 1731.' See M. A. Sarsembaev, *Международное право* [International Law] (Almaty, Zheti zhargy, 1996), pp. 79–80.

28 Decree of the RSFSR Supreme Soviet on the Denunciation of the Treaty on the Formation of the USSR, adopted 12 December 1991. *Российская газета*, 17 December 1991, p. 1, cols. 4–5; transl. in W. E. Butler, *Basic Legal Documents of the Russian Federation* (Dobbs Ferry, Oceana Publications, 1992), p. 53.

Representations in Moscow on 13 January 1992,[29] although the term 'legal-continuer' or 'State-continuer' was not actually used. The editors of the official collection of Russian foreign policy documents prepared by the Ministry of Foreign Affairs of the RF commenced their series as from 12 June 1990, the date of the proclamation of the Declaration of State Sovereignty of Russia.[30] After the termination of the existence in December 1991 of the USSR, 'a new era commenced in the formation and confirmation of the foreign policy of Russia as a policy of a sovereign great power-continuer of the Soviet Union'.[31]

The other fourteen union republics which comprised the USSR have each regarded themselves as legal successors to the former USSR to the individual obligations and property apportioned to them (although the Baltic republics each had their own positions on their statehood, which does not concern us here).[32]

In fact, the situation is immensely complicated. On 4 December 1991 nine union republics of the USSR assembled in Moscow to sign the Treaty on Legal Succession with Respect to the External State Debt and Assets of the USSR; that Treaty referred to the USSR as the 'predecessor-State' and all the union republics were deemed to be 'legal successor States'. Four days later, on 8 December 1991, the RF, Belarus, and Ukraine signed an agreement in which they denounced the 1922 Treaty of the Union. On 24 December 1991 the President of the RF sent a message to the UN Secretary-General which affirmed that the RF would retain responsibility in full for all the rights and obligations of the USSR in accordance with the UN Charter, including financial obligations. In addition to the Note sent to the heads of diplomatic representations in Moscow on 13 January 1992, a Commission for Legal Succession with Respect to Treaties was formed within the framework of the CIS. In July 1992 it produced a Memorandum on Mutual Understanding with Regard to Questions of Legal Succession in Respect of Treaties of the

29 *Дипломатический вестник*, no. 2–3 (1992), p. 34; Iu. M. Kolosov and E. S. Krivchikova (comps.), *Действующее международное право в трех томах* [Prevailing International Law in Three Volumes] (M., izd-vo Moskovskogo nezavisimogo instituta mezhdunarodnogo prava, 1996), I, p. 476.

30 *Ведомости СНД и ВС РСФСР* (1990), no. 2, item 22.

31 See *Внешняя политика России: сборник документов 1990–1992* [Foreign Policy of Russia: Collection of Documents 1990–1992] (M., Mezhdunarodnye otnosheniia, 1996–). The editors state that 'In January 1992, 131 States recognized Russia' (p. 5).

32 In the view of some jurists, the other eleven members of the CIS (excluding Russia) are both legal successors in relevant part of the former USSR and 'continue the legal personality of the former union republics, that is, effectuate continuity'. See I. Klapas, 'Правопреемство и континуитет в международном праве' [Legal Succession and Continuity in International Law], *Московский журнал международного права*, no. 4 (1992), p. 33.

Former USSR of Mutual Interest. The Memorandum was preceded and followed by six agreements concerned with, principally, debt and property questions.

The confusion between the concepts of 'continuer' and 'legal-successor' was compounded by inconsistent statements by State officials and public figures from the CIS countries, although, as one observer has commented, the two concepts are 'incompatible'. Elementary logic dictates that 'one cannot simultaneously be the continuer and the legal successor'.[33]

This position had a number of practical consequences, among them the fact that the RF replaced the USSR on the Security Council of the United Nations, whereas those other union republics who were not members of the United Nations (only Ukraine and Belarus were) each joined the Organization anew.[34] The RF also moved quickly to absorb on the basis of individual agreement with each former union republic the proportionate share of each for the foreign indebtedness of the USSR.[35]

The RF is in the process of agreeing with individual countries one by one the extent to which treaties concluded with the USSR may remain in force. An example of the approach taken is the Agreement in the Form of an Exchange of Letters between the Government of the Russian

[33] See the analysis, and literature cited, in I. N. Bartsits, *Правовое пространство России: вопросы конституционной теории и практики* [Legal Space of Russia: Questions of Constitutional Theory and Practice] (M., izd-vo MGU, 2000), p. 241.

[34] See the Message of B. N. Eltsyn to the Secretary-General of the United Nations, 24 December 1991: 'membership of the Union of Soviet Socialist Republics in the United Nations, including in the Security Council and in all organs and organizations of the United Nations system, shall be continued by the Russian Federation with the support of the countries of the Commonwealth of Independent States. In this connection I request that the name "Russian Federation" be used in the United Nations in place of the name "Union of Soviet Socialist Republics". The Russian Federation shall retain in full the responsibility for all the rights and obligations of the USSR in accordance with the United Nations Charter, including financial obligations'. *Дипломатический вестник*, no. 1 (1992), p. 13; Iu. M. Kolosov and E. S. Krivchikova (comps.), *Действующее международное право в трех томах* [Prevailing International Law in Three Volumes] (M., izd-vo Moskovskogo nezavisimogo instituta mezhdunarodnogo prava, 1996), p. 475.

[35] See, respectively, the Treaty on Legal Succession with Respect to the Foreign State Debt and Assets of the USSR, signed 4 December 1991; the Agreement on Additions to the Treaty on Legal Succession with Respect to the Foreign State Debt and Assets of the Former USSR, signed 13 March 1992; the Agreement on the Heads of States of the Commonwealth of Independent States on the Ownership of the Former USSR Abroad, signed 30 December 1991, and the Agreement on the Distribution of All Ownership of the Former USSR Abroad, signed 6 July 1992; and the Agreement on Legal Succession with Respect to the State Archives of the Former USSR, signed 6 July 1992. The texts are respectively published in Iu. M. Kolosov and E. S. Krivchikova (comps.), *Действующее международное право в трех томах* [Prevailing International Law in Three Volumes] (M., izd-vo Moskovskogo nezavisimogo instituta mezhdunarodnogo prava, 1996), I, pp. 476–92.

Federation and the Government of the Republic of Bulgaria with Regard to the Results of the Inventorization of Inter-State and Intergovernmental Treaties and Agreements Concluded between the USSR and PRB During the Period from 1945 through 1991, done at Moscow on 27 April 1996.[36] In this document reference is made to the RF in its capacity as the 'State-continuer' of the USSR, as set out in the Note of 13 January 1992. The Parties divided the relevant treaties into four annexes: (i) treaties and agreements which continue to operate in relations between the RF and Bulgaria; (ii) treaties and agreements which remain in force but require some adjustments; these will be revised or replaced by new treaties; (iii) treaties and agreements to be considered individually in order to clarify the extent of rights and obligations for the two parties and for third States for which such rights and obligations arise as a consequence of the termination of the existence of the USSR; and (iv) treaties and agreements which are terminated, with the proviso that certain internal procedures are required to fully terminate them. Treaties and agreements in which the possibility of unilateral termination was provided are considered to have been terminated after expiry of the respective period from the date of receipt of first notification thereof unless the second notification is made before the expiry of the said period. The Parties also agreed to conduct individual consultations with regard to a group of 'treaties of a confidential character'. Finally, in the course of the negotiations the Parties agreed that the inventorying of treaties and agreements does 'not affect the rights and obligations of third countries emanating from their legal succession with regard to international treaties of the former USSR in accordance with generally-recognized principles and norms of international law'.

The Russian role as 'State-continuer' has not been without inconsistencies. First, in some documents the term 'legal successor' has been used. Read literally, the so-called Minsk Agreement of 8 December 1991 between Belarus, Russia, and Ukraine stated that the 'USSR as a subject of international law and a geopolitical reality terminates its existence' (Preamble).[37] It has been suggested that the example of Russia 'proves

[36] *БМД*, no. 10 (1996), pp. 66–79.

[37] Translated in W. E. Butler, *Basic Legal Documents of the Russian Federation* (Dobbs Ferry, Oceana Publications, 1992), p. 3. This was an ambitious statement, for although the three States were original founders of the USSR in 1922, there was a fourth (the Transcaucasian SFSR) which later split up into Armenia, Azerbaidzhan, and Georgia – each arguably a continuer or legal successor to the Transcaucasian SFSR and each having a voice in the ultimate existence of the USSR. Moreover, in December 1991, there were yet another six union republics who were undeniably part of the USSR, whatever the absence of treaty formalities to confirm their accession to the 1922 Treaty of the Union. Had two or more of the union republics decided to retain the USSR and

that in certain circumstances the same State may simultaneously act as the legal successor with respect to some rights and as the State-continuer with respect to others'.[38] However, the 'decision in principle of Russia to assume treaty obligations of the former Soviet Union merely confirms the continuity thereof, and not legal succession'.[39]

CIS

Only one CIS treaty law, besides that of the RF, addresses the issue of State succession to treaties of the former USSR. The *Georgian* (Article 2[2]) treaty law provides that it extends to international treaties of the former USSR with regard to which Georgia has declared itself to be a legal successor. This can relate only to relevant provisions of the said treaty law, which would preclude those regulating the conclusion of treaties.

A Kazakh jurist has written on this issue that 'The demise of the USSR, its disappearance from the political map of the world, entailed the termination of a significant portion of the treaties concluded by the USSR during the 70 years of its existence.'[40] This would seem to be an overstatement which ignores the role of both continuity and legal succession. On the other hand, a Russian jurist referred to 'international legal documents of which the USSR was a participant and to which all State-successors became participants unless they declared otherwise',[41] by which he meant all treaties of the former USSR. The State practice of the CIS countries has been otherwise; they have not declared those treaties to which they do not wish to be a party, but rather gradually have ratified or acceded to multilateral treaties to which the USSR was a party in their own right.

merely recognized the withdrawal of the other republics from the Union, there would have been substantial legal arguments in support of that position.

[38] See M. V. Kuchin, *Договорная правоспособность Российской Федерации* [Treaty Legal Capacity of the Russian Federation] (Kazan, n.p., 1994), p. 14. (Abstract of dissertation for kandidat of legal sciences).

[39] See S. V. Chernichenko, 'Континуитет, идентичность и правопреемство государств' [Continuity, Identity, and Legal Succession of States], *РЕМП 1996–1997* (Spb., 1998), p. 27. On the other hand, note the use of this concept by a member of the Supreme Court of the RF: 'The integration of the Russian Federation into the system of basic international human rights documents as the country-successor of the USSR.' See V. N. Solov'ev, 'О некоторых вопросах практики применения норм международного права судами Российский Федерции' [On Certain Questions of the Practice of the Application of Norms of International Law by Courts of the Russian Federation], *РЕМП 1998–1999* (Spb., 1999), p. 273.

[40] See M. A. Sarsembaev, *Международное право* [International Law] (Almaty, Zheti zhargy, 1996), p. 83.

[41] See I. P. Blishchenko, 'Международно-правовые проблемы государств, входящих в СНГ' [International Legal Problems of States Within the CIS], *РЕМП 1996–1997* (Spb., 1998), p. 273.

Article 2 Use of Terms

For the purposes of the present Federal Law:

(a) 'international treaty of the Russian Federation' means an international agreement concluded by the Russian Federation with a foreign State(s) or with an international organization in written form and regulated by international law, irrespective of whether such agreement is contained in one or in several related documents, and also irrespective of its specific name;

(b) 'ratification', 'confirmation', 'adoption' and 'accession' mean, depending upon the event, the form of expression of the consent of the Russian Federation to the bindingness of an international treaty upon it;

(c) 'signature' means either the stage of concluding a treaty, or the form of expression of consent by the Russian Federation to the bindingness of an international treaty upon it if the treaty provides that signature has such force, or an arrangement of the Russian Federation and other States participating in negotiations has established otherwise that the signature must have such force, or the intention of the Russian Federation to attach such to the signature arises from the powers of its representative or was expressed during the negotiations;

(d) 'conclusion' means the expression of the consent of the Russian Federation to the bindingness of the international treaty for it;

(e) 'powers' means a document which emanates from a competent agency of the Russian Federation and by means of which one person or several persons are appointed to represent the Russian Federation for the purposes of:

conducting negotiations;

adopting the text of a treaty or establishing the authenticity thereof;

expressing the consent of the Russian Federation to the bindingness of the treaty for it;

performing any other act relating to the treaty;

(f) 'reservation' means a unilateral declaration made when signing, ratifying, confirming, or adopting a treaty or acceding thereto by means of which the wish is expressed to exclude or change the legal operation of specified provisions of the treaty in their application to the Russian Federation;

(g) 'international organization' means an inter-State or intergovernmental organization;

(h) 'depositary' means a State, international organization, or its chief executive official to whom the original of the international treaty is handed over

for keeping and who fulfils with respect to this treaty the functions provided for by international law.

Russia

This Article follows in substantial form and substance Article 2 of the 1969 Vienna Convention.

The 1995 Law follows the 1969 Vienna Convention in stipulating that the 1995 Law extends only to international treaties concluded in written form. Neither the 1969 Vienna Convention nor the 1995 Law purports to restrict States in general or the RF in particular from concluding oral international treaties, for such treaties are binding under international law. Nonetheless, the Commentary takes the view that the 1995 Law would apply to oral treaties of the RF by analogy (the Commentary does not stipulate whether by analogy of *jus* or of *lex*), with due regard being taken of the specific features of oral treaties.[42]

The Commentary is of the view that the RF may not conclude a treaty concerning human rights without requiring the ratification thereof and may not conclude an oral treaty concerning human rights. Further, it is declared that agreements between States which contain merely political substance and no legal obligations do not fall within the 1969 Vienna Convention nor the 1995 Law.[43] The Commentary has in view certain agreements concluded within the framework of the OSCE, where obligations of the States-parties are characterized as 'political obligations'.

Article 2(b) of the 1995 Law reproduces Article 2(b) of the 1969 Vienna Convention.

Article 2(c) is based on the 1969 Vienna Convention and in substance distinguishes, although this terminology is not used, between preliminary signature (initialling) by those empowered individuals who took direct part in negotiating the text and final signature indicating full approval by the Government of the text negotiated. Depending upon the formalities required, full signature may constitute final formal confirmation or approval or the readiness of the Government to submit the text for ratification. In some cases initialling is transformed into final signature by decision of the respective Government.

Article 2(d) offers a definition of 'conclusion' which is more precisely defined in the 1995 Law as the final acceptance of the treaty, that is, the ultimate stage of the conclusion thereof. The 1995 Law in this respect

42 Lukashuk, Commentary, p. 9.
43 Lukashuk, Commentary, p. 10.

offers a more concrete definition with respect to international treaties than does the 1995 Russian Civil Code with respect to the conclusion of contracts.[44] While there is some procedural overlap between treaties and contracts under Russian Law, the concept retains a certain vagueness, in particular where registration of the document is mandatory (or deposit, in the case of a treaty). In the latter instance 'conclusion' is associated with entry into force.

Powers may be partial or full, and therefore encompass all of the actions which must be performed to conclude a treaty of the RF or only certain of them (see Gloss on Articles 23 and 13, below).

Reservations were extensively used by the former USSR to consolidate certain ideological positions of the day, including reservations to the 1969 Vienna Convention itself. The RF has removed a number of reservations to individual treaties previously entered by the former USSR. See Gloss on Article 25, below.

The reference to international organizations in Article 2(g) is to so-called 'classical' international organizations and institutions founded by States, almost invariably on the basis of an international treaty, and enjoying the status of subjects of international law. Such organizations have limited international legal personality in accordance with their charters and as a rule have the right to conclude or participate in international treaties in their own names.

The texts of bilateral treaties are, as a rule, retained by each of the signatories, although they have the right to refer the text to an international organization or third State for keeping. Multilateral treaties usually are drawn up in a single document, albeit in several languages, which is signed by each State-party and then placed in the keeping of a designated international organization, State-party, or third State as depositary. The depositary then sends to each State-party a certified copy of the treaty and may prepare translations of the treaty in the languages of the States-parties. See Gloss on Articles 28 and 29, below.

CIS

The treaty laws of *Armenia*, *Azerbaidzhan*, *Moldova*, and *Turkmenistan* do not contain definitions of terms. Ukraine defines 'conclusion of a treaty' (Article 1[2]) and *Uzbekistan* defines the concept of an international treaty only (Article 3).

44 Article 432 of the Civil Code of the Russian Federation provides: 'A contract shall be considered to be concluded when agreement regarding all the material conditions of the contract has been reached in the form required in appropriate instances.' See W. E. Butler, *Russian Civil Legislation* (London, Simmonds & Hill, 1999), p. 212.

The articles of CIS treaty laws containing definitions introduce a number of clarifications into the 1969 Vienna Convention terminology, which does not entirely suit the legal traditions and terminology of the CIS legal systems. The term 'party' in the 1969 Vienna Convention will commonly appear in the Russian language as 'participant' because the word 'party' is usually used only for bilateral agreements and the word 'participant' for either bilateral or multilateral ones. The 1969 Vienna Convention defines an 'international organization' as an 'intergovernmental organization', which in the Russian language would be a very narrow concept indeed and not reach most international organizations. The Belarus treaty law (Article 2) clarifies the position: an 'inter-State (or intergovernmental) organization created for the fulfilment of determined tasks of an international character in accordance with the constitutive act of this organization'. The terms 'acceptance' and 'approval' in the 1969 Vienna Convention do not fit long-standing CIS legislative practice; the Russian text of the 1969 Vienna Convention translates those terms, respectively, as 'adoption' and 'confirmation', and all CIS treaty laws follow this practice. The stipulation in the 1969 Vienna Convention that these terms mean the 'international act so named' does not, and cannot, save the clause from the impact of municipal law terminology used to designate normative legal acts connected with international treaties of an individual State.

Several CIS treaty laws, including the 1995 Law, contain a definition of the 'conclusion' of an international treaty in varying levels of detail. The same question can arise in domestic civil-law contract practice in the CIS countries: precisely when does the process of conclusion commence and when is it completed? The civil codes do not offer a definitive answer.[45] In the realm of treaty law, the CIS countries frequently provide a full explanation that could be applied by analogy to civil-law contracts, an analogy perhaps the more compelling when one bears in mind that the word in Russian for 'contract' and 'treaty' is the same: *договор*. However, the definition offered by the Kyrgyzstan treaty law is no definition at all and begs the question as to what 'conclusion' means: 'conclusion shall mean the expression of consent of the Kyrgyz Republic to the bindingness of the

[45] Article 402 of the Belarus Civil Code reads: 'A contract shall be considered to be concluded when agreement regarding all the material conditions of the contract has been reached in the form required in appropriate instances.' See W. E. Butler, *Civil Code of the Republic Belarus* (The Hague, Kluwer Law International, 2000), p. 203. Article 341 of the Turkmenistan Civil Code stipulates: 'A contract shall be considered to be concluded if the parties have reached consent with regard to all of the material conditions thereof in compliance with the form established for this.' See W. E. Butler, *Turkmenistan Civil Code of Saparmurat Turkmenbashi* (The Hague, Kluwer Law International, 1999), p. 114.

international treaty for it' (Article 2). Similarly, the Kyrgyzstan treaty law defines 'municipal procedures' as ratification or confirmation, omitting other types of municipal procedure contained in the same treaty law.

The treaty law of *Belarus* contains several definitions not to be found in the 1969 Vienna Convention and 1995 Federal Law: inter-State and intergovernmental treaty, respectively, of the Republic Belarus; bilateral and multilateral international treaty; depositary. In the definitions article (Article 2) Belarus determines that the treaty law extends solely to treaties in written form.

The treaty law of *Georgia* offers definitions of signature, denunciation, and abrogation (Article 3). That of *Kazakhstan* includes definitions of 'exchange of instruments of ratification, documents concerning confirmation (or adoption) or accession' and of 'authentic text of treaty' (Article 2). The *Kyrgyzstan* treaty law also defines 'municipal procedures' and 'initialling' (Article 2).

Article 3 International Treaties of Russian Federation

1. In accordance with the Constitution of the Russian Federation the conclusion, termination, and suspension of the operation of international treaties of the Russian Federation is within the jurisdiction of the Russian Federation.

2. International treaties of the Russian Federation shall be concluded with foreign States, and also with international organizations, in the name of the Russian Federation (inter-State treaties), in the name of the Government of the Russian Federation (intergovernmental treaties), and in the name of federal agencies of executive power (treaties of an interdepartmental character).

Russia

1 This point originates in the federative nature of the RF. The 1993 Constitution provides in Article 71 (l) that international treaties are within the jurisdiction of the RF. It follows, as set out in point 1 of this Article, that all legal actions relating to international treaties of the RF also are within the jurisdiction of the RF.

The formulation is not conclusive with respect to treaties that may be concluded by subjects of the RF. However, it is clear that no subject of the RF may itself conclude, terminate, or suspend treaties of the RF.

CIS

Only the *Georgian* treaty law (Article 5) addresses the issue of whether territorial entities within Georgia may have treaty powers. The competence of the Abkhazian and Adzharian autonomous republics and other territorial entities with respect to international treaties is to be determined after the establishment of the territorial State system of Georgia. This formulation reflects the 1995 Constitution of Georgia, which provides that the 'State-territorial system of Georgia shall be determined by a constitutional law on the basis of the principle of delimitation of powers after the full restoration of the jurisdiction of Georgia to the entire territory of the country' (Article 2[3]).[46]

[46] Translated in W. E. Butler, *Constitutional Foundations of the CIS Countries* (The Hague, Kluwer Law International, 1999), p. 170.

Russia

2 The 1995 Law establishes a hierarchy of levels at which international treaties of the RF may be concluded. Inter-State treaties are those concluded in the name of the RF at the highest level. Those concluded in the name of the Government of the RF are designated as intergovernmental. So-called interdepartmental treaties are concluded by individual ministries, State committees, or other empowered departments. The Commentary is of the view that 'Despite these distinctions they all are treaties of the State as a whole, and it bears responsibility for the fulfilment thereof. Irrespective of the level of agencies representing the State, treaties according to international law possess equal legal force.'[47]

The hierarchy is not without legal importance. Bilateral treaties concluded at the highest level with the RF will, as a rule, take precedence over bilateral treaties concluded by the same State with the RF at a lower level. Unusual variations can occur. For example, on 4 April 1992 the Governments of the RF and of the United States signed an Agreement Regarding Cooperation to Facilitate the Provision of Assistance (from the Russian point of view, an intergovernmental agreement). On 17 June 1992, pursuant to the Agreement of 4 April 1992, the RF and the United States concluded a so-called Umbrella Agreement, an Agreement Concerning the Safe and Secure Transportation, Storage, and Destruction of Weapons and the Prevention of Weapons Proliferation, signed for each party, respectively, by the President of the country (from the Russian point of view, an inter-State agreement). On 15 and 16 June 1999, the Umbrella Agreement was extended for seven years by the Protocol to the Agreement Between the United States of America and the Russian Federation Concerning the Safe and Secure Transportation, Storage, and Destruction of Weapons and the Prevention of Weapons Proliferation, which for the United States was signed by the Ambassador of the United States in Moscow. It is unusual to see an implementing agreement concluded at a higher level than a framework agreement. In any event, this hierarchical principle would not extend to treaties involving States other than the RF. See Gloss on Article 5, below.

The *vires* of an individual department to conclude a treaty need to be examined in each individual instance. They may originate in general legislation creating and regulating the particular ministry or State committee or in a special empowerment, commonly in the form of a normative act.

It will be noted that the hierarchy of treaties does not take into account the stature of an international organization. It may therefore be presumed

[47] Lukashuk, Commentary, p. 12.

that it is the stature of the Russian party which determines the level of the treaty. In practice, the RF has concluded treaties with international organizations at all three levels of the hierarchy of treaties.

CIS

All CIS countries without exception accept the hierarchy and nomenclature of international treaties (inter-State, intergovernmental, and interdepartmental), which was originally set out in the 1978 USSR Law. To this classification the *Kyrgyzstan* treaty law has added a fourth type of treaty: interparliamentary (Article 3[3]), concluded by the Zhogorku Kenesh of Kyrgyzstan with other parliaments. As a rule, the category of treaty will determine who signs in the name of the respective CIS country. The Head of State commonly signs inter-State treaties; the Head of Government, intergovernmental treaties; and the head of the respective department, interdepartmental treaties. Where, as in Turkmenistan, the same individual is both Head of State and the Head of Government, care must be taken to determine in which capacity the treaty is being signed.

The Constitution of the Republic Tadzhikistan, adopted 6 November 1994, as amended 26 September 1999, contains an unusual formulation in Article 10: 'international legal acts recognized by Tadzhikistan shall be an integral part of the legal system of the Republic. In the event laws of the Republic do not conform to recognized international legal acts, the norms of the international legal acts shall apply. Laws and international legal acts recognized by Tadzhikistan shall enter into force after their official publication.' Tadzhikistan has the sole constitution among the CIS members which refers to 'acts' instead of international treaties. The term 'acts' is sufficiently broad to encompass documents concluded with entities which may or may not enjoy autonomous international legal personality. The 1999 Tadzhikistan law on treaties does not use the term 'acts', but rather refers throughout to international treaties.

The *Ukrainian* treaty law (Article 2[1]) stipulates certain treaties that must be concluded in the name of Ukraine: (a) political, territorial, peace; (b) concerning the rights and freedoms of man; (c) concerning citizenship; (d) concerning the participation of Ukraine in inter-State unions and other inter-State associations (or organizations) and collective security systems; (e) concerning military assistance and relative to sending a contingent of the Armed Forces of Ukraine to another country or admitting the armed forces of foreign States to the territory of Ukraine; (f) concerning the use of the territory and natural resources of Ukraine; and (g) to which with the consent of the Parties an inter-State character is imparted.

Most CIS treaty laws provide that both States and international organizations may be parties to international treaties; that is, that the treaty laws extend to treaties concluded with States and with international organizations. *Uzbekistan* (Article 3) provides that treaties may be concluded with 'other subjects of international law'. In practice other Central Asian jurisdictions have concluded treaties to which entities other than States or international organizations were parties. On 31 August 2000, at Astana, Kazakhstan, the Republic Tadzhikistan, the Kyrgyz Republic, the Republic Kazakhstan, and the Ismaili Imamate concluded a Treaty for the Establishment of the University of Central Asia.[48] The leader of the Ismaili Imamate is His Highness The Aga Khan.

The Council for National Reconciliation in Tadzhikistan was a signatory to a number of agreements during the 1990s concluded with the United Nations and several interested States.

[48] The Law of the Kyrgyz Republic concerning ratification of the Treaty was adopted by the Legislative Assembly of the Zhogorku Kenesh on 26 December 2000; approved by the Assembly of People's Representatives of the Zhogorku Kenesh on 29 December 2000; and signed by the President of the Kyrgyz Republic on 14 January 2001. The text of the Law (but not the Treaty) appears in *Нормативные акты Кыргызской Республики*, no. 3 (2001), p. 11.

Article 4 International Treaties of Russian Federation Affecting the Powers of a Subject of Russian Federation

1. An international treaty of the Russian Federation affecting questions relegated to the jurisdiction of a subject of the Russian Federation shall be concluded by agreement with the agencies of State power of the interested subject of the Russian Federation on which the respective function has been placed.

2. The basic provisions or draft international treaty affecting the powers of a subject of the Russian Federation with regard to subjects of joint jurisdiction of the Russian Federation and subjects of the Russian Federation shall be sent by federal agencies of executive power to the agencies of State power of the interested subject of the Russian Federation on which the respective function has been placed. The proposals received shall be considered when preparing the draft treaty.

3. When effectuating the agreeing of questions of the conclusion of an international treaty of the Russian Federation, the agencies of State power of the interested subject of the Russian Federation on which the respective function has been placed shall be informed by federal agencies of executive power about the maximum periods for sending proposals, comprising not less than two weeks. The failure to submit a reply within the said period shall not prevent the making of proposals concerning the conclusion of the international treaty of the Russian Federation.

4. Questions of the participation of representatives of agencies of State power of a subject of the Russian Federation in the preparation of a draft international treaty affecting questions relegated to the jurisdiction of a subject of the Russian Federation or its powers relating to subjects of joint jurisdiction of the Russian Federation and subjects of the Russian Federation, and also in negotiations and the procedure for the signature thereof, shall be decided by federal agencies of executive power by agreement with the agencies of State power of the interested subject of the Russian Federation on which the respective function has been placed.

Russia

1 The RF is a federative State structure comprising eighty-nine subjects of the Federation. Although the 1993 Constitution has relegated

international treaties of the RF to the jurisdiction of the Federation (Article 71[j]), the fulfilment of such treaties falls within the joint jurisdiction of the RF and subjects of the RF (Article 72[n]).[49] This is a distinction which was elaborated in the 1993 Constitution and does not exist in the Treaty on the Delimitation of Subjects of Jurisdiction and Powers Between Federal Agencies of State Power of the Russian Federation and Agencies of Power of the Sovereign Republics Within the Russian Federation, signed on 31 March 1992, where the reference to the fulfilment of international treaties is lacking.[50]

The constitutions of certain subjects of the RF adopted before the 1993 Russian Constitution contain provisions based on the presumption of the sovereignty of the respective subject. The Constitution of the Republic Tatarstan, adopted 6 November 1992, for example, provides that Tatarstan is a sovereign State and a subject of international law and 'enters into relations with other States, concludes international treaties, exchanges diplomatic, consular, trade, and other representations, and participations in the activity of international organizations' (Articles 60–62). The Tatarstan Constitution further provides that 'Laws of the Republic Tatarstan shall have supremacy throughout all of its territory unless they are contrary to international obligations of the Republic Tatarstan' (Article 59). There are analogous provisions in the constitutions of the Republic Adygei, Republic Bashkortostan, Republic Ingushetia, Republic Komi, and Republic Northern Osetia-Alania. By a Ruling of 27 June 2000, the Constitutional Court of the Russian Federation declared these provisions to be unconstitutional, although the Ruling left unimpaired the right of Republics to effectuate international and foreign economic links in accordance with Articles 72 and 76 of the 1993 Constitution of the RF so long as such links did not affect the powers and prerogatives of the RF as a sovereign State provided for by Article 71 of the 1993 Russian Constitution and that the coordination thereof was determined by a federal law.[51]

The variety of provisions to be found in the constitutions, charters, and other enactments of the subjects of the RF concerning international

[49] W. E. Butler, *Constitutional Foundations of the CIS Countries* (The Hague, Kluwer Law International, 1999), p. 445.

[50] For the text of the Treaty, see B. A. Strashun (comp.), *Федеральное конституционное право России. Основные источники по состоянию на 15 сентября 1996 года* [Federal Constitutional Law of Russia. Basic Sources as of 15 December 1996] (M., izd-vo Norma, 1996), pp. 191–7; trans. in W. E. Butler and J. Henderson, *Russian Legal Texts* (London, Simmonds & Hill, 1998), pp. 51–72; W. E. Butler, *Constitutional Foundations of the CIS Countries* (The Hague, Kluwer Law International, 1999), pp. 477–503.

[51] See T. P. Kolpakova, 'Конституционно-договорные основы международных и внешнеэкономических связей субъектов Российской Федерации' [Constitutional-Treaty Foundations of International and Foreign Economic Links of Subjects of the Russian Federation], *Журнал российского права*, no. 6 (2001), pp. 80–7.

treaties is quite remarkable and worthy of a separate study. The Charter of the Voronezh Region, for example, follows the 1993 Russian Constitution by incorporating generally-recognized principles and norms of international law and international treaties of the RF and Voronezh Region into the legal system of the Region (Article 8); these propositions are elaborated in the Law of the Voronezh Region on Legal Normative Acts of the Voronezh Region: 'Agencies of State power of the Region may conclude treaties which are legal normative acts with foreign States with regard to questions of common, mutual interest thereof' (Article 17).[52]

The 1995 Law in this Article distinguishes between international treaties of the RF which affect questions relegated to the jurisdiction of a subject of the RF and those international treaties of the RF which affect the powers of a subject of the RF with regard to matters of joint jurisdiction of the RF and the particular subject(s) of the RF.

The 1993 Constitution (Article 73) reserves to subjects of the RF the entire plenitude of residual State power which has not been relegated to the jurisdiction of the RF or to the powers of the RF in respect of the matters of joint jurisdiction of the RF and subjects of the RF. It follows that the RF may not conclude an international treaty which affects questions relegated to the jurisdiction of a subject of the RF without the consent of the agencies of State power of the subject of the RF.

The 1995 Law does not refer to the network of Treaties of the Federation concluded in March 1992 between the RF and the subjects of the RF. Whether the 1969 Vienna Convention and the 1995 Law are applicable to the Treaties of the Federation is a delicate issue circumvented in doctrinal writings to date.[53] Noting the divergence of views amongst Russian jurists, one observer comments: 'The treaties of subjects of the Federation between themselves and the Federation arouse especially vigorous discussions. Some jurists prove that intra-Federation treaties are regulated

[52] Cited in I. N. Bartsits, *Правовое пространство России: вопросы конституционной теории и практики* [Legal Space of Russia: Questions of Constitutional Theory and Practice] (M., izd-vo MGU, 2000), p. 212. Bartsits adds: 'International law does not deny subjects of federative States the right to conclude international agreements nor international legal personality as a whole; however, neither does it consolidate it . . . questions of the conclusion, performance and termination of the operation of international treaties are determined by the 1969 Vienna Convention on the Law of Treaties, in which there is no mention of the right of subjects of federated States to participate in international agreements' (p. 213).

[53] But see the view of Kovalev that the subjects of the RF possess 'partial international legal personality'. A. A. Kovalev, 'Проблемы разграничении полномочий между Российской Федерации и субъектами федерации в вопросах заключения международных договоров' [Problems of Delimitation of Powers Between the Russian Federation and Subjects of the Federation on Questions of the Conclusion of International Treaties], *Московский журнал международного права*, no. 3 (1994), p. 5.

by State law and the elimination of violations thereof is a matter for competent Federal agencies (for example, the Constitutional Court). Other jurists, both in Russia and abroad, allow the application of international law to them, in particular, international conciliation procedures, basing their view on the fact that one is speaking of international treaties. In our view this is an unsubstantiated position entailing the extension of international law to municipal life.'[54] From the standpoint of international law, the only serious candidate would be the Treaty of the Federation delimiting the jurisdiction and powers between Federal agencies of State power of the RF and the agencies of power of the 'sovereign republics within the Russian Federation'.[55] The 1993 Constitution was adopted after the Treaties of the Federation were concluded and takes precedence over those Treaties in the event of any inconsistency between the two, pursuant to Section two, point one, of the Constitution.[56]

Other Russian jurists reach a similar conclusion on other grounds. Constitutional lawyers argue that the Treaties of the Federation and other such treaties 'are not international treaties in the meaning of Article 15(4) of the Constitution. Their legal force cannot be greater than the force of federal laws adopted with regard to Article 71 of the Constitution'. It is further contended that the chamber of the Federal Assembly may have a role in 'legitimising' treaties signed by the President of Russia with individual subjects of the RF.[57]

After the 1993 Constitution entered into force and on the basis of the 1992 Treaties of the Federation, the RF has been concluding treaties with individual subjects of the RF which clarify and, in some cases, extend the powers of the subjects of the RF with respect to international treaties or to matters likely to be regulated by international treaties. Such treaties have been concluded with the Republic Tatarstan (15 February

[54] See V. V. Pustogarov, *Субъекты Федерации. Правовые проблемы международной деятельности. Учебное пособие* [Subjects of the Federation. Legal Problems of International Activity. Instructional Manual] (Ufa, Vostochnyi universitet, 1995), p. 22. For the view that the Treaties of the Federation are a 'State-law agreement between the Federation and its subjects' see N. A. Mikhalev, in B. S. Krylov, I. P. Il'inskii, *et al.*, *Проблемы суверенитета в Российской Федерации* [Problems of Sovereignty in the Russian Federation] (M., Respublika, 1994), pp. 139–46.

[55] For the view that the Treaties of the Federation are purely internal documents not governed by international law, see G. M. Vel'iaminov, 'Правовой статус субъектов Российской Федерации' [Legal Status of Subjects of the Russian Federation], *Московский журнал международного права*, no. 2 (1995), pp. 3–12.

[56] W. E. Butler, *Constitutional Foundations of the CIS Countries* (The Hague, Kluwer Law International, 1999), p. 473.

[57] See V. A. Chetvernin (ed.), *Конституция Российской Федерации: Проблемный комментарий* [Constitution of the Russian Federation: Problem Commentary] (M., n.p., 1997), pp. 54–5.

1994),[58] the Kabardino–Balkarian Republic (1 July 1994), the Republic Bashkortostan (3 August 1994), the North Osetian–Alania Republic (23 March 1995), the Republic Sakha (Iakutia) (29 June 1995), the Republic Buriatia (29 August 1995), the Udmurt Republic (17 October 1995), the Chuvash Republic (27 May 1996), as well as with a territory and several regions.[59] Each of these documents needs to be individually consulted in order to determine the precise role the respective subject of the RF may have with respect to an international treaty of the RF.

CIS

There are no equivalent provisions in the other CIS treaty laws. *Georgia* has deferred the regulation of treaty powers for territorial entities of Georgia pending the enactment of further legislation. See Gloss on CIS Article 3.1, above.

Russia

2 The basic provisions of or the text of a draft international treaty affecting the powers of a subject of the RF with regard to matters of joint jurisdiction of the RF and the subjects of the RF are to be sent by federal ministries, State committees, or other departments to the agencies of State power of the interested subject. Proposals received from subjects of the RF are to be considered when preparing the draft treaty. The 1995 Law imposes no periods for the process to be undertaken or completed (except a minimum two-week period for submitting proposals), nor does it require that proposals made are binding upon the Federal Government, nor does it address what should happen if subjects of the RF share divergent views as to the substance of the proposals made or the draft treaty.

Read in combination with Articles 9(5), 36(1), and 37(5) of the 1995 Law, the present Article in effect gives subjects of the RF the right, with respect to the questions which directly affect the interests of the subject of the RF, to veto the conclusion, termination, or suspension of an international treaty of the RF. However, the 1995 Law does not clarify whether the requirement of agreeing an international treaty of the RF affecting

[58] Five treaties with Tatarstan are translated in W. E. Butler and J. E. Henderson, *Russian Legal Texts* (London, Simmonds & Hill, 1998), pp. 73–86.

[59] For the Russian-language texts, see B. A. Strashun, *Федеральное конституционное право России* [Federal Constitutional Law of Russia] (M., izd-vo Norma, 1996), pp. 219–352.

such questions with the subjects of the RF would enable individual subjects of the RF to opt out of the treaty or whether the withholding of agreement by one subject of the RF is sufficient to determine the entire fate of the international treaty of the RF for all other subjects of the RF.

Direct foreign relations between subjects of the RF and foreign States are regulated also by the Decree of the Government of the RF concerning the giving of consent for those relations adopted 1 February 2000 in furtherance of Article 1(1) of the Federal Law on the Coordination of International and Foreign Economic Relations of Subjects of Russian Federation.[60] The Decree, translated in the annexes, below, is relevant insofar as those relations may take the form of treaty relations.

This requirement of agreeing the text of an international treaty of the RF does not extend to international treaties of the RF concerning cooperation with regard to matters relegated by the 1993 Constitution to the joint jurisdiction of the RF and subjects of the RF and not affecting directly the interests of any specific subject of the RF, e.g. culture, public health, nature protection, sport, and the like.

Precisely which agencies of State power of a subject of the RF have responsibility for agreeing a draft international treaty of the RF affecting the powers of the subject of the RF is not determined in the 1995 Law. The subjects of the RF may make this determination, but most have not done so, or have not done so exhaustively. Federal agencies will as a rule address those agencies of State power of the respective subject of the RF which perform the respective function or will send the draft treaty or basic provisions thereof to them.

CIS

There are no equivalent provisions in the other CIS treaty laws.

Russia

3 The 1995 Law gives Federal agencies the right to determine the maximum period during which subjects of the RF may submit proposals regarding the proposed treaty. Failure to reply will not obstruct the treaty process, and the agency which takes the decision to sign an international treaty may exclude or alter provisions of the draft treaty, send the draft for agreement to agencies of State power of the interested subject of the RF, or return the documents to the federal department and request it

[60] *СЗ РФ* (2000), no. 6, item 771.

to complete the process of agreeing the draft with the subject of the RF. The 1995 Law seems to presume that the process of agreeing the draft will ultimately be achieved, and contains no provisions to cover situations in which the subject of the RF explicitly refuses to endorse or agree the draft.

CIS

There are no equivalent provisions in the other CIS treaty laws.

Russia

4 While the 1995 Law expects federal departments to interact with the agencies of State power of subjects of the RF in the process of concluding an international treaty of the RF, no procedure is laid down to address the situation where the respective parties cannot resolve the issue confronting them.

CIS

There are no equivalent provisions in the other CIS treaty laws.

Article 5 International Treaties of Russian Federation in Legal System of Russian Federation

1. International treaties of the Russian Federation shall, together with generally-recognized principles and norms of international law, be an integral part of its legal system in accordance with the Constitution of the Russian Federation.

2. If other rules have been established by an international treaty of the Russian Federation than those provided for by a law, then the rules of the international treaty shall apply.

3. The provisions of officially published international treaties of the Russian Federation which do not require the publication of intra-State acts for application shall operate in the Russian Federation directly. Respective legal acts shall be adopted in order to effectuate other provisions of international treaties of the Russian Federation.

Russia

1 Point one of this Article reproduces verbatim the formulation of Article 15(4) of the 1993 Constitution and the first sentence of paragraph two of the Preamble to the 1995 Law (see Gloss on Preamble, above). The formal recognition of generally-recognized principles and norms of international law, that is, customary rules of international law, to be an integral part of the Russian legal system is among the most momentous changes of the twentieth century in the development of Russian Law.[61] It was foreshadowed by an amendment to the 1978 Constitution of the RSFSR introduced in December 1992 (Article 32): 'Generally-recognized international norms relating to human rights shall have preference over laws of the Russian Federation and directly shall give rise to rights and duties

[61] 'The incorporation of international legal norms into the Russian legal system furthers the formation of the institutes of a rule-of-law State and a civil society since the possibilities for the defence of rights and freedoms of man and citizen in the country are significantly broadened.' See G. D. Sadovnikova, *Комментарий к Конституции Российской Федерации* [Commentary on the Constitution of the Russian Federation (Article-by-Article)] (M., Iurait, 2001), p. 53.

of citizens of the Russian Federation', although point one of this Article goes farther.

The Commentary specifically singles out the 1966 Covenant on Civil and Political Rights as containing norms which are deemed to be generally-recognized, whereas its sister 1966 Covenant on Economic and Social Rights, given objections to certain clauses by ratifying States, is regarded as containing treaty norms binding only upon the States-Parties. The 1948 Universal Declaration of Human Rights, technically merely a Resolution of the UN General Assembly and therefore having only recommendatory force, is nonetheless characterized as containing norms of general international law because the international community has so deemed them to be.[62]

The criticism has been made in Russian doctrinal writings that many rules of customary international law concern only inter-State relations and need not be incorporated into domestic law. The Commentary observes that such norms, in being incorporated into Russian Law, acquire a 'new legal quality'; a constitutional guarantee of compliance by Russian State agencies with such generally-recognized principles and norms has been established.[63] Examples already have arisen of the Constitutional Court of the RF citing generally-recognized principles of international law and the 1970 Declaration of the Principles of International Law.[64] The Constitutional Court also has cited non-binding resolutions of UN organs when construing provisions of the 1993 Constitution.[65]

The view of the Constitutional Court would appear to be that 'Generally-recognized principles and norms of international law, and also international treaties of Russia, are applied by the Constitutional Court of Russia as being norms incorporated into national law. Such incorporation is a variety of general incorporation. This means that any principles and norms of international law which are generally-recognized in international relations are part of the Russian legal system. These are not only those generally-recognized principles and norms which are applied by States in the modern period, but also those which emerge in the future . . . The introduction of new generally-recognized international

[62] Lukashuk, Commentary, p. 15.
[63] Lukashuk, Commentary, p. 16.
[64] *СЗ РФ* (1995), no. 33, item 3224.
[65] See, for example, the Decree of the Constitutional Court of the RF adopted 28 November 1996 regarding the Case concerning the verification of the constitutionality of Article 418 of the RSFSR Code of Criminal Procedure in Connection with a Request of the Karatuzsk District Court, Krasnoiarsk Territory. In holding Article 418 to be unconstitutional, the Court made reference to the Resolution of the United Nations Economic and Social Council 1989/60, adopted 24 May 1989. *СЗ РФ* (1996), no. 50, item 5679.

legal principles and norms into the system of Russian national law is effectuated, thus, automatically.'[66]

Although the 1993 Constitution has incorporated generally-recognized norms of international law into the legal system, their place in the legal system is not determined with precision by the 1993 Constitution. Depending upon their subject-matter, generally-recognized norms of international law appear to enjoy two separate statuses with respect to the Russian Legal System. The 1993 Constitution (Chapter 2) placed human rights at the very foundation of the legal system, stipulating that those basic rights and freedoms set out in the Constitution must not be interpreted as a denial of or impingement of other generally-recognized rights and freedoms of man and citizen and that laws repealing or reducing the rights and freedoms of man and citizen may not be adopted (Article 55). Article 17 of the 1993 Constitution further provides that: 'The rights and freedoms of man and citizen shall be recognized and guaranteed in the Russian Federation according to generally-recognized principles and norms of international law and in accordance with the present Constitution.' This formulation places international law ahead of the Constitution and, in so doing, confers upon international law a special status in the Russian Legal System.

That same status is not accorded to other generally-recognized norms of international law.

CIS

The CIS treaty laws of *Armenia, Azerbaidzhan, Belarus, Kazakhstan, Moldova, Ukraine*, and *Uzbekistan* do not regulate the status of international treaties within the domestic legal system.

The *Georgian* treaty law (Article 6) provides that an 'international treaty of Georgia is an integral part of the legislation of Georgia'. *Kyrgyzstan* adopts an analogous formulation but places it in the Preamble of the treaty law: international treaties of Kyrgyzstan are 'an integral and directly operating part of the legislation of the Kyrgyz Republic'. In a Decree of 10 December 1991 (translated in the annexes, below), *Ukraine* took an analogous but narrower position and explained its implications:

[66] O. I. Tiunov, 'Конституционный суд Российской федераци и международное право' [Constitutional Court of the Russian Federation and International Law], *РЕМП 1995* (1996), p. 180. Tiunov is a Judge of the Constitutional Court of the RF. However, for a view that Article 15 effects the transformation of international law into Russian Law, see E. T. Usenko, 'Соотношение и взаимодействие международного и национального права в Российская Конституция' [Correlation and Interaction of International and National Law in the Russian Constitution], *Московский журнал международного права*, no. 2 (1995), pp. 13–28.

'international treaties concluded and duly ratified by Ukraine shall constitute an integral part of the national legislation of Ukraine and be applied in the procedure provided for norms of national legislation.' That position is reiterated in the Constitution of Ukraine (Article 9). Ukraine is 'incorporating' only ratified treaties into national legislation, leaving the status of lesser treaties ambiguous and excluding general principles and customary rules of international law entirely. The Azerbaidzhan Constitution (Article 148) contains a similar provision.[67] Each of these formulations have been construed variously; some suggest that treaties enjoy the same stature as national legislation and therefore imply that the principle *lex posteriori derogat priori* governs and that *lex specialis* takes precedence over general norms. The view that an international norm loses that international status when it becomes part of a national legal system has been rejected because, first, if the norm is self-executing it has direct effect on the territory of the State and preserves its international status and, second, if incorporated into national legislation, one is speaking of a new national norm brought into conformity with the international obligation of the State. And the rule that the law latest in time governs is not relevant to a norm of international law which has become part of a national legal system because the international legal norm is of a different legal nature than a national legal norm. The international norm is subject to the 1969 Vienna Convention, which provides under Articles 27 and 45 that a treaty can not be terminated or suspended by reason of domestic law.[68]

Tadzhikistan has adopted a formulation closer to the 1995 Law. The 1999 Tadzhikistan treaty law provides in an Article devoted specially to the place of international treaties in the legal system of Tadzhikistan that international treaties 'recognized by Tadzhikistan in accordance with the Constitution of the Republic Tadzhikistan' are 'an integral part of its legal system' (Article 4). The reference in Article 4 to the rather unusual formulation 'recognized by Tadzhikistan' is taken verbatim from the Constitution of Tadzhikistan (Article 10).[69] Indeed, the constitutional formula is broader: it refers not to international treaties, but to 'international acts'. The breadth of this formulation would incorporate into Tadzhikistan law such international acts as the complex of agreements concluded with, *inter*

[67] Translated in W. E. Butler, *Constitutional Foundations of the CIS Countries* (The Hague, Kluwer Law International, 1999), p. 104.

[68] See L. A. Pavlova, 'Международное право в правовой системе Республики Беларусь' [International Law in the Legal System of the Republic Belarus], *РЕМП 1998–1999* (Spb., 1999), p. 347.

[69] Translated in W. E. Butler, *Constitutional Foundations of the CIS Countries* (The Hague, Kluwer Law International, 1999), p. 521.

alia, the participation of the Commission for National Reconciliation as part of the peace-making process within Tadzhikistan.[70]

Although *Armenia* does not address the issue in its treaty law, the Armenian Constitution provides that 'ratified international treaties shall be an integral part of the legal system of the Republic' (Article 6).[71]

Under the 1995 Law, generally-recognized principles and norms of international law are an integral part of the legal system of the RF. Other CIS treaty laws do not mention international law generally in this context. Turkmenistan (Article 3) declares that it will be 'guided by generally-recognized principles and norms of international law' when concluding and performing international treaties but does not incorporate these into Turkmenistan law; a similar approach is taken by *Armenia* (Article 2). In its Constitution, *Belarus* recognizes the 'priority' of generally- recognized principles of international law and undertakes to ensure the conformity of legislation to them (Article 8), but does not expressly stipulate that such principles automatically override inconsistent provisions of Belarus legislation.[72] The *Georgian* Constitution (Article 6[2]) requires also that legislation conform to generally-recognized principles and norms of international law without establishing the consequences of the failure to do so.

Russia

2 The formulation of this point is drawn from the last sentence of Article 15(4) of the 1993 Constitution. A literal interpretation of this provision requires that it extend to all treaties of the RF, including interdepartmental ones. Some Russian jurists have taken the view that this point, read against Article 15(1) of the 1995 Law, must be construed to mean that only ratified treaties take precedence over laws of the RF, with the result that treaties which are not subject to ratification fall outside the scope of Article 15(4) of the 1993 Constitution and the present point of the 1995 Law. This view was accepted in a Decree of the Plenum of the Supreme Court of the RF adopted on 31 October 1995, which provided that other rules of a treaty are subject to application only if the decision

[70] The principal agreements are translated in W. E. Butler, *Tadzhikistan Legal Texts* (The Hague, Kluwer Law International, 1999), pp. 101–34.

[71] Translated in W. E. Butler, *Constitutional Foundations of the CIS Countries* (The Hague, Kluwer Law International, 1999), p. 10.

[72] A Belorussian jurist has, however, written that 'generally-recognized principles of international law stand at the apex of the hierarchical ladder', followed by the Constitution. The 'provisions of Article 8 of the [Belarus] Constitution concerning recognition of the priority of generally-recognized principles of international law can be classified as recognition of their supremacy over the Constitution'. See L. V. Pavlova, 'Международное право в правовой системе Республики Беларусь' [International Law in the Legal System of the Republic Belarus], *РЕМП 1998–1999* (Spb., 1999), p. 344.

concerning consent to their bindingness was adopted in the form of a federal law.[73] The Decree of the Plenum is binding upon courts. It should be noted, however, that this question has not been placed before the Constitutional Court of the RF. There is a strong argument that reading Article 15(1) of the 1995 Law so as to limit the operation of Article 15(4) of the 1993 Constitution and the present point of the 1995 Law produced a result which is unconstitutional, and that Article 15(4) of the 1993 Constitution means exactly what it says: all treaties of the RF.[74] In both the Constitutional Conference,[75] which drafted the 1993 Constitution, and in the working groups which prepared the draft 1995 Law proposals were made to insert the requirement of 'ratification' with respect to this supremacy clause, and both times the proposals were rejected.[76]

This view has been doubted by many Russian jurists.[77] Narrower constructions of the clause have been suggested, although these constructions too are reluctant to accept the literal meaning of the present point. One such approach observes that two variants may arise with respect to a treaty establishing rules other than those laid down by a law. The first arises when a treaty introduces appreciable changes in legislation by adding to or replacing norms or laying down different general rules, whereas in

[73] Point 5, Decree of the Plenum of the Supreme Court of the RF, no. 8, 31 October 1995. *Бюллетень Верховного Суда Российской Федерации*, no. 11 (1995). The practice of the Supreme Court of the RF accepts this position. See V. N. Solov'ev, 'О некоторых вопросах практики применения норм международного права судами Российский Федерации' [On Certain Questions of the Practice of the Application of Norms of International Law by Courts of the Russian Federation], *РЕМП 1998–1999* (Spb., 1999), p. 268.

[74] See, for example, G. M. Danilenko who, while acknowledging that Article 15 does not use the word 'ratified', says it must refer 'above all to such treaties. At the same time, in principle, the application is permitted also of those treaties which were concluded in the name of the Russian Federation by respective agencies competent to do so without the obligation of submitting them to the Federal Assembly for ratification.' B. N. Topornin, Iu. M. Baturin, and R. G. Orekhov (eds.), *Конституция Российской Федерации* [Constitution of the Russian Federation] (M., Iuridicheskaia literatura, 1994), pp. 117–18.

[75] For the verbatim transcripts of the Constitutional Conference, see Конституционное совещание. Стенограммы. Материалы. Документы. *29* апреля–*10* ноября *1993* г. [Constitutional Assembly. Verbatim Transcripts. Materials. Documents. 29 April-10 November 1993] (M., Iuridicheskaia literatura, 1995–96), 21 vols.

[76] See Lukashuk, in V. M. Zhuikov (ed.), *Международные нормы о правах человека и применение их судами Российской Федерации. Практическое пособие* [International Norms on Human Rights and the Application Thereof by Courts of the Russian Federation. Practical Manual] (M., Prava cheloveka, 1996), p. 10.

[77] See, for example, S. Polenina, who criticized the 1993 Constitution for not including the term 'ratification' and urging that the provision be interpreted as though the word had been included. See S. Polenina, in L. A. Morozova, 'Российская правовая система и международное право: современные проблемы взаимодействия' [Russian Legal System and International Law: Contemporary Problems of Interaction], *Государство и право*, no. 2 (1996), p. 5.

the second instance the treaty establishes 'other rules' only for a specific situation without affecting the operation of the rules of a normative act as a whole, for example by creating an exception from the general legislative norm for a determined particular case. 'In the first instance one speaks of the priority of the rule of a treaty over a rule of law. In the second, about the priority of the application of the rule of a treaty in specific conditions.'[78] Understanding these two variant situations, it is argued, helps explain why the criterion of ratification was excluded from Article 15(4) of the 1993 Constitution and from the present point of the 1995 Law. Refusing to apply a treaty concluded without ratification would prejudice the authority of the State, which bears State responsibility for the obligations it has assumed under such treaties and would severely limit the role of intergovernmental treaties in the regulation of international relations.

Nonetheless, there is great reluctance to extend this point to interdepartmental treaties. The Commentary argues that interdepartmental treaties do not fall within Article 15(4) of the 1993 Constitution and the present point of the 1995 Law, but rather enjoy priority only with respect to acts of the respective ministry, State committee, or other department.[79] Another line of reasoning is that: first, 'only the Russian Federation has been endowed with the legal personality to conclude international treaties; second, an international treaty of the Russian Federation must acquire the form and status of a federal law. Therefore, neither intergovernmental treaties nor treaties of an interdepartmental character fall under the . . . definition of an international treaty of the Russian Federation.'[80]

The symmetry of the hierarchy of sources of Russian Law preoccupies many commentators with respect to the types of international treaties.[81]

[78] Lukashuk, in Zhuikov, *Международные нормы о правах человека и применение их судами Российской Федерации* [International Norms on Human Rights and the Application Thereof by Courts of the Russian Federation] (M., Prava cheloveka, 1996), p. 10.

[79] Also see Lukashuk and Naumov, who observe: 'Other treaties also enter the legal system of the country, but only at their own level. Treaties confirmed by the Government have priority with respect to governmental and other inferior acts. Agreements of an interdepartmental character do not fall within the operation of Article 15 of the Constitution at all and enjoy priority only with respect to acts which the department has concluded.' See I. I. Lukashuk and A. V. Naumov, *Международное уголовное право.* Учебник [International Criminal Law. Textbook] (M., Spark, 1999), pp. 21–2.

[80] V. M. Volzhenkina, *Нормы международного права в российском уголовном процессе* [Norms of International Law in Russian Criminal Procedure] (Spb., Iuridicheskii tsentr press, 2001), p. 78. The author goes on to suggest that Article 15(4) of the present Law, insofar as it does include intergovernmental and interdepartmental treaties within the category of international treaties of the Russian Federation, is unconstitutional.

[81] For a detailed study of the hierarchical interaction of international and Russian law, see V. A. Tolstik, *Иерархия российского и международного права* [Hierarchy of Russian and International Law] (M., Iurait, 2001).

Although the 1995 Law on Treaties identifies the forms or types of treaties, it does not link these distinctions to levels of legislation. Chernichenko suggests that although the 'automatic incorporation of treaties into the legislation of a State (and, consequently, the incorporation of the provisions contained therein into the internal law of a State) is the shortest path to the maximum synchronisation of international and municipal law-creation. It should extend to all treaties, taking into account the level of the treaties: treaties of the highest level as a result of incorporation should have the status of laws; those to be concluded by the Government and not subject to incorporation – the status of acts of the Government; and interdepartmental treaties – the status of acts adopted by departments'. This, he adds, is essential in order to determine the priority of incorporated treaties, depending on their level, *vis-à-vis* municipal acts of the respective level.[82]

There is no language in the present point to sustain this view, and most interdepartmental treaties address general normative issues within the competence of the respective department. The editors of a treaty collection observe: 'Treaties concluded by the Ministry of Internal Affairs of Russia with the respective ministries of internal affairs of other States are relegated to the category of international treaties of the Russian Federation of an interdepartmental character. This legal status of these treaties means that they are an integral part of the Russian legal system and binding upon personnel of internal affairs agencies of Russia.'[83]

There is disagreement as to what the word 'laws' encompasses in this point. Some would extend the word to include the Constitution itself. Others would extend the primacy of international treaties of the RF to Federal laws, including constitutional laws, laws adopted by subjects of the RF, and all other normative acts. 'These norms affect all laws

[82] S. V. Chernichenko, *Теория международного права: старые и новые теоретические проблемы* [Theory of International Law: Old and New Theoretical Problems] (M., izd-vo NIMP, 1999), II, pp. 350–51, 357. The equation has been expressed as follows: 'Recently the notion has begun to form in doctrine, correct in our view, that a ratified international agreement is a normative act possessing in the municipal sphere legal force equal to the force of that act by which it was ratified.' See M. A. Pshenichnov, 'Юридико-технические средства обеспечения соответствия российского законодательства международному праву' [Juridical–Technical Means of Ensuring the Conformity of Russian Legislation to International Law], in V. M. Baranov (ed.), *Проблемы юридической техники: сборник статей* [Problems of Legal Technique: Collection of Articles] (Nizhnii Novgorod, Nizhegorodskaia pravovaia akademiia, 2000), p. 189.

[83] See T. N. Moskal'kova and N. B. Sliusar' (comps.), *Сборник международных соглашений МВД России* [Collection of International Agreements of the Ministry of Internal Affairs of Russia] (M., Spark, 1996), p. 4.

irrespective of the time of their adoption: before or after the conclusion of the treaty.'[84]

Occasionally the legislator strays from this proposition. The 1996 Federal Constitutional Law on the Judicial System provided (Article 3) that all courts are to apply the Russian Constitution, 'federal constitutional laws, federal laws, generally-recognized principles and norms of international law and international treaties of the Russian Federation', a hierarchy of legal norms which is contrary to the Russian Constitution itself.[85]

Several Russian jurists take a restrictive view of the word 'laws'. It is maintained that the 1993 Russian Constitution, 'in recognizing the priority of international law over municipal legislation, does not extend this supremacy to the Basic Law of the country'.[86] Others would exclude federal constitutional laws and consider even federal laws to be disputable.[87]

CIS

The primacy of international treaties in the event of an inconsistency between the provision of a treaty and a provision of domestic legislation was a fundamental principle of Soviet Law.[88] The treaty laws of several CIS countries do not address the question: *Azerbaidzhan, Belarus, Kazakhstan, Kyrgyzstan, Moldova, Ukraine*, and *Uzbekistan*. The constitutions of CIS countries commonly do so provide. In *Armenia* the Constitution provides that the norms of a ratified treaty apply if they establish other rules than are provided for in laws (Article 6). The *Azerbaidzhan* Constitution (Article 151) gives priority to international treaties unless they are inconsistent with the Constitution itself, acts adopted by referendum, and other inter-State treaties to which Azerbaidzhan is a party. The *Belarus*

[84] V. I. Andrianov, in Iu. V. Kudriavtsev (ed.), *Комментарий к Конституции Российской Федерации* [Commentary on the Constitution of the Russian Federation] (M., Fond 'Pravovaia kul'tura', 1996), pp. 80–1.

[85] Translated in W. E. Butler and J. E. Henderson, *Russian Legal Texts* (London, Simmonds & Hill, 1998), p. 142.

[86] V. A. Kartashkin, *Права человека в международном и внутригосударственном праве* [Human Rights in International and Municipal Law] (M., Institut gosudarstva i prava RAN, 1995), p. 17. Also see B. S. Ebzeev, 'Прямое действие Конституции Российской Федерации (некоторые методологические аспекты)' [Direct Operation of the Constitution of the Russian Federation (Certain Methodological Aspects)], *Правоведение*, no. 1 (1996), p. 12.

[87] See I. I. Lukashuk, *Конституция государств и международное право* [The Constitution of States and International Law] (M., n.p., 1998), p. 69; V. M. Volzhenkina, *Нормы международного права в российском уголовном процессе* [Norms of International Law in Russian Criminal Procedure] (Spb., izd-vo Iurid. tsentr Press, 2001), p. 100.

[88] See for the debate surrounding the extent to which this rule was all-embracing or confined to individual branches of law, W. E. Butler, *Soviet Law* (2nd edn., London, Butterworths, 1988), pp. 342–4.

Constitution does not expressly make provision for the priority of treaties generally over inconsistent legislative provisions but does in individual instances (Articles 11 and 116, for example) so stipulate. The *Kazakhstan* Constitution (Article 4[3]) expressly stipulated that ratified international treaties have 'priority over its laws'. Both the *Uzbekistan* Constitution and treaty law are silent on the point. Individual provisions of some Uzbekistan laws establish the priority of international treaty provisions, but the general rule does not apply in Uzbekistan.

In *Armenia* the treaty law (Article 15) gives priority to a treaty over inconsistent domestic legislation. The *Georgian* treaty law gives 'preferential legal force' to an international treaty over 'municipal normative acts' (Article 6[2]). The word 'municipal' in this context has the meaning of international law and refers therefore to Georgian normative acts generally. The 1999 *Tadzhikistan* (Article 4) and *Turkmenistan* (Article 3) treaty laws accord priority to an international treaty if it does not conform to laws of the respective State.

The primacy of international treaties, where recognized, does not extend to the Constitution itself. *Armenia* provides that international treaties which are contrary to the Constitution may be ratified after a respective amendment is made to the Constitution (Article 6); the *Moldovan* Constitution (Article 8[2]) and *Ukrainian* Constitution (Article 9) contain an identical requirement.

The *Belarus* Constitution provides that the conclusion of international treaties which are contrary to the Constitution is not permitted (Article 8).[89] A Belorussian jurist has set out the hierarchical structure of normative acts within the legal system of Belarus as follows: 1. generally-recognized principles of international law; 2. the Belarus Constitution; 3. ratified international treaties; 4. laws, dekrets, edicts of the President, international obligations of Belarus arising from treaties not subject to ratification and customary norms of international law; 5. acts of inter-State formations of which Belarus is a participant, subordinate acts adopted by the Council of Ministers, Supreme Court, Supreme Economic Court, and Procurator General.[90] An analogous conclusion is reached by a Belorussian civil lawyer, who observes that the Constitution of Belarus affirms the vertical dependence of the Constitution on universal human values of world culture. The priority of generally-recognized principles of international law is a reflection and expression

[89] Translated in W. E. Butler, *Constitutional Foundations of the CIS Countries* (The Hague, Kluwer Law International, 1999), p. 121.

[90] See L. A. Pavlova, 'Международное право в правовой системе Республики Беларусь [International Law in the Legal System of the Republic Belarus]', *РЕМП 1998–1999* (Spb., 1999), p. 344.

of such dependence.[91] He further points out that the Belarus Constitution does not prohibit the direct operation of supranational norms in the Republic and observes that Article 6 of the Belarus Civil Code provides that norms of civil law contained in international treaties of the Republic Belarus which have entered into force are subject to direct application by subjects of civil turnover and by judicial and other State agencies.[92]

The *Georgian* treaty law (Article 6[2]) and the Georgian Constitution (Article 6[2]) acknowledge the primacy of the Georgian Constitution.

Some countries of the CIS have adopted laws on normative legal acts which are intended to define the concept of a normative legal act and establish the position of each in the hierarchy of normative legal acts. These are noteworthy both for what they contain and may not contain. The Law of the Republic Kazakhstan on Normative Legal Acts of 24 March 1998 (Article 4) and the Law of Turkmenistan on Normative Legal Acts of 18 June 1996 (Article 3), for example, offer an exhaustive enumeration of the hierarchy of normative legal acts with a distinction being drawn in Kazakhstan between basic and derivative types of normative legal acts. Neither law mentions international treaties in any connection whatsoever, whereas a 1997 Law of Georgia on the same subject does so.

Russia

3 The standards laid down in Article 15(3) of the 1993 Constitution[93] are extended by the present point of the 1995 Law to international treaties. Secret, that is, unpublished treaties, do not have direct effect in the Russian legal system. The 1995 Law does not use the terminology of 'self-executing' and 'non-self-executing', although Russian doctrinal

[91] V. A. Vitushko, *Курс гражданского права. Общая часть* [Cours of Civil Law. General Part] (Minsk, BGEU, 2001), I, pp. 54–5.

[92] Article 6 provides 'The Republic Belarus recognizes the priority of generally-recognized principles of international law and shall ensure the conformity of civil legislation to them. Norms of civil law contained in international treaties of the Republic Belarus which have entered into force shall be part of the civil legislation prevailing on the territory of the Republic Belarus, shall be subject to direct application except for instances when it follows from the international treaty that the issuance of a municipal act is required for the application of such norms, and shall have the force of a legal act to which the consent of the Republic Belarus has been expressed.' See W. E. Butler (transl.), *Civil Code of the Republic Belarus* (The Hague, Kluwer Law International, 2000), p. 5.

[93] Article 15(3) provides: 'Laws shall be subject to official publication. Unpublished laws shall not be applied. Any normative legal acts affecting the rights, freedoms, and duties of man and citizen may not be applied if they have not been published officially for general information.' W. E. Butler, *Constitutional Foundations of the CIS Countries* (The Hague, Kluwer Law International, 1999), p. 426. Also see V. V. Oksamytnyi and T. V. Rakhmanina, *Комментарий к Конституции Российской Федерации* [Commentary on the Constitution of the Russian Federation] (M., izd-vo BEK, 1994).

writings equate the two when differentiating between treaties which have direct effect and those which do not.[94]

When the adoption of implementing municipal legislation is required in order to give effect to treaty obligations, the courts and other agencies applying the law should be guided by the implementing legislation as an official expression of how the State understood its obligations under the particular treaty unless there is a clear divergence between the treaty and the implementing legislation. In the last instance, the treaty should prevail by virtue of Article 15(4) of the 1993 Constitution.

The State Duma produced a set of Recommendations of the Unified Commission for the Coordination of Legislative Activity on the Question 'On the Realization of International Legal Acts in the Russian Legal System' which proposed, *inter alia*, the adoption of a Federal Law 'On the Procedure for the Realization of International Legal Acts in the Legal System of the Russian Federation'. One measure under consideration is the obligatory expert assessment of draft federal laws from the standpoint of their conformity to the requirements of 'ratified' international legal acts by a special commission whose membership would be drawn from the Ministry of Foreign Affairs, the Ministry of Justice, law faculties, and the like.[95]

CIS

The treaty laws of *Armenia, Azerbaidzhan, Belarus, Kazakhstan, Moldova, Turkmenistan, Ukraine*, and *Uzbekistan* do not address the question of direct effect or operation of international treaties on their territory.

The treaty law of *Georgia* (Article 6[3]) is analogous to the 1995 Law except that it adds an additional requirement which the international treaty must satisfy: the establishment of 'rights and duties of a specific character'. It follows from the position of *Kyrgyzstan* that all treaties are of direct operation (Preamble) because they are part of Kyrgyzstan legislation, and the treaty law so provides. *Tadzhikistan* (Article 4) has reproduced the 1995 Law without change in relevant part.

[94] See, for example, V. M. Zhuikov, in Zhuikov, *Международные нормы о правах человека и применение их судами Российский Федерации* [International Norms on Human Rights and the Application Thereof by Courts of the Russian Federation] (M., Prava cheloveka, 1996), pp. 30–53. Also see Lukashuk, Commentary, p. 18.

[95] The text of the Recommendations appears in *Журнал российского права*, no. 3/4 (1999), pp. 95–6. The Commission was chaired by V. A. Ryzhkov.

Article 6 Expression of Consent of Russian Federation to Bindingness of International Treaty for It

1. The consent of the Russian Federation to the bindingness for it of an international treaty may be expressed by means of:

signature of the treaty;

the exchange of documents which form a treaty;

ratification of the treaty;

confirmation of the treaty;

adoption of the treaty;

accession to the treaty;

the use of any other means of expressing consent which the contracting parties have stipulated.

2. Decisions concerning consent to the bindingness for the Russian Federation of international treaties shall be adopted by agencies of State power of the Russian Federation in accordance with their competence established by the Constitution of the Russian Federation, by the present Federal Law, and by other acts of legislation of the Russian Federation.

Russia

1 Consent, or agreement, is the foundation stone of the international legal system. All norms of international law to be such required in their formative stage the consent of States as to formation and substance. Late Soviet international legal doctrine placed particular emphasis upon the 'concordant wills' of States in the formation of rules of international law.[96]

Procedurally, consent is a formal requirement of entry into force. Point one of this Article contains an exemplary list of the methods most commonly used in Russian practice for expressing consent to the text of a treaty, or to part thereof. Most often the method to be used is specified in the treaty itself. Although other methods may be used to express consent than those enumerated in the Law, such has not yet occurred in Russian practice.

[96] See G. I. Tunkin, *Theory of International Law*, transl. W. E. Butler (Cambridge, Mass., Harvard University Press, 1974), pp. 89–160.

Formal signature is the most extensively utilized method of expressing consent in international practice, including Russian practice. Signature may be either the full and final stage of expressing consent, or it may be an intermediate stage to be followed by ratification, acceptance, confirmation, or approval. When signature is the final stage of consent, entry into force follows either immediately thereafter or within a stipulated period. Further steps are not necessary.

In the second instance entry into force does not follow unless and until the additional procedure for expressing consent has been completed. The Commentary observes that pursuant to Article 18 of the 1969 Vienna Convention a State is obliged to refrain from actions which would deprive a treaty of its object and purposes.[97]

In both senses used above signature is to be distinguished from initialling the text of a treaty. While a form of signature is physically affixed to the text of a treaty when initialling, the initials merely establish the authenticity of the text and the agreement of the parties that they have completed work thereon. The accepted practice is that changes, additions, or amendments may not be made in the initialled text, although exceptions are known to have occurred in international practice. A decision of the President of Russia or of the Government of Russia, depending upon the nature of the treaty, is required for the text to be initialled. Initials are placed in the corner of each page, but the full signature of the individuals empowered to initial are not placed on the document nor are the initials placed where the signature will eventually be affixed. Having drawn the distinctions above, it also must be noted that the 1969 Vienna Convention permits the parties to stipulate that initialling is tantamount to signature and the treaty is in force. Such instances are uncommon and as yet unknown to Russian practice.

The Commentary observes that as a rule the text of a treaty will specify whether it enters into force upon signature by the parties, but that numerous examples are known in Russian practice where the text is silent. The preferred view is that where the treaty is silent on this point, it should be regarded as having entered into force upon signature.[98] Although formal statistics are not available, it would appear that the majority of Russian treaties enter into force upon signature.

While it is common for treaties to be signed by the parties at the same place and simultaneously, Russian practice knows instances when treaties have been signed by the Heads of State or Government in their respective countries and not necessarily on the same day. The Commentary believes

[97] A. G. Khodakov, in Commentary, p. 20.
[98] Khodakov, Commentary, p. 21.

a presumption operates to the effect that entry into force occurs from the moment of the last signature, unless the treaty stipulates otherwise.[99] An example of State practice is the Protocol to the Agreement Between the United States of America and the Russian Federation Concerning the Safe and Secure Transportation, Storage, and Destruction of Weapons and the Prevention of Weapons Proliferation. The Protocol recites that it was 'Done in duplicate . . . at Moscow and Washington DC this 15th & 16th day of June 1999'. Article 7 provides that 'This Protocol shall be applied provisionally from the date of signature', but Article 1 stipulates that the Agreement is being extended from 17 June 1999. Presumably the logic of the parties was that the Protocol, which amended the Agreement in certain respects, entered into force on 16 June, the date of last signature, duly amended the Agreement being provisionally applied and due to expire according to its provisions of 17 June 1999, and then extended the Agreement for seven years from 17 June 1999.[100]

The signature of treaties observes a sequence of affixing signatures long established in international practice but not addressed in the 1995 Law. The signatures of the plenipotentiaries follow the heading of the treaty, preamble, and text and are placed on the left side of the text (unless a language text is used which flows from right to left, e.g., Arabic, Hebrew, in which case from the right). If a seal is to be used, it is affixed from the left side.

For multilateral treaties the practice varies to take into account the multilateral character of the document. When a treaty text is the result of an international conference, it is common for all of the States which participated and which have decided to sign to assemble on a designated day to sign the document. Often the text is left open for signature by States within a stipulated period, especially when signature must be followed by ratification or similar expression of consent. Signature proceeds alphabetically by country according to the language in which the text was drafted unless the treaty stipulates otherwise. Where more than one copy of the treaty text has been drawn up and each has a different depositary, it is sufficient to sign any one of the texts.

Consent to the binding nature and entry into force of a treaty often is expressed by way of an exchange of notes or letters between the parties to the treaty. In Russian practice such notes or letters are conducted through the Ministry of Foreign Affairs: 'Other State committees, ministries, or departments do not conduct correspondence by Notes. Notes, as a rule, are exchanged by the Ministry of Foreign Affairs with the embassy of the

99 Khodakov, Commentary, p. 21.

100 The Russian-language text of the Protocol appears in *Ядерный контроль*, no. 6 (November–December 1999), p. 38.

respective State in Moscow or the embassy of Russia with the foreign policy department of the receiving country. However, in practice the sending of Notes by the Ministry of Foreign Affairs directly to the foreign policy department of another State is encountered.'[101]

Russian practice, according to the Commentary, relies principally upon the *note verbale*, which is not signed and which is drafted in the third person. The seal of the Ministry of Foreign Affairs is affixed, together with the date. When personal notes are used, they are addressed to a specific official, are signed by the person in whose name the Note is being sent (usually the Minister of Foreign Affairs or his deputy), and the date is affixed, but not the seal. An exchange of Letters follows the same procedure and formalities as does a Note, except that the exchange is effectuated not through the Ministry of Foreign Affairs, but through other departments, ministries, or State committees. As a rule, the Letter is drawn up in the name of the head of the department or his deputy.

Agreements reached in the form of an Exchange of Notes or an Exchange of Letters are normally of a narrow technical nature and brief in length. Examples include waiver of visa fees, lease of buildings, and others. An Exchange of Notes or an Exchange of Letters is often used to clarify individual provisions of a treaty, the exchange occurring simultaneously upon signature of the treaty or subsequently and the text of the Notes or Letters constituting an integral part of the treaty. In some instances, however, the Exchange of Notes or Letters is concluded by the parties to the treaty as an autonomous agreement which supplements the treaty or has the independent stature of a treaty itself. An example of the last is the Agreement in the Form of an Exchange of Letters between the Government of the Russian Federation and the Government of the Republic of Bulgaria Regarding the Results of Inventorization of Inter-State and Intergovernmental Treaties and Agreements Concluded between the USSR and the PRB in the Period from 1945 through 1991.[102]

The form of and procedures for the exchange of Notes or Letters varies. In form the Notes or Letters may be identical in substance, or one may contain an offer to conclude an agreement and the terms thereof which is then accepted in the Note or Letter of reply. Although extensively used in bilateral treaty practice, there is no limitation as to the number of parties to an exchange of Notes or Letters. When the text of the Notes or Letters is identical, the exchange usually occurs on the same day by way of being personally handed over to one another. Each party drafts the respective Note or Letter in its own language and appends an unofficial translation

[101] Khodakov, Commentary, p. 22.
[102] Dated 27 April 1996. *БМД*, no. 10 (1996), pp. 66–79.

into the language of the other party(ies). Except for the salutation and signatures, the texts of the Notes or Letters must coincide precisely.

In Russian practice, and perhaps international practice too, an exchange of Notes or Letters in the form of an offer and acceptance is encountered more commonly than an exchange of identical texts. As a rule, the text of the offer is known to and probably has been agreed with the other party. The formula is quite standard in international practice: an offer in the name of the sending State, Government, or department is made to reach agreement on a particular matter. The text of the proposed agreement is set out in full. The concluding section contains a clause to the effect that if the recipient State, Government, or department agrees with the offer, then the reply to that effect shall constitute an agreement between the respective parties which enters into force from the date of the Note or Letter of reply unless the parties have stipulated a different date.

Ratification of a treaty is not obligatory according to international law. This is a requirement stipulated by the parties, usually as a consequence of municipal law, especially the Constitution of the States concerned. In Russia the 1993 Constitution provides that certain treaties must be ratified by the Federal Assembly as a precondition of entry into force. Certain international conventions subject to ratification do not require signature of the treaty as a preliminary stage before ratification; among these are certain conventions of the International Labour Organization (ILO) which allow ratification without signature.

The term ‘confirmation’ is widely encountered in Russian legislative, executive, and governmental practice. Many types of normative acts are ‘confirmed’ by way of a Law [*закон*], Edict, or Decree. In Russian treaty practice confirmation is more commonly found with respect to treaties whose final consent to entry into force is given by the President of the Russian Federation or by the Government of the Russian Federation. Signature will almost always precede confirmation. According to the Commentary, confirmation with respect to bilateral treaties is encountered rather rarely.[103] When confirmation is completed, a Note communicating this is sent to the other party to a bilateral treaty or to the depositary of the respective multilateral treaty.

The Commentary stresses that confirmation of a treaty after signature in no way repeals the approval of a proposal to conclude or sign a treaty which must be submitted according to Article 9 of the 1995 Law to the Government, President, or other department. It follows that the confirmation of treaties signed without obtaining a decision of the President or the Government concerning the proposal to do so would constitute a

[103] Khodakov, Commentary, p. 24.

departure from the 1995 Law and in principle should not be permitted.[104] However, the 1995 Law attaches no consequences or sanctions of any kind to such a departure.

Acceptance of a treaty as a means of expressing consent to the treaty being binding and entering into force is not a term of Russian Law and appears in the 1995 Law by reason of the 1969 Vienna Convention. In Russian practice the term is used when the treaty to be 'accepted' expressly uses this term. It is treated as the equivalent of confirmation, and when Russian Law requires that acceptance be the equivalent of ratification, the form used is that of a Federal Law and the legal consequences are analogous to ratification, and notice of acceptance is communicated by Note or Letter.

Accession is not used in bilateral treaty practice unless the intention is to make a bilateral treaty multilateral by allowing a third State to become a party thereto. As a rule, accession is available to a State which did not take part in the negotiations or is otherwise not a party to the treaty from the very beginning. The conditions of accession may be stipulated in the treaty itself. Open accession is an accession available to any State, or to a State sharing the object and purposes of the treaty, as is sometimes provided; semi-closed accession is available only with the consent of all the other parties to the treaty; and closed accession is limited to States which satisfy certain criteria. The procedures for accession may take various forms: a special protocol of accession may be drawn up stipulating the conditions of accession; a Note or Letter may be sent by the acceding party to the depositary; or an instrument of accession may be formalized (see Gloss on Article 18, below).

While there is a view that accession may occur only with respect to a treaty which already has entered into force, such limitation, the Commentary observes, does not follow from the 1969 Vienna Convention. Treaties do exist which make provision for accession before their entry into force.[105]

CIS

Some treaty laws of CIS countries contain a provision identical or similar to point 1 of the 1995 Law, among them: *Azerbaidzhan* (Article 3), *Belarus* (Article 3), *Georgia* (Article 7[1]), *Kyrgyzstan* (Article 5), *Turkmenistan* (Article 2).

Others are silent on the point: *Armenia, Kazakhstan, Moldova, Tadzhikistan, Ukraine*, and *Uzbekistan*. However, these countries all

[104] Khodakov, Commentary, p. 24.
[105] Khodakov, Commentary, p. 25.

recognize the enumerated means by which a State may give consent to be bound by a treaty and use them in practice.

Russia

2 This point concerns the delimitation of power among Russian agencies of State power with respect to the conclusion of international treaties. In substance it requires an express delegation of power to give consent to the entry into force of an international treaty of the RF in the form of a competence established by the 1993 Constitution, the 1995 Law, or other acts of RF legislation. The Commentary indicates that the rule is intended to avoid a situation in which a Russian State agency which under legislation has no right to consent to a treaty being binding upon Russia nonetheless does so.[106]

One commentator, incorrectly in my view, has gone so far as to suggest that 'One must emphasize that international treaties of an interdepartmental character are binding only upon the departments which concluded them; neither the State nor the Government bears any responsibility for them'.[107]

Article 46 of the 1969 Vienna Convention would prevent the Russian Federation from invoking such an instance against the validity of the treaty in the absence of circumstances prescribed by the Convention. The failure to demarcate properly in this domain also could lead to a situation where pursuant to Article 15(4) of the 1993 Constitution the priority of the international treaty over a municipal law is established, legislative power could be usurped by a Russian State agency which improperly consented to the entry of a treaty into force.

The general provisions of this point are elaborated in Articles 9, 11, 15, 20, 21, and 22 of the 1995 Law (see Gloss, below). Articles 9, 11, 20, and 21 contain rules which enable the powers of the President and the Government to be delimited and which clarify the competence of Federal departments and agencies to adopt decisions concerning the entry of a treaty into force. Article 15 sets out the treaties which are subject to ratification. Articles 20 and 21 determine the distribution of competence between the agencies of legislative and executive power with regard to concluding international treaties of the RF. In addition the competence of individual State agencies with respect to treaties is to be found in individual Federal laws, edicts of the President, decrees and regulations

106 Osminin, Commentary, p. 26.

107 V. G. Boiarshinov, 'Междунаролные логоворы в правовой системе российской федерации' [International Treaties in the Legal System of the Russian Federation]. Available on the Computer Data Base GARANT 4.0.

of the Government, and especially the Statutes on individual Federal agencies.

The Commentary has characterized the delimitation of competence among agencies of State power with respect to termination and suspension of international treaties as a mirror reflection of the competence to conclude[108] (see Gloss on Articles 36 and 37, below).

CIS

Although this point of the 1995 Law has a particular meaning in the RF context, two CIS countries have adopted an identical or equivalent paragraph in their treaty laws even though they are unitary States: *Belarus* (Article 3) and *Kyrgyzstan* (Article 5(2)). *Georgia*, which is not a unitary State, has also included the provision (Article 7[2]).

[108] Osminin, Commentary, p. 27.

Article 7 Informing Federal Assembly of Russian Federation About International Treaties of Russian Federation

1. The Ministry of Foreign Affairs of the Russian Federation shall inform the Soviet of the Federation and the State Duma of the Federal Assembly of the Russian Federation about international treaties of the Russian Federation concluded in the name of the Russian Federation and in the name of the Government of the Russian Federation, and also about the termination of such treaties or the suspension of their operation.

2. The Government of the Russian Federation shall ensure the provision of information concerning international treaties being readied for signature at the requests of the chambers of the Federal Assembly of the Russian Federation.

Russia

1 To Western eyes point one of this Article would seem to address essentially the separation of powers between legislative and executive branches of the State. In fact, however well or badly the information process operates in practice, Russian doctrine attributes considerably more importance to the conceptual underpinnings of the provision.

The Commentary is illustrative in this respect. Given that international treaties of the RF are part of the legal foundation of inter-State relations and that the preparation, conclusion, termination, suspension, or introduction of policies to ensure compliance or take into account changes in treaty practice all influence Russian legislation as well as foreign and domestic policies, it is imperative that the two branches of government are aware of what one another is doing. Accordingly, the Ministry of Foreign Affairs is charged with keeping the chambers of the Federal Assembly abreast of what is happening in Russian treaty relations.[109]

[109] V. P. Zvekov, Commentary, p. 27.

Treaties are an integral part of foreign policy and accordingly also fall within the procedures laid down in the Reglaments of the State Duma[110] and of the Soviet of the Federation[111] for considering foreign policy issues. The chambers of the Federal Assembly are expected to have regard to treaty obligations when preparing their own foreign policy documents.

Article 15(4) of the 1993 Constitution affects the present Article as well, for insofar as international treaties and generally-recognized principles of international law are an integral part of the legal system, the legislator must have regard to them when legislating on any matter of relevance.

CIS

The treaty laws of the other CIS countries do not contain a provision similar to this point.

Russia

2 The requirement that the Government submit information to the Federal Assembly at its request concerning international treaties being prepared for signature also is intended to promote a unified foreign policy. Pursuant to Article 8 of the 1995 Law, the two chambers of the Federal Assembly each have the right to submit recommendations to the President or to the Government concerning the conclusion of an international treaty (see Gloss on Article 8, below).

Each chamber of the Federal Assembly enjoys under Article 125 of the 1993 Constitution the right to request the Constitutional Court of the RF to determine whether an international treaty of the RF which has not entered into force is in conformity with the 1993 Constitution.

CIS

The treaty laws of the other CIS countries do not contain a provision similar to this point.

[110] Section 5. *Ведомости ФС РФ* (1994), no. 3, item 160. These have been repeatedly amended since.

[111] Chapter 24. *СЗ РФ* (1996), no. 7, item 655.

Section II

Conclusion of International Treaties of Russian Federation

Article 8 Recommendations Concerning Conclusion of International Treaties of Russian Federation

1. Recommendations concerning the conclusion of international treaties of the Russian Federation may be submitted, depending upon the character of the questions affected, for consideration of the President of the Russian Federation or the Government of the Russian Federation, by each of the chambers of the Federal Assembly of the Russian Federation and by subjects of the Russian Federation in the person of their respective agencies of State power.

Such recommendations may also be submitted by the Supreme Court of the Russian Federation, the Supreme Arbitrazh Court of the Russian Federation, the General Procuracy of the Russian Federation, the Central Bank of the Russian Federation, and the Plenipotentiary for Human Rights with regard to questions of their jurisdiction.

2. The President of the Russian Federation, the Government of the Russian Federation, or on their behalf a federal minister or the director of another federal agency of executive power shall give a reply within a month to the recommendation.

Russia

1 The 1995 Law draws a distinction which did not exist in previous Soviet or Russian legislation on treaties: between a 'recommendation' and a 'proposal' to conclude an international treaty of the RF. This Article addresses the 'recommendation'; Article 9 is concerned with the 'proposal'.

Of the two terms, 'recommendation' appears to be the weaker, amounting in essence to a wish or desire of the issuing agency that an international treaty be concluded with regard to a particular issue. The 1995 Law contains no formal requirements which a recommendation must meet; it merely enumerates the bodies which have the right to make a recommendation: each chamber of the Federal Assembly, the Supreme Court, the Supreme Arbitrazh Court, the General Procuracy, the Central Bank of Russia, and the Plenipotentiary for Human Rights.

A proposal, on the other hand, must contain certain documents and be submitted by a different group of agencies (see Gloss on Article 9, below).

To whom the recommendation is submitted depends, according to Article 8, upon the competence of the President or the Government to conclude the respective treaty. The competence of each is defined rather broadly in Russian legislation. The 1993 Constitution (Article 86) provides merely that the President directs the foreign policy of Russia, conducts negotiations, and signs international treaties or instruments of ratification.[112] The competence of the Government in foreign relations is addressed in Article 114(1)(e) even more generally: measures relating to ensuring the defence of the country, State security, and the realization of the foreign policy of the RF.[113] However, the Law on the Council of Ministers – Government of the Russian Federation provides (Article 20[5]) that the Government: (a) effectuates direction in the domain of the relations of the RF with foreign States and international organizations; (b) ensures the representation of the RF in foreign States and in international organizations, concludes intergovernmental agreements, takes measures for the execution of international treaties of the RF; (c) effectuates direction in the domain of foreign trade and other types of foreign economic activity and of scientific – technical and cultural cooperation.[114]

Neither of these formulations of the competence of the President and the Government is sufficiently precise so as to enable the agency submitting a recommendation concerning the conclusion of an international treaty to determine to which the recommendation should be presented. Embryonic practice in Russia suggests that the President should receive recommendations concerning international treaties on major issues, such as collective security, friendship and cooperation, disarmament, and the like. It would follow that the Government should entertain recommendations relating to matters within the jurisdiction of the Government: foreign economic activity, scientific – technical and cultural cooperation, and the like.

The Reglaments of the State Duma and the Soviet of the Federation do not expressly contain procedures for the adoption of a Recommendation to conclude an international treaty. In the case of the State Duma one may suppose that the provisions of the Reglament determining how an Appeal or a Statement is enacted by the Duma would suffice to encompass

112 W. E. Butler, *Constitutional Foundations of the CIS Countries* (The Hague, Kluwer Law International, 1999), p. 452.
113 W. E. Butler, *Constitutional Foundations of the CIS Countries* (The Hague, Kluwer Law International, 1999), p. 463.
114 Adopted 22 December 1992. *Ведомости СНД и ВС РФ* (1993), no. 1, item 14.

a Recommendation. The Reglament of the Soviet of the Federation offers less scope for such a conclusion.

None of the other entities mentioned by the 1995 Law have been expressly endowed with the right to make a Recommendation to conclude an international treaty, although some of them may be inferred to have been so endowed by *renvoi* norms. The courts are governed generally by the 1996 Federal Constitutional Law on the Judicial System of the Russian Federation, adopted 23 October 1996.[115] The Supreme Court of the Russian Federation also is governed by the Law of the RSFSR on Court Organization of the RSFSR, adopted 8 July 1981, as amended.[116] Article 56 of the said Law, as amended, gives the Supreme Court the right to 'effectuate other powers granted to it by legislation'. The specific reference to international treaties in the Law concerns only treaties which have entered into force. However, the wording of Article 56 is sufficient, it would appear, to embrace the conferral of competence by Article 8(1) of the 1995 Law.

The Federal Constitutional Law of the Russian Federation on Arbitrazh Courts in the Russian Federation, adopted 5 April 1995,[117] preceded by several months the 1995 Law and did not take into account the possibility of making Recommendations. The Supreme Arbitrazh Court may decide within the limits of its competence questions arising from international treaties. The formulation is such that only treaties in force fall within its ambit.

The Federal Law of the Russian Federation on Making Changes in and Additions to the Law of the Russian Federation on the Procuracy of the Russian Federation, adopted 18 October 1995,[118] did follow the 1995 Law in time. In determining the competence of the General Procuracy, reference was made to its participating 'in the working out of international treaties'. This formulation is sufficiently broad to include the right of the Procuracy to make a Recommendation to conclude an international treaty.

The legislation making changes in and additions to the Federal Law on the Central Bank of the RSFSR (Bank of Russia), adopted 12 April 1995,[119] also preceded the 1995 Law and did not expressly empower the Central Bank to make a Recommendation concerning the conclusion of an international treaty. However, a new provision was included providing that the Central Bank 'effectuates other functions in accordance with federal laws'. Article 8(1) of the 1995 Law would therefore fall within

[115] Entered into force 1 January 1997. *Российская газета*, 6 January 1997, p. 3.
[116] *Ведомости Верховного Совета РСФСР* (1981), no. 28, item 976; *Ведомости СНД и ВС РФ* (1992), no. 27, item 1560; no. 30, item 1794; *СЗ РФ* (1994), no. 32, item 3300.
[117] *СЗ РФ*(1995), no. 18, item 1598.
[118] *СЗ РФ* (1995), no. 47, item 4472.
[119] *СЗ РФ*(1995), no. 18, item 1593.

this category and the Central Bank may be deemed to be so empowered with respect to a Recommendation.

The 1995 Law endows subjects of the RF with the right to make a Recommendation with regard to the conclusion of an international treaty but does not determine precisely which agencies of State power of a subject of the RF may act in this respect. This must be determined by examining the constitutional and other documents of each individual subject of the RF.

CIS

Only *Georgia* (Article 8) has chosen to introduce the distinction between a recommendation and a proposal to conclude a treaty first set out in the 1995 Law. The power to recommend is granted only to the Parliament of Georgia, which submits its recommendations concerning the conclusion of an international treaty to the President of Georgia. The autonomous republics within Georgia are not mentioned in this connection. The Supreme Court and the People's Defender of Georgia, following the Russian model but more narrowly, may make recommendations concerning their 'competence'. The recommendation must be accompanied by a substantiation explaining why the treaty should be concluded, a requirement not present in the Russian 1995 Law.

Russia

2 The 1995 Law requires that the President or the Government respectively reply to a Recommendation within a month and stipulates by whom such reply should be given. The procedure for calculating the month's period is not stipulated in the 1995 Law, but the procedure for calculating periods of limitation laid down by the Civil Code of the Russian Federation may be taken as guidance.[120]

The 1995 Law imposes no requirements with respect to the reply: whether it must be reasoned, whether it must be in writing, whether it must be debated, and the like.

CIS

Unlike the Russian case, where the President must reply within a month to the recommendation, the President of *Georgia* (Article 8[4]) need not reply; however, if the Georgian President approves the recommendation, he must within two months charge the Georgian Ministry of Foreign Affairs to prepare a proposal to conclude the treaty.

[120] W. E. Butler (transl.), *Russian Civil Legislation* (London, Simmonds & Hill, 1999), pp. 109–11.

Article 9 Proposals Concerning Conclusion of International Treaties of Russian Federation

1. Proposals concerning the conclusion of international treaties in the name of the Russian Federation shall be submitted to the President of the Russian Federation, and proposals concerning the conclusion of international treaties in the name of the Russian Federation relating to questions relegated to the jurisdiction of the Government of the Russian Federation shall be submitted to the Government of the Russian Federation.

2. Proposals concerning the conclusion of international treaties in the name of the Russian Federation shall be submitted to the President of the Russian Federation by the Ministry of Foreign Affairs of the Russian Federation.

Other federal agencies of executive power shall submit to the President of the Russian Federation proposals concerning the conclusion of international treaties in the name of the Russian Federation with regard to questions within their competence jointly with the Ministry of Foreign Affairs of the Russian Federation or by agreement with it.

Proposals concerning the conclusion of international treaties in the name of the Russian Federation which are subject to submission to the President of the Russian Federation and which require the preliminary consideration thereof by the Government of the Russian Federation shall be submitted to the Government of the Russian Federation. Decisions of the Government of the Russian Federation concerning the submission to the President of the Russian Federation of proposals concerning the conclusion of international treaties in the name of the Russian Federation shall be adopted in the form of a decree.

Proposals concerning the conclusion of international treaties in the name of the Russian Federation with regard to questions relegated to the jurisdiction of the Government of the Russian Federation shall be submitted in the procedure established by point 3 of the present Article.

3. Proposals concerning the conclusion of international treaties in the name of the Government of the Russian Federation shall be submitted to the Government of the Russian Federation by the Ministry of Foreign Affairs of the Russian Federation.

Other federal agencies of executive power shall submit to the Government of the Russian Federation proposals concerning the conclusion of international treaties in the name of the Government of the Russian Federation regarding questions within their competence jointly with the Ministry of Foreign Affairs of the Russian Federation or by agreement with it.

4. Proposals concerning the conclusion of international treaties of the Russian Federation of an interdepartmental character shall be submitted to the Government of the Russian Federation by federal agencies of executive power with regard to questions within their competence jointly with the Ministry of Foreign Affairs of the Russian Federation or by agreement with it.

5. Proposals concerning the conclusion of international treaties of the Russian Federation shall, before their submission to the President of the Russian Federation or to the Government of the Russian Federation, be agreed with the interested federal agencies of executive power, other agencies of State power of the Russian Federation, and agencies of State power of the respective subjects of the Russian Federation.

Proposals concerning the conclusion of an international treaty must contain the draft treaty or its basic provisions, a substantiation of the advisability of the conclusion thereof, a determination of the conformity of the draft treaty to legislation of the Russian Federation, and also an evaluation of the possible financial – economic and other consequences of the conclusion of the treaty.

6. Federal agencies of executive power shall have the right to conduct, by agreement with the Ministry of Foreign Affairs of the Russian Federation, consultations with respective agencies of foreign States or international organizations for the purpose of preparing draft international treaties for the submission of proposals in the procedure established by points 1–5 of the present Article concerning the conclusion thereof to the President of the Russian Federation or to the Government of the Russian Federation.

Russia

1 This Article distinguishes between inter-State treaties concluded in the name of the RF and intergovernmental treaties regulating issues relegated to the Government by the Constitution, the Law on the government, other federal laws, and edicts and regulations of the President. There is a certain flexibility in this distinction which enables a policy judgement to be made as to at which level a treaty will be concluded, including by agreement with the other Contracting Party. The Commentary rightly rejects as erroneous the widely shared view that Proposals to conclude an international treaty in the name of the RF should be submitted only to the President and Proposals in the name of the Government, only to the Government. [121] The Government also may act in the name of the RF.

[121] Osminin, Commentary, p. 35.

CIS

All CIS treaty laws (except *Belarus*) contain an article concerning the submission of proposals to conclude an international treaty. They differ in the apparent rationale for the distinctions drawn between an inter-State and an intergovernmental treaty and in the assignment of bureaucratic channels for submission of the respective proposals.

The *Armenian* (Article 3) treaty law makes no distinction for this purpose between the President and the Government but does require that the Armenian Ministry of Foreign Affairs be the key channel through which any proposals are submitted. This formulation would suggest that the Ministry of Foreign Affairs has considerable latitude in deciding whether the proposal should go to the President or to the Government, depending upon the subject-matter of the proposed treaty and other factors. The *Azerbaidzhan* (Article 4) treaty law is concerned more with who makes the proposal than the substance. The Cabinet of Ministers and the Ministry of Foreign Affairs of Azerbaidzhan have the right to make proposals to the President of Azerbaidzhan. Ministries, State committees, and the like make their proposals to the Cabinet of Ministers or to or with the Ministry of Foreign Affairs.

In the *Georgian* (Article 9) scheme the Ministry of Foreign Affairs has direct access to the President of Georgia with its proposals, and all others in Georgia must submit their proposals through the Ministry of Foreign Affairs. The *Kazakhstan* (Article 4[1]) treaty law authorizes both the Government and the Ministry of Foreign Affairs to make proposals to the President of Kazakhstan, but only with respect to inter-State treaties. The Kyrgyzstan (Article 6[1]), *Tadzhikistan* (Article 5), *Turkmenistan* (Article 4), and *Uzbekistan* (Article 8) treaty law formulations follow that of the 1995 Law. In *Moldova* (Article 10) and *Ukraine* (Article 3[1]) proposals for the conclusion of treaties are the matter of the Government.

Only *Georgia* (Article 9[9]) has made express provision for the possibility that a foreign State or international organization might propose the conclusion of an international treaty. Such proposal of a foreign State or international organization concerning the conclusion of an international treaty the Ministry of Foreign Affairs of Georgia shall submit to the President of Georgia in the procedure established by Article 9 generally.

Russia

2 Point two regulates the procedure for Federal agencies of executive power to submit a proposal to conclude an international treaty in the name of the RF. These are submitted to the President of the RF by the

Ministry of Foreign Affairs. Other Federal agencies of executive power submit such proposals to the President with regard to questions within their competence either jointly with the Ministry of Foreign Affairs or by agreement with that Ministry.

The Ministry of Foreign Affairs thus occupies a central place in the treaty process, acting both as a principal and coordinator. This follows from the Statute on the Ministry, confirmed by Edict of the President of the RF on 14 March 1995, No. 271, [122] and is elaborated in the Edict of the President of the RF on the Coordinating Role of the Ministry of Foreign Affairs of the Russian Federation in Conducting a Unified Foreign Policy Line of the Russian Federation, adopted 12 March 1996, No. 375.[123] The last provides that the Ministry of Foreign Affairs is the head agency within the system of Federal agencies of executive power and effectuates general control over compliance with international obligations by the RF. The Ministry coordinates the activity of other federal agencies of executive power in this domain and the international links of subjects of the RF. A proposal affecting the foreign policy interests of Russia, including a proposal to conduct negotiations and conclude an international treaty, even a treaty of an interdepartmental character, is subject 'in an obligatory procedure' to being agreed by Federal agencies of executive power with the Ministry of Foreign Affairs before being submitted to the President or to the Government. The Administration of the President and the Government are not to accept a proposal for consideration unless it has been agreed with the Ministry.

Competence is a key issue in this provision, and the competence of agencies of executive power is determined by the Statutes on such agencies, many of which were confirmed before the 1995 Law and do not fully reflect its provisions.

Point two also contains an exception to the general rule with regard to making proposals to the President of the RF. If the proposal to conclude a treaty in the name of the RF requires preliminary consideration by the Government of the RF, the proposal must be first submitted to the Government, which will then determine by way of a Decree whether to submit the proposal to the President. Major treaties are subjected to this procedure. An example is the Agreement on Partnership and Cooperation between the Russian Federation and the European Union and its member-States; the draft was submitted jointly by the Ministry of Foreign Economic Relations and the Ministry of Foreign Affairs for approval by the Government and then to the President of the RF. [124]

[122] *СЗ РФ* (1995), no. 12, item 1033.
[123] *СЗ РФ* (1996), no. 12, item 1061.
[124] Decree of 19 June 1994, No. 742. *СЗ РФ* (1994), no. 9, item 1054.

A proposal to conclude an international treaty in the name of the RF with regard to questions relegated to the jurisdiction of the Government are submitted to the Government in the same procedure established for a proposal to conclude an intergovernmental treaty in the name of the Government.[125]

CIS

The other CIS treaty laws contain more laconic provisions on the matter of jurisdiction over treaty proposals than does the 1995 Law. Often the relevant clause is incorporated into point one above: *Armenia* (Article 3), *Azerbaidzhan* (Article 4), *Kazakhstan* (Article 4), *Kyrgyzstan* (Article 6), *Tadzhikistan* (Article 4), *Turkmenistan* (Article 4), and *Uzbekistan* (Article 8).

The *Georgian* treaty law (Article 9) does not distinguish the Government from central agencies of executive power for the purposes of proposals to conclude a treaty. The *Ukrainian* treaty law (Article 3), on the other hand, refers all treaty proposals to the Government of Ukraine. The President has no role in this process.

In nearly all cases the Ministry of Foreign Affairs is given the central and coordinating role for submitting and/or evaluating the proposals. Some treaty laws involve the Government directly or alternatively in this process. The *Moldovan* treaty law is silent on the question of proposals to conclude treaties. The principal exception is *Uzbekistan,* which has made special provision in its treaty law (Article 9) for proposals to conclude treaties concerning questions of foreign economic activity, including questions of trade and economic cooperation and rendering technical assistance. Treaties of this nature may be submitted by the Ministry of Foreign Economic Relations autonomously to the Government with mere 'notification' to the Ministry of Foreign Affairs of Uzbekistan. Other ministries and departments of Uzbekistan may circumvent the Ministry of Foreign Affairs with treaty proposals on foreign economic activity, submitting them directly to the Ministry of Foreign Economic Relations without notifying the Ministry of Foreign Affairs.

Russia

3 Pursuant to point three of this Article, the following Federal agencies have been endowed with the right to make a proposal to conclude an international treaty in the name of the RF: first, the Ministry of Foreign Affairs; and second, other Federal agencies of executive power within their competence and jointly with the Ministry of Foreign Affairs or by

[125] Osminin, Commentary, p. 36.

agreement with that Ministry. The same procedure applies to a proposal to conclude an international treaty of the RF with regard to questions relegated to the jurisdiction of the Government. An example was the proposed Franco-Russian Agreement on cooperation in outer space. The Ministry of Foreign Affairs of the RF submitted a draft Agreement jointly with the Russian Space Agency by agreement with the State Customs Committee of the RF and the Russian Agency for Patents and Trademarks, which draft was approved by the Government on 26 November 1996. [126]

The official submission of such proposals is the prerogative of Federal agencies of executive power. The Commentary observes that 'this right has been consolidated for Federal agencies of executive power as agencies of special competence to be realized in various spheres of State administration and effectuated by them in each instance within the limits of respective competence. Other agencies and organizations, including those functioning attached to the Government, do not possess such a right.'[127]

CIS

The other CIS treaty laws mostly follow this pattern. The Ministry of Foreign Affairs, being the central governmental agency charged with conducting foreign affairs, is the principal conduit for circulating treaty proposals to the Government. When other agencies of executive power have competence to make a proposal to conclude a treaty, that proposal, as a rule, must be submitted jointly with, or by agreement with, the Ministry of Foreign Affairs. See, for example, the *Ukrainian* treaty law (Article 3[2]).

Russia

4 Only Federal agencies of executive power may with regard to questions within their competence jointly with the Ministry of Foreign Affairs or by agreement with that Ministry submit a proposal to the Government to conclude an international treaty of an interdepartmental character. The same observations regarding the prerogative power of Federal agencies in the preceding point apply here.

CIS

The other CIS treaty laws fall into three groups with respect to proposals to conclude interdepartmental treaties. The first group, comprising

[126] See Decree No. 1424. *СЗ РФ* (1996), no. 51, item 5827.
[127] Zvekov, Commentary, p. 36.

Georgia (Article 9[8]), *Kazakhstan* (Article 4[6]), *Kyrgyzstan* (Article 6[5]), and *Turkmenistan* (Article 4), contains a provision analogous to that of the 1995 Law. The *Georgian* treaty law makes provision in this connection only for interdepartmental treaties which involve the making of changes in or additions to normative acts of Georgia; *Azerbaidzhan* (Article 4) and *Turkmenistan* (Article 4) extend this requirement to all such treaties. The second group, comprising *Ukraine* (Article 3[3]) and *Uzbekistan* (Article 8), relegates the issue to special decrees or other normative acts which are to be enacted with respect to interdepartmental treaties. A third group, comprising *Armenia, Azerbaidzhan, Belarus, Moldova, Tadzhikistan,* makes no reference whatsoever to interdepartmental treaties in this connection.

The *Kyrgyzstan* treaty law (Article 6[3]) is unique in the CIS in making provision for so-called 'inter-parliamentary' treaties. Proposals concerning the conclusion of inter-parliamentary treaties are to be submitted by the Torag of the Legislative Assembly, the Torag of the Assembly of People's Representatives of the Zhorogku Kenesh of the Kyrgyz Republic or by deputies of the Zhorogku Kenesh of the Kyrgyz Republic for consideration of the chambers of the Zhorogku Kenesh of the Kyrgyz Republic. Neither the Ministry of Foreign Affairs nor the President and Government of Kyrgyzstan has any express role in the proposals to conclude this category of treaty.

Russia

5 The agreeing of a Proposal to be submitted to the President or to the Government is mandatory by interested Federal agencies irrespective of whether they are Federal agencies of executive power or not. This includes agencies which are not part of the executive branch, such as the Supreme Court of the RF or the Supreme Arbitrazh Court of the RF.

The requirement that a Proposal to conclude an international treaty of the RF must be agreed with agencies of State power of subjects of the RF must be read against Article 4 of the 1995 Law (see Gloss on Article 4, above). Article 4 uses the term 'interested subject' of the RF, which is understood to mean, first, subjects of the RF within whose jurisdiction fall the questions affected by the international treaty, and second, subjects of the RF whose powers with regard to matters of joint jurisdiction of the RF and subjects of the RF are affected by the draft international treaty or by basic provisions thereof. In the first instance Article 4 of the 1995 Law speaks of the treaty being concluded 'by agreement' with the agencies of State power of the subject of the RF on which the respective function has been placed (point one), whereas in the second instance a Proposal received 'shall be considered when preparing the draft of the treaty' (point two). The differences arise from the nature of the powers of the subject of the RF being exercised in each instance on the basis of constitutional norms (see Gloss on Article 4, above).

As noted above in the Gloss on Article 4, Federal agencies of executive power decide by agreement with agencies of State power of the interested subject of the RF which have been charged with the respective function the issues of the participation of representatives of agencies of State power of the subject of the RF in preparing the draft treaty, in negotiations, and in signature of the treaty. No provision is made for resolving disagreements over these matters.

The proposal to conclude an international treaty of the RF must be accompanied by certain materials set out in point five of the 1995 Law. These include submission of the text of the draft treaty or the basic provisions thereof, a substantiation of the advisability of concluding the treaty, a view as to the conformity of the draft to Federal legislation in force, and an assessment of the financial and economic or other (for example, environmental) implications or consequences of the treaty. Projections should be made as to the expenditure implications for the Federal budget.

CIS

The formal requirement of obtaining the agreement of interested State agencies before submitting a proposal to conclude a treaty, as set out in the 1995 Law, is found in only two CIS treaty laws and even then in modified form. *Uzbekistan* does make this requirement, specifically instructing that the views of the Ministry of Justice be obtained (Article 8). *Ukraine* requires the agreement of the Ministry of Justice to such a proposal only if the treaty would require changes in Ukrainian legislation (Article 3[7]).

The 1995 Law extends the requirement of obtaining agreement to subjects of the RF. Ukraine does not make this requirement of its constituent republic, *Crimea*, but does permit the Crimea to make proposals with regard to the conclusion of international treaties of Ukraine in the person of its highest agencies of legislative and executive power (Article 3[6]).

In five CIS treaty laws there are requirements with respect to the documents and substantiation which must accompany a proposal to conclude an international treaty. They vary from those of the RF in that they require a broader substantiation of the consequences of concluding the proposed treaty, including political, economic, legal, and material consequences (*Azerbaidzhan, Georgia, Kyrgyzstan, Ukraine,* and *Uzbekistan*). In *Georgia* (Article 9[4]) and *Ukraine* (Article 3[4]) the proposal should contain the proposed composition of the delegation which would negotiate the treaty, together with a draft text.

The treaty laws of *Armenia, Belarus, Kazakhstan, Moldova,* and *Tadzhikistan* contain no relevant provisions.

Russia

6 The preparation of a draft treaty presupposes consultations with competent agencies of foreign States or international organizations with a view to determining the positions of the parties, overcoming possible differences, finding agreed solutions, and agreeing texts. By agreement with the Ministry of Foreign Affairs, Federal agencies of executive power have the right to conduct such consultations. The 1995 Law is silent as to what happens if the Ministry of Foreign Affairs declines to authorize such consultations or prefers to conduct them by itself.

CIS

Although the *Georgian* treaty law (Article 9[9]) recognizes that a proposal to conclude a treaty may originate with a foreign State or international organization, only the *Kyrgyzstan* treaty law (Article 7[2]) contains a provision analogous to point six of the present Article of the 1995 Law.

Article 10 Functions of Ministry of Justice of Russian Federation in Connection with Conclusion of International Treaties of Russian Federation

1. Proposals concerning the conclusion of international treaties of the Russian Federation establishing other rules than those provided for by legislation of the Russian Federation shall be submitted to the President of the Russian Federation or to the Government of the Russian Federation by agreement with the Ministry of Justice of the Russian Federation.

2. The Ministry of Justice of the Russian Federation shall give, in particular if this is provided for by the international treaty of the Russian Federation or is a necessary condition of the entry thereof into force, an opinion regarding the questions of the conformity of the provisions of the treaty to legislation of the Russian Federation and the legal force thereof in the Russian Federation, and also with regard to other questions connected with the entry into force and fulfilment of such treaty.

Russia

1 Point one sets out the general rule that proposals concerning the conclusion of international treaties which would establish other rules than those provided for by Russian legislation in force must be agreed with the Ministry of Justice of the RF. Neither the procedure nor the form for such agreement is stipulated by the 1995 Law.

This provision is analogous to that contained in the 1978 Law of the USSR (Article 6). The practice under the 1978 Law of the USSR resulted in the USSR Ministry of Justice issuing an Opinion concerning the conformity of the Proposal to Soviet legislation.

A Proposal is likely to contain the view of the Federal agency of executive power concerning the conformity of the draft international treaty to Russian legislation. The Ministry of Justice therefore in verifying such non-conformity is in fact addressing a related issue: whether it is possible or advisable to introduce into the Russian legal system rules of an international treaty which differ from legislation in force. The 1995 Law is silent as to what implications should flow from the Opinion of the Ministry of Justice. A negative assessment would not preclude the draft being submitted to the President or to the Government, for otherwise the Ministry of Justice would have a virtual veto over treaty-making of the RF.

CIS

The CIS treaty laws fall into three groups with respect to the role of their ministries of justice in treaty-making. Most make no express provision.

The treaty law of *Ukraine* (Article 3[7]) follows the model of the RF and requires involvement of the Ministry of Justice when the proposed treaty would establish other rules than those provided for by legislation of the respective State.

A third category of treaty laws stipulates that the ministry of justice must be involved in any proposal to conclude a treaty: *Kyrgyzstan* (Article 7[1]), *Uzbekistan* (Article 8).

Russia

2 Point two consolidates State practice of relatively recent origin in the RF by authorizing the Ministry of Justice of the RF to issue a formal legal Opinion as to the conformity of an international treaty of the RF to Russian legislation and the legal force thereof for the RF. Such Opinions also may require the Ministry to opine that all internal procedures have been complied with in the RF with respect to empowering individual officials to sign the treaty and similar issues. International financial institutions have been among those whose credit agreements required such an Opinion of the Ministry, including The World Bank and the European Bank for Reconstruction and Development (EBRD). The Statute on the Ministry of Justice of the RF did not make provision for the Ministry to issue such Opinions. The present point creates the legal basis for the Ministry of Justice to do so.

There are facile Western assumptions about the legal value of such Opinions which have no basis in Russian legislation. First, there is an assumption of due diligence on the part of the Ministry, although there is no legal requirement that such be conducted. Neither is there any indication as to what agencies have the right to request such an Opinion from the Ministry of Justice, nor whether the Ministry of Justice may issue an Opinion at its own initiative and to whom, nor what the legal consequences of a Ministry of Justice Opinion may be. Some of the early Opinions issued appear to have been drafted on the basis of Western legal requirements and were not responsive to the real issues of Russian Law purportedly addressed in them.

CIS

The other CIS treaty laws do not contain a requirement of this nature.

Article 11 Decisions Concerning Conducting of Negotiations and Signature of International Treaties of Russian Federation

1. Decisions concerning the conducting of negotiations and the signature of international treaties of the Russian Federation shall be adopted:

(a) with respect to treaties to be concluded in the name of the Russian Federation: by the President of the Russian Federation, and with respect to treaties to be concluded in the name of the Russian Federation with regard to questions relegated to the jurisdiction of the Government of the Russian Federation: by the Government of the Russian Federation;

(b) with respect to treaties to be concluded in the name of the Government of the Russian Federation: by the Government of the Russian Federation.

2. The President of the Russian Federation shall adopt decisions concerning the conducting of negotiations and the signature of international treaties with regard to questions relegated to the jurisdiction of the Government of the Russian Federation if there is need to do so.

3. Decisions concerning the conducting of negotiations concerning the conclusion of international treaties of the Russian Federation of an interdepartmental character shall be adopted by the Government of the Russian Federation.

Decisions concerning the signature of international treaties of an interdepartmental character shall be adopted by a federal minister or director of another federal agency of executive power within whose competence the questions are which are to be regulated by such treaties, by agreement with the Ministry of Foreign Affairs of the Russian Federation.

4. The Government of the Russian Federation shall adopt decisions concerning the signature of international treaties of an interdepartmental character if the respective questions have important significance for the State interests of the Russian Federation.

Russia

1 This Article lays down the procedure for adopting a decision to conduct negotiations and to sign international treaties of the RF. The decision

as to who will sign an international treaty of the RF will predetermine the procedure for submitting the treaty for ratification (see Article 16, 1995 Law) and the procedure for adopting a decision to apply an international treaty provisionally (Article 23, 1995 Law). And these decisions in turn predetermine the procedure for submitting a Proposal to terminate or suspend an international treaty (Article 36, 1995 Law) and play a role in establishing the procedure for terminating and suspending such a treaty (Article 37, 1995 Law).

According to subpoint (a) of point one of this Article, the President of the RF adopts decisions to conduct negotiations and sign international treaties concluded in the name of the RF. Examples include the decision to sign the Treaty on Friendship and Cooperation between the RF and the Republic of Albania,[128] the Treaty between the RF and Turkmenistan on Cooperation for the Purpose of Ensuring the Rights of the Russian Minority in Turkmenistan and of the Turkmen Minority in the RF,[129] and the Treaty between the RF and the Kingdom of Spain on Rendering Legal Assistance with Regard to Criminal Cases.[130]

Decisions to conduct negotiations and sign treaties concluded in the name of the RF with regard to questions relegated to the jurisdiction of the Government are adopted by the Government. Examples are numerous: the Agreement between the RF and the International Bank for Reconstruction and Development (IBRD) on a Loan for Financing the Project 'Urban Public Transport'.[131] This Decree was enacted on the basis of Article 114 of the 1993 Constitution and in execution of Article 3 of the Federal Law on State Foreign Borrowings of the Russian Federation and State Credits to be Granted by the Russian Federation to Foreign States, Juridical Persons Thereof, and International Organizations. Article 3 of the said Law provided that State foreign borrowings of the RF shall be effectuated by the Government on the basis of international treaties concluded in the name of the RF or in the name of the Government. The Decree of the Government of the Russian Federation of 26 November 1996 on Signing the Agreement between the Government of the Russian Federation and the Government of the French Republic on Cooperation in the Domain of Research and Use of Outer Space for Peaceful Purposes 'considered it advisable to sign the said Agreement on the level of Heads of Governments in the course of the second session of the Russo-French Commission for Questions of Bilateral Cooperation'.[132]

[128] Regulation of 20 February 1995, No. 85-рп. *СЗ РФ* (1995), no. 9, item 741.
[129] Regulation of 17 May 1995, No. 226-рп. *СЗ РФ* (1995), no. 21, item 1964.
[130] Regulation of 24 August 1995, No. 393-рп. *СЗ РФ* (1995), no. 35, item 3523.
[131] Decree of 11 August 1995, No. 810. *СЗ РФ* (1995), no. 33, item 3406.
[132] *СЗ РФ* (1996), no. 51, item 5827.

The Government of the RF formalizes decisions to sign international treaties of the RF in the form of a Decree (excluding treaties of an interdepartmental character).

The language of subpoint (b) of point one of the present Article is extremely broad, reflecting the breadth of the 1993 Constitution in empowering the Government to adopt decisions relating to the realization of Russian foreign policy.

CIS

The CIS treaty laws fall into two groups with respect to decisions concerning the conducting of negotiations and signature of international treaties. The first group follows the model of the 1995 Law and distinguishes between treaties to be concluded in the name of the respective State and those to be concluded in the name of the Government of the respective State, and on the basis of that distinction empowering the President and the Government or Head of Government, respectively: *Armenia* (Article 4), *Azerbaidzhan* (Article 5), *Belarus* (Articles 4 and 5), *Kazakhstan* (Article 7), *Kyrgyzstan* (Article 8),[133] *Tadzhikistan* (Article 6), *Ukraine* (Article 4), and *Uzbekistan* (Article 11).

The treaty law of Belarus regulates the issues of negotiation and signature in separate articles as separate decisions and in exceeding detail. The proposal concerning either negotiations or signature must be supported by:

- the draft international treaty or basic provisions of the position in negotiations;
- the draft of the respective decision of the President of the Republic Belarus or Council of Ministers of the Republic Belarus;
- the substantiation of the advisability of concluding the international treaty;
- the opinion of the respective State agencies of the Republic Belarus within whose competence the questions contained in the draft international treaty are relegated;
- the opinion of the Ministry of Foreign Affairs of the Republic Belarus concerning the conformity of the draft international treaty to international obligations of the Republic Belarus;
- the opinion of the Ministry of Justice of the Republic Belarus concerning the conformity of the draft international treaty to

[133] But with respect to signature only. Kyrgyzstan does not require a special decision-making process to enter into negotiations to conclude a treaty. Consistent with its category of interparliamentary treaties, the Kyrgyzstan treaty law (Article 8[2]) makes provision for the decision to sign such treaties.

the Constitution and other legislation of the Republic Belarus;
the list of norms of laws of the Republic Belarus, acts of the President of the Republic Belarus, and Government of the Republic Belarus subject to change, addition, repeal, or adoption in connection with the conclusion of the international treaty;
the proposals concerning the working out of acts of legislation of the Republic Belarus necessary for the realization of the international treaty;
the list of persons who have taken part in working out the draft international treaty and proposed for participation in the negotiation process;
the financial – economic substantiation of the expenditures proposed which are connected with the realization of the international treaty (Article 4).

The second group of treaty laws grants to the President of the country the right to make the decision for both categories of treaties: *Azerbaidzhan* (Article 4), *Georgia* (Article 11[1]), *Moldova* (Article 2), *Turkmenistan* (Article 5).

The *Georgian* (Article 11[1]) treaty law specifies the form in which the President expresses his decision concerning negotiation and signature of a treaty: the regulation.

Russia

2 Point two of this Article creates an exception from the provisions of point one by granting to the President of the RF the right to adopt a decision to conduct negotiations and sign international treaties with regard to questions relegated to the Government if necessity so requires. The definition of 'necessity' is evidently a political one, and the exception illustrates the special role of the President under the 1993 Constitution (Article 86) in directing the foreign policy of Russia.

The decision to conclude an Agreement between the Government of the Russian Federation and NATO concerning the Financial Participation of the Russian Federation in Operations of Multinational Forces in Bosnia and Herzogovina[134] was taken by the President of the RF, having regard to the fact that the Agreement was closely linked to another Agreement, also approved at Presidential level, between the RF and NATO on interaction within the multinational forces in Bosnia and Herzogovina.

Instances also are known of a Presidential decision to conduct negotiations and conclude international treaties of the RF of an interdepartmental character where such treaties touch upon questions relegated to

[134] Regulation of 13 February 1996, No. 65-рп. *СЗ РФ* (1996), no. 10, item 921.

the competence of the President or Federal agencies of executive power within the President's jurisdiction. An example is the Agreement between the Federal Security Service of the Russian Federation and the General Staff of the Bulgarian Army on Cooperation in the Sphere of Military Counterintelligence,[135] the decision to conclude which was taken by the President of the RF.

The Commentary indicates that when a draft treaty is approved by the Government and a proposal is submitted to the President of the RF concerning the signature thereof, a decision is adopted authorizing both signature and the making of changes in and additions to the draft which do not involve questions of principle in comparison with the draft approved by the Government.[136] This practice also was followed in respect of the Agreement on Partnership and Cooperation between the Russian Federation and the European Union and its Member-States.[137]

Ambiguity can arise in Russian treaty practice over the use of the words 'conclusion' and 'signature' in this connection. When an international treaty of the RF is to enter into force from the moment of signature, the decision authorizing action with regard to the treaty probably actually has in view authorizing the 'conclusion' of the treaty, whereas when signature is a preliminary and not the final stage, but must be followed by ratification or confirmation, the decision authorizing action does have 'signature' in view. This distinction is reinforced in Article 2(d) of the 1995 Law, where the word 'conclusion' is used to signify the expression of consent of the RF to an international treaty binding upon it. The word 'conclusion' as a legal term has several meanings, some of which are as applicable to the Law of Treaties as to the Law of Obligations under Russian Civil Law; in both international and domestic usage 'conclusion' commonly encompasses an entire series of stages or processes which end with the entry of the document into force.

While there are ample examples in practice of the President of the RF adopting a single decision authorizing both the conducting of negotiations and the signature of an international treaty, instances are known of decisions treating these as separate stages requiring separate authorizations. The President of the RF authorized negotiations to be conducted with Switzerland concerning the preparation of a draft treaty on conciliation and arbitration, on condition that if any agreement were reached a proposal should be submitted for consideration.[138]

[135] Regulation of 25 December 1995, No. 554-рп. *СЗ РФ* (1995), no. 52, item 5162. This approach was based on Article 12, paragraph two, [3], of the Federal Law on Foreign Intelligence. *СЗ РФ* (1996), no. 3, item 143.

[136] Osminin, Commentary, p. 43.

[137] Regulation of 22 June 1994, No. 322-рп. *СЗ РФ* (1994), no. 9, item 1002.

[138] Regulation of 21 June 1994, No. 31-рп. *СЗ РФ* (1994), no. 9, item 996.

A more or less standard formulation is followed in drafting a decision to sign an international treaty. Approval of the draft treaty text is given, as a rule, as the basis for negotiations or as being agreed preliminarily with the other party, and authorization to make changes in and additions to the draft appended to the decision which are not ones of principle. The Commentary reports that it is uncommon in Russian practice not to approve the text of the draft treaty, but instead to instruct the negotiators to be guided by relevant treaty practice, Russian legislation, and norms of international law.[139] An example was the Consular Convention between the Russian Federation and Bulgaria.[140] Submission of the basic provisions of a draft treaty, rather than the draft text, although permitted by the 1995 Law, is reportedly virtually never done in practice.[141]

A multilateral convention raises different problems in this context as the text is to be adopted at an international conference or within an international organization and authorizing changes and additions would not have any meaning. Instead a text officially certified is sent to the official or agency who is adopting the decision to authorize signature. An example is the decision to sign the Convention on the safety of United Nations personnel, adopted by the UN General Assembly; Russia participated in the drafting.[142]

CIS

The other CIS treaty laws do not contain this provision.

Russia

3 Decisions of the Government of the RF to conclude treaties may take a general form or be addressed to an individual treaty. The Ministry of Internal Affairs of the RF, for example, concluded a series of agreements on cooperation with similar departments of foreign States on the basis of the Decree of the Government of the RF 'On the Conclusion of Agreement on Cooperation between the Ministry of Internal Affairs of the Russian Federation and Competent Departments of Foreign States, No. 653, 29 June 1995'.[143]

139 Osminin, Commentary, p. 44.

140 See the Decision set out in Regulation of 20 September 1995, No. 425-рп. *СЗ РФ* (1995), no. 39, item 3766.

141 Osminin, Commentary, p. 44.

142 Regulation of 23 June 1995, No. 291-рп. *СЗ РФ* (1995), no. 26, item 2474.

143 *СЗ РФ* (1995), no. 28, item 2705. For the view that the Ministry of Internal Affairs abused its powers under this Decree to conclude agreements or provisions not authorized by the Decree, see V. M. Volzhenkina, *Нормы международного права в российском*

Ministers, Chairmen of State committees, and the heads of other Federal agencies of executive power whose respective departments have competence over questions regulated by an international treaty of the RF of an interdepartmental character have the right to adopt decisions, by agreement with the Ministry of Foreign Affairs, to sign such treaties, provided that the Government has adopted a decision to conduct negotiations to conclude the respective treaty. A formulation commonly encountered is as follows: 'To accept the Proposal of the Minprirody of Russia, agreed with the MID of Russia, on conducting negotiations concerning the conclusion of an Agreement between the Ministry of Protection of the Environment and Natural Resources of the Russian Federation and the Ministry of Environmental Protection of the Slovak Republic on Cooperation in the Domain of Environmental Protection.'[144] The Commentary observes that if a protocol or memorandum is under consideration, the words 'concerning the conclusion' will be replaced by 'concerning the signature'.

CIS

The CIS treaty laws fall into several groups with regard to the conducting of negotiations and signature of interdepartmental treaties.

One group of laws refers the question to subordinate legislation: *Armenia* (Article 4), *Belarus* (Article 1), *Ukraine* (Article 4), and *Uzbekistan* (Article 11).

A second group is silent on the subject: *Azerbaidzhan* (Article 5).

A third group determines that the head of the Ministry of Foreign Affairs may take the decision to negotiate and sign by agreement with the respective department: *Georgia* (Article 11 [2]).

A fourth group grants to the head of the respective department the right to negotiate and sign by agreement with the Government: *Kyrgyzstan* (Article 7), *Moldova* (Article 4), *Tadzhikistan* (Article 6), *Turkmenistan* (Article 5).

Russia

4 The 1995 Law creates two exceptions to the rules for adopting decisions concerning the signature of interdepartmental international treaties. First, if the questions dealt with in the treaty are deemed to be of important significance for the State interests of Russia, the decision to sign the interdepartmental treaty may be adopted by the Government. The

уголовном процессе [Norms of International Law in Russian Criminal Procedure] (Spb., izd-vo Iurid. tsentr Press, 2001), pp. 81–2.

144 Regulation of 29 June 1995, No. 893p. *СЗ РФ* (1995), no. 28, item 2731.

second arises when an act is issued by the President under which a decision may be taken to conduct negotiations and sign an interdepartmental treaty with regard to matters relegated to the jurisdiction of the Government. What falls into the category of 'important significance for the State interests' of Russia is a policy decision, but one which must be addressed in the Proposal submitted. The Commentary advises that as a rule the draft text of the interdepartmental treaty is appended to the authorizing Regulation.[145]

The Government takes decisions to conduct negotiations or sign interdepartmental treaties in the form of a Regulation. Inter-State or intergovernmental treaties are normally the platform for concluding an interdepartmental treaty. Russian treaty practice knows instances of several departments being involved on the Russian side. In Western experience difficulty is sometimes experienced in determining precisely what the statutory competence of the Russian department is, a reflection of imprecise drafting of the Statutes on the particular department.

CIS

The other CIS laws do not contain an analogous provision.

[145] Zvekov, Commentary, p. 46.

Article 12 Conducting of Negotiations and Signature of International Treaties of Russian Federation Without Need to Present Powers

1. The President of the Russian Federation as the Head of State shall represent the Russian Federation in international relations and in accordance with the Constitution of the Russian Federation and international law shall conduct negotiations and sign international treaties of the Russian Federation without the need to present powers.

2. The Chairman of the Government of the Russian Federation as the Head of Government and the Minister of Foreign Affairs of the Russian Federation by virtue of his functions and in accordance with international law shall conduct negotiations and sign international treaties of the Russian Federation without the need to present powers.

3. A federal minister or director of another federal agency of executive power shall have the right within the limits of his competence to conduct negotiations and to sign international treaties of the Russian Federation of an interdepartmental character without presenting powers.

4. The head of a diplomatic representation of the Russian Federation in a foreign State or the head of a representation of the Russian Federation attached to an international organization shall have the right to conduct negotiations for the purposes of adopting the text of an international treaty between the Russian Federation and the receiving State or within the framework of the said international organization without presenting powers.

Russia

1 Point one reflects the constitutional stature of the President of the RF as the Head of State and the provisions of Article 7(2) of the 1969 Vienna Convention which deem the Head of State to be *ex officio* empowered to sign international treaties in the name of the State. Accordingly, there is no requirement that the President submit 'powers', a special document confirming his right to conduct negotiations or to sign a treaty.

CIS

The stature of the President of the country *ex officio* to conduct negotiations and sign treaties is affirmed in the treaty laws of *Armenia* (Article 5), *Azerbaidzhan* (Article 7), *Georgia* (Article 12[1]), *Kazakhstan* (Article 9[1]), *Kyrgyzstan* (Article 9[1]), *Moldova* (Article 2), *Tadzhikistan* (Article 6), *Turkmenistan* (Article 7), *Ukraine* (Article 5), and *Uzbekistan* (Article 13).

The *Belarus* treaty law is silent on the powers of the President to conduct negotiations and sign international treaties, but his right to do so is provided for by the Constitution of the Republic Belarus (Article 84[20]).[146]

The *Kyrgyzstan* treaty law (Article 9[2]) authorizes, with respect to interparliamentary treaties, the Toraga of the Legislative Assembly and the Toraga of the Assembly of People's Representatives of the Zhogorku Kenesh of the Kyrgyz Republic to conduct negotiations and sign in the name of the Zhogorku Kenesh of the Kyrgyz Republic international treaties of the Kyrgyz Republic without special powers.

Russia

2 The same applies to the Head of Government, in the case of the RF, the Chairman of the Government, and to the Minister of Foreign Affairs. In this case point two of the 1995 Law also reflects the provisions of Article 7(2) of the 1969 Vienna Convention.

CIS

The CIS treaty laws differ as to whether both the Head of Government and the Minister of Foreign Affairs may conduct negotiations and sign treaties without a special power. The Head of Government may do so according to the treaty laws of: *Armenia* (Article 5), *Azerbaidzhan* (Article 7, subject to an exclusion), *Kazakhstan* (Article 9[1]), *Kyrgyzstan* (Article 9[3]), *Moldova* (Article 5), *Tadzhikistan* (Article 6, which empowers both the Head of Government and the Prime Minister), and *Ukraine* (Article 5).

The Minister of Foreign Affairs is so authorized according to the treaty laws of: *Armenia* (Article 5), *Azerbaidzhan* (Article 7, subject to an exclusion), *Georgia* (Article 12[1]), *Kazakhstan* (Article 9[1]), *Kyrgyzstan* (Article 9[4]), *Moldova* (Article 5), *Tadzhikistan* (Article 6), *Turkmenistan* (Article 7), *Ukraine* (Article 5), and *Uzbekistan* (Article 13).

[146] Translated in W. E. Butler, *Constitutional Foundations of the CIS Countries* (The Hague, Kluwer Law International, 1999), p. 138.

In the case of *Azerbaidzhan,* however, neither the Head of Government nor the Minister of Foreign Affairs may conduct negotiations or sign international treaties of the following types unless they have been granted a special power by the President: (1) treaties concerning friendship, cooperation, and mutual assistance (or solidarity) and treaties establishing principles of inter-State relations; (2) peace treaties; (3) treaties of the Azerbaidzhan Republic with other States in regard to territorial and frontier questions and questions of the separation or alienation of territories and clarification of boundaries; (4) treaties of a defence character and with regard to military cooperation; (5) treaties concerning legal assistance; (6) treaties concerning the entry of the Azerbaidzhan Republic into international organizations of a universal and regional character; (7) multilateral and long-term economic treaties; (8) treaties establishing other rules than those which are contained in laws of the Azerbaidzhan Republic; (9) treaties whose ratification is provided for by laws or international treaties of the Azerbaidzhan Republic; (10) treaties with regard to questions of receiving credits; (11) treaties concerning participation in inter-State unions and other inter-State associations; (12) treaties concerning the despatch of a contingent of the Armed Forces of the Azerbaidzhan Republic to other countries or admittance of a contingent of armed forces of other States to the territory of the Azerbaidzhan Republic (Article 7).

Neither the Head of Government nor the Minister of Foreign Affairs may act without a special power to conduct negotiations or sign treaties in *Belarus* (Article 6).

Russia

3 The 1995 Law goes beyond the 1969 Vienna Convention in authorizing a Federal Minister or the head of another Federal agency of executive power to conduct negotiations and sign treaties of an interdepartmental character without presenting powers. The Commentary suggests that this provision arises from the fact that a Minister is responsible for the activity of his department and under the Statute on the department may act in its name by virtue of his official position.[147]

The exemption from presenting powers does not, however, mean that the Minister or head of another Federal agency of executive power can avoid complying with the requirement of obtaining an authorization in the form of a decision to conduct negotiations and sign an international treaty of the RF. Even the issue of powers can be a problem with respect to

[147] Khodakov, Commentary, p. 47.

a Minister if there is doubt as to whether the interdepartmental treaty may transcend the competence of his particular Ministry into the competence of others.

CIS

The CIS treaty laws differ in their regulation of this question. One group does not address the question at all: *Belarus, Georgia, Tadzhikistan, Turkmenistan,* and *Ukraine.*

A second group permits such officials to conduct negotiations and sign treaties only with the issuance of a special power: *Azerbaidzhan* (Article 7) and *Moldova* (Article 5).

A third group follows the model of the 1995 Law: *Armenia* (Article 5), *Kazakhstan* (Article 9[4]), *Kyrgyzstan* (Article 9[6]), and *Uzbekistan* (Article 13).

Russia

4 Point four of the 1995 Law is based on Article 7(2) of the 1969 Vienna Convention, except that the 1995 Law refers to the receiving State, whereas the 1969 Vienna Convention refers to the accrediting State. The Commentary observes that the 1995 Law has in view only the acceptance of the text of a treaty as a stage of concluding it, and not signature of the treaty: 'To sign a treaty the ambassador or head of representation must receive powers.'[148]

CIS

Some CIS treaty laws adopt the position of the 1995 Law: *Azerbaidzhan* (Article 7), *Georgia* (Article 12[2]), *Kazakhstan* (Article 9[2]), *Kyrgyzstan* (Article 9[5], but on condition of receiving special instructions from the Ministry of Foreign affairs), *Tadzhikistan* (Article 6), *Turkmenistan* (Article 7), *Ukraine* (Article 5[3]), and *Uzbekistan* (Article 13).

Others permit the head of a diplomatic representation to both conduct negotiations and sign an international treaty only with special powers: *Moldova.*

A third group does not address the issue at all: *Armenia, Belarus.*

The *Kazakhstan* (Article 9[3]) treaty law expressly stipulates that the head of a diplomatic representation may sign an international treaty only if he has the requisite special powers.

[148] Khodakov, Commentary, p. 47.

Article 13 Powers to Conduct Negotiations and to Sign International Treaties of Russian Federation

Powers to conduct negotiations and to sign international treaties of the Russian Federation shall be provided:

(a) with respect to treaties to be concluded in the name of the Russian Federation: by the President of the Russian Federation, and with respect to treaties to be concluded in the name of the Russian Federation with regard to questions relegated to the jurisdiction of the Government of the Russian Federation: by the Government of the Russian Federation. Powers to conduct negotiations and to sign the said treaties shall be formalized in the name of the President of the Russian Federation or in the name of the Government of the Russian Federation by the Ministry of Foreign Affairs of the Russian Federation;

(b) with respect to treaties to be concluded in the name of the Government of the Russian Federation: by the Government of the Russian Federation. Powers to conduct negotiations and to sign the said treaties shall be formalized in the name of the Government of the Russian Federation by the Ministry of Foreign Affairs of the Russian Federation;

(c) with respect to treaties of an interdepartmental character: by a federal minister or director of another federal agency of executive power.

Russia

The word 'powers' is used in this Article in two senses. With respect to the President and the Chairman of the Government, who are empowered *ex officio*, 'powers' is not a form of empowerment but rather an indication that in the decision to conduct negotiations and sign a treaty pursuant to Article 11 of the 1995 Law it has been expressly determined whether the President or the Government will act.

The Commentary indicates that in Russian practice with respect to Federal agencies of executive power, that Federal agency from which the proposal emanated to conduct negotiations or sign a treaty will be empowered, rather than a specifically named individual. This formulation gives greater flexibility when a specific individual is ill or otherwise unable to act; he may be replaced by a deputy or by another person acting in his stead.[149]

Nothing, however, precludes a specific individual from being named, in which event the individual may or may not be an official of the respective Federal agency.

The formalization of powers in the second sense of the word, a special document empowering a particular agency or individual, is the responsibility of the Ministry of Foreign Affairs. This document confirms the right of the specified individual or agency to conduct negotiations and sign a treaty. In the case of an interdepartmental treaty, the powers are issued by the respective Federal agency of executive power.

According to the Commentary, the Ministry of Foreign Affairs issues powers on the basis of a decision adopted by the President or by the Government in accordance with Article 11 of the 1995 Law, which decision specifies who has been charged to conduct negotiations and sign the treaty. Without such a decision, the Ministry will not formalize powers. Depending upon the substance of the decision, powers may be issued to conduct negotiations, or to sign the treaty, or to do both. The powers are issued on a special letterhead bearing the Arms of Russia. The printed text reads: 'The Ministry of Foreign Affairs of the Russian Federation hereby certifies that the President of the Russian Federation empowered.' There follows the full surname, name, and patronymic of the empowered individual and his office and a specification of what actions the person is empowered to perform. Such powers bear two signatures: either the Minister of Foreign Affairs or his deputy, and the Head of the Legal Department of the Ministry. The mastic seal of the Ministry is affixed.

Powers issued with respect to an interdepartmental treaty are formalized by the respective department in accordance with its own practice and are issued on the basis of a decision adopted by the head of the department.[150]

If the signature of a treaty is accompanied by a reservation or a statement, the text thereof must be contained in the powers of the person signing on behalf of the RF.

It has been argued in Russian doctrinal writings that this Article 'arbitrarily enlarged the powers of the Government and of federal agencies of executive power for the right to conclude a treaty together with the Russian Federation in its own name'. This view argued that the powers granted to the Government under this Article can in turn be delegated

[149] Khodakov, Commentary, p. 48.
[150] Khodakov, Commentary, p. 49.

to federal ministers and executives of other federal agencies of executive power with respect to treaties of an interdepartmental character.[151]

CIS

The CIS treaty laws differ in referring to the powers issued to conduct negotiations and to sign international treaties. Some refer to 'powers'; *Armenia* (Articles 6 and 7) refers to 'special powers'.

The basic pattern follows the model of the 1995 Law. The President issues powers to be concluded in the name of the respective State; the Government issues powers to be concluded in the name of the Government; and, where so mentioned, the head of the department or a minister issues powers for the conclusion of interdepartmental treaties: *Armenia* (Articles 6 and 7), *Azerbaidzhan* (Article 6), *Belarus* (Article 6), *Georgia* (Article 13), *Kazakhstan* (Article 8), *Kyrgyzstan* (Article 10), *Moldova* (Article 5), *Ukraine* (Article 5[4]), and *Uzbekistan* (Article 12).

In *Tadzhikistan* powers are issued by decision of the Government only (Article 6).

Some CIS treaty laws exclude any mention of interdepartmental treaties in this respect: *Azerbaidzhan* (Article 6), *Belarus* (Article 6), *Georgia* (Article 13), and *Uzbekistan* (Article 12).

The formalization of powers in *Belarus* (Article 6), *Georgia* (Article 13), *Kyrgyzstan* (Article 10), *Moldova* (Article 5) is the responsibility of the Ministry of Foreign Affairs. In *Turkmenistan* the formalization of powers is by acts of the President and the Government (Article 6).

The *Turkmenistan* treaty law (Article 6) provides that the President issues powers to conclude and sign both inter-State and intergovernmental treaties. The Government issues powers with respect to interdepartmental treaties.

Powers are issued in *Kyrgyzstan* (Article 10) with respect to interparliamentary treaties by the designated official of the Kyrgyzstan parliament.

The *Ukrainian* treaty law (Article 6) additionally makes provision for the issue of powers to a delegation or representative of Ukraine.

[151] V. M. Volzhenkina, *Нормы международного права в российском уголовном процессе* [Norms of International Law in Russian Criminal Procedure] (Spb., izd-vo Iurid. tsentr Press, 2001), pp. 79–80.

Article 14 Ratification of International Treaties of Russian Federation

In accordance with the Constitution of the Russian Federation the ratification of international treaties of the Russian Federation shall be effectuated in the form of a Federal Law.

Russia

This Article is based on Article 106(d) of the 1993 Constitution, which provides that Federal laws on the ratification and denunciation of international treaties are adopted by the State Duma and subject to obligatory consideration by the Soviet of the Federation.[152] Accordingly, the 1995 Law requires that ratification of international treaties of the RF be in the form of a Federal Law.

CIS

The ratification of international treaties is regulated in the constitutions of all CIS countries. As a rule, the ratifying branch of State is also designated in the CIS treaty laws, although not necessarily following the 1995 Law by stipulating the form in which ratification should take place.

The National Assembly of *Armenia* ratifies international treaties (Constitution, Article 81; treaty law (Article 8)); the Constitution provides that the group of international treaties subject to ratification by the National Assembly shall be established by a law, which is in fact the treaty law.[153]

The ratification of international treaties in *Azerbaidzhan* is a matter decided by the Milli Medzhlis which is adopted in the form of a law, according to the Azerbaidzhan Constitution (Article 95(I)[4] and Article

[152] W. E. Butler, *Constitutional Foundations of the CIS Countries* (The Hague, Kluwer Law International, 1999), p. 460. See, for example, the Decree of the Soviet of the Federation on the Federal Law 'on the Ratification of the Agreement between the Russian Federation and the Federal Republic of Germany on Avoiding Double Taxation With Respect to Taxes on Revenues and Property'. *СЗ РФ* (1996), no. 50, item 5618.

[153] The Armenian treaty law dates from 1992, whereas the Armenian Constitution was enacted in 1995. Under the new Constitution the former Supreme Soviet is renamed the National Assembly. Armenian sources report that the 1992 treaty law has not yet been amended or replaced.

95(II); also see the treaty law (Article 8)). The position is the same in *Belarus* (Constitution, Article 97; treaty law, Article 9) and in Ukraine (Constitution, Article 9; treaty law, Article 7[1]).

In *Georgia* treaties are ratified by the Parliament (Constitution, Article 65[1]; treaty law, Article 14[1]). The same is true in *Kazakhstan* (Constitution, Article 54[7]; treaty law, Article 10[1]), *Moldova* (Constitution, Article 66(g); treaty law, Article 6).

The ratification of treaties in *Kyrgyzstan* is divided between the Parliament and the President. The parliament ratifies treaties (Constitution, Article 58(9); treaty law, Article 11[1]), except for international financial treaties and credit agreements, which are ratified by the President (Constitution, Article 48; treaty law, Article 11[3]). The Constitution of Kyrgyzstan was amended on 16 February 1996 to introduce this division of ratification power and the pre-existing 1994 treaty law amended on 7 September 1996 to incorporate the change.

The international treaties of *Tadzhikistan* are ratified by the upper chamber of the parliament, called the Madzhlisi Namoiandagon (Constitution, Article 57(5); treaty law, Article 70)). International treaties of *Turkmenistan* are ratified by the Halk Maslakhaty of Turkmenistan and by the Madzhlis of Turkmenistan, unless they concern inter-State unions and other formations, in which event they are subject to ratification of the Halk Maslakhaty of Turkmenistan (Constitution, Article 50; treaty law, Article 9).

In *Uzbekistan* treaties are ratified by the Olii Mazhlis (Constitution, Article 78[21]; treaty law, Article 14).

Article 15 International Treaties of Russian Federation Subject to Ratification

1. International treaties of the Russian Federation shall be subject to ratification:

(a) the performance of which requires changes of prevailing or the adoption of new federal laws, and also the establishing of other rules than those provided for by a law;

(b) the subject of which is the basic rights and freedoms of man and citizen;

(c) concerning the territorial demarcation of the Russian Federation with other States, including treaties on the course of the State boundary of the Russian Federation, and also the demarcation of the exclusive economic zone and continental shelf of the Russian Federation;

(d) on the basic principles of inter-State relations, regarding questions affecting the defence capability of the Russian Federation, regarding questions of disarmament or international control over armaments, regarding questions of ensuring international peace and security, and also peace treaties and treaties on collective security;

(e) on the participation of the Russian Federation in inter-State unions, international organizations, and other inter-State associations, if such treaties provided for the transfer to them of the effectuation of part of the powers of the Russian Federation or establish the legal bindingness of decisions of their organs for the Russian Federation.

2. International treaties of the Russian Federation likewise shall be subject to ratification when during the conclusion of which the parties have stipulated subsequent ratification.

Russia

1 Point one(a) of this Article sets down the general rule that international treaties whose execution requires a change of legislation in force or the enactment of new Federal Laws, or which establishes other rules than those provided for by a Law, are subject to ratification. This clause needs to be read against Article 6(2) of the 1995 Law, which provides that the decision to consent to an international treaty of the RF becoming binding upon the RF is adopted by agencies of State power of the

RF in accordance with their competence (see Gloss on Article 6, above). A comparison of Article 6(2) and of Article 15(1)(a), read together with Article 14, leads one to conclude that an international treaty whose performance requires a change of prevailing or the adoption of new Federal laws can be consented to by the RF only in the form of a Federal Law.

It is argued by some jurists that a ratified treaty gives rise with the same degree of definitude as an internal law to respective intra-State relations. From the standpoint of subjects of intra-State law, a ratified international treaty is a normative act possessing legal force in the intra-State sphere equal to the force of that act by which it was ratified; that is, the force of a law.[154]

There is some ambiguity in connection with the phrase 'which establish other rules than provided for by a law', as the word 'law' [*закон*] is not modified by the word 'federal' and could be construed to mean a law adopted by a subject of the RF. The Commentary, it should be said, does not understand the word 'law' in this broader sense, but rather assumes the legislator had in view a Federal Law.[155]

The 1995 Law thus gives the legislator a paramount role in treaty-making. The Commentary is of the view that neither the President, nor the Government, nor any Federal agency of executive power has the right to adopt a decision consenting to an international treaty becoming binding upon the RF if the execution of that treaty requires a change of prevailing or the adoption of new Federal laws or establishes other rules than provided for by a law. This view finds confirmation in the 1993 Constitution, which establishes that edicts and regulations of the President must not be contrary to the Constitution and Federal Laws (Article 90), the Government issues entirely subordinate acts, decrees and regulations, on the basis of and in execution of the Constitution, Federal Laws, and normative edicts of the President (Article 115), and federal departments may operate only within their competence and also issue only subordinate normative acts.[156]

The 1993 Russian Constitution does not enumerate the international treaties which are subject to ratification. Article 15(1)(b)–(e) above enumerates the subject-matter of international treaties which qualify them for ratification irrespective of whether they require a change in Russian

[154] M. A. Pshenichnov, 'Юридико-технические средства обеспечения соответствия российского законодательства международному праву' [Juridical–Technique Means of Ensuring the Conformity of Russian Legislation to International Law], in V. M. Baranov (ed.), *Проблемы юридической техники* [Problems of Legal Technique] (Nizhnii Novgorod, Nizhegorodskaia pravovaia akademiia, 2000), p. 189.

[155] Osminin, Commentary, p. 51.

[156] Osminin, Commentary, p. 51.

legislation or the enactment of new Russian legislation. The formulation of subpoint (1)(e) is obscure, for few international organizations will fail to meet these criteria, although the extent to which they do so is controversial under international law.

Neither the 1977 USSR Constitution nor the 1978 RSFSR Constitution contained an enumeration of treaties subject to ratification. Compared with the 1978 USSR Law, which was in force in the RF until the enactment of the 1995 Law, the list of types of international treaties which require ratification is greatly enlarged.

Should a dispute arise between the legislative and executive branch as to whether a particular treaty is subject to ratification, it is subject to resolution in the Constitutional Court of the RF on the basis of Article 125 of the 1993 Constitution and Article 3, paragraph one, (2)(a) of the Federal Constitutional Law on the Constitutional Court of the RF.[157] The question before the Constitutional Court would be to determine whether a particular agency of the RF had the right to give consent to the treaty entering into force for the RF. If the Constitutional Court gives a negative decision, this agency would be obliged to take measures in accordance with the provisions of the treaty and international law to terminate the treaty or to change it.

CIS

The CIS treaty laws fall into two groups when determining the international treaties which are subject to ratification. The first group determines those treaties in the Constitution of the respective CIS country and replicates the enumeration of such treaties in the treaty law. The group consists of *Georgia* (Constitution, Article 65[2]; treaty law, Article 14).

The second group determines the list of treaties subject to ratification solely in the treaty law, according to the model of the 1995 Law, and confines itself in the Constitution to a general statement as to which organs of State will actually ratify. *Armenia* (Constitution, Article 81; treaty law, Article 9), *Azerbaidzhan* (Constitution, Article 94[22]; treaty law, Article 8), *Belarus* (Constitution, Article 97; treaty law, Article 8), *Kazakhstan* (Constitution, Article 54; treaty law, Article 11), *Kyrgyzstan* (Constitution, Articles 48 and 49; treaty law, Article 11), *Moldova* (Constitution, Article 66; treaty law, Article 6), *Tadzhikistan* (Constitution, Article 57; treaty law, Article 8), *Turkmenistan* (Constitution, Article 50; treaty law, Article 9), *Ukraine* (Constitution, Article 85[32]; treaty law,

[157] See L. V. Lazarev, in N. V. Vitruk, L. V. Lazarev, and B. S. Ebzeev (eds.), *Федеральный конституционный закон о конституционном суде Российской Федерации. Комментарий* [Federal Constitutional Law on the Constitutional Court of the Russian Federation. Commentary] (M., Iuridicheskaia literatura, 1996), pp. 41–2.

Article 7[2]), and *Uzbekistan* (Constitution, Article 78[21]; treaty law, Article 14).

The general position of CIS doctrinal writings is that ratified international treaties are not higher than the respective Constitution of each country. Not enumerating the treaties subject to ratification in the constitutions gives the State flexibility to enlarge or reduce the types of treaties subject to ratification and, therefore, an integral part of the legal system or of national legislation.

Russia

2 Point two of this Article gives the Russian side flexibility in agreeing with a foreign State that a particular treaty will be subject to ratification notwithstanding the possibility under Russian legislation that ratification is not obligatory.

Of the various ways of expressing consent in the form of a Federal Law to the binding nature of an international treaty for the RF, ratification is by far the preferred method. In 1994–5 ninety international treaties were ratified in the form of a Federal Law; only once was a Federal Law used to give consent in another form (accession).

CIS

All CIS treaty laws except those of *Georgia* and *Moldova* include this provision.

Article 16 Procedure for Submitting International Treaties for Ratification

1. International treaties, decisions concerning the signature of which were adopted by the President of the Russian Federation, shall be submitted to the State Duma of the Federal Assembly of the Russian Federation for ratification by the President of the Russian Federation.

International treaties, decisions concerning the signature of which were adopted by the Government of the Russian Federation, shall be submitted to the State Duma for ratification by the Government of the Russian Federation.

The Government of the Russian Federation shall have the right, when necessary, to submit to the President of the Russian Federation a proposal concerning the submission for ratification of an international treaty, the decision to sign which was adopted by the Government of the Russian Federation.

2. Proposals concerning the approval and submission for ratification of international treaties shall be submitted respectively to the President of the Russian Federation and to the Government of the Russian Federation by the Ministry of Foreign Affairs of the Russian Federation autonomously or jointly with other federal agencies of executive power if the treaty affects questions within their competence.

International treaties which are subject to submission to the President of the Russian Federation for submission for ratification, the fulfilment of which requires the preliminary consideration thereof by the Government of the Russian Federation, shall be submitted to the Government of the Russian Federation.

3. Decisions of the Government of the Russian Federation concerning the approval and the submission for ratification of international treaties, and also concerning approval and submission to the President of the Russian Federation for the submission of international treaties for ratification shall be adopted in the form of a Decree.

4. The proposal concerning ratification of an international treaty must contain a certified copy of the official text of the international treaty, a substantiation of the advisability of its ratification, a determination of the conformity of the treaty to legislation of the Russian Federation, and also an evaluation of the possible financial–economic and other consequences of ratification of the treaty, including, when necessary, an Opinion of the Government of the Russian Federation as provided for by Article 104 of the Constitution of the Russian Federation.

5. In the event a subject of the right of legislative initiative submits to the State Duma on the basis of Article 104 of the Constitution of the Russian Federation a draft law not mentioned in point 1 of the present Article regarding a question of the ratification of an international treaty which has not yet entered into force for the Russian Federation but is subject to ratification in accordance with Article 15 of the present Federal Law, the State Duma shall send the draft law submitted to the President of the Russian Federation for proposals regarding this draft law.

Russia

1 Point one of this Article addresses the general procedure for submitting a draft treaty to the State Duma for ratification. If the President adopted the decision to sign the treaty, the President is to submit the treaty to the State Duma for ratification, together with a draft Federal Law on ratification.

If the Government adopts the decision to sign the treaty, the Government submits the treaty to the State Duma for ratification, also with the draft of the respective Federal Law on ratification. However, the Government has the right to propose to the President that he submit the treaty to the State Duma for ratification. Whether the Government chooses to ask the President to act in this respect is a policy decision with respect to which the 1995 Law is neutral. An example of governmental practice is the Letter of the Government of the Russian Federation, 28 April 1997, No. 1316п-П4, to the State Duma which accompanied several treaties with Kazakhstan concerning nuclear testing, draft federal laws concerning ratification, the decree of the Government to refer the treaties for ratification, an explanatory memorandum, and certified copies of the international treaties themselves.[158]

The fact that only the President and the Government are mentioned as having the right to submit a treaty for ratification is reflective of Article 11 of the 1995 Law, which confers on them the right to adopt a decision concerning the signature of a treaty. Others who have the right of legislative initiative under Article 104 of the 1993 Constitution are treated in point five of the 1995 Law.

CIS

The procedure set out in the 1995 Law is that the submission of an international treaty for ratification should follow the official or agency which adopted the decision to sign the treaty. This general pattern has been adopted in the treaty laws of the CIS countries: *Armenia* (Article 10),

[158] Available on the Computer Data Base GARANT 4.0.

Kyrgyzstan (Article 12), *Ukraine* (Article 7[4]), and *Uzbekistan* (Article 15).

In *Azerbaidzhan* the government has no role in the submission process except in the person of the Ministry of Foreign Affairs. The President takes the decision to submit the treaty to the Supreme Soviet for ratification irrespective of the type of treaty (Article 9).

The *Belarus* (Article 9) procedures are more complex and involve both the President and the Government. A time-limit of three months is laid down for proposals concerning ratification to be submitted after signature.

The *Georgian* (Article 15[1]), *Tadzhikistan* (Article 9), and *Turkmenistan* (Article 10) treaty laws permit only the President of the Republic to submit a treaty for ratification.

In *Kazakhstan* (Article 13[1]) the President plays the principal role in submitting treaties for ratification upon the proposal of the Government, which in turn acts upon the proposal of the Ministry of Foreign Affairs and other interested State agencies.

Provision is made in the *Kyrgyzstan* treaty law (Article 12[3]) for proposals concerning the ratification of international financial treaties and credit agreements, which are submitted to the President of the Kyrgyz Republic by the Government of the Kyrgyz Republic in accordance with the Constitution of the Kyrgyz Republic. Such agreements are in Kyrgyzstan subject to ratification by the President.

The *Moldovan* treaty law does not regulate the procedure for submitting international treaties for ratification.

Russia

2 The Ministry of Foreign Affairs under point two of the 1995 Law submits proposals concerning the approval of or the submission for ratification of international treaties to the President and to the Government. These proposals may be submitted by the Ministry alone, or together with other Federal agencies of executive power provided that in the last instance the treaty affects questions within the competence of those Federal agencies. The provision is reflective of the 'head' role played by the Ministry of Foreign Affairs in conducting and coordinating the foreign policy of Russia.

The second paragraph of point two of this Article stipulates that if compliance with an international treaty requires the preliminary consideration of the Government, the text must be submitted first to the Government and then to the President, to be submitted to the State Duma for ratification. The turn of phrase is a curious one, for the 1995 Law contains no standard by which 'fulfilment' of a treaty may require consideration of the Government. The Commentary refers to the Government evaluating the 'financial – economic and other consequences' of ratifying a treaty, to complying with other obligations arising out of the treaty, or to taking measures with regard to 'other questions within the competence of the Government'.[159] It is not clear what form such 'consideration' takes, although it would appear from practice that 'Government' means not merely the ministers collegially but individual departments of the Government.

CIS

The CIS treaty laws do not contain a provision which corresponds fully to this point of the 1995 Law, particularly the second paragraph. The first point deals with the role of the Ministry of Foreign Affairs and other federal State agencies, which does have an equivalent in several CIS treaty laws: *Belarus* (Article 9), *Kazakhstan* (Article 13[2]–[5]), *Kyrgyzstan* (Article 12[4]), *Tadzhikistan* (Article 9), *Turkmenistan* (Article 10), *Ukraine* (Article 7[4]), and *Uzbekistan* (Article 15).

The *Moldovan* treaty law contains no equivalent provision.

Russia

3 Point three of this Article is not expressly linked with the preceding point; no reference is made to consideration. The Commentary does link the two subpoints, however, which leads to the result that consideration by the Government as to whether a treaty should be submitted to the State Duma for ratification must take the form of a positive decision, an approval, expressed in the form of a Decree.[160] This is true whether the Government itself submits the treaty directly to the State Duma for ratification, or whether it submits the treaty to the President, who in turn will submit it to the State Duma for ratification.

CIS

Only the *Kyrgyzstan* (Article 12[5]) and Uzbekistan (Article 15) treaty laws determine the form of the enactment by which the Government submits a treaty for ratification. In each case the form is a decree.

Russia

4 Point four of this Article addresses the formal requirements for a Proposal concerning ratification of an international treaty of the RF. The

159 Osminin, Commentary, p. 56.
160 Osminin, Commentary, p. 56.

Proposal must contain a certified copy of the official text of the treaty, a substantiation of the advisability of ratifying the treaty, a determination whether the treaty is in conformity with Russian legislation, and an assessment of possible financial–economic and other consequences of ratifying the treaty.

The procedure for certifying copies of official texts of international treaties is regulated by a Regulation of the President of the Russian Federation, adopted 8 September 1994. The Regulation provided that any Proposal submitted to the President or to the Government concerning the ratification, confirmation, acceptance, or accession to an international treaty, including provisional application, termination, or suspension, must contain an official text of the treaty, if necessary with an official translation into the Russian language, certified by the federal agency of executive power making the submission.[161] What constitutes an 'official translation' for these purposes is not regulated either by the 1995 Law or by the preceding Regulation, however. At best, the agency supplying the 'official translation' is acting in its own behalf, and the translation can be 'official' only for it and not necessarily for the Russian State as a whole.[162]

An assessment of possible financial–economic and other consequences of ratification includes, when necessary, an Opinion of the Government provided for by Article 104 of the 1993 Constitution. Article 104 in particular has in view draft laws concerning the introduction or repeal of taxes, exemption from the payment of taxes, the issuance of State loans, a change in the financial obligations of the State, and those entailing expenditures to be covered from the Federal budget.

The consequences of ratification of a treaty subject to being evaluated are not exhaustively enumerated in the 1995 Law (also see Articles 9, 20, 21, and 36, 1995 Law).

CIS

Several CIS treaty laws impose requirements similar to those of point 4 of the 1995 Law. The *Belarus* treaty law (Article 9) requires that the proposal to ratify must be supported by: the draft law on ratification of the international treaty of the Republic Belarus; a copy of the international treaty of the Republic Belarus; a substantiation of the need for ratification of the international treaty of the Republic Belarus; the opinion of the

[161] No. 458-рп. *СЗ РФ* (1994), no. 20, item 2269.

[162] See P. A. Laptev, 'Проблемы перевода международно-правовых актов и новые технико-юридические процедуры их имплементации в правовую систему Российской Федерации' [Problems of Translation of International Legal Acts and New Legal-Technique Procedures for the Implementation Thereof in the Legal System of the Russian Federation], in V. M. Baranov (ed.), *Проблемы юридической техники* [Problems of Legal Technique] (Nizhnii Novgorod, Nizhegorodskaia pravovaia akademiia, 2000), p. 150.

Ministry of Justice of the Republic Belarus concerning the conformity of the international treaty of the Republic Belarus to the Constitution and other legislation of the Republic Belarus; a list of norms of laws of the Republic Belarus, acts of the President of the Republic Belarus and Government of the Republic Belarus subject to change, addition, repeal, or adoption for the purposes of performance of the international treaty of the Republic Belarus; other opinions of interested State agencies; a financial–economic substantiation of the proposed expenditures in connection with the realization of the international treaty of the Republic Belarus submitted for ratification; a list of persons who took part in working out this international treaty.

The *Kyrgyzstan* (Article 12[4]) and *Tadzhikistan* (Article 9) treaty laws are virtually identical in this respect to the 1995 Law, except that Tadzhikistan does not require an evaluation of financial and economic consequences.

A second group does not impose such requirements: *Armenia, Azerbaidzhan, Moldova, Turkmenistan, Ukraine,* and *Uzbekistan.*

Russia

5 As noted in the Gloss on Article 14 of the 1995 Law above, the ratification of treaties of the RF takes the form of a Federal Law. Article 104(1) of the 1993 Constitution grants the right of legislative initiative, in addition to the President and the Government, also to the Soviet of the Federation, members of the Soviet of the Federation, deputies of the State Duma, and legislative or representative agencies of subjects of the RF. On a stipulated range of questions, legislative initiative also may be exercised by the Constitutional Court, the Supreme Court, and the Supreme Arbitrazh Court.[163]

Legislative initiative includes the right to submit a draft Federal Law concerning ratification of an international treaty provided that such treaty is subject to ratification in accordance with Article 15 of the 1995 Law and assuming that the treaty is not already in force. The Commentary is of the view that the right of legislative initiative may not be exercised with respect to an international treaty which is not subject to ratification and falls within the competence of the President or the Government.[164] Given the pre-eminent role of the legislative branch with respect to treaty-making and the absence of a constitutional limitation in this regard on the right of legislative initiative, that view must be open to doubt.

[163] W. E. Butler, *Constitutional Foundations of the CIS Countries* (The Hague, Kluwer Law International, 1999), p. 459.

[164] Osminin, Commentary, p. 58.

The sole requirement of point five of the present Article is that the State Duma refer to the President the draft Federal Law concerning ratification of a treaty and seek his proposals. No deadline is fixed in the 1995 Law for the President to reply. If the President were to disagree with the proposal for ratification by way of legislative initiative, there is no indication in the 1995 Law as to what the consequences may be. Presumably the State Duma is at liberty to ratify the treaty, which would seem entirely logical since the Federal Assembly is not required necessarily to concur with a Presidential or Governmental proposal to ratify. By right of legislative initiative the Federal Assembly has the opportunity to consider ratification of a treaty which may, for various reasons of policy, not ever be submitted to it by the President or the Government.

CIS

The other CIS treaty laws do not contain a provision equivalent to this point of the 1995 Law.

Article 17 Decisions Concerning Ratification of International Treaties of Russian Federation

1. The State Duma shall consider proposals concerning the ratification of international treaties and after preliminary discussion in committees and commissions of the State Duma shall adopt respective decisions.

Federal laws adopted by the State Duma concerning the ratification of international treaties of the Russian Federation shall be subject in accordance with the Constitution of the Russian Federation to obligatory consideration in the Soviet of the Federation.

2. A Federal Law adopted by the Federal Assembly of the Russian Federation concerning the ratification of an international treaty of the Russian Federation shall be sent in accordance with the Constitution of the Russian Federation to the President of the Russian Federation for signature and promulgation.

Russia

1 The State Duma considers proposals to ratify international treaties in accordance with its Reglament. Consideration includes preliminary discussion, and possibly hearings, in committees and commissions of the State Duma. Plenipotentiaries of the President or Government may be specially appointed to oversee the course of the draft Law in the Federal Assembly, and such representatives, if appointed, will participate in the Committee or Commission deliberations. Outside experts may be invited to take part, and special subcommittees created. The Committee for International Affairs and the Committee for Affairs of the CIS normally have a key role with respect to an international treaty. The Committee responsible for the draft Law reports to the plenary State Duma on the results of its deliberations.

On the floor of the State Duma the draft Federal Law concerning ratification of a treaty is in the same position as any other draft Federal Law. It may be adopted at first reading, rejected, adopted in full, or deferred. If adopted in full, the Federal Law is sent by the State Duma within five days to the Soviet of the Federation for consideration; referral to the Soviet of the Federation is by way of a Decree of the State Duma.

The Reglament of the State Duma does not address what should happen if the draft Federal Law on ratification of the treaty is rejected. This has happened on rare occasion. In one case involving a Russo-Turkish Agreement on double taxation, signed 9 September 1993, the State Duma asked the Government to reopen negotiations with the Turkish side and make adjustments to the text or to negotiate a new Agreement and resubmit it.[165] Rejection also could be reconsidered by the Duma itself, or the President or the Government could resubmit the draft Law and request reconsideration.

The Soviet of the Federation considers Federal Laws adopted by the State Duma concerning ratification of an international treaty in accordance with its own Reglament. Its internal procedure is analogous on the whole with that followed in the State Duma. The results of the internal discussion are reported to the plenary session of the Soviet of the Federation, which is then invited either to approve the Law or to reject it. The decision is recorded in the form of a Decree of the Soviet of the Federation.

The remaining formalities within the Federal Assembly are completed in accordance with the Constitution and the Reglaments of the two chambers.

The 1995 Law leaves open, as do the Reglaments of the two chambers of the Federal Assembly, what happens if an international treaty has been signed but the President or the Government decide against proceeding with ratification, or the Federal Assembly rejects ratification. A Russo-Turkmenistan Treaty on joint measures in connection with the creation of the Armed Forces of Turkmenistan, signed on 31 July 1992, was never submitted for ratification in Russia, and on 13 April 1995 the President of the RF decided not to seek ratification, so informing the Turkmenistan side after bilateral consultations. In this instance a formal Decision was adopted by the President recording the final result of the deliberations.[166] Had this decision been taken by the State Duma, the Reglament made no provision for formally recording the result in the form of a Decree.

It should also be observed that had there been disagreement in the State Duma with the Presidential decision not to submit the treaty for ratification, by right of legislative initiative the treaty might have been placed before the State Duma for consideration.

CIS

The CIS treaty laws vary in the amount of detail in which the process of consideration of a proposal to ratify an international treaty is specified.

[165] Regulation of 24 October 1995, No. 1477-p. *СЗ РФ* (1995), no. 44, item 4231.
[166] Regulation of 13 April 1995, No. 174-рп. *СЗ РФ* (1995), no. 16, item 1412.

Provision is made for consideration of the proposal to ratify a treaty in the committees and commissions of the parliament in the *Armenian* (Article 11), *Azerbaidzhan* (Article 10), and *Georgian* (Article 16) treaty laws.

Usually the treaty is ratified by the entire parliament (see the treaty laws of *Armenia* (Article 11), *Azerbaidzhan* (Article 11), *Belarus* (Article 9), *Georgia* (Article 15), *Kazakhstan* (Article 10), *Ukraine* (Article 7[1]), and *Uzbekistan* (Article 16)), but in some instances by a stipulated chamber of parliament: in *Kazakhstan,* the two chambers separately and in succession (Article 14[1]); in *Kyrgyzstan* (Article 13[1]) first by the Legislative Assembly and then approved by Assembly of People's Representatives; in *Tadzhikistan* (Article 7), by the upper chamber, the Madzhlisi Namoiandagon; in *Turkmenistan* (Article 11) certain treaties are ratified by a special assembly, the Halk Maslakhaty.

The type of enactment used to ratify a treaty is a law (*Belarus, Kazakhstan, Kyrgyzstan, Ukraine*), a decree (*Armenia, Azerbaidzhan, Georgia, Moldova, Tadzhikistan, Turkmenistan, Uzbekistan*), or a decision (*Turkmenistan*). In *Kyrgyzstan* (Article 13[2]), when the President acts to ratify certain categories of treaty the type of enactment is the edict.

In some countries or special situations a special majority of the parliament is required to ratify a treaty. The *Georgian* (Article 17) treaty law requires a majority of the total number of deputies in the parliament (and not those present). The *Ukrainian* (Article 7(2) and [3]) treaty law imposes a two-thirds majority of the entire Supreme Rada for the ratification of treaties concerning territory, citizenship, and participation in inter-State unions and other inter-State associations (or organizations), and collective security systems.

Russia

2 Point two of this Article merely reiterates the status of a Federal Law concerning ratification of an international treaty as being an ordinary Federal Law subject to the same constitutional formalities as any other Federal Law.

CIS

This issue is addressed in several CIS treaty laws: *Armenia* (Article 11), *Azerbaidzhan* (Article 11), *Georgia* (Article 17[2]), *Kazakhstan* (Article 14[2]), *Kyrgyzstan* (Article 13[1]), *Tadzhikistan* (Article 10), *Turkmenistan* (Article 11), and *Uzbekistan* (Article 18).

In *Ukraine* the law adopted is signed not by the President, but by the head of the Supreme Rada, who also signs the instrument of ratification.

Article 18 Signature of Instrument of Ratification

On the basis of the Federal Law concerning the ratification of an international treaty of the Russian Federation, the instrument of ratification shall be signed by the President of the Russian Federation, which shall be affixed with his seal and the signature of the Minister of Foreign Affairs of the Russian Federation.

Russia

The formalities for drawing up and signing instruments of ratification are set out in the Commentary. The instruments of ratification are a folder made of thin white card on which is printed in gold or black lettering 'The President of the Russian Federation announces that'. The internal left side is blank. On the internal right side is printed: 'The Federal Assembly of the Russian Federation by a Law of "..." ________ 200_ has ratified the following act(s):.' There follows the full and precise name of the ratified treaty. If the treaty was ratified with a reservation or statement, the text is set out in the instrument of ratification. Should the text of the reservation or statement be so long that it is impossible to set it out in full in the instrument of ratification itself, then after the name of the treaty it is said that 'with a reservation (or statement) contained in the Annex.' Thereafter there is again printed text as follows: 'and declares that all set out in the said act(s) will be strictly fulfilled'. Below are the words: 'Moscow, Kremlin' and a place for inserting the date. The date is added on the date of signature of the instrument by the President.

Before sending the instrument for signature of the President the instrument is signed by the Minister of Foreign Affairs. After the President signs the instrument, the seal of the President is affixed by his chancellery.

An instrument of accession is virtually identical, except that the text refers to the Federal Assembly adopting 'a decision concerning accession to the following acts(s)'.[167]

[167] Khodakov, Commentary, pp. 61–2.

CIS

The majority of CIS treaty laws contain an analogous provision either as a separate article or incorporated in a more general provision concerning the procedures for ratification.

Those CIS treaty laws having a separate Article concerning signature of the instrument of ratification which is similar to the 1995 Law regulate the elements of signature, the affixing of a seal, and the signature of the Minister of Foreign Affairs: *Tadzhikistan* (Article 10) and *Uzbekistan* (Article 18). In the treaty law of *Armenia* (Article 11), *Kyrgyzstan* (Article 14), and *Moldova* (Article 12) the President affixed the State seal rather than his own.

The treaty laws of *Azerbaidzhan* (Article 11), *Georgia* (Article 17[2]), *Kazakhstan* (Article 14[2]) mention only signature by the President. In the case of Georgia, the Ministry of Foreign Affairs 'certifies' the instrument of ratification.

In the *Turkmenistan* (Article 11) treaty law the form of the instrument of ratification is determined by the President of Turkmenistan.

The *Ukrainian* (Article 7[11]) treaty law takes a different approach. The instrument of ratification is signed by the Chairman of the Supreme Rada, whose signature is certified by the Minister of Foreign Affairs of Ukraine.

The treaty law of *Belarus* does not contain relevant provisions.

Article 19 Exchange of Instruments of Ratification and Handing Over Instruments Concerning Ratification of International Treaties of Russian Federation for Keeping by Depositaries

The exchange of instruments of ratification and the handing over of instruments concerning ratification of international treaties of the Russian Federation for keeping by depositaries shall be done, unless there is another arrangement, by the Ministry of Foreign Affairs of the Russian Federation or on its behalf by a diplomatic representation of the Russian Federation in the foreign State or by the representation of the Russian Federation attached to an international organization.

Russia

This Article is essentially a 'default' clause which enabled the RF to take full advantage of international practice or any agreement of the parties with regard to the exchange and handing over of instruments of ratification, but otherwise to place full responsibility with the Ministry of Foreign Affairs.

The general patterns of Russian practice, which correspond fully with international practice, are set out in the Commentary. As a rule instruments of ratification are exchanged with respect to bilateral treaties and multilateral treaties which have a small number of parties. Most treaties specifically address the issue of exchanging the instruments of ratification and provide where the exchange shall occur. If the text of the treaty is silent and the treaty is bilateral, the exchange is likely to occur in the State where the treaty was not signed. But any arrangement is possible by agreement of the parties.

When the instruments of ratification are exchanged, a protocol is drafted containing the full names of the persons effecting the exchange, their posts, the full name of the treaty, possibly the acts of legislation by which the treaty was ratified or confirmed, and the date and place where the exchange occurs. The protocol also may specify that the persons making the exchange have satisfied themselves that the instruments of ratification are duly formalized; these persons will sign the protocol.

Powers are not issued to sign a protocol concerning the exchange of instruments of ratification.

Instruments of ratification are usually exchanged at the level of ambassador, on one side, and deputy minister on the other. For various policy reasons, however, more senior officials may act, including the Head of State or the Head of Government.

Instruments of ratification are handed over for keeping by a depositary, as a rule, under multilateral treaties. Where multiple depositaries are designated, the depositing State may deposit with any of them unless the treaty provides otherwise, or even all of them. The State handing over an instrument of ratification receives in return a certified protocol by way of receipt, and the depositary notifies other parties to the treaty about the date of receipt of the instrument of ratification, which as a rule also is the date of entry into force of the treaty for the depositing State. Simplified practices are followed in some international organizations, whereby a *note verbale* or a personal note is handed over to the proper official of the international organization together with the instrument of ratification, and a note of reply is sent to confirm receipt. The Russian representative attached to the international organization will normally perform this role. Where treaties provide for an exchange of notices of ratification rather than instruments, the confirmation of the ratification commonly occurs by way of a *note verbale*.[168]

CIS

The treaty laws of several CIS countries determine internal responsibility for exchanging or handing over instruments of ratification to depositaries. In all cases where the issue is addressed, the Ministry of Foreign Affairs is the designated State agency, which in turn has the right to subdesignate its diplomatic representation in a foreign State or attached to an international organization.

This approach is followed in the treaty laws of: *Armenia* (Article 12), *Tadzhikistan* (Article 11), *Azerbaidzhan* (Article 12), *Kazakhstan* (Article 15), *Kyrgyzstan* (Article 15), *Turkmenistan* (Article 12), *Ukraine* (Article 8), *Uzbekistan* (Article 19). *Armenia* and *Turkmenistan* add the possibility of a specially empowered envoy. *Azerbaidzhan* includes an international conference among the places where an instrument of ratification

[168] Khodakov, Commentary, pp. 62–4.

may be handed over. The *Kazakhstan* treaty law includes, together with instruments of ratification, documents concerning the confirmation of or accession of the Republic Kazakhstan to multilateral international treaties.

The treaty laws of *Belarus, Georgia,* and *Moldova* do not regulate this question.

Article 20 Confirmation and Adoption of International Treaties

1. The confirmation and adoption of international treaties which are subject to confirmation and adoption shall be effectuated:

(a) with respect to treaties to be concluded in the name of the Russian Federation with regard to questions specified in Article 15(1) of the present Federal Law: in the form of a Federal Law in the procedure established by Article 17 of the present Federal Law for the ratification of international treaties;

(b) with respect to treaties to be concluded in the name of the Russian Federation (except for treaties provided for by subpoint (a) of the present point): by the President of the Russian Federation, and with respect to treaties to be concluded in the name of the Russian Federation with regard to questions relegated to the jurisdiction of the Government of the Russian Federation: by the Government of the Russian Federation;

(c) with respect to treaties to be concluded in the name of the Government of the Russian Federation: by the Government of the Russian Federation.

2. The President of the Russian Federation shall adopt decisions concerning the confirmation and adoption of international treaties with regard to questions relegated to the jurisdiction of the Government of the Russian Federation if such is necessary.

3. The confirmation or adoption of international treaties of an interdepartmental character which provide for the entry into force thereof after confirmation or adoption shall be effectuated by federal agencies of executive power in whose name such treaties were signed.

4. Proposals concerning the confirmation or adoption of international treaties in the form of a Federal Law shall be submitted in the procedure established by Article 16 of the present Federal Law, and in other instances – in the procedure provided for by Article 9 of the present Federal Law.

Russia

1 This Article is a rather unsuccessful attempt, in compliance with Article 11 of the 1969 Vienna Convention, to import terminology from the Convention by using Russian equivalents which have a long-established meaning in Russian (and Soviet) norm-formation. Confirmation, in the

sense of Article 20(1), has in view the final consent of the State to the respective treaty entering into force and does not connote any form of preliminary endorsement. Insofar, therefore, as confirmation means the final consent by the Federal Assembly in the form of a Federal Law to an international treaty being binding upon the RF, it is identical to ratification and, as a term, is redundant. The same applies to the term 'acceptance' (in the 1969 Vienna Convention) and 'adoption' (in Russian legislative practice) insofar as the Federal Assembly is concerned. No wonder that in Russian State practice the use of both terms is virtually unknown. The Commentary cites but one example, when in 1992 the Supreme Soviet of the RF adopted a decision 'to accept' the respective Agreements concerning Russia joining the World Bank and the International Monetary Fund (IMF). No examples are known since the enactment of the 1995 Law. It also follows from this Article that ratification, where required, can not be evaded by having the parties agree to 'confirmation'.

CIS

The terminological Gloss with respect to the 1995 Law applies equally to the treaty laws of the CIS countries which contain an analogous Article: *Azerbaidzhan* (Article 13), *Belarus* (Article 10), *Kazakhstan* (Article 16), *Kyrgyzstan* (Article 16), *Tadzhikistan* (Article 12), *Ukraine* (Article 9), and *Uzbekistan* (Article 20).

The treaty law of *Armenia* (Article 13) provides that either the President or the Government of Armenia may confirm international treaties not requiring ratification. The criteria for one or the other acting are not specified.

The treaty law of *Georgia* (Article 18) avoids the terminology discussed above and provides that the President of Georgia confirms a treaty not subject to ratification. In *Moldova* this is left to the Government (Article 8).

The *Tadzhikistan* treaty law devotes separate articles to confirmation and adoption (Articles 12 and 13) and combines accession to a treaty with adoption. The text becomes confusing because Article 8 of the Tadzhikistan treaty law enumerates those treaties which are subject to ratification; Article 13 allows for the adoption of or accession to treaties falling under Article 8, which suggests that treaties subject to ratification might be adopted or acceded to instead without ratification. Under the Tadzhikistan treaty law interdepartmental treaties subject to confirmation by the Government under Article 12 appear to be also subject to adoption under Article 13 also by the Government. And in either instance proposals to confirm or adopt must originate with the Ministry of Foreign Affairs of Tadzhikistan (Article 14).

In *Turkmenistan* the President confirms both inter-State and intergovernmental treaties. The concept of 'adoption' is not used in the Turkmenistan treaty law.

The form by which confirmation takes place is not widely addressed in the CIS treaty laws. In *Georgia* the form is a presidential edict. The *Ukrainian* (Article 9) treaty law provides that the form of confirmation is an edict when the President so acts, and a decree when the Government acts.

Russia

2 The term 'confirmation' and, less so, 'acceptance' make sense in the Russian legal lexicon when applied to instances when the President or the Government has the competence to give final consent to an international treaty entering into force for the RF. In the interests of clarity the legislator perhaps missed an opportunity to reserve the term 'acceptance' for decisions of the President and 'confirmation' for decisions of the Government.

Neither term, however, changes the competence of the President or the Government with respect to international treaties (see Gloss on Article 11, above). The Government of the RF has used both terms in treaty practice. The Agreement between the RF and the IBRD on the Second Rehabilitation Loan was 'confirmed' by a Decree of 9 September 1995,[169] and the Protocol on Changing Article X, Point 2, of the 1966 International Convention on the Preservation of Atlantic Tuna was 'accepted' by a Decree of 3 May 1994.[170] Although the 1995 Law does not so stipulate in this case, as it does with ratification (which takes the form of a Federal Law), the form of expressing confirmation or acceptance; in practice the Government uses the Decree to 'confirm' or 'accept' an international treaty; that is, 'confirmation' and 'acceptance' are not themselves the denomination for the normative act containing confirmation or acceptance.

With respect to international treaties concluded in the name of the Government or those concluded in the name of the RF but with regard to questions within the jurisdiction of the Government the term 'confirmation' or 'acceptance' may be used, and indeed would appear to be the ideal expression.

[169] No. 914. *СЗ РФ*(1995), no. 38, item 3690.
[170] No. 439. *СЗ РФ* (1994), no. 3, item 223.

The Commentary observes that the term 'confirmation' sometimes is used in another context, to endorse changes 'of principle' made in the final stages of a treaty after preliminary approval had been given to the Draft.[171] In this case the treaty is 'confirmed', which in fact seems closer to the ordinary legislative use of the term in Government practice. There is a certain analogy with commercial practice, when the Government 'confirms' certain contracts and thereby, at least in the foreign view, recognizes and accepts contractual provisions of those contracts and any obligations they may contain with respect to the State.

However, under the 1995 Law the process of 'confirmation' cannot be utilized to repair a failure to comply with the requirements of preliminary approval of a draft treaty laid down in Articles 9–11 of the 1995 Law.

Having embarked upon carving out a special regime for 'confirmation' and 'acceptance', point two of this Article is a logical extension, creating the same exception from the general rule with respect to the President as does Article 11 of the 1995 Law (see Gloss on Article 11, above). The President may adopt a decision to confirm or accept an international treaty on questions relegated to the jurisdiction of the Government, when necessary.

CIS

The treaty laws of the CIS countries do not contain such a provision.

Russia

3 Point three of this Article reflects Article 11(4) of the 1995 Law, providing that interdepartmental international treaties are confirmed or adopted/accepted when the treaty provides that entry into force occurs after such confirmation or adoption/acceptance, in this instance by the Federal agencies of executive power in whose name the treaty is signed.

CIS

The CIS treaty laws fall into three groups. The first contains a provision analogous to that of the 1995 Law. *Kazakhstan* (Article 16), *Tadzhikistan* (Articles 12 and 13), and *Turkmenistan* (Article 13) fall into the first group, but reserves the power of confirmation for the Government rather than agencies of executive power.

[171] Osminin, Commentary, p. 66.

The second reserves the confirmation or adoption/acceptance of interdepartmental treaties for subordinate legislation: *Armenia* (Article 13), *Ukraine* (Article 9), and *Uzbekistan* (Article 20).

The third group does not mention interdepartmental treaties in this connection.

Russia

4 Proposals regarding the confirmation or adoption/acceptance of an international treaty in the form of a Federal Law follow the same procedures as Proposals for ratification in the form of a Federal Law (see Gloss on Article 16, above). Otherwise, proposals are to be submitted in accordance with the procedure laid down by Article 9 of the 1995 Law (see Gloss on Article 9, above).

CIS

The *Belarus* (Article 10) treaty law makes provision in detail for the supporting documentation to be submitted when confirmation of a treaty is required: proposals relative to the confirmation of an international treaty of the Republic Belarus by agreement with the Ministry of Foreign Affairs of the Republic Belarus are submitted to the Council of Ministers within a three-month period from the day of signature thereof by republic agencies of State administration and other State agencies of the Republic Belarus within whose competence are the questions regulated by this treaty. They must contain: the draft decision concerning confirmation of the international treaty of the Republic Belarus; a copy of the international treaty of the Republic Belarus; a substantiation of the need for confirmation of the international treaty of the Republic Belarus; the opinion of the Ministry of Justice of the Republic Belarus concerning the conformity of the international treaty of the Republic Belarus to the Constitution and other legislation of the Republic Belarus; a list of norms of laws of the Republic Belarus, acts of the President of the Republic Belarus and Government of the Republic Belarus subject to change, addition, repeal, or adoption for the purposes of performance of the international treaty of the Republic Belarus; other opinions of interested State agencies, remarks, and proposals with regard to the particular international treaty, if there are any; a financial–economic substantiation of the proposed expenditures in connection with the realization of the international treaty of the Republic Belarus submitted for confirmation; a list of persons who took part in working out this international treaty.

The *Tadzhikistan* treaty law (Article 14) contains an analogous provision, requiring that proposals concerning confirmation and adoption of international treaties or accession thereto be submitted in compliance with the requirements laid down for proposals concerning the conclusion of treaties (Article 5). A similar approach is taken by the *Kyrgyzstan* (Article 16[2]) treaty law.

Article 21 Accession of Russian Federation to International Treaties

1. Decisions concerning accession of the Russian Federation to international treaties shall be adopted:

(a) with respect to treaties to which accession is made in the name of the Russian Federation with regard to questions specified in Article 15(1) of the present Federal Law: in the form of a Federal Law in the procedure established by Article 17 of the present Federal Law for the ratification of international treaties;

(b) with respect to treaties to which accession is made in the name of the Russian Federation (except for treaties provided for by subpoint (a) of the present point): by the President of the Russian Federation, and with respect to treaties to which accession is made in the name of the Russian Federation with regard to questions relegated to the jurisdiction of the Government of the Russian Federation: by the Government of the Russian Federation;

(c) with respect to treaties to which accession is made in the name of the Government of the Russian Federation: by the Government of the Russian Federation.

2. The President of the Russian Federation shall adopt decisions concerning accession to international treaties with regard to questions relegated to the jurisdiction of the Government of the Russian Federation if such is necessary.

3. Accession to international treaties of an interdepartmental character shall be effectuated in the procedure established by Article 11(3) and (4) of the present Federal Law.

4. Proposals concerning accession to international treaties to be effectuated in the form of a Federal Law shall be submitted in the procedure established by Article 16 of the present Federal Law, and in other instances – in the procedure provided for by Article 9 of the present Federal Law.

Russia

1 Accession is one of the forms of a State expressing its consent to an international treaty being binding upon it which is recognized in Article 11 of the 1969 Vienna Convention and accordingly is recognized in the 1995 Law.

The basic approach of Article 21 is to ensure that the same procedures apply to the RF becoming a party to a treaty after the treaty has entered into force or signature has been closed as would apply had the RF been an initial party to the treaty. Accession as a rule is applicable to multilateral treaties.

Article 21(1)(a) refers to the types of treaties regulated by Article 15(1) and Article 17 of the 1995 Law, requiring that accession in these instances occurs in the form of a Federal Law. The procedure for adopting decisions concerning accession in the form of a Federal Law are analogous to the procedure laid down in Article 17 of the 1995 Law for the ratification of a treaty. Russia acceded to the Charter of the Council of Europe and to the General Agreement on the privileges and immunities of the Council of Europe and protocols thereto in this manner.[172]

Subpoint (1)(b) of this Article establishes for the President and the Government of the RF the same rights with respect to accession as they enjoyed with respect to confirmation and adoption (Article 20, 1995 Law). The President has the right to accede to international treaties provided that the decision concerning accession is not already reserved to the Federal Assembly, and the Government, with respect to treaties within its jurisdiction (see Gloss on Article 11, above).

Subpoint (1)(c) of this Article authorizes the Government to accede to international treaties in the name of the Government of the RF.

CIS

The CIS treaty laws vary as to whether accession is treated as a separate and distinct process to which a separate Article of the law is devoted, or whether it is combined with ratification, confirmation, and/or adoption/acceptance. The basic pattern of regulation, as in the 1995 Law, follows that for ratification or confirmation.

The treaty law of *Armenia* (Article 14) draws the following distinctions: decisions concerning the accession of the Republic Armenia to international treaties are adopted by: (a) the Supreme Soviet of the Republic Armenia: upon the submission of the President of the Republic Armenia – with respect to treaties subject to ratification; (b) the President of the Republic Armenia: with respect to those treaties not subject to ratification, accession to which is in the name of the Republic Armenia; and (c) the Government of the Republic Armenia: with respect to intergovernmental and interdepartmental treaties not subject to ratification. *Turkmenistan* (Article 14), *Ukraine* (Article 10), and *Uzbekistan* (Article 21) follow similar procedures. The treaty law of

172 *СЗ РФ* (1996), no. 9, items 774 and 775.

Azerbaidzhan (Article 14) takes an analogous approach, eliminating any reference to interdepartmental treaties.

The *Kazakhstan* (Article 18) treaty law contains a variant of the above formulations: decisions concerning accession are adopted (1) with respect to international treaties of an inter-State character submitted by the President of the Republic Kazakhstan, and also with respect to international treaties submitted by the Government of the Republic Kazakhstan and subject to ratification with regard to questions relegated to the jurisdiction of the Government – the Parliament of the Republic Kazakhstan; and (2) with respect to international treaties relegated to the jurisdiction of the Government of the Republic Kazakhstan and not subject to ratification – the Government of the Republic Kazakhstan. The *Kyrgyzstan* treaty law (Article 17[1]) follows closely the scheme of Kazakhstan.

The form of enactment with respect to accession is expressly addressed in a few treaty laws. That of *Belarus* (Article 11) requires a law in the case of an inter-State or intergovernmental treaty subject to ratification; an edict in the case of an inter-State treaty not subject to ratification; and a decree in the event of an intergovernmental treaty not subject to ratification.

The treaty law of *Georgia* (Article 18) combines accession with ratification or confirmation, and of *Tadzhikistan* (Article 13) combines accession with adoption/acceptance.

The *Kyrgyzstan* (Article 17[2]) treaty law makes provision for the accession to interparliamentary treaties, a decision which is taken by the respective parliamentary organs.

Russia

2 Point two of this Article contains an exception similar to that found in Article 20 of the 1995 Law. The President has the right to adopt the decision to accede to an international treaty with regard to questions within the jurisdiction of the Government, when necessary (see Gloss on Articles 11 and 20, 1995 Law).

CIS

There is no equivalent provision in the other CIS treaty laws.

Russia

3 Accession to interdepartmental treaties occurs in the same procedure as for concluding such treaties. Unless the treaty is of such importance that the Government itself decides to accede, the Government will

adopt a decision to conduct negotiations concerning accession and the respective Ministry, State Committee, or other department will adopt the decision concerning accession by agreement with the Ministry of Foreign Affairs.

CIS

Many CIS treaty laws do not address the question of accession to interdepartmental treaties.

The *Armenian* (Article 14), *Kazakhstan* (Article 18[2]), and *Turkmenistan* (Article 14) treaty laws provide that decisions concerning accession to international treaties of an interdepartmental character are adopted by the Government. In *Kyrgyzstan* (Article 17) accession to interdepartmental treaties is procedurally handled as in the case of the signature of an international treaty. In *Ukraine* (Article 10[2]) and *Uzbekistan* (Article 21[4]) decisions concerning accession to interdepartmental treaties are adopted in the procedure established by the Government.

Russia

4 Point four requires that accession in the form of a Federal Law comply with the procedures set out in Article 16 of the 1995 Law which apply to a proposal for the ratification of an international treaty. Otherwise, such proposals are submitted in the procedure laid down in Article 9 of the 1995 Law (see Gloss on Articles 9 and 16, above).

CIS

Several CIS treaty laws regulate the procedure for making proposals concerning accession to international treaties, usually by cross-reference to other Articles of the treaty law. In *Belarus* proposals for accession to a treaty are procedurally equated to those for conducting negotiations to conclude a treaty. The *Kyrgyzstan* (Article 17[4]) treaty law is influenced in this respect by the form of enactment to be used for accession. If in the form of a law, the procedures follow those for ratification of a treaty. If another form is to be used, the procedures concerning the conclusion of treaties, agreement of the said proposals with interested departments, and the confirmation of treaties not subject to ratification are to be followed.

The *Moldovan* (Articles 6, 12) treaty law requires that accession to a treaty which would require ratification according to Article 6 must also be ratified and that the internal documents 'consolidating' accession are the same as those for ratification of a treaty.

Article 22 Special Procedure for Expression of Consent to Bindingness of International Treaties for Russian Federation

If an international treaty contains rules requiring the change of individual provisions of the Constitution of the Russian Federation, the decision concerning consent to its bindingness for the Russian Federation shall be possible in the form of a Federal Law only after making the respective amendments to the Constitution of the Russian Federation or a revision of its provisions in the established procedure.

Russia

This Article aims to reduce the possibility of conflict between the 1993 Constitution and treaty obligations of the RF by laying down a procedure for resolving the conflict and confirming that the Constitution takes precedence over a treaty unless and until the Constitution is changed, added to, or amended to eliminate the conflict between the treaty and the Constitution. The 1993 Constitution contains formulations which themselves contain the seeds of possible conflict with treaty obligations.

Article 79 of the 1993 Constitution provides that the RF may transfer part of its powers to 'inter-State associations' in accordance with international treaties 'if this does not entail a limitation of the rights and freedoms of man and citizen and is not contrary to the foundations of the constitutional system of the Russian Federation'.[173]

International treaties concerning the rights and freedoms of man and citizen and requiring a change of, addition to, or amendment of the 1993 Constitution would have to await, under this Article, the completion of special procedures applicable to Chapters 1 and 2 of the 1993 Constitution. These procedures make changing the 1993 Constitution extremely difficult with respect to Chapters 1 and 2. However, international treaties

[173] W. E. Butler, *Constitutional Foundations of the CIS Countries* (The Hague, Kluwer Law International, 1999), p. 448.

expanding or improving the rights and duties of man and citizen would not meet with these procedural difficulties.

Although this Article does not address the issue of constitutional federal laws of the RF, there is the question of Article 76(3) of the 1993 Constitution, which provides that 'federal laws may not be contrary to federal constitutional laws'.[174] Treaties subject to ratification are ratified in the form of a federal law, and in the hierarchy of constitutional sources of law, constitutional federal laws are of higher stature than federal laws. Some Russian jurists are of the view that international treaties which would make changes in federal constitutional laws should be adopted in the same procedure as the federal constitutional law or changes thereto.[175] Others suggest that only changes in the Constitution itself are contemplated by Article 22 of the 1995 Law.[176]

CIS

The majority of CIS treaty laws do not contain an analogous provision, and where they do so provide, it is usually not in the form of a separate Article.

The *Georgian* (Article 21) treaty law provides, however, that in the event a constitutional suit is brought by an empowered subject before an international treaty is deemed by Georgia to be binding, the Constitutional Court of Georgia shall adopt a decision concerning the constitutionality of the international treaty. If a constitutional suit is brought to the Constitutional Court of Georgia, consideration of the question of deeming the respective international treaty to be binding upon Georgia before the rendering of a decision by the Constitutional Court shall not be permitted. Should the Constitutional Court establish the non-conformity of an international treaty to the Constitution of Georgia, the deeming of a treaty to be binding upon Georgia is permitted only after respective changes are made in the Constitution in the established procedure.

In Georgia the filing of a suit is required in the Constitutional Court in order to address the constitutionality of the ratification of an international treaty. A different approach is taken in the *Kazakhstan* (Article 12) treaty law. There the Constitutional Council, upon the application of the President of the Republic Kazakhstan, Chairman of the Senate, Chairman of the Mazhilis, not less than one-fifth of the total number of

[174] W. E. Butler, *Constitutional Foundations of the CIS Countries* (The Hague, Kluwer Law International, 1999), p. 447.

[175] Lukashuk, Commentary, p. 72.

[176] V. I. Andrianov, in Iu. V. Kudriavtsev (ed.), *Комментарий к Конституции Российской Федерации* [Commentary on the Constitution of the Russian Federation] (M., Iuridicheskaia literatura, 1996), p. 81.

deputies of Parliament, or the Prime Minister, is empowered to consider before ratification international treaties of the Republic Kazakhstan for their conformity to the Constitution. In the event of an application to the Constitutional Council with regard to the questions specified, the running of the periods for the ratification of international treaties is suspended. International treaties deemed not to conform to the Constitution of the Republic Kazakhstan may not be ratified and introduced into operation.

The *Kyrgyzstan* (Article 19) treaty law follows the model of the 1995 Law.

In *Ukraine* (Article 7[4]) it is for the commissions of the Supreme Rada to determine whether a constitutional issue is raised by an international treaty. If divergencies between the treaty submitted for ratification and the Constitution of Ukraine are discovered, the treaty is sent to the Constitutional Court of Ukraine in order to receive an opinion concerning the conformity thereof to the Constitution of Ukraine.

Although none of the CIS treaty laws makes this formal linkage, several also require a legal evaluation of a proposed international treaty which includes an assessment of any consequential changes in domestic legislation that may be required if the treaty is ratified. One would expect that such a legal assessment would not overlook constitutional issues.

Article 23 Provisional Application of International Treaty by Russian Federation

1. An international treaty or part of a treaty may, before its entry into force, be applied by the Russian Federation provisionally if such has been provided for in the treaty or if an arrangement was reached concerning this with the parties who have signed the treaty.

2. Decisions concerning the provisional application by the Russian Federation of an international treaty or part thereof shall be adopted by the agency which adopted the decision to sign the international treaty in the procedure established by Article 11 of the present Federal Law.

If an international treaty the decision concerning consent to the bindingness of which for the Russian Federation is subject in accordance with the present Federal Law to adoption in the form of a Federal Law provides for the temporary application of the treaty or part thereof or an arrangement concerning this has been reached with the parties in any other way, it shall be submitted to the State Duma within a period of not more than six months from the date of the commencement of the provisional application thereof. By a decision adopted in the form of a Federal Law in the procedure established by Article 17 of the present Federal Law for the ratification of international treaties, the period of provisional application may be extended.

3. Unless provided otherwise in an international treaty or the respective States agree otherwise, the provisional application by the Russian Federation of a treaty or part thereof shall terminate upon informing the other States which provisionally are applying the treaty of the intention of the Russian Federation not to become a participant of the treaty.

Russia

1 The term 'provisional' or 'temporary' is used in Russian treaty practice in two senses. The first refers to a 'provisional' or 'temporary' Agreement which the parties conclude with a view to replacing it with a more comprehensive or more elaborated Agreement in the future. In this sense the concept of 'provisional' is relative. The Provisional Agreement

concluded between the former Soviet Union and the United Kingdom on 22 May 1930 remained in force for more than fifty years.

This Article, based on Article 25 of the 1969 Vienna Convention, uses the concept of 'provisional' or 'temporary' in the sense that a treaty duly agreed to by the parties but not yet in force may be applied by them temporarily as though it were in force until the necessary formalities to introduce it into force have been completed. Under this approach the parties are not under an obligation to not deprive the treaty of its object and purpose (Article 18, 1969 Vienna Convention), but rather to fully perform the treaty as though it were in force. Neither is this position the same as a set of unilateral declarations by the parties that they will adhere to the provisions of the treaty in practice, for this Article contemplates full compliance with treaty obligations as set out in the treaty. The last are mutual obligations, and these are not created by unilateral declarations, even if identical.

Application of the concept of provisionality can be complex in State practice. An instructive example is the Agreement between the United States of America and the Russian Federation Concerning the Safe and Secure Transportation, Storage, and Destruction of Weapons and the Prevention of Weapons Proliferation concluded on 17 June 1992 and the Protocol to the said Agreement signed on 15 and 16 June 1999, which extended the duration of the said Agreement for seven years as from 17 June 1999. This Agreement and Protocol, *inter alia*, granted certain tax and customs privileges to designated civilian and military personnel. Neither the Agreement nor the Protocol were ratified or submitted for ratification in the RF.

The 1992 Agreement was concluded between the United States and the Russian Federation after the Union of Soviet Socialist Republics had been dissolved. The RF at the time had no special legislation on the procedure for the conclusion and ratification of international treaties. The 1978 Constitution of the RSFSR, as amended, which was in force when the 1992 Agreement was concluded, provided that: 'The Supreme Soviet of the RSFSR' shall 'ratify and denounce international treaties of the RSFSR' (Article 109[15]) and that the President of Russia shall 'conduct negotiations and sign in the name of the RSFSR international and inter-republic treaties, which shall enter into force after ratification by the Supreme Soviet of the RSFSR' (Article 121^5).

The 1978 constitutional formulation, as amended, did not determine which international treaties were subject to ratification. The 1992 Agreement itself provided 'This Agreement shall enter into force upon signature and shall remain in force for seven years' (Article XIV), that is, 17 June 1992. Foreign contractors operating under the 1992 Agreement experienced difficulties in obtaining the tax and customs exemptions provided for by the Agreement. The Russian Ministry of Finances took the view that under both Soviet and Russian legislation, the 1992 Agreement fell into the category of those treaties which required ratification. At the time the 1992 Agreement was signed, in the view of the Russian Ministry of Finances, the 1978 USSR Law remained in force on the territory of the RF. According to the 1978 USSR Law, 'international treaties of the USSR. . .establishing rules other than those which are contained in legislative acts of the USSR shall be subject to ratification'.[177] Since no other language in Article 12 of the 1978 USSR Law can be applicable, the Russian Ministry of Finances apparently considered that the 1992 Agreement established an exemption from the provisions of certain tax laws.[178] That view of the Russian Ministry of Finances has been set out officially to local Russian tax agencies and enterprises on several occasions.[179] The view of the Russian side regarding the legal requirement to ratify the 1992 Agreement was plainly otherwise at the time of signature, in light of Article XIV.

In practice the parties to the 1992 Agreement treated it as provisionally in force, subject to tax and customs exemptions only for military and civilian government personnel from the United States (and not to contractors of the US Government). That view is confirmed by the text of the 1999 Protocol to the 1992 Agreement, which refers in Articles 4, 5, and 6 to 'taking into account established practice'. The 'established practice' would appear to include the positions adopted by the Russian Ministry of Finances.

When the 1999 Protocol was signed, the situation had changed. The 1995 Law had lengthened the list of treaties subject to ratification: treaties 'regarding questions affecting the defence capability of the Russian Federation, regarding questions of disarmament or international control over armaments, regarding questions of ensuring international peace and security' (Article 15[1]). Under this formulation the 1992 Agreement and 1999 Protocol thereto would clearly be subject to ratification. Moreover,

[177] See W. E. Butler, *Basic Documents on the Soviet Legal System* (Dobbs Ferry, Oceana Publications, 1983), p. 288. The full text of the Law appears in an annex below.

[178] It is an interesting point as to whether a treaty creating an exemption from tax and customs legislation is 'establishing a rule other than contained' in legislation. That is, does the exemption established in a bilateral treaty from a rule constitute a rule in and of itself or does the exemption merely represent the suspension or non-application of the rule contained in legislation?

[179] See the Letter of the Department of Tax Police of the Ministry of Finances of the Russian Federation, 27 July 1998, No. 04-06-05/1, and another Letter of the same agency dated 3 August 1998, No. 04-06-05/2, both of which rely upon Article 12 of the 1978 USSR Law.

the 1995 Law made subject to ratification treaties which establish rules that differ from those laid down in federal laws; that is, the same position taken in the 1978 USSR Law which the Department of Tax Police of the Ministry of Finances of the Russian Federation invoked in their Letters of 27 July and 3 August 1998.

Under Article 7 of the 1999 Protocol, Russia and the United States agreed that the Protocol 'shall be applied provisionally from the date of signature and shall enter into force on the date of the last written notification that the Parties have fulfilled the national procedures required for its entry into force'. This formulation satisfied the requirements of point one of the present Article.

The 1995 Law makes no distinction between bilateral and multilateral treaties in this respect. It therefore is possible for some of the parties to a multilateral treaty to agree that the treaty is provisionally in force as between themselves, or to agree that stipulated parts of the treaty are provisionally in force. In Russian treaty practice the text of the treaty itself normally makes provision for temporary application of its provisions, although in some instances a protocol signed after the treaty itself records this agreement. Where the treaty itself provides for temporary application, a separate decision to this effect by the President or the Government is not required on the premise that the decision to sign the treaty constituted approval of provisional application. However, if the agreement concerning provisional application was reached later, after signature, the Proposal to this effect and the decision would be adopted by the same agency which decided to sign the treaty.

CIS

The CIS countries have approached the provisional application of a treaty variously in their treaty laws. The model of the 1995 Law is followed in substance by *Uzbekistan* (Article 22).

The *Belarus* (Article 14) treaty law permits provisional application, but only on condition that the treaty as a whole or part thereof does not contain provisions establishing other rules than those which are contained in laws of the Republic Belarus, acts of the President of the Republic Belarus, or provisions not regulated by laws of the Republic Belarus and acts of the President of the Republic Belarus.

Georgia (Article 20) effectively precludes the possibility of the provisional application of a treaty by requiring that notwithstanding agreement to the contrary by the parties, it will apply in *Georgia* only from the moment of entry into force for Georgia.

The treaty laws of some CIS countries make no formal provision for the provisional application of a treaty: *Armenia, Azerbaidzhan, Kazakhstan, Kyrgyzstan, Moldova, Tadzhikistan, Turkmenistan,* and *Ukraine*.

Russia

2 Treaties subject to ratification may be applied provisionally, and this has been done in Russian practice. In principle treaties subject to confirmation or acceptance or accession may also be applied provisionally, although in Russian practice this has not yet occurred.

Point two of this Article lays down the procedure for adopting decisions concerning the temporary application of a treaty, or part thereof, by the RF. The 1995 Law requires that such decisions be taken, pursuant to Article 11 of the 1995 Law, by the agency which adopted the decision to sign the treaty irrespective of whether the treaty text itself contains a provision on temporary application or not. This approach retains intact the decision-making procedure for the treaty followed with respect to other actions regarding it.

A special procedure is laid down in point two of this Article with respect to treaties which are subject to ratification, confirmation, or adoption in the form of a Federal Law, presumably with a view towards preserving the delimitation of competence with respect to international treaties laid down by the 1993 Constitution and the 1995 Law between the legislative and executive branches of State. Accordingly, the 1995 Law establishes a six-month period during which the treaty is to be submitted to the State Duma for consideration. No limitation is placed on the length of time which the State Duma may devote to consideration, nor does any limitation extend to the Soviet of the Federation. The Reglaments of the State Duma and the Soviet of the Federation make no mention of special procedures or limitations in this connection.

After the 1995 Law entered into force, the President of the RF issued a Regulation[180] which addressed the issue of certain international treaties whose temporary application commenced before the 1995 Law entered into force and which under the 1995 Law now required ratification in the form of a Federal Law. On 9 October 1995 the Government of the RF required the Ministry of Foreign Affairs of Russia and other Federal agencies of executive power to make proposals in accordance with Presidential Regulation No. 370-рп and submit a list of relevant treaties.[181]

[180] Regulation of 7 August 1995, No. 370-рп. *СЗ РФ* (1995), no. 33, item 3363.
[181] Regulation of 9 October 1995, No. 1388-р. *СЗ РФ* (1995), no. 43, item 4083.

Although a six-month period for submitting such treaties to the State Duma for ratification has been laid down in point two of this Article, the Commentary is of the view that the failure to submit the treaty within the six-month period would not automatically terminate the temporary application thereof. This, it is argued, would be contrary to Article 23 of the 1995 Law and to Article 18 of the 1969 Vienna Convention. The failure to submit a treaty to the State Duma is not an unequivocal expression of the intention not to become a party to the respective treaty. It follows that if the treaty is submitted to the State Duma within the six-month period and the Duma fails to consider the matter, the temporary application of the treaty continues. If the State Duma ratifies the treaty, temporary application ceases from the date the treaty enters into force. If the period of temporary application is extended by the State Duma, the temporary application continues to the date specified in the Federal Law authorizing continuance or to entry into force if ratification occurs, or for a new period of extension. If the State Duma rejects the treaty (having regard to problems identified in the Gloss on Article 17 above, with respect to the indefiniteness of Duma procedures), provisional application must cease from the date of rejection. If continuance of the temporary application is refused, so too must the temporary application cease from the date of refusal.[182] The Commentary further argues that the provisional application may be terminated before the six-month period for submission to the State Duma elapses by the agency which adopted the decision to sign the treaty, or upon the expiry of the six-month period, or if the Proposal to ratify has been withdrawn from the State Duma.[183]

While these scenarios have merit, they would appear to overlook the mutual obligations inherent in this Article of the 1995 Law, that the parties have *agreed* to temporary application.

This Article would appear to give scope to the executive branch of State to achieve the application of an international treaty subject to ratification without achieving a final consent of the Federal Assembly to ratification in the form of a Federal Law for a very extended period of time. No sanctions attach if the President or the Government fail to submit a treaty temporarily being applied for ratification. The Commentary suggests that this situation be viewed as an 'exception' from the procedures of the 1995 Law. Their reasoning is that the possibility of temporary application is expressly provided for by the 1995 Law, and that this position is consistent with Article 25 of the 1969 Vienna Convention. To speak of temporary application as being the equivalent of fulfilment of a treaty would be incorrect, as both the 1969 Vienna Convention and the 1995 Law treat

[182] Khodakov and Osminin, Commentary, pp. 74–5.
[183] Khodakov and Osminin, Commentary, p. 75.

them separately and mirror one another in this respect.[184] However, to speak of complicated and complex procedures with respect to ratification is usually to speak of political complications between the executive and the legislative branches of State. The Agreement between the former Soviet Union and the United States Concerning the Line of Demarcation of Sea Expanses, signed at Washington DC on 1 June 1990, has been subject to temporary application for some time.[185]

CIS

In *Belarus* (Article 14) the decision concerning the provisional application of an international treaty by the Republic Belarus or part thereof is adopted with respect to: inter-State treaties of the Republic Belarus – by the President of the Republic Belarus; intergovernmental treaties of the Republic Belarus – by the Council of Ministers of the Republic Belarus.

The treaty law of *Georgia* contains no provision analogous to this point of the 1995 Law.

The treaty law of *Uzbekistan* (Article 22) contains a clause substantially similar to the first paragraph of point 2 of the 1995 Law. It does not contain a provision similar to the second paragraph.

Russia

3 Point three of this Article is based on Article 25(2) of the 1969 Vienna Convention. A State which has agreed to the temporary application of a treaty is required to give notice to the other States concerning its intention not to become a party, unless the States have agreed otherwise or there is no agreement on this issue. It follows from the 1995 Law that such notice must be explicit, and not merely an inference from, for example, the failure of the State Duma to consider a treaty text submitted for ratification or the failure of the Federal Law ratifying a treaty to obtain the requisite number of votes in the State Duma or in the Soviet of the Federation.

CIS

Only the *Belarus* (Article 14) treaty law contains an equivalent provision.

184 Khodakov and Osminin, Commentary, p. 77.

185 See Regulation of the President of the RF of 9 March 1996, No. 109-рп. *СЗ РФ* (1996), no. 13, item 1326. The US Senate gave its advice and consent to the Agreement in 1991 by a vote of 86 to 6. On the background to the Agreement from a Russian perspective, see V. Zilanov, 'А после Аляски еще одна клякса' [And After Alaska Yet Another Blot], *Российская газета*, 14 January 1997, p. 3. Zilanov wrote in this capacity as Deputy Chairman of the State Committee for Fisheries of Russia.

Article 24 Entry into Force of International Treaties of Russian Federation

1. International treaties shall enter into force for the Russian Federation in accordance with the present Federal Law and in the procedure and periods provided for in the treaty or agreed between the contracting parties.

2. Official communications of the Ministry of Foreign Affairs of the Russian Federation concerning the entry into force of international treaties of the Russian Federation concluded in the name of the Russian Federation and in the name of the Government of the Russian Federation shall be published in the procedure provided for by Article 30 of the present Federal Law.

Russia

1 Although this Article speaks of treaties entering into force 'in accordance with the present Federal Law', this language is not construed as meaning that the failure to comply with the Federal Law will *ipso facto* mean that the treaty did not enter into force for the RF. The Commentary suggests a narrow construction: 'the necessity to comply with the requirements of the Law when formulating the provisions of the treaty affecting entry into force'.[186] The procedure and periods for entry into force, in the wording of point one of this Article, are a matter of agreement for the parties.

Russian treaty practice contains a vast variety of variables with respect to entry into force. Signature is commonly the moment of entry into force unless the treaty requires ratification, confirmation, acceptance, or approval. The formulations are several: 'from the date', 'from the day', 'from the moment' of signature. Sometimes a specific date is inserted, or a specified number of days, upon the elapsing of which the treaty enters into force. Where no date in any form is specified in the treaty, the presumption in Russian practice is that the date of signature operates.[187]

The same principle applies when documents are exchanged. As a rule, entry into force occurs when instruments of ratification, notes, or letters are exchanged, or when the last communication constituting agreement is

[186] Khodakov, Commentary, p. 81.
[187] Khodakov, Commentary, p. 80.

the date of entry into force. When the instruments, documents, or notice are handed over to a depositary, the date of handing over becomes the date of entry into force.

CIS

The CIS treaty laws contain a similar provision: *Georgia* (Article 24), *Kyrgyzstan* (Article 21[1]), *Tadzhikistan* (Article 15), and *Uzbekistan* (Article 23).

The *Belarus* (Article 12) adds to the formulation, in the interests of greater precision, the phrase: 'after the expression of consent of the Republic Belarus to the bindingness for it of the international treaty'.

In *Georgia* (Article 24[2]) if legislation of Georgia requires for the entry of an international treaty into force the fulfilment of any municipal procedure, such treaty shall enter into force for Georgia only after the fulfilment of the respective procedure. This is an obscure formulation which could be construed to include ratification or confirmation. In light of other provisions regarding them, this Article might be construed to encompass non-self-executing treaties.

No similar provision concerning entry into force is to be found in the treaty laws of *Armenia, Azerbaidzhan, Kazakhstan, Moldova, Turkmenistan*, and *Ukraine*.

Russia

2 Official communications are not to be confused with publication of the text of the treaty itself. The 1995 Law contains no obligation to publish such communications, so that 'secret diplomacy' from this standpoint may still operate. If, however, an official communication is to be issued, this Article requires that publication be in the procedure provided for by Article 30 of the 1995 Law. With regard to the entry into force, the purpose of publication is to officially announce the respective event for informational purposes and does not, unless the treaty provides otherwise, have any constitutive effect.

CIS

The treaty laws of *Georgia* (Article 23) and *Kyrgyzstan* (Article 21[2]) contain a similar requirement.

Article 25 Reservations to International Treaties of Russian Federation

1. When signing, ratifying, confirming, or adopting international treaties of the Russian Federation or acceding to treaties, reservations may be made while complying with the conditions of the treaty and respective norms of international law.

2. Reservations may be removed at any time (unless provided otherwise by an international treaty of the Russian Federation) in the same procedure in which they were made.

3. The acceptance of a reservation made by another contracting State to an international treaty of the Russian Federation or an objection to such shall be effectuated in accordance with the conditions of the treaty itself and the norms of international law by the agency which adopted the decision concerning consent to the bindingness of the international treaty for the Russian Federation.

Proposals concerning the acceptance or objection to reservations to be effectuated in the form of a Federal Law shall be submitted in the procedure established by Article 16 of the present Federal Law, and in other instances – in the procedure provided for in Article 9 of the present Federal Law.

Russia

1 Point one of this Article reflects the provisions of Article 19 of the 1969 Vienna Convention. Reservations may be entered to a treaty upon signature, ratification, confirmation, acceptance, or accession on two conditions: compliance with the treaty provisions themselves, and compliance with the respective norms of international law. Compliance with the treaty provisions would mean that a reservation may not be entered if the treaty prohibits reservations or limits reservations to certain matters. As regards norms of international law, at a minimum reservations may not be made which are incompatible with the principles and purposes of the treaty or with general principles of international law.

The former Soviet Union routinely entered reservations to international treaties during the 1950s–1980s on certain matters of ideological consequence in those days. The reservations practice of the RF has been far more restrained. From 1994 to 1998 Russia concluded or acceded to more than 270 treaties subject to ratification in the State Duma, both bilateral and multilateral. Reservations were declared to six, and other unilateral declarations were made with regard to twenty four. Of the some 270 treaties, about 114 were agreements concluded within the framework of the CIS and with States that are members of the CIS. One reservation and seven declarations were made with regard to those agreements.[188] More precise data for 1996 indicates that of the fifty bilateral and multilateral treaties submitted to the Soviet of the Federation of the RF, six were submitted with reservations and declarations.[189]

The Soviet reservations are being gradually reviewed by the RF. The pivotal moment was the withdrawal by the USSR of the reservations not recognizing the compulsory jurisdiction of the International Court of Justice in the Edict of the Presidium of the USSR Supreme Soviet 'On the Withdrawal of Reservations of the USSR Previously Made Concerning the Nonrecognition of the Compulsory Jurisdiction of the United Nations International Court With Regard to Disputes on the Interpretation and Application of a Number of International Treaties'.[190] Reservations were removed from the 1948 genocide convention, the 1966 convention on the elimination of all forms of racial discrimination, the 1979 convention on eliminating all forms of discrimination against women, and the 1989 convention on torture.[191] The removal of the reservations was not retroactive. The Edict provided that: 'The provisions of the treaty will extend to disputes . . . with respect to instances which may arise after the date of notification of the Secretary-General of the United Nations on withdrawal of the reservations.'

The Commentary recommends that reservations not be declared unilaterally by one branch of State without coordinating the position with other branches. With respect to an international treaty subject to ratification, such an approach would entail the reservation being formulated during the first reading of the Federal Law concerning ratification of the treaty and then agreed with other agencies of State power.[192]

The 1995 Law is silent about reservations to bilateral treaties but imposes no restriction with respect to them. The possibility of such reservations was recognized by Soviet international legal doctrine in the

188 See A. V. Zharskii, 'Reservations to International Treaties in CIS Practice', *Sudebnik*, IV (1999), 564.

189 T. I. Spivakova, 'Оговорки и заявления в договорной практике Российской Федерации' [Reservations and Declarations in Treaty Practice of the Russian Federation], *Московский журнал международного права*, no. 3 (1998), p. 137.

190 *Ведомости СССР* (1989), no. 11, item 79.

191 A. V. Zharskii, 'Reservations to International Treaties in CIS Practice', *Sudebnik*, IV (1999), 563.

192 Lukashuk, Commentary, p. 83.

mid-1950s.[193] This view finds support among contemporary international lawyers,[194] although 'the majority of representatives of the Russian doctrine of international law theoretically deny the very possibility of a reservation to a bilateral treaty. Nonetheless, instances are known in practice of reservations to international treaties of the Russian Federation, as well as when an interpretative statement may be treated as a reservation to a bilateral treaty.'[195]

CIS

Within the CIS there are two aspects to reservations. The first concerns the CIS treaty laws; the second concerns the practice of entering reservations to treaties concluded within the framework of the CIS.

Several CIS treaty laws contain a provision similar to this point of the 1995 Law: *Belarus* (Article 13), *Georgia* (Article 22[1]), *Kyrgyzstan* (Article 22[1]), *Uzbekistan* (Article 24). The Decision of the Council of Heads of States of 17 May 1996 'On Confirmation of the Rules of Procedure of the Council of Heads of States and the Council of Heads of Governments of the CIS' provides that reservations may be entered but omits the qualifying language of the 1995 Law 'while complying with the conditions of the treaty and respective norms of international law' (Article 21[1]).[196] Two procedural requirements are added: a time-period of forty five days is laid down for a State-Participant to object to a reservation, and both the reservation and objection thereto must be fixed in the form of an annex to the principal text of the treaty (Article 21(2) and [3]).

The *Tadzhikistan* treaty law (Article 16) strengthens the formulation of the 1995 law by referring to 'provisions' rather than 'conditions' and to norms of international law generally rather than to 'respective' norms of international law.

The *Georgian* (Article 22[1]) and *Tadzhikistan* (Article 16) treaty laws add the stipulation that a reservation may not be incompatible with the

193 See V. N. Durdenevskii, 'К вопросу об оговорках в международных договорах' [On the Question of Reservations to International Treaties], *Советское государство и право*, no. 4 (1956), p. 102.

194 R. A. Kalamkarian, 'К вопросу о допустимости формулирования оговорок согласно Венской конвенции о праве международных договоров 1969 г.' [On the Question of the Admissability of Formulating Reservations According to the 1969 Vienna Convention on the Law of Treaties], *Государство и право*, no. 10 (1998), p. 92; A. N. Talalaev, *Венская конвенция о праве международных договоров. Комментарий* [Vienna Convention on the Law of Treaties. Commentary] (M., Iuridicheskaia literatura, 1997), pp. 50–1.

195 T. O. Orlova, 'Legal Technique in International Treaties of the Russian Federation', *Sudebnik*, V (2000), 136.

196 Quoted in A. V. Zharskii, 'Reservations to International Treaties in the Practice of the CIS', *Sudebnik*, IV (1999), 591.

object and purpose of the treaty. The *Georgian* (Article 22[2]) treaty law adds a procedural requirement: a reservation made when signing, ratifying, and confirming an international treaty or while acceding to the treaty shall be formalized in writing, the depositary or other contracting party being notified thereof.

The treaty laws of *Armenia, Azerbaidzhan, Kazakhstan, Moldova, Turkmenistan,* and *Ukraine* omit any mention of reservations.

Within the framework of the CIS, reservations were declared to the very earliest agreements concluded: the Agreement of the Council of the Heads of States-Participants of the CIS on Armed Forces and Border Guards of 30 December 1991, and the Agreement on Strategic Forces, also of 30 December 1991. The practice of declaring reservations within the CIS framework has been described as 'widespread'.[197] Although more than a thousand such treaties and agreements have been concluded, it has been said by CIS experts themselves that only 10 percent actually operate.[198]

The Economic Court of the CIS[199] has issued a Decision and an Advisory Opinion[200] in which the validity of reservations made to CIS treaties is examined. In an Advisory Opinion given at the request of the Inter-State Economic Committee of the Economic Union on 15 May 1996 concerning whether reservations made to certain agreements concluded within the CIS framework were compatible with the 1969 Vienna Convention, the Economic Court determined which categories of CIS documents fell into the category of a treaty. Documents which met the criteria of an international treaty were:

(1) decisions of the heads of States and governments approving draft agreements and annexes thereto and instituting organs provided for by international agreements; (2) statements of heads of States and governments, if they were an annex to a treaty; and (3) memorandums and declarations of heads of States and governments, if they have the respective attributes of international agreements.

Reservations to such documents were regulated by the 1969 Vienna Convention. The Economic Court declared that the decisions of organs of the CIS affecting budgetary questions and statutes on the personnel or organizations or founding auxiliary agencies of the organization were the internal law of the international organizations, and unilateral declarations

197 A. V. Zharskii, 'Reservations to International Treaties in CIS Practice', *Sudebnik*, IV (1999), 580.

198 *Вестник Межпарламентской Ассамблея СНГ*, no. 1 (1998), p. 45.

199 The Agreement on the Status of the Economic Court of the CIS and Statute thereon are translated by W. E. Butler in *Sudebnik*, IV (1999), 679–88.

200 These are translated by W. E. Butler in *Sudebnik*, IV (1999), 937–72.

with respect to such, if made by States, did not fall under the 1969 Vienna Convention. Most treaties concluded within the CIS are silent on the subject of reservations; a very few stipulate what kind of reservations might be entered.

Russia

2 This point of the Article incorporates the provisions of Article 22(1) of the 1969 Vienna Convention. Since reservations are a unilateral position adopted by a State with respect to an international treaty, it follows that the State which made the reservation has the right to remove it at any time, unless the treaty itself provides otherwise.

CIS

Some CIS treaty laws contain a similar provision: *Belarus* (Article 13), *Georgia* (Article 22[3]), *Kyrgyzstan* (Article 22[2]), *Tadzhikistan* (Article 16), *Uzbekistan* (Article 24).

The Decision of the Council of Heads of States of 17 May 1996 'On Confirmation of the Rules of Procedure of the Council of Heads of States and the Council of Heads of Governments of the CIS' provides that reservations to a treaty may be withdrawn at any time by means of a notification sent to the Executive Secretariat of the CIS as depositary. Withdrawal of the reservation enters into force on the day of receipt of the notification (Article 21[4]).

Russia

3 Point 3 of this Article addresses the procedural implications of a reservation being entered by another Contracting Party or of an objection being entered against a reservation. Preserving the basic scheme of the 1995 Law, the agencies which adopted the decision to consent to the treaty entering into force for the RF have the right to determine whether to accept the reservation or to object against it. If the treaty concerned is one subject to ratification in the form of a Federal Law, the reservations and objections thereto must also be formalized in the form of a Federal Law in the procedure of Article 16 of the 1995 Law. In other instances the procedure laid down in Article 9 of the 1995 Law is applicable. For example, when ratifying the Agreement between the Russian Federation and Norway on the construction of housing for military servicemen of the Armed Forces of the RF who withdrew from the countries of the Baltic, the following Statement was made and recorded in the Federal Law on

ratification: 'The Russian Federation for the purposes of the Agreement understands by the term "countries of the Baltic" the Estonian Republic and the Latvian Republic.'[201]

The legislative procedure is a cumbersome one, and has been criticized by Russian jurists who observe that it departs from 'international practice', which normally vests the executive branch with the right to accept or object to a reservation. [202]

CIS

Several CIS treaty laws contain a provision analogous to the first paragraph of this point of the 1995 Law: *Belarus* (Article 13), *Kyrgyzstan* (Article 22[3]), *Tadzhikistan* (Article 16).

The *Georgian* (Article 22[4]) treaty law contains a provision somewhat analogous to point two of the 1995 Law, formulating it as follows: 'The recognition by another Contracting State of a reservation to an international treaty made by Georgia, or the expression of a protest with respect to it in compliance with the conditions of the international treaty and according to norms of international law shall be effectuated by the State agency deciding the question of deeming an international treaty to be binding upon Georgia.'

The *Kyrgyzstan* (Article 22[3]) treaty law follows the second paragraph of point two of the 1995 Law closely.

201 Signed at Oslo on 11 September 1995. *БМД*, no. 12 (1996), p. 51.
202 For example, Lukashuk, Commentary, p. 84.

Section III

Registration and Official Publication of International Treaties of Russian Federation

Article 26 Unified State System for Registration and Recording of International Treaties of Russian Federation

A unified State system for the registration and recording of international treaties of the Russian Federation shall be within the jurisdiction of the Ministry of Foreign Affairs of the Russian Federation.

Russia

The Ministry of Foreign Affairs is vested with jurisdiction over a unified State system for the registration and recording of international treaties of the RF. Within the Ministry, the Legal Department maintains two card indexes to register and record treaties, one for bilateral and the other for multilateral treaties.

The Commentary describes the system as follows: a special card is prepared for each multilateral treaty to which the RF is a party containing a registration number of the treaty, the number of parties, the name of the treaty, the date and place of signature, the depositary(ies), the conditions for entry into force, the date of entry into force, the period of operation of the treaty, the date of signature by Russia, the date of entry into force for Russia, information concerning municipal-law procedures within Russia essential for entry into force, publication data regarding the treaty, and data concerning registration of the treaty with an international organization, if such occurred. The index entry also contains a complete list of parties to the treaty, specifying the date of signature, date of handing over the ratification, confirmation, acceptance, accession, or legal succession document, and date of handing over documents concerning denunciation, if there are such.

An analogous card is compiled for each bilateral treaty, although the data recorded varies somewhat: registration number of the treaty, the name of the treaty, the place and date of signature, the persons who signed for the RF and for the foreign State, ratification and confirmation data, entry into force, period of operation, period for declaring extension or denunciation, conditions for extension, and publication data. Work is underway to transfer the two card indexes to a computer data base.

The card indexes also include data concerning treaties concluded by the former USSR to which the RF remains a party in its capacity as the 'State-continuer' of the former Soviet Union.[203]

On the principle that the RF is not the legal successor of the former Soviet Union, but rather the 'State-continuer', it follows that the date of entry into force for the RF of multilateral treaties which were in force for the former USSR is the date of entry into force for the USSR. The RF simply replaced the former USSR in such treaties, and did not succeed it. With regard to bilateral treaties, the RF has operated the presumption that those concluded by the former Soviet Union remain in force for the RF, although in certain circumstances the changed frontiers of the RF or the economic realities of a transition to a market economy make it impossible to apply these treaties in their original sense. At the time of its dissolution in December 1991, the former Soviet Union had concluded more than 15,000 bilateral treaties, all of which are being reviewed by the RF with a view to determining their status and the need in some cases to renegotiate or replace them.[204]

CIS

Most CIS treaty laws contain a similar provision establishing a unified system for registering and recording treaties and placing it within the jurisdiction of the Ministry of Foreign Affairs: *Armenia* (Article 20), *Azerbaidzhan* (Article 26), *Belarus* (Article 18), *Kazakhstan* (Articles 29, 30), *Kyrgyzstan* (Article 24), *Moldova* (Article 16), *Tadzhikistan* (Article 17), *Ukraine* (Article 22[1]).

Sometimes a time period is established during which the originals of the treaty must be handed over for keeping. In *Armenia* (Article 20) and *Kazakhstan* (Article 30[2]) that period is two weeks unless the treaty provides otherwise; in *Moldova* (Article 16) the period is fifteen days.

In *Armenia* (Article 20) the Ministry of Foreign Affairs is required to circulate copies of the treaty to the relevant parliamentary commissions and State agencies. The *Tadzhikistan* (Article 17) treaty law adds the requirement that copies of international treaties be sent to the Ministry of Justice for inclusion in the State Register of Legal Acts.

The *Kazakhstan* (Article 30[3]) treaty law makes provision for the keeping of interdepartmental treaties. The originals remain with the respective ministries and departments, but attested copies must be supplied to the Ministry of Foreign Affairs within two weeks.

The treaty law of *Uzbekistan* omits any reference to this.

203 Khodakov, Commentary, pp. 84–5.
204 Khodakov, Commentary, p. 85.

Article 27 Registration of International Treaties of Russian Federation in International Organizations

The registration of international treaties of the Russian Federation in the Secretariat of the United Nations and in corresponding organs of other international organizations shall be effectuated by the Ministry of Foreign Affairs of the Russian Federation.

Russia

This Article places on the Ministry of Foreign Affairs responsibility for registering international treaties of the RF with the Secretariat of the United Nations or with other international organizations.

The registration of international treaties at the Secretariat of the United Nations originates in Article 102 of the UN Charter, which provides that any treaty and any international agreement concluded by a member of the Organization after the entry of the Charter into force must at first opportunity be registered at the Secretariat of the United Nations and published by it. The UN Secretariat publishes the *United Nations Treaty Series* to this end. In practice it has proved impossible to realize the dream of a single central repository for international treaties. The *United Nations Treaty Series* is published with great delay, and far from all treaties are registered with the Secretariat. Article 80 of the 1969 Vienna Convention elaborates the requirements of Article 102 of the UN Charter, although publication by the United Nations is not mandatory under this formulation.

In the case of Russia the Permanent Representation of the RF attached to the United Nations transfers treaties to the UN Secretariat for registration, accompanied as a rule by a *note verbale*.[205]

The constitutive documents of certain other international organizations require that treaties in stipulated domains be registered with their Secretariat. In some cases the precise formalities to be complied with differ from those of the United Nations.

[205] Khodakov, Commentary, p. 86.

CIS

The CIS treaty laws of *Armenia* (Article 21), *Azerbaidzhan* (Article 26), *Belarus* (Article 21), *Georgia* (Article 27), *Kazakhstan* (Article 30[1]), *Kyrgyzstan* (Article 25), *Moldova* (Article 14), *Tadzhikistan* (Article 18), *Ukraine* (Article 21), and *Uzbekistan* (Article 26) contain a similar provision.

Article 28 Keeping of Texts of International Treaties of Russian Federation

1. The originals (or certified copies, official translations) of international treaties of the Russian Federation concluded in the name of the Russian Federation and in the name of the Government of the Russian Federation shall be handed over for keeping to the Ministry of Foreign Affairs of the Russian Federation within a two-week period from the date of signature thereof (or the receipt from the depositary of certified copies, official translations), and copies of these treaties shall within a two-week period from the date of their entry into force be circulated to the respective federal agencies of executive power and agencies of State power of the respective subjects of the Russian Federation.

2. The originals of international treaties of the Russian Federation of an interdepartmental character shall be kept in the archives of the respective federal agencies of executive power, and certified copies of these treaties shall within a two-week period from the date of their signature (or receipt from the depositary of certified copies, official translations) be sent to the Ministry of Foreign Affairs of the Russian Federation.

Russia

1 This Article regulates the internal procedure for keeping the texts of international treaties of the RF. The originals of bilateral inter-State and intergovernmental treaties are lodged with the Historico-Documentary Department of the Ministry of Foreign Affairs. The powers of the person who signed the treaty in the name of the foreign Party are kept together with the text of the treaty, together with any annexes to the treaty or written statements. If the treaty is subject to ratification, the instruments of ratification of the foreign State also are retained.[206]

No sanction is attached to the failure to lodge the text of a treaty with the Ministry within the two-week stipulated period. The circulation of texts to respective federal agencies of executive power and agencies of State power within two weeks after entry into force is an internal procedure not linked with official publication.

[206] Khodakov, Commentary, pp. 86–7.

In the case of multilateral treaties the depositary as a rule keeps the originals of the treaty. When the RF is the designated depositary, the original of the treaty also is kept by the Historico-Documentary Department of the Ministry of Foreign Affairs, which also keeps certified copies and official translations sent to the RF by another depositary. Correspondence relating to the particular treaty is preserved by the Legal Department of the Ministry of Foreign Affairs.

CIS

The CIS treaty laws take various approaches to the keeping of texts of international treaties and their subsequent circulation. The *Armenian* (Article 20) treaty law provides that 'the originals of international treaties of the Republic Armenia shall within a two-week period after the signature thereof be handed over for keeping to the Ministry of Foreign Affairs of the Republic Armenia unless provided otherwise by the treaty. The Ministry of Foreign Affairs of the Republic Armenia shall send copies of the treaties to the permanent commission for questions of foreign relations of the Supreme Soviet of the Republic Armenia and respective Republic agencies of State administration and departments of the Republic Armenia.' The treaty laws of *Kazakhstan* (Article 30[2]), *Kyrgyzstan* (Article 26), *Moldova* (Article 16), *Tadzhikistan* (Article 19), *Ukraine* (Article 22) impose an analogous requirement. *Belarus* (Article 18) requires the Ministry of Foreign Affairs to keep originals, certified copies, and official translations. *Georgia* (Article 28) imposes a similar requirement and further provides that the original of the treaty must have appended information concerning the persons who signed it and, when necessary, documents confirming their powers.

Some CIS treaty laws do not address the issue at all: *Azerbaidzhan*, *Uzbekistan*.

Russia

2 The position is reversed with respect to interdepartmental treaties of the RF. The originals are kept in the archives of the respective Federal agencies of executive power, and certified copies are supplied to the Ministry of Foreign Affairs, where they repose in the Legal Department of that Ministry. No sanction or other legal consequence attaches to the failure to transfer certified copies to the Ministry of Foreign Affairs.

CIS

The treaty laws of *Kazakhstan* (Article 30[3]), *Kyrgyzstan* (Article 26) follow the example of the 1995 Law.

Several treaty laws of the CIS countries leave the question of keeping interdepartmental treaties to other legislation: *Armenia* (Article 21), *Ukraine* (Article 22[2]).

Article 29 Effectuation of Functions of Depositary

1. The Ministry of Foreign Affairs of the Russian Federation shall effectuate the functions of depositary of multilateral international treaties if in accordance with the conditions of such treaties these functions have been entrusted to the Russian Federation.

2. Correspondence with agencies of foreign States, international organizations, or their chief executive officials which are fulfilling the functions of depositary of multilateral international treaties shall be effectuated by the Ministry of Foreign Affairs of the Russian Federation.

Russia

1 Point one of this Article charges the Ministry of Foreign Affairs with acting as the depositary of multilateral international treaties if the RF is designated as depositary in the respective treaty. It should be noted that neither international practice nor the 1995 Law requires that the RF necessarily be a party to such multilateral treaty, nor that the RF necessarily consent in advance to performing such functions.

The functions of depositary performed by the Ministry of Foreign Affairs, unless specified otherwise in the respective multilateral treaty, are laid down in Article 77 of the 1969 Vienna Convention.

CIS

One group of CIS treaty laws follows the example of the 1995 Law: *Belarus* (Article 19), *Georgia* (Article 29[1]), *Kazakhstan* (Article 31[1]), *Kyrgyzstan* (Article 27[1]), and *Tadzhikistan* (Article 20).

Some CIS treaty laws omit any mention of the functions of depositary: *Armenia*, *Azerbaidzhan*, *Moldova*, *Ukraine*, and *Uzbekistan*.

Russia

2 The Ministry of Foreign Affairs conducts all correspondence in connection with the Russian Federation performing the functions of

depositary of a multilateral treaty. Such correspondence is, as a rule, conducted through diplomatic channels.[207]

CIS

This function of the Ministry of Foreign Affairs also is regulated in the treaty laws of *Belarus* (Article 19), *Georgia* (Article 29[2]), *Kazakhstan* (Article 31[2]), and *Kyrgyzstan* (Article 27[1]).

207 Khodakov, Commentary, p. 88.

Article 30 Official Publication of International Treaties of Russian Federation

1. International treaties which have entered into force for the Russian Federation, decisions concerning consent to the bindingness of which for the Russian Federation have been adopted in the form of a Federal Law, shall be subject to official publication upon the recommendation of the Ministry of Foreign Affairs of the Russian Federation in the Собрание законодательства Российской Федерации.

2. International treaties which have entered into force for the Russian Federation (except for treaties of an interdepartmental character) shall be officially published upon the recommendation of the Ministry of Foreign Affairs of the Russian Federation also in the Бюллетень международных договоров.

3. International treaties of the Russian Federation of an interdepartmental character shall be published by decision of the federal agencies of executive power in whose name such treaties were concluded in official publications of these agencies.

Russia

1 Traditionally the publication of international treaties in the twentieth century was associated with the demise of secret diplomacy and the rise of more democratic foreign policies. Soviet diplomacy played its own role in that process,[208] although by the time the Soviet period had come to an end, only a small percentage of the 15,000 plus bilateral treaties concluded by the former USSR had been published.

The 1993 Constitution placed the issue of treaty publication in a rather different context. The 1993 Constitution does not itself explicitly make official publication a requirement for the domestic applicability of treaties in the national legal system.[209] Article 15(4) of the 1993 Constitution

[208] See, for example, the Decree on Peace, 8 November 1917; the text is translated in the annexes, below.

[209] See G. Danilenko, 'The New Russian Constitution and International Law', *American Journal of International Law*, LXXXVIII (1994), 456. Such a requirement was recommended by many Russian specialists. See Danilenko, '*Международно-правовые аспекты новой Конституции России*' [International Legal Aspects of the New Constitution of Russia], *Конституционный вестник*, no. 13 (1992), p. 135.

provides that international treaties of the RF are an integral part of the legal system and that treaties in force take priority over inconsistent laws in the event of a contradiction between them. Moreover, Article 15(3) of the 1993 Constitution prohibits the application of any normative legal acts affecting the rights, freedoms, and duties of man and citizen unless thay have been published officially for general information.[210] And while the presumption of knowledge of the law operates generally in the RF, as in other legal systems, that presumption is difficult to operate if international treaties of all levels are not accessible to the general public, for treaty-making is inherently not as open an operation as is domestic norm-creation. It has accordingly been suggested that a broad interpretation of 'normative legal act' could encompass international treaties of the RF in force, as they too are part of the national legal system and are normative in character.[211]

Under point one of this Article only international treaties which have entered into force may be officially published. Upon their entry into force, such treaties become part of the legal system pursuant to Article 15(4) of the 1993 Constitution. However, point one further qualifies the position by requiring that the Ministry of Foreign Affairs recommend publication and that publication occur in the *Собрание законодательства Российской Федерации*. The 1993 Constitution imposes no requirement of 'recommendation', which implies a discretion to publish a treaty or not. Moreover, the 1995 Law does not take full account of the distinction between publication of the Federal Law concerning ratification of an international treaty and publication of the text of the treaty. The Federal Law concerning ratification falls into the category of all Federal Laws and therefore is subject to publication not only in the *СЗ РФ*, but also in *Российская газета*. There is an appreciable time lag between the appearance of the newspaper and the *СЗ РФ*, which would allow in many cases for the text of the treaty to appear in a timely manner.

The Federal Law on the Procedure for the Publication and Entry into Force of Federal Constitutional Laws, Federal Laws, and Acts of the Federal Assembly, adopted 25 May 1994, provides: 'International treaties ratified by the Federal Assembly shall be published simultaneously with the Federal laws concerning the ratification thereof' (Article 3).

It also should be noted that the 1995 Law, with respect to publication, draws distinctions between treaties subject to ratification and

[210] W. E. Butler, *Constitutional Foundations of the CIS Countries* (The Hague, Kluwer Law International, 1999), p. 426.

[211] See G. Danilenko, 'The New Russian Constitution and International Law', *American Journal of International Law*, LXXXVIII (1994), 456.

international treaties of an interdepartmental character. The 1993 Constitution does not recognize such a distinction, regarding all of them as part of the legal system.

CIS

The CIS treaty laws differ substantially among themselves with respect to the publication of treaties. Distinctions are drawn on the basis of the type of treaty, whether it was ratified or not, and the media designated for official publication.

The treaty law of *Armenia* (Article 19) provides, first, that inter-State and intergovernmental treaties of the Republic Armenia which have entered into force are subject to publication. Second, they are published only upon the recommendation of the Ministry of Foreign Affairs of the Republic Armenia. What criteria the Ministry of Foreign Affairs may use to recommend publication is not mentioned in the treaty law. Treaties are published respectively in the *Ведомости Верховного Совета Республики Армения* and the *Сборник постановлений Правительства Республики Армения*, which are the official gazettes for parliamentary and governmental normative acts in Armenia. This formulation omits the newspapers which have the stature of official gazettes in Armenia.

An analogous pattern exists in *Azerbaidzhan* (Article 25). International treaties of the Azerbaidzhan Republic ratified, and also confirmed or accepted in accordance with the present Law, or international treaties to which the Azerbaidzhan Republic has acceded, shall be published upon the recommendation of the Ministry of Foreign Affairs of the Azerbaidzhan Republic in the *Ведомости Верховного Совета Азербайджанской Республики* and in the official State newspaper of the Azerbaidzhan Republic. However, in Azerbaidzhan there is no requirement that the treaty has entered into force before publication. The newspaper designated as an official gazette is also required to publish treaties.

In *Belarus* (Article 20) the treaty law provides that ratified international treaties of the Republic Belarus are to be published in the *Ведомости Национального Собрания Республики Беларусь*, and those not subject to ratification and which have entered into force, in an annex to the *Собрание декретов, указов Президента и постановлений Правительства Республики Беларусь.*

The *Georgian* (Article 30) treaty law requires that an international treaty of Georgia, consent to the deeming of the bindingness of which for Georgia was expressed by the Parliament of Georgia, should after entry of the treaty into force be published officially upon the recommendation of the Ministry of Foreign Affairs of Georgia in the *Парламентис уцкубани*. An international treaty of Georgia, consent to the deeming of the bindingness of which for Georgia was expressed by the President of Georgia, is after entry of the treaty into force to be published officially upon the recommendation of the Ministry of Foreign Affairs of Georgia in the *Сборник указов и распоряжений Президетна Грузии*. An international treaty of Georgia, the deeming of the bindingness of which for Georgia does not require consent on the part of the Parliament of Georgia and the President of Georgia, is to be published officially in accordance with the provisions of the Law of Georgia on Normative Acts.

In *Kazakhstan* the treaty law provides that inter-State and intergovernmental treaties which have entered into force for the Republic Kazakhstan and undergone in accordance with the present Edict ratification in the Parliament of the Republic Kazakhstan are to be published in official publications of the Parliament. Inter-State and intergovernmental treaties which have entered into force for the Republic Kazakhstan and are not subject to ratification, and also intergovernmental treaties, the accession to which by the Republic Kazakhstan is effectuated in the procedure established by the present Edict, are to be published in the *Собрание актов Президента Республики Казахстан и Правительства Республики Казахстан*.

The *Kyrgyzstan* (Article 23) treaty law stipulates that international treaties which have entered into force for the Kyrgyz Republic (except for treaties of an interdepartmental character) are to be published officially in the *Ведомости Жогорку Кенеша Кыргызской Республики*, collection of acts and laws of the President of the Kyrgyz Republic, and official publications of the Government of the Kyrgyz Republic in accordance with laws of the Kyrgyz Republic 'On Normative Legal Acts of the Kyrgyz Republic' and 'On the Procedure for the Publication of Laws of the Kyrgyz Republic'.

The *Moldovan* (Article 14) treaty law mentions only the 'official publications' of the Parliament and the Government as the place where treaties are to be published.

In *Tadzhikistan* (Article 21) treaties, excluding interdepartmental, are to be published in the *Свод законов Республики Таджикистан*.

The *Ukrainian* (Article 20) treaty law provides that treaties which have entered into force for Ukraine – ratified treaties and treaties whose confirmation or adoption, or accession to which, is effectuated in the basis of decisions respectively of the Supreme Rada of Ukraine or President of Ukraine and treaties which have entered into force from the moment of their signature by the President of Ukraine – are to be published in the *Ведомости Верховного Совета Украины* and in the *Собрание действующих международных договоров Украины*. Treaties which have entered into force for Ukraine, international treaties not requiring ratification, confirmation, adoption, or accession respectively by the Supreme Rada of Ukraine or by the President of Ukraine, and also treaties, the adoption or accession to which was effectuated on the basis of decisions of the Government of Ukraine, are to be published in the *Собрание постановлений Правительства Украины* and in the newspaper of the Government of Ukraine.

The *Uzbekistan* (Article 25) treaty law contains a renvoi clause, referring questions of treaty publication to the Government.

The language of treaty publication is not treated in the 1995 Law, although where drafts and proposals are submitted the assumption clearly is that the relevant documents will be in the Russian language. In the CIS treaty laws the issue of language is sometimes addressed in the Article concerned with publication and sometimes in a separate Article. The *Azerbaidzhan* (Article 25) treaty law contains a requirement often encountered in the CIS but impossible to realize in practice; namely, that international treaties of the Azerbaidzhan Republic whose authentic texts have been drawn up in foreign languages shall be published in one of these languages with an official translation into the Azerbaidzhan language. The aspiration commonly remains unmet for one of two reasons: either there does not exist an official or satisfactory text in the local language, or there are difficulties with the typefaces and limited budgets when printing foreign language texts (Persian, Chinese, Arabic, English, Greek, and the like). In some Independent States there has been a reaction against the Russian language sufficiently strong to preclude the publication of legislation and of treaty texts officially in Russian, as used to be the practice.

There is an analogous requirement in the *Georgian* (Article 30) treaty law: when one of the authentic texts of an international treaty of Georgia is drawn up in the Georgian language, the treaty shall be published in the Georgian language. An international treaty of Georgia whose authentic text is drawn up only in foreign languages shall be published in one of these languages with an official Georgian translation appended. A similar practice is provided for by the *Kyrgyzstan* treaty law (Article 23[3]).

The *Kazakhstan* (Article 5) treaty law contains an article specifically devoted to the language of treaties. It provides that bilateral treaties are, as a rule, in the State languages of the contracting parties, whereas the languages of the texts of multilateral treaties are determined by consent of the parties. Article 28(4) of the same treaty law requires that International treaties of the Republic Kazakhstan whose authentic texts have been drawn up in foreign languages be published in one of these languages with an official translation into the Kazakh and Russian languages.

Uzbekistan (Article 5) is the other CIS treaty law to contain a separate Article on language. Formulated more assertively than that of Kazakhstan, it provides that 'The State language of the Republic Uzbekistan and the language of the other Contracting Party(ies) shall be the language of an international treaty of the Republic Uzbekistan. By agreement of the subjects of the international treaty another language may be selected as the language of the treaty. The language in which the text of the international treaty is drawn up shall be specified in the text of the particular treaty, where the authenticity and official nature thereof shall be determined.' Article 25 of the same treaty law says that international treaties of the Republic Uzbekistan, the authentic texts of which have been drawn up in foreign languages, shall be published in the State language. International treaties of the Republic Uzbekistan may also be published in other languages.

The *Ukrainian* (Article 20) treaty law, with respect to the language of treaties, stipulates that if an international treaty of Ukraine has an authentic text in the State language of Ukraine, the authentic text shall be published in the State language of Ukraine. When an international treaty of Ukraine does not have an authentic text in the State language of Ukraine, one of the authentic texts in a foreign language is published, and also an official translation into the State language of Ukraine effectuated by the Ministry of Foreign Affairs of Ukraine.

Russia

2 Point two offers a second source of official publication. The *БМД* commenced publication in March 1993 and is issued monthly on the basis of Edict of the President of the RF, No. 11, adopted on 11 January 1993, with the changes and additions of 1 December 1995, On the Procedure for the Publication of International Treaties of the RF.[212] The *БМД*, however, contains only a fraction of the international treaties of the RF to be published 'on the recommendation' of the Ministry of Foreign Affairs.

The *БМД* also contains the texts of international treaties of the RF which are not subject to ratification by the Federal Assembly and are not interdepartmental, that is, international treaties which enter into force on the basis of a decision of the President of the RF or of the Government. By Edict of the President of the RF adopted 23 May 1996 'On the Procedure for the Publication and Entry into Force of Acts of the President of the Russian Federation and Government of the Russian Federation and

[212] *САПП РФ* (1993), no. 3, item 182; *СЗ РФ* (1995), no. 49, item 4777.

Normative Legal Acts of Federal Agencies of Executive Power', edicts and regulations of the President and decrees and regulations of the Government are subject to obligatory official publication, except for those acts or individual provisions thereof whose content comprises a State secret or information of a confidential character. This formulation includes edicts, decrees, and regulations concerning international treaties.

Pursuant to the Edict of the President of the RF on the Procedure for the Publication and Entry into Force of Federal Laws, issued 5 April 1994 as changed and added to on 9 August 1994 and 1 December 1995: 'Federal laws adopted with regard to questions of the ratification of international treaties also shall be published in the *Бюллетень международных договоров*' (point 4).

The *БМД* has been called 'an example of the incorporation of international treaties' in its capacity as an official publication of the Administration of the President of the RF. By 'incorporation' the learned author had in view a type of systematization of the norms of international law, combining and placing international legal norms without changing their essence in individual collections in chronological, alphabetical, thematic, or other order.[213]

CIS

Most Independent States do not have a separate gazette devoted solely to international treaties. Those which do include: *Georgia* (Article 30[4]) and *Kazakhstan* (Article 29[3]), whose gazette includes interdepartmental treaties.

Russia

3 Point three makes the publication of international treaties of the RF of an interdepartmental character discretionary upon the decision of the Federal agency of executive power in whose name the treaty was concluded. There is no centralized official gazette designated for such treaties, nor are the *СЗ РФ* and the *БМД* authorized to include such. Most Federal agencies of executive power do not publish their own gazettes, so

[213] See P. A. Laptev, 'Проблемы перевода международно-правовых актов и новые технико-юридические процедуры их имплементации в правовую систему Российской Федерации' [Problems of Translation of International-Legal Acts and New Legal-Technique Procedures of the Implementation Thereof in the Legal System of the Russian Federation], in V. M. Baranov (ed.), *Проблемы юридической техники* [Problems of Legal Technique] (Nizhnii Novgorod, Nizhegorodskaia pravovaia akademiia, 2000), p. 142n.

that for many the possibility opened by the 1995 Federal Law is unrealistic.

Recognizing the difficulty, individual departments have issued normative legal acts to regulate the publication of interdepartmental treaties. Because such acts are normative, they require registration with the Ministry of Justice of the Russian Federation as a condition of validity. The Minister of Railways on 5 July 2001 issued an Order which provided that 'international treaties of an interdepartmental character which have entered into force for the Russian Federation (hereinafter: international treaties of the Ministry of Railways of the Russian Federation) shall be subject to publication in the monthly journal *Экономика железных дорог* and the daily newspaper *Гудок*, which shall be the official publication'. The choice of treaties to be published officially in those media lies with the Legal Administration and the Foreign Affairs Administration of the Ministry of Railways.[214]

The constitutionality of points two and three of the 1995 Law must be open to doubt.

CIS

The position is very much the same in the other CIS countries. Only the treaty laws of *Georgia*, *Kazakhstan*, *Kyrgyzstan*, *Tadzhikistan*, and *Ukraine* address the issue.

[214] See the Order of the Ministry of Railways of the Russian Federation, No. 17, 5 July 2001; registered at the Ministry of Justice of the Russian Federation, No. 2911, 30 August 2001, 'On the Procedure for the Publication of Normative Acts of the Ministry of Railways of Russia Deemed by the Ministry of Justice of Russia Not to Need State Registration, and also International Treaties of the Russian Federation of an Interdepartmental Character, Concluded in the Name of the Ministry of Railways of Russia', *Российская газета*, 11 September 2001, p. 4, col. 5.

Section IV

Fulfilment of International Treaties of Russian Federation

Article 31 Fulfilment of International Treaties of Russian Federation

1. International treaties of the Russian Federation shall be subject to good-faith fulfilment in accordance with the conditions of the international treaties themselves, norms of international law, the Constitution of the Russian Federation, the present Federal Law, and other acts of legislation of the Russian Federation.

2. The Russian Federation shall, before the entry into force for it of an international treaty, refrain from actions which would deprive the treaty of its object and purposes, taking into account the respective norms of international law.

3. An international treaty shall be subject to fulfilment by the Russian Federation from the moment of the entry into force thereof for the Russian Federation.

Russia

1 Point one of this Article incorporates the most fundamental principle of international law, *pacta sunt servanda*, as laid down in Article 26 of the 1969 Vienna Convention. Without this rule, the international legal system could not function.

'Norms of international law' in this context include the UN Charter and generally-recognized principles and norms of international law, including customary international law. 'Good faith' in Russian doctrine has 'autonomous significance' in international law and includes: eliciting the factual circumstances relating to the application of norms; determining the norms subject to application; ensuring that the letter and spirit of norms are complied with; determining the limits of the applicable norms so as not to prejudice the rights and legal interests of other States; and not to permit abuse of right.[215]

Point one lays the foundation for the President of the RF to take measures to ensure compliance with international obligations. On 8 August 1997, for example, an Edict of the President of the Russian Federation, No. 848, 'On Measures with Regard to the Fulfilment of International

[215] Lukashuk, Commentary, p. 91.

Treaties in the Domain of Outer Space' required the Ministry of Finances of the Russian Federation and the Government of the Russian Federation to attract credits from foreign banks under guarantee of the Russian Government for activities of the Russian Space Agency undertaken pursuant to international treaties.

CIS

The formulations of the CIS treaty laws differ in their formulation of the principle of *pacta sunt servanda.*

The *Armenian* (Article 15) treaty law refers to 'performance' of treaties. Such performance is to be 'undeviating'. It is here that the Armenian treaty law invokes the priority of the treaty over inconsistent Armenian legislation. Although the *Azerbaidzhan* (Article 15) and *Ukrainian* (Article 12[1]) treaty laws refer to 'compliance', they are in other respects essentially the same as the Armenian treaty law on this point. In the interests of 'good-faith' compliance, the Azerbaidzhan and Ukrainian treaty laws require the Republics to make efforts to ensure that the contracting parties of Azerbaidzhan do their part to comply with treaties. The *Turkmenistan* (Article 15) treaty law contains an analogous stipulation and, indeed, imposes the requirement of 'good-faith' compliance only upon State agencies.

The *Belarus* (Article 15) treaty law follows the example of the 1995 Law and interpolates in this Article the provision that makes generally-recognized principles of international law and norms of international law part of the law operating on the territory of Belarus.

The *Georgian* (Article 31[1]), *Kazakhstan* (Article 21[1]), *Kyrgyzstan* (Article 28[1]), and *Tadzhikistan* (Article 22) treaty laws contain essentially the same language as the 1995 Law, using the terms 'performance', 'compliance', and 'fulfilment', respectively.

The *Moldovan* (Article 13) treaty law makes a fleeting reference to the Government taking necessary measures for control over the performance thereof.

The *Uzbekistan* (Article 27) treaty law speaks not of 'fulfilment', but of 'compliance'. Treaties are to be absolutely and obligatorily complied with in accordance with norms of international law. The element of 'good faith' is not stipulated.

Russia

2 Point two of this Article is based on Article 18 of the 1969 Vienna Convention. A State may not take actions before an international treaty

enters into force for it which would deprive the treaty of its object and purpose, that is, not take actions which would make compliance with the treaty impossible or difficult. The duty arises from general international law and not from the treaty itself; the 1969 Vienna Convention also recorded the principle of general international law.

CIS

Only the treaty laws of *Georgia* (Article 31[2]), *Kyrgyzstan* (Article 28[2]), and *Tadzhikistan* (Article 22) address this issue.

Russia

3 Point three of this Article restates the generally accepted proposition that a treaty must be complied with from the moment of entry into force unless the parties have agreed otherwise. Some treaties enter into force on the basis of conditions subsequent or precedent, and, as noted above (see Gloss on Article 23, above), the parties may agree to temporary application of a treaty.

CIS

The treaty laws of *Georgia* (Article 31[3]), *Kyrgyzstan* (Article 28[2]), and *Tadzhikistan* (Article 22) include a provision on this question.

Article 32 Ensuring Fulfilment of International Treaties of Russian Federation

1. The President of the Russian Federation and the Government of the Russian Federation shall take measures directed towards ensuring the fulfilment of international treaties of the Russian Federation.

2. Federal agencies of executive power within whose competence the questions are which are to be regulated by international treaties of the Russian Federation shall ensure the fulfilment of obligations of the Russian Party under the treaties and the effectuation of the rights of the Russian Party arising from such treaties, and also observe the fulfilment by other participants of the treaties of their obligations.

3. Agencies of State power of the respective subjects of the Russian Federation shall ensure within the limits of their powers the fulfilment of international treaties of the Russian Federation.

4. General observation over the fulfilment of international treaties of the Russian Federation shall be effectuated by the Ministry of Foreign Affairs of the Russian Federation.

Russia

1 While it is entirely natural under the Russian constitutional system that the President of the RF and the Government should be charged with taking measures to ensure compliance with international treaties of the RF, it is curious that the legislative branch omitted itself from the 1995 Law in this respect, not least given the fact that certain treaties require implementing legislation that only the Federal Assembly can enact.

Insofar as the President of the RF is concerned, as Head of State the President personifies the State responsibility of the RF for compliance with its international obligations under general principles of international law and international treaties of the RF. Measures to be taken which are directed towards ensuring the fulfilment of international treaties may include submitting Proposals to the State Duma for implementing legislation, issuing Edicts on his own volition with regard to matters within the competence of the President, or instructing the Government of the

RF to take appropriate measures. In some cases special organs, agencies, commissions, or committees may have to be formed, appointed, and financed. Reviews of existing legislation may need to be undertaken and proposals for the revision or repeal of subordinate legislation considered. Becoming a party to one international treaty may involve becoming a party to others, and the appropriate actions must be initiated.

Several Federal laws of the RF do not comply with the 1993 Constitution with respect to the relationship between international law and Russian Law. For example, Article 109 of the Fundamental Principles of Legislation of the Russian Federation on the Notariat, adopted 11 February 1993, provides that the performance of notarial actions by a notary which are not provided for by legislation of the RF but are provided for by an international treaty shall be in the procedure established by the Ministry of Justice of the RF.[216] If the treaty is of direct effect within the Russian legal system, Article 109 is unconstitutional. Similarly, Article 52 of the Law of the RF on the Subsoil, adopted 24 November 1992,[217] regulates the application of norms of international treaties previously concluded and in doing so operates as a clause of limitation, whereas this is now governed by the 1993 Constitution. The Law of the RF on Forced Resettlements, adopted 19 February 1993 (Article 14) and the Law on Refugees, adopted also 19 February 1993 (Article 15), actually attempt to give themselves primacy over international treaties, providing that provisions of international treaties shall not apply in instances when this may lead to a limitation of the rights and freedoms, respectively, of the forced resettlers and refugees regulated by those laws.[218]

The powers of the Government in this respect follow from the exemplary listing in Article 114 of the 1993 Constitution.[219]

CIS

Some of the CIS treaty laws contain analogous provisions. The *Armenian* (Article 16), *Tadzhikistan* (Article 23), *Turkmenistan* (Article 16), and *Ukrainian* (Article 13) treaty laws follow the model of the 1995 Law.

The *Belarus* (Article 16) treaty law designates specific decisions to be taken so as to ensure the fulfilment of treaty obligations. Such decisions, as a rule, contain: the determination of the State agency (or official)

216 *Ведомости РФ* (1993), no. 10, item 357.
217 *Ведомости РФ*(1992), no. 16, item 834.
218 See, respectively, *Ведомости РФ* (1993), no. 12, items 425 and 427.
219 W. E. Butler, *Constitutional Foundations of the CIS Countries* (The Hague, Kluwer Law International, 1999), pp. 463–4.

responsible for performance of the international treaty or coordinating performance of the international treaty; the commission to the competent State agency to make proposals concerning the bringing of legislation of the Republic Belarus into conformity with the international treaty which has entered into force.

The *Azerbaidzhan* (Article 16), *Kazakhstan* (Article 21), *Kyrgyzstan* (Article 29[1]), and *Uzbekistan* (Article 28) treaty laws place on the President the duty to ensure compliance with treaties and obligations assumed. The Governments in Kazakhstan, Kyrgyzstan, and Uzbekistan are to work out measures with regard to the fulfilment of international treaties of the Republic Uzbekistan and determine the ministries, departments, and officials on which responsibility for the performance of obligations under international treaties of the Republic Uzbekistan is placed. In Azerbaidzhan the role of the Government is to ensure the fulfilment of obligations assumed under treaties.

Russia

2 Federal agencies of executive power are charged with fulfilling the obligations and effectuating the rights of the RF arising from international treaties of the RF. Unlike the President and the Government, they also are specially charged with watching over compliance by the other parties to the treaty – all in accordance with their competence.

The Statutes on some Federal agencies of executive power expressly refer to ensuring the fulfilment of international obligations. The Statute on the Ministry of Foreign Economic Links of the RF, confirmed on 26 February 1993 by Decree of the Council of Ministers – Government of the RF, No. 85 – requires that Ministry to 'ensure the realization of international treaties relating to questions of trade–industrial cooperation, cooperation in construction and operation of objects abroad and on the territory of the Russian Federation with the participation of foreign firms and organizations, to take part in the realization of international treaties in the domain of transport' and others.[220]

CIS

The treaty laws of the CIS countries vary in their approach to this question. Several follow the model of the 1995 Law: *Armenia* (Article 17), *Belarus* (Article 16), *Kazakhstan* (Article 22), *Kyrgyzstan* (Article 29), *Turkmenistan* (Article 17), and *Uzbekistan* (Article 28).

[220] *САПП РФ* (1993), no. 10, item 830.

The *Ukrainian* (Article 14[1]) treaty law omits the reference in the 1995 Law concerning the effectuation of rights arising from treaties. Such agencies are required to supply information to the Ukrainian Ministry of Foreign Affairs affecting the fulfilment of international treaties of Ukraine. The Ministry of Foreign Affairs of the Azerbaidzhan Republic is regularly to inform the President of the Azerbaidzhan Republic concerning the fulfilment of obligations under international treaties both by the Azerbaidzhan Republic and also by other participants of the said treaties (Article 17).

Russia

3 The federative structure of the RF is reflected in point three of this Article. The 1993 Constitution has relegated the fulfilment of international treaties to the joint jurisdiction of the RF and subjects of the RF. Accordingly, the 1995 Law requires subjects of the RF to ensure the fulfilment of international treaties of the RF within the limits of their powers. Insofar as subjects of the RF may enact normative legal acts to this purpose, those acts must correspond to Article 76 of the 1993 Constitution which governs the interaction of the RF and subjects of the RF on matters of joint jurisdiction.[221]

CIS

The CIS treaty laws do not contain a provision equivalent to this point of the 1995 Law.

Russia

4 The role of the Ministry of Foreign Affairs as the 'head' organization in matters of foreign policy is underscored by point four of this Article (see Gloss on Article 9, above). The role of the Ministry is modestly formulated, being limited to 'general observation' over the fulfilment of treaties.

CIS

The model of the 1995 Law is emulated by the treaty laws of *Armenia* (Article 17), *Azerbaidzhan* (Article 18), *Kazakhstan* (Article 23), *Tadzhikistan* (Article 23), and *Turkmenistan* (Article 18).

221 W. E. Butler, *Constitutional Foundations of the CIS Countries* (The Hague, Kluwer Law International, 1999), pp. 446–7.

Several CIS treaty laws do more in this connection than merely draw attention to the role of the Ministry of Foreign Affairs.

Under some CIS treaty laws the Ministry of Foreign Affairs is charged with 'general supervision' over the fulfilment of or compliance with treaties: *Belarus* (Article 15), *Georgia* (Article 33), *Ukraine* (Article 15[1]). Upon the demand of agencies applying international treaties of Ukraine, the Ministry of Foreign Affairs of Georgia and Ukraine must provide official information relative to questions arising in connection with the fulfilment of the international treaty of Ukraine. In the event of the improper fulfilment of obligations assumed under international treaties by the Georgian or Ukrainian Party, the Ministry of Foreign Affairs of Georgia or Ukraine is to inform the Ministry of Foreign Affairs of Georgia or the President of Ukraine or the Government of Ukraine thereof so that necessary measures can be taken.

The *Kyrgyzstan* (Article 30) treaty law divides the role of 'general observation' over the performance of treaties. The Ministry of Foreign Affairs has the principal responsibility, except for 'financial treaties of the Kyrgyz Republic, credit agreements, and agreements concerning a grant', which fall within the purview of the Ministry of Finances.

The *Uzbekistan* (Article 29) treaty law places on the Ministry of Foreign Affairs the duty to 'watch over' the performance of international treaties of Ukraine.

Article 33 Measures Applicable in Event of Violation of International Treaty of Russian Federation by Other Participants Thereof

In the event of a violation of obligations under an international treaty of the Russian Federation by other participants thereof, the Ministry of Foreign Affairs of the Russian Federation or other federal agencies of executive power shall, jointly with the Ministry of Foreign Affairs of the Russian Federation, submit to the President of the Russian Federation or to the Government of the Russian Federation, depending upon within whose competence the questions are, proposals concerning the taking of necessary measures in accordance with norms of international law and the conditions of the treaty itself.

Russia

Article 60 of the 1969 Vienna Convention provides for the options of States in the event of a material breach of a treaty. Article 33 of the 1995 Law addresses any kind of breach by a party other than the RF to an international treaty of the RF. It is essentially a procedural Article; it does not in any way dictate what the response of the RF should be to such a violation. Moreover, it addresses only a violation of an international treaty. A violation of a customary norm of international law by analogy might be handled in the same procedure.

The approach taken by the Article centralizes a response to the alleged violation. A proposal must be submitted to the President or to the Government, depending upon whose competence the questions regulated by the treaty falls within, to take the necessary measures in accordance with the norms of international law and the conditions of the treaty itself. The Ministry of Foreign Affairs plays a key role, for it must either submit the proposal or do so jointly with other Federal agencies of executive power.

Short of invoking Article 60 of the 1969 Vienna Convention, the RF has an almost unlimited range of lesser measures which may be taken, both political and legal. It should be noted that certain treaties may contain their own sanctions in the event of a violation. Some require financial sanctions or penalties in the event of non-compliance. Members of an international organization may suffer consequences provided for in the Charter or other documents of the organization in the event of the failure to fulfil obligations.

The 1995 Federal Law on the State Regulation of Foreign Trade Activity authorizes the RF to take retaliatory measures against a foreign State which fails to fulfil international treaty obligations to the RF.[222]

The 1995 Law does not address procedures to be followed in the event an international treaty of the RF is violated by the Russian side.

CIS

The CIS treaty laws fall into three categories with respect to treaty violations. The first group follows the example of the 1995 Law and makes provision for proposals to be made to the President and/or the Government concerning necessary measures that might be taken. Within this group are *Armenia* (Article 18), *Azerbaidzhan* (Article 19), *Belarus* (Article 17), *Georgia* (Article 34), *Kazakhstan* (Article 24[1] and [2]), *Kyrgyzstan* (Article 31), *Tadzhikistan* (Article 24), *Ukraine* (Article 16[1]), and *Uzbekistan* (Article 31).

The second group of treaty laws additionally addresses the question of material violations and provides for the possibility of the treaty being terminated in accordance with the denunciation procedures laid down in the treaty law: *Armenia* (Article 18), *Azerbaidzhan* (Article 19), *Kazakhstan* (Article 24[3]). In the case of Armenia, however, the formulation is not apt. The Armenian treaty law speaks of a treaty being declared 'invalid' in the event of a material violation. The Azerbaidzhan, Kazakhstan, Ukrainian, and Uzbekistan treaty laws correctly speak of a treaty being 'terminated' or 'denounced' for a material violation by way of denunciation. All formulations, however, are contrary to Article 60 of the 1969 Vienna Convention for their failure to distinguish between a material violation of a bilateral and a multilateral treaty.

The third group of treaty laws does not regulate the issue of violation: *Moldova*.

222 Article 34. *СЗ РФ* (1995), no. 42, item 3923; transl. in *Sudebnik*, I (1996), 427–55.

Article 34 Conformity of International Treaties to Constitution of Russian Federation

1. The Constitutional Court of the Russian Federation shall in the procedure determined by a federal constitutional law settle cases concerning the conformity to the Constitution of the Russian Federation of international treaties which have not entered into force for the Russian Federation, or individual provisions thereof, and shall settle disputes concerning the competence between federal agencies of State power, and also between agencies of State power of the Russian Federation and agencies of State power of subjects of the Russian Federation in connection with the conclusion of international treaties of the Russian Federation.

2. International treaties which have not entered into force for the Russian Federation and are deemed by the Constitutional Court of the Russian Federation to not conform to the Constitution of the Russian Federation shall not be subject to introduction into operation and application.

Russia

1 This Article is based on Article 125(2) of the 1993 Constitution, which sets out the principal jurisdiction of the Constitutional Court of the RF.[223] According to Article 3(1)(d) of the 1994 Federal Constitutional Law on the Constitutional Court of the RF, the Court settles cases concerning 'international treaties of the Russian Federation which have not entered into force'. The procedures by which the Court does so are set out in Chapter X of the 1994 Federal Constitutional Law on the Court. It is a function traditionally associated with constitutional control rather than judicial review.[224] The phrase is extremely broad. First, treaties at

[223] W. E. Butler, *Constitutional Foundations of the CIS Countries* (The Hague, Kluwer Law International, 1999), p. 468.

[224] L. V. Lazarev, in N. V. Vitruk, L. V. Lazarev, and B. S. Ebzeev (eds.), *Федеральный конституционный закон о конституционном суде Российской федерации. Комментарий* [Federal Constitutional Law on the Constitutional Court of the Russian Federation. Commentary] (M., Iuridicheskaia Literatura, 1996), p. 40. On the early experience of the Constitutional Court with international law, prior to the 1993 Constitution, see J. Henderson, 'Reference to International Law in Decided Cases of the First Russian Constitutional Court', in R. Müllerson, M. Andenas, and M. Fitzmaurice

virtually any stage of being concluded fall into this category. Even ratification by the RF may not constitute the final stage, for certain treaties do not enter into force, in accordance with their provisions, until a determined number of ratifications have been deposited, or the instruments of ratification have been exchanged, or other formalities completed. Second, an international treaty 'of the RF' is vague, for on one reading a treaty does not become a treaty of the respective State party unless and until it is in force.

The 1969 Vienna Convention provides that a party may not refer to provisions of its municipal law as justification for the failure to comply with a treaty. This rule operates without prejudice to Article 46 of the 1969 Vienna Convention, pursuant to which a State does not have the right to refer to the fact that its consent to the bindingness of a treaty was expressed in violation of a provision of its municipal law affecting the competence to conclude the treaty as the grounds for the invalidity of its consent unless the violation was clear and affected norms of municipal law of special importance.

The Commentary concludes that deeming a treaty of the RF which has been finally accepted but not yet entered into force to be unconstitutional would be a violation of international law.[225] Article 91(2) of the Law on the Constitutional Court provides that from the moment the Court deems a treaty, or individual provisions thereof, which has not entered into force to be unconstitutional, the treaty or respective provisions 'are not subject to introduction into operation and application, that is, may not be ratified, confirmed, or otherwise may not enter into force for the Russian Federation'. The Commentary is of the view that the reference to 'introduction into operation and application' means acts of expressing consent to the bindingness of a treaty. It follows in this view that the phrase 'treaties which have not entered into force' in the context of the Law on the Constitutional Court means treaties with respect to which consent has not been given to their being binding. This construction, the Commentary observes, would correspond to international law and to the general principle of law, including Russian law, that a presumption exists in favour of the legislator not intending to violate norms of international law.

The Law on the Constitutional Court further provides that deeming a treaty or individual provisions thereof to be unconstitutional is grounds for vacating the provisions of other normative acts of the RF based on the treaty or reproducing or otherwise containing provisions of the treaty. The Commentary observes that this formulation does not take satisfactory account of the fact that if the treaty does not exist because it has not

(eds.), *Constitutional Reforms in Central and Eastern Europe and Russia and International Law* (The Hague, Kluwer Law International, 1998).

225 Lukashuk, Commentary, p. 98.

entered into force, its provisions are not subject to being implemented. If a treaty of the RF were placed in force temporarily, the declaration by the Constitutional Court of its provisions to be unconstitutional would terminate application of the treaty even temporarily. It also should be borne in mind that some international treaties of the RF enter into force upon signature.

The law of international treaties accepts the principle of separability of treaty provisions under limited circumstances (Article 44, 1969 Vienna Convention), but assumes the unity of the text of a treaty unless the treaty provides otherwise or the other parties consent to such separability. Accordingly, a decree of the Constitutional Court declaring individual provisions of a treaty to be unconstitutional could be tantamount to rejecting the treaty as a whole.

The jurisdiction of the Constitutional Court to review the constitutionality of international treaties of the RF does not extend to general principles of international law, including customary international law, nor to other forms of international acts which may be binding upon the RF; for example, binding decisions of organs of international institutions.

This Article of the 1995 Law also gives the Constitutional Court the right to settle disputes concerning competence with respect to international treaties of the RF between Federal agencies of State power, and also between agencies of State power of the RF and agencies of State power of subjects of the RF.

The Commentary, resting on Article 89 of the 1994 Federal Constitutional Law on the Constitutional Court, accepts the proposition laid down in Article 89(1) that only treaties subject to ratification or confirmation by a Federal agency of State power may be the subject of judicial review with respect to constitutionality. This formulation would preclude all treaties of the RF which enter into force upon signature, as well as interdepartmental treaties. The Commentary attempts to dismiss the issue by suggesting that the quantity of such treaties is 'comparatively few' and in substance are unlikely to 'affect constitutional problems',[226] whereas in reality the numbers are quite substantial. Specialists on the Constitutional Court incline to another view, suggesting that in this respect Article 89(1) of the 1994 Federal Constitutional Law on the Constitutional Court may be unconstitutional. They observe that Article 125(2)(d) of the 1993 Constitution conferred on the Constitutional Court the right to settle cases concerning the conformity to the Russian Constitution of 'international treaties of the Russian Federation which have not entered

[226] Lukashuk, Commentary, p. 99.

into legal force'.[227] The 1993 Constitution contains no qualification as to what treaties may be examined: 'From a literal interpretation of this provision one should hardly draw the conclusion that all other international treaties which have not entered into legal force and which provide for their entry into force by a means other than ratification and confirmation which are enumerated in the Vienna Convention and in the Law on International Treaties of the Russian Federation are inadmissable for verification of their constitutionality in the Constitutional Court. However, such a limited interpretation of the said provisions of Article 89 would be incorrect ... a limitation of those means in the Law on the Constitutional Court would not correspond to those purposes which the Constitution pursues: to grant to the applicants the right to initiate cases concerning the verification of any international treaties of the Russian Federation which have not entered into force'.[228]

The conclusion is therefore compelling that treaties subject to any form of expression of consent with respect to being binding that have been enumerated in the 1969 Vienna Convention fall within the purview of the Constitutional Court of the RF with respect to their constitutionality. This view is reinforced by the last paragraph of Article 91 of the 1994 Federal Constitutional Law on the Constitutional Court, which addresses the final result in such a verification: if the Constitutional Court finds that the respective treaty does not correspond to the Constitution of the RF, the treaty 'may not be ratified, confirmed, nor may not otherwise enter into force for the Russian Federation'. In this context the word 'otherwise' must refer to treaties which are not subject to ratification or confirmation; that is, any of the generally-recognized means of expressing consent to the bindingness of an international treaty.

The Constitutional Court is not endowed with the right of control, or supervision, over the conformity of Federal laws to international treaties generally. The Commentary commends the Constitutional Court for its initiative in recommending, as part of a Decree on 31 July 1995 to the Federal Assembly of the RF the desirability of putting in order Russian legislation concerning the use of the Armed Forces and the regulation of other matters arising during armed conflicts, including those arising out of the Additional Protocol to the 1949 Geneva

227 W. E. Butler, *Constitutional Foundations of the CIS Countries* (The Hague, Kluwer Law International, 1999), pp. 467–8.

228 E. M. Ametistov, in N. V. Vitruk, L. V. Lazarev, and B. S. Ebzeev (eds.), *Федеральный конституционный закон о конституционном суде Российской Федерации. Комментарий* [Federal Constitutional Law on the Constitutional Court of the Russian Federation. Commentary] (M., Iuridicheskaia literatura, 1996), pp. 271–2.

Convention on defending the victims of armed conflicts of a non-international character.[229]

Although the Constitutional Court does not have a supervisory function with respect to international treaties, all courts and judges, as part of their lawful autonomy, are required under the 1996 Federal Constitutional Law on the Judicial System, 'having established when considering a case the nonconformity of the act of a State or other agency, and likewise of an official, . . . to generally-recognized principles and norms of international law, to an international treaty of the Russian Federation . . . , shall adopt a decision in accordance with the legal provisions having the highest legal force'.[230]

Article 125(3) of the 1993 Constitution confers on the Constitutional Court the right to settle disputes concerning competence.[231] This point of the present Article also reflects the jurisdiction of the Constitutional Court to settle disputes arising in connection with the competence of Federal agencies of State power, or between Federal agencies of State power and agencies of State power of subjects of the RF, in connection with the conclusion of international treaties of the RF. The consideration of cases by the Constitutional Court of the RF relating to disputes concerning competence is regulated by Chapter XI of the 1994 Federal Constitutional Law on the Constitutional Court (Articles 92–95). Both the 1993 Constitution and the Federal Laws and Statutes on individual Federal agencies of executive and of State power often are ambiguous with respect to delimiting competence, and it is entirely plausible that a dispute could arise over competence connected with the conclusion of a treaty, or, for that matter, denunciation or termination in other form. The Federal agencies of State power and agencies of power of the subjects of the RF who have the right to seek settlement of a dispute concerning competence are narrower than is the case with respect to seeking verification of the constitutionality of an international treaty of the RF; compare Articles 88 and 92 of the 1994 Federal Constitutional Law on the Constitutional Court.

CIS

Several CIS countries have a similar provision in their constitutions and/or treaty laws. The Constitutional Court of *Armenia* (Constitution, Article 100[2]) is empowered to 'establish before the ratification of an

229 Lukashuk, Commentary, p. 100.
230 Article 5(3). *Российская газета*, 6 January 1997, p. 3.
231 W. E. Butler, *Constitutional Foundations of the CIS Countries* (The Hague, Kluwer Law International, 1999), p. 467.

international treaty the conformity to the Constitution of the obligations consolidated therein'.[232] The *Armenian* treaty law does not refer to the Constitutional Court.

In *Azerbaidzhan* the Constitution (Article 130[6]) empowers the Constitutional Court decide questions on the basis of an enquiry of the President, parliament, government, Supreme Court, or Procuracy of the conformity of, first, inter-State treaties which have not entered into force to the Constitution and, second, the conformity of intergovernmental treaties, irrespective of whether they have entered into force, to the Constitution and laws of Azerbaidzhan.[233] The Azerbaidzhan Constitution thus attaches major significance to the categories of international treaties. The Azerbaidzhan treaty law makes no mention of the Constitutional Court.

The Constitution of *Belarus* (Article 116) empowers the Constitutional Court to give opinions concerning, first, the constitutionality of laws, decrets, and edicts of the President, international treaty and other obligations of the Republic Belarus both to the Constitution and to international legal acts ratified by Belarus and, second, the conformity of acts of inter-State formations (such as the CIS itself) which Belarus joins to the Constitution, international legal acts ratified by Belarus, laws, and decrets, and, third, the conformity of decrees of the Council of Ministers, acts of the Supreme Court, Supreme Economic Court, and Procurator General and any other State agency to, *inter alia*, international acts ratified by Belarus.[234] The Belarus treaty law does not refer to the role of the Constitutional Court.

In *Georgia* the Constitution (Article 89) provides merely that the Constitutional Court shall 'consider questions of the constitutionality of international treaties and agreements'.[235] The *Georgian* treaty law (Article 21) establishes standing to bring a suit in this connection. It provides that if a constitutional suit is brought by an empowered subject before an international treaty is deemed by Georgia to be binding, the Constitutional Court of Georgia is to adopt a decision concerning the constitutionality of the international treaty. In the event a constitutional suit is brought to the Constitutional Court, the question of deeming the respective international treaty to be binding upon Georgia may not be considered until the Constitutional Court renders a decision. If the Constitutional

232 Translated in W. E. Butler, *Constitutional Foundations of the CIS Countries* (The Hague, Kluwer Law International, 1999), p. 32.

233 Translated in W. E. Butler, *Constitutional Foundations of the CIS Countries* (The Hague, Kluwer Law International, 1999), pp. 94–5.

234 Translated in W. E. Butler, *Constitutional Foundations of the CIS Countries* (The Hague, Kluwer Law International, 1999), pp. 154–5.

235 Translated in W. E. Butler, *Constitutional Foundations of the CIS Countries* (The Hague, Kluwer Law International, 1999), pp. 205–6.

Court establishes the non-conformity of an international treaty to the Constitution of Georgia, the treaty may be deemed to be binding upon Georgia only after respective changes are made in the Constitution in the established procedure.

Kazakhstan does not have a Constitutional Court. Rather it has established a Constitutional Council, which is empowered by the Constitution (Article 72[3]) to 'consider before ratification international treaties of the Republic for their conformity to the Constitution'.[236] The treaty law of *Kazakhstan* (Article 12) provides that the Constitutional Council will consider treaties upon the application of the President of the Republic Kazakhstan, Chairman of the Senate, Chairman of the Mazhilis, not less than one-fifth of the total number of deputies of Parliament, or the Prime Minister. Once an application is filed with the Constitutional Council, the running of the periods for the ratification of international treaties is suspended. As in the case of most other countries, only treaties subject to ratification are within the jurisdiction of the Constitutional Council.

In *Tadzhikistan* the Constitution (Article 89) provides that the Constitutional Court has the power to determine, *inter alia*, the conformity to the Constitution of treaties of Tadzhikistan which have not entered into legal force.[237] The Tadzhikistan treaty law does not mention the Constitutional Court.

The *Ukrainian* Constitution (Article 151[2]) provides that the Constitutional Court of Ukraine shall give opinions upon the recourse of the President of Ukraine or Cabinet of Ministers of Ukraine concerning the conformity to the Constitution of prevailing international treaties of Ukraine or those treaties which are submitted to the Supreme Rada for 'the giving of consent to their bindingness'.[238] This formulation must be read against the Ukrainian treaty law (Article 7[7]), which says that if 'the Permanent Commission of the Supreme Rada of Ukraine for Foreign Affairs or other permanent commissions of the Supreme Rada of Ukraine establishes the existence of divergencies between the treaty submitted for ratification and the Constitution of Ukraine, the treaty shall be sent to the Constitutional Court of Ukraine in order to receive an opinion concerning the conformity thereof to the Constitution of Ukraine'. The treaty law does not determine who should refer the treaty to the Constitutional Court for evaluation.

236 Translated in W. E. Butler, *Constitutional Foundations of the CIS Countries* (The Hague, Kluwer Law International, 1999), pp. 270–1.

237 Translated in W. E. Butler, *Tadzhikistan Legal Texts* (The Hague, Kluwer Law International, 1999), p. 33. W. E. Butler, *Constitutional Foundations of the CIS Countries* (The Hague, Kluwer Law International, 1999), p. 547.

238 Translated in W. E. Butler, *Constitutional Foundations of the CIS Countries* (The Hague, Kluwer Law International, 1999), p. 650.

The Constitutional Court of *Uzbekistan* (Constitution, Article 109) has the right, *inter alia*, to determine the conformity to the Constitution of the Republic Uzbekistan of inter-State treaty and other obligations of the Republic Uzbekistan.[239] The Uzbekistan treaty law makes no mention of the role of the Constitutional Court. The jurisdiction of the Constitutional Court extends only to an inter-State treaty unless the term 'other obligations' is construed to embrace other categories of treaties.

The Constitutional Courts of *Kyrgyzstan* and *Moldova* do not have jurisdiction over international treaties, and the Kyrgyzstan and Moldovan treaty laws make no mention of a judicial power with respect to treaties. *Turkmenistan* does not have a constitutional court.

It will be seen from the account of the CIS treaty laws above that the 1995 Law is broader in several respects from the CIS treaty laws. First, the 1995 Law refers to 'international treaties' generally and does not confine the Constitutional Court of the RF to merely inter-State and intergovernmental treaties. The formulation of Ukraine, awkward though it may be ('the giving of consent to their bindingness'), encompasses treaties subject to ratification, confirmation, adoption/acceptance, and the like; that is, all treaties to which Ukraine consents to be bound. *Tadzhikistan* takes a similarly broad view.

Second, the 1995 Law empowers the Constitutional Court of the RF to settle disputes concerning competence between designated State agencies in connection with the conclusion of treaties. The CIS treaty laws do not contain such a provision.

Russia

2 This provision is based on Article 125(6) of the 1993 Constitution and elaborated in Article 91, paragraph two, of the 1994 Federal Constitutional Law on the Constitutional Court. If a treaty or individual parts thereof are deemed by the Constitutional Court not to be in conformity with the 1993 Constitution, they may not be introduced into force or applied not only by means of ratification or confirmation, but also by any other means of expressing final consent. This follows from the constitutional right (Article 125, 1993 Constitution) of the Constitutional Court to verify the constitutionality of any international treaty of the RF and precludes evasion of the Constitutional Court's powers of verification by having resort to methods of expressing consent other than ratification or confirmation. Such prohibition operates from the moment the Decree of

[239] Translated in W. E. Butler, *Constitutional Foundations of the CIS Countries* (The Hague, Kluwer Law International, 1999), p. 697.

the Constitutional Court is proclaimed in open session in full immediately after signature (Article 77, 1994 Federal Constitutional Law on the Constitutional Court).

The reference to 'application' would appear to encompass at least two situations. The first is the provisional application of an international treaty (see Gloss on Article 23, above), and the application of a treaty or treaty provision by way of analogy of *jus* or *lex*, or other aid to interpretation.

CIS

The treaty law of *Kazakhstan* (Article 12[3]) provides that international treaties deemed not to conform to the Constitution of the Republic Kazakhstan may not be ratified and introduced into operation. Unlike the 1995 Law, however, the Kazakhstan formulation extends only to treaties subject to ratification.

Section V

Termination and Suspension of Operation of International Treaties of Russian Federation

Article 35 Recommendations Concerning Termination or Suspension of Operation of International Treaties of Russian Federation

1. Recommendations concerning the termination or suspension of international treaties of the Russian Federation may be submitted, depending upon within whose competence the questions are which are regulated by the treaty, for the consideration of the President of the Russian Federation or the Government of the Russian Federation by each chamber of the Federal Assembly of the Russian Federation and by subjects of the Russian Federation in the person of their respective agencies of State power.

Such recommendations also may be submitted by the Supreme Court of the Russian Federation, Supreme Arbitrazh Court of the Russian Federation, General Procuracy of the Russian Federation, Central Bank of the Russian Federation, and Plenipotentiary for Human Rights with regard to questions of their jurisdiction.

2. The President of the Russian Federation, the Government of the Russian Federation, or on their behalf a federal minister or director of other federal agency of executive power shall within a month's period give a reply to the recommendation.

Russia

1 This Article of the 1995 Law regulates an internal procedural matter for the RF. General international law does not expressly regulate this matter nor necessarily require a State to lay down an internal procedure for making such recommendations.

The right to make recommendations concerning termination or suspension of the operation of international treaties of the RF is distinct from the right of legislative initiative (see Gloss on Article 36(5), below), and also from the submission of Proposals to the President or to the Government on the basis of Article 36(1) of the 1995 Law.

CIS

The CIS treaty laws use various terminology in addressing termination of treaties. Many favour 'denunciation', and one (*Georgia*) uses and defines the term 'abrogation'.

The word 'denunciation' is sometimes used as the synonym of 'termination', but in some treaty laws both terms are used in the same Article and are not regarded as synonyms.

The treaty laws of *Armenia, Azerbaidzhan, Belarus, Georgia, Kazakhstan, Kyrgyzstan, Moldova, Tadzhikistan, Turkmenistan, Ukraine*, and *Uzbekistan* do not contain a provision concerning the submission of recommendations to terminate or suspend the operation of a treaty.

Russia

2 A period of one month is granted for a reply to be given by the President of the RF or by the Government to a recommendation concerning termination or suspension. There is no indication as to whether the reply need be a reasoned one or not.

CIS

The CIS treaty laws do not contain a provision similar to point two of the 1995 Law.

Article 36 Proposals Concerning Termination or Suspension of Operation of International Treaties of Russian Federation

1. Proposals concerning the termination or suspension of the operation of international treaties of the Russian Federation concluded in the name of the Russian Federation and in the name of the Government of the Russian Federation shall be submitted, depending upon who adopted the decision concerning consent to the bindingness of the treaty for the Russian Federation, to the President of the Russian Federation or to the Government of the Russian Federation by the Ministry of Foreign Affairs of the Russian Federation autonomously or by agreement with other federal agencies of executive power, other agencies of State power of the Russian Federation, or agencies of State power of the respective subjects of the Russian Federation.

2. Proposals concerning the termination or suspension of the operation of international treaties of the Russian Federation, the decisions concerning consent to the bindingness of which for the Russian Federation were adopted in the form of a Federal Law, shall be submitted to the State Duma by the President of the Russian Federation or by the Government of the Russian Federation, depending upon to whom the proposal was submitted on the basis of which the Federal Assembly of the Russian Federation gave consent to the conclusion of the international treaty of the Russian Federation.

The President of the Russian Federation shall submit, if such is necessary, to the State Duma proposals concerning the termination or suspension of the operation of international treaties of the Russian Federation, the decisions concerning consent to the bindingness of which for the Russian Federation were adopted in the form of a Federal Law on the basis of a recommendation of the Government of the Russian Federation.

The Government of the Russian Federation shall have the right, when necessary, to submit to the President of the Russian Federation a proposal concerning the submission to the State Duma of a proposal concerning the termination or suspension of the operation of an international treaty of the Russian Federation, the decision concerning consent to the bindingness of which for the Russian

Federation was adopted in the form of a Federal Law on the basis of a recommendation of the Government of the Russian Federation.

Proposals which are subject to submission to the President of the Russian Federation for submission to the State Duma concerning the termination or suspension of the operation of international treaties of the Russian Federation which require preliminary consideration by the Government of the Russian Federation shall be submitted to the Government of the Russian Federation.

3. The proposal concerning the termination or suspension of the operation of an international treaty of the Russian Federation must contain a certified copy of the official text of the international treaty, a substantiation of the advisability of its termination or the suspension of its operation, and also an evaluation of the possible financial–economic and other consequences of termination or suspension of the operation of the treaty, including, when necessary, an Opinion of the Government of the Russian Federation provided for by Article 104 of the Constitution of the Russian Federation.

4. Decisions of the Government of the Russian Federation concerning the submission to the State Duma of proposals concerning termination or suspension of the operation of international treaties of the Russian Federation, and also concerning the submission to the President of the Russian Federation for submission to the State Duma of proposals concerning the termination or suspension of the operation of international treaties of the Russian Federation shall be adopted in the form of a Decree.

5. In the event of a subject of the right of legislative initiative which is not mentioned in point two of the present Article submitting to the State Duma on the basis of Article 104 of the Constitution of the Russian Federation a draft law with regard to the question of the termination or suspension of the operation of an international treaty of the Russian Federation, the State Duma shall send the draft law submitted to the President of the Russian Federation for proposals regarding the said draft law.

Russia

1 Point one addresses the procedure for the submission by Federal ministries, State committees, and other departments of Proposals concerning the termination or suspension of international treaties of the RF. Depending upon whether the President or the Government adopted a decision concerning the bindingness of the treaty upon the RF, the Proposals concerning termination or suspension are sent, respectively, to one or the other, bearing in mind that the President may adopt decisions concerning the bindingness of treaties relating to matters within the jurisdiction of the Government.

The MID plays the leading role in submitting Proposals to the President or the Government, acting autonomously or by agreement with other Federal departments, other agencies of State power of the RF, or agencies of State power of the subjects of the RF. The reference to 'other agencies of State power of the RF' indicates that when necessary the Proposal for termination or suspension may be agreed with such agencies as the Supreme Court, Supreme Arbitrazh Court, General Procuracy, Central Bank, or Plenipotentiary for Human Rights.

Thus, the MID by agreement with the Ministry of Defence of the Russian Federation submitted to the President a Proposal concerning termination by mutual consent the Treaty between the Russian Federation and Poland concerning the withdrawal of forces of the RF from the territory of Poland.[240] The Proposal to terminate by mutual consent the intergovernmental Russo-Turkmenistan agreements in the domain of material–technical supply and financial provision for military formation on the territory of Turkmenistan was submitted by the MID and Ministry of Defence to the Government.[241]

The involvement of agencies of State power of subjects of the RF with regard to termination and suspension of international treaties of the RF is likely to be identical virtually with that procedure used when agreeing the conclusion of such treaties.

With regard to subjects of the RF, a distinction must be drawn between those international treaties of the RF which affect questions relegated to the jurisdiction of a subject of the RF, and, second, international treaties of the RF affecting the powers of a subject of the RF with regard to matters of joint jurisdiction of the RF and subjects of the RF. Termination or suspension of treaties of the first category must be agreed with agencies of State power of the respective subject of the RF. Proposals concerning termination and suspension of treaties within the second category, if they directly affect the interests of a particular subject of the RF, are submitted approximately according to the procedure for the conclusion of such treaties (see Gloss on Article 4, above).

The determination of the respective jurisdiction and joint jurisdiction of subjects of the RF must in the case of each individual subject of the RF be assessed not only against the provisions of the 1993 Constitution, but also in light of the 1992 Treaties of the Federation and individual treaties concluded between the RF and subjects of the RF concerning the clarification of the delimitation of jurisdiction. Depending upon the subject-matter of the respective international treaty of the RF, the treaties

240 See Regulation of 1 April 1996, No. 157-рп. *СЗ РФ* (1996), no. 15, item 1585.
241 Decree of 6 September 1995, No. 898. *СЗ РФ* (1995), no. 38, item 3693.

between the RF and subjects of the RF may materially affect the role of subjects of the RF in this process.[242]

CIS

The treaty laws of the CIS contain extensive provisions on making proposals to terminate or suspend the operation of treaties. As a rule, they are a mirror image of the provisions on making proposals to conclude a treaty. In comparison with the 1995 Law, they omit concern for subjects of the Federation, which occupy a significant place in the procedures of consultation and consent for treaties in the RF.

The simplest system is laid down in the treaty law of *Armenia* (Article 22). Proposals and supporting documents are submitted to the President by the Ministry of Foreign Affairs by agreement with the Government. There is a slight variation in *Azerbaidzhan* (Article 21), where the proposal is submitted to the President by the Government or by the Ministry of Foreign Affairs either alone or jointly with other departments. Neither the Armenian nor the Azerbaidzhan treaty laws treat the suspension of treaties. Both treaty laws speak of 'denunciation', although that term is generally understood to be one form of termination among others. The *Georgian* (Article 35[1] and [2]) treaty law belongs basically to the same group.

The *Belarus* (Article 22) treaty law refers to termination, 'including denunciation', or suspension of a treaty. Proposals are submitted in the same procedure as proposals to conduct negotiations (Article 4) laid down in the same law. The Belarus treaty law provides for the form of taking a decision to terminate or suspend; an edict in the case of the President, and a decree when the decision is adopted by the Government.

Kazakhstan regulates the suspension (Article 19) and denunciation (Article 32) of treaties in separate Articles which are not placed in the same section of the treaty law. The procedures are different. With respect to denunciation, the Government of the Republic Kazakhstan upon the recommendation of the Ministry of Foreign Affairs of the Republic Kazakhstan submits to the President of the Republic Kazakhstan proposals concerning the denunciation of international treaties of the Republic Kazakhstan of an inter-State character. The Ministry of Foreign Affairs of the Republic Kazakhstan submits to the Government of the

242 The 1992 Treaties of the Federation and individual treaties between the RF and certain subjects of the RF are published in B. A. Strashun (ed.), *Федеральное конституционное право России. Основные источники по состоянию на 15 сентября 1996 года* [Federal Constitutional Law of Russia. Principal Sources as of 15 September 1996] (M., izd-vo Norma, 1996).

Republic Kazakhstan proposals concerning the denunciation of international treaties of the Republic Kazakhstan with regard to questions relegated to the jurisdiction of the Government.

As regards suspension (Article 19), the Government of the Republic Kazakhstan upon the recommendation of the Ministry of Foreign Affairs of the Republic Kazakhstan submits to the President of the Republic Kazakhstan proposals concerning the suspension of the operation of international treaties of the Republic Kazakhstan of an inter-State character. The Ministry of Foreign Affairs of the Republic Kazakhstan submits to the Government of the Republic Kazakhstan proposals concerning the suspension of the operation of international treaties of the Republic Kazakhstan with regard to questions relegated to the jurisdiction of the Government.

Kyrgyzstan (Article 34) basically follows the 1995 Law. The *Tadzhikistan* (Article 25) treaty law is similar. Proposals to denounce or suspend a treaty ratified by the Madzhlisi Namoiandagon are submitted by the President of Tadzhikistan to that legislative chamber. Proposals with regard to other treaties are submitted, depending upon who adopted the decision to consent to the treaty, to the President or Government of Tadzhikistan by the Ministry of Foreign Affairs autonomously or by agreement with other State agencies.

In *Ukraine* (Article 23) all proposals are submitted by the Ministry of Foreign Affairs or other departments to the Government, following the procedures for the conclusion of a treaty. The Government in turn makes respective proposals to the President of Ukraine or to the Supreme Rada. The Ukrainian treaty law makes no mention of the suspension of treaties.

The *Uzbekistan* (Article 38) treaty law follows the example of the 1995 Law, making an exception for certain types of treaty. The Ministry of Foreign Economic Relations has the right to submit proposals concerning the termination, denunciation, or suspension of the operation of international treaties of the Republic Uzbekistan with regard to questions of foreign economic activity to the Government of the Republic Uzbekistan, simultaneously notifying the Ministry of Foreign Affairs of the Republic Uzbekistan. Other ministries and departments submit proposals concerning termination, denunciation, or suspension of the operation of international treaties to the Ministry of Foreign Affairs.

The *Georgian* (Article 35[3]) treaty law is unique in that it makes provision for a proposal of a foreign State or international organization concerning the suspension or termination of the operation of an international treaty of Georgia. Such a proposal should be submitted by the Ministry of Foreign Affairs of Georgia to the President of Georgia in the form of a proposal in the procedure established for internal suggestions of the same type.

The *Moldovan* treaty law contains no provisions on the matter.

Russia

2 This point addresses the submission of proposals concerning the termination or suspension of international treaties of the RF, the decisions concerning the bindingness of which were adopted in the form of a Federal law. In general the submission of proposals to the State Duma concerning the termination or suspension of international treaties of the RF is done in virtually the same procedure as submitting proposals concerning ratification of international treaties. With certain peculiarities the procedure also extends to termination and suspension of international treaties to which the RF is a party in its capacity as the legal-continuer of the former Soviet Union (see Gloss on Article 37, below).

The President and Government submit proposals concerning the termination or suspension of international treaties of the RF together with a draft of the respective Federal law, the decision concerning the consent to the bindingness of which for the RF was adopted in the form of a Federal law. Other subjects of the right of legislative initiative specified in Article 104 of the 1993 Constitution may submit proposals in this connection as set out in point five of this Article of the 1995 Law (see below).

CIS

The CIS treaty laws either contain no provisions equivalent to the matter dealt with in this point of the 1995 Law or subsume it within the provisions discussed in the preceding point of this Article.

Russia

3 The requirements laid down in this point are analogous to those set out in Article 16(4) of the 1995 Law. The Proposal concerning termination or suspension of an international treaty of the RF must contain a certified copy of the official text of the treaty, a substantiation of the advisability of terminating or suspending its operation, and an assessment of the possible financial–economic, and other consequences of termination or suspension. An Opinion of the Government must be provided for as necessary pursuant to Article 104 of the 1993 Constitution. The consequences of termination or suspension to be addressed are those also

set out in Articles 38 and 39 of the 1995 Law (see Gloss on Articles 38 and 39, below).

If the treaty makes provision for termination or suspension, the procedures laid down therein must be complied with.

CIS

Most CIS treaty laws do not contain a provision concerning the supporting documentation to accompany a proposal to terminate or suspend a treaty.

The *Georgian* (Article 35[5]) treaty law requires the submission of an attested copy of the original of the treaty (in the Georgian language), opinions of the Ministry of Foreign Affairs of Georgia concerning possible foreign policy consequences of the suspension or termination thereof, Ministry of Justice of Georgia concerning the legal consequences, Ministry of Finances of Georgia concerning possible financial–economic consequences of suspension or termination of the present treaty, and also the opinion of a respective central agency of executive power of Georgia.

In *Kyrgyzstan* (Article 34[4]) and *Tadzhikistan* (Article 25) the treaty laws require the submission of an attested copy of the official text of the international treaty, a substantiation of the advisability of the denunciation thereof, and also an evaluation of possible financial–economic or other consequences of the termination of the operation of an international treaty. Proposals for the suspension of a treaty require the same supporting materials.

Russia

4 Decisions of the Government concerning the submission of proposals to the State Duma concerning the termination or suspension of an international treaty of the RF or a recommendation to the President to make such a proposal to the State Duma are to be adopted in the form of a Decree.

CIS

The *Belarus* (Article 22) treaty law provides that the decision of the President regarding a proposal to terminate or suspend a treaty shall be adopted in the form of an edict, and the decision of the Government, in the form of a decree.

The other CIS treaty laws do not contain an equivalent provision.

Russia

5 The right of legislative initiative provided for in Article 104 of the 1993 Constitution also extends to submitting proposals to terminate or suspend an international treaty of the RF. The same procedure is applicable in this instance as applies to Proposals concerning the conclusion of international treaties of the RF (see Gloss on Article 9, above).

The procedure for actions of the State Duma in the event it disagrees with the arguments of the President with regard to the inadvisability of terminating or suspending a treaty, if the decision to agree to the bindingness of the treaty for the RF was adopted in the form of a Federal law, is not regulated by the 1995 Law. In principle a confrontation between the branches of State could occur over such an issue.

If consent to an international treaty of the RF being binding upon the RF were given by the President or by the Government and if the State Duma disagreed with the arguments of the President concerning the inadvisability of terminating or suspending the treaty, the provisions of Article 37(1) of the 1995 Law are applicable and the decision is to be taken by the President or by the Government, respectively. The State Duma is effectively excluded from becoming involved in such termination or suspension.

Consequently, submitting a draft normative act to terminate or suspend an international treaty of the RF, the consent to the bindingness of which for the RF was adopted not in the form of a Federal Law, is comparable in its legal consequences to submitting a recommendation to terminate or suspend the operation of an international treaty of the RF (see Gloss on Article 35, above).

CIS

The other CIS treaty laws do not contain a provision equivalent to this point of the 1995 Law.

Article 37 Termination and Suspension of Operation of International Treaties of Russian Federation

1. The termination (including denunciation) and suspension of the operation of international treaties of the Russian Federation shall be effectuated in accordance with the conditions of the treaty itself and norms of international law by the agency which adopted the decision concerning consent to the bindingness of the international treaty for the Russian Federation.

2. The President of the Russian Federation shall adopt, if this is necessary, decisions concerning the termination or suspension of the operation of international treaties of the Russian Federation, the consent to the bindingness of which for the Russian Federation was given by the Government of the Russian Federation.

3. The State Duma shall consider proposals concerning the termination or suspension of the operation of international treaties of the Russian Federation and after the preliminary discussion in committees and commissions of the State Duma shall adopt respective decisions.

Federal Laws adopted by the State Duma concerning termination (including denunciation) or suspension of the operation of international treaties of the Russian Federation shall be subject, in accordance with the Constitution of the Russian Federation, to obligatory consideration in the Soviet of the Federation.

A Federal Law adopted by the Federal Assembly of the Russian Federation concerning the termination (including denunciation) or suspension of the operation of an international treaty of the Russian Federation shall be sent, in accordance with the Constitution of the Russian Federation, to the President of the Russian Federation for signature and promulgation.

4. The operation of an international treaty of the Russian Federation, the decision concerning consent to the bindingness of which for the Russian Federation was adopted in the form of a Federal Law may be suspended by the President of the Russian Federation in instances requiring the taking of urgent measures, with the obligatory immediate informing of the Soviet of the Federation and the State Duma and the submission to the State Duma of a draft respective Federal Law.

In the event the State Duma rejects the draft Federal Law concerning the suspension of the operation of an international treaty of the Russian Federation, the operation of the treaty shall be subject to immediate renewal.

5. The termination and suspension of the operation of international treaties of the Russian Federation of an interdepartmental character shall be done by federal agencies of executive power in whose name such treaties were concluded by agreement with the Ministry of Foreign Affairs of the Russian Federation, by other interested federal agencies of executive power, by agencies of State power of respective subjects of the Russian Federation, and with the authorization of the Government of the Russian Federation.

6. The Government of the Russian Federation shall adopt decisions concerning the termination or suspension of the operation of international treaties of the Russian Federation of an interdepartmental character if the respective questions have important significance for State interests of the Russian Federation.

7. Decisions concerning the termination (including denunciation) and suspension of the operation of international treaties in which the Russian Federation is a party as the State-continuer of the USSR shall be adopted by agencies of State power of the Russian Federation in accordance with their competence established by the Constitution of the Russian Federation, by the present Federal Law, and by other acts of legislation of the Russian Federation.

The making of respective proposals and draft laws shall be effectuated according to the procedure established by Article 36 of the present Federal Law.

Russia

1 Termination of an international treaty of the RF means that it has lost binding force in the relations between the parties and ceased to give rise to rights and obligations for them (see Gloss on Article 38, below). In most instances of termination the parties invoke the provisions of the treaty itself or rest upon the provisions of the 1969 Vienna Convention and general principles of international law. Unlawful termination is a breach of international law and engages the State responsibility of the offending State.

It is for each State itself to determine the internal procedures for arriving at a decision to terminate or suspend the operation of a treaty, provided that those procedures are not arbitrary and are consistent with international law. Under this point of the 1995 Law, the agency which adopted the decision to consent to the bindingness of the international treaty for the RF is to effectuate the termination, including denunciation, of that treaty in accordance with the conditions of the treaty itself and norms of international law. Accordingly, only lawful means of termination are authorized under the 1995 Law. The distribution of competence to decide the question is resolved by making that dependent upon the allocation of competence to adopt the decision to give consent to the

RF being bound by the respective treaty (with the exception set down in point two of this Article of the 1995 Law).

CIS

Several CIS treaty laws contain provisions which substantially address the matters regulated in Article 37 of the 1995 Law.

The *Belarus* (Article 22) and *Kyrgyzstan* (Article 36[1]) treaty laws reproduce verbatim the provision of the 1995 Law.

The *Tadzhikistan* (Article 26) treaty law, which uses the terminology of denunciation and suspension (without termination), is otherwise identical to point one of the 1995 Law. However, the Tadzhikistan treaty law felt obliged to add that denunciation relieves, unless the treaty provides otherwise, Tadzhikistan from the obligation to fulfil the treaty thereafter.

The treaty laws of *Armenia, Azerbaidzhan, Georgia, Kazakhstan, Moldova, Ukraine*, and *Uzbekistan* contain no provision equivalent to this point of the 1995 Law.

Russia

2 Point two of this Article creates an exception from the rule set down in point one of this Article, giving the President the right to adopt, if necessary, a decision to terminate or suspend an international treaty of the RF, the original decision to consent to its being binding upon the RF was adopted by the Government. This exception reflects the same right granted to the President under Article 11(2) of the 1995 Law to adopt a decision to sign an international treaty of the RF even though the treaty regulates questions relegated to the jurisdiction of the Government.

CIS

The CIS treaty laws do not contain a provision of this nature.

Russia

3 The State Duma considers proposals concerning the termination or suspension of an international treaty of the RF in accordance with its Reglament. If a Federal Law is enacted by the State Duma to terminate or suspend an international treaty of the RF, the text is referred within five days to the Soviet of the Federation for consideration, the decision to refer being adopted in the form of a Decree of the State Duma.

The 1993 Constitution provides (Article 106) that Federal laws adopted by the State Duma with regard to the denunciation of international treaties of the RF are subject to obligatory consideration in the Soviet of the Federation. On the premise that denunciation in Article 106 is meant broadly to mean any form of lawful unilateral termination, the better view is that the Soviet of the Federation can not be circumvented simply by avoiding use of the term 'denunciation' in the draft Federal Law on termination of a treaty. This argument, however, is not persuasive with respect to suspension, for the 1993 Constitution is silent in this respect.

The procedures within the State Duma and Soviet of the Federation with respect to termination are the same as those applicable to ratification of an international treaty of the RF (see Gloss on Article 17, above).

CIS

The *Armenian* (Article 25) treaty law requires that the permanent commission for questions of foreign relations of the Supreme Soviet of the Republic Armenia shall consider in advance an international treaty submitted for denunciation to the Supreme Soviet of the Republic Armenia and the proposal concerning denunciation and give a respective opinion. A similar procedure is provided for by the *Azerbaidzhan* (Article 23) treaty law.

The treaty law of *Georgia* (Article 36) provides that an international treaty submitted to the Parliament of Georgia for the purpose of the termination or suspension of operation shall be considered preliminarily by the Committee for foreign relations of the Parliament of Georgia, and, when necessary, jointly with other committees of the Parliament of Georgia and render a respective opinion. Under the same law (Article 37), the Parliament of Georgia by a majority of the full composition in the form of a decree adopts a decision concerning the suspension or termination of the international treaty, the deeming of the bindingness of which for Georgia it expressed consent. The President of Georgia in the form of an edict adopts a decision concerning the suspension or termination of the operation of an international treaty, the deeming of the bindingness of which for Georgia he expressed consent. The Minister of Foreign Affairs of Georgia in the form of an order adopts a decision concerning the suspension or termination of an international treaty, the deeming of the bindingness of which for Georgia he expressed consent.

In *Kazakhstan* the treaty law (Article 33) requires that the Parliament of Kazakhstan in a separate session of the Chambers by means of consecutive consideration of the questions, first in the Mazhilis and then in the Senate, denounce: (1) international treaties of the Republic Kazakhstan of an inter-State character ratified and not subject to ratification upon the recommendation of the President of the Republic Kazakhstan; (2) international treaties of the Republic Kazakhstan relegated to the jurisdiction of the Government, and also international treaties of the Republic Kazakhstan accession to which was effectuated on the basis of decisions of the Government of the Republic Kazakhstan upon the recommendation of the Government of the Republic Kazakhstan.

The *Ukrainian* (Article 24[4]) treaty law authorizes the submission of the question of denouncing a treaty to the Permanent Commission of the Supreme Rada of Ukraine for Foreign Affairs, and when necessary also other permanent commissions of the Supreme Rada of Ukraine, to consider preliminarily the international treaties of Ukraine submitted for denunciation and give respective opinions.

In *Uzbekistan* (Article 39) the parliament plays a key role in the denunciation of treaties. The termination or denunciation of international treaties of the Republic Uzbekistan concluded in the name of the Republic Uzbekistan is performed by the Olii Mazhlis upon the recommendation of the President of the Republic Uzbekistan, and treaties concluded in the name of the Republic Uzbekistan with regard to questions relegated to the jurisdiction of the Government of the Republic Uzbekistan, upon the recommendation of the Government of the Republic Uzbekistan. The termination and denunciation of ratified international treaties of the Republic Uzbekistan concluded in the name of the Government of the Republic Uzbekistan is performed by the Olii Mazhlis upon the recommendation of the Government of the Republic Uzbekistan.

Russia

4 Point four of this Article gives the President of the RF an exceptional power to suspend the operation of an international treaty of the RF even though consent to the bindingness of the treaty was given in the form of a Federal Law. Such decision is to be taken under urgent circumstances and on condition that the Soviet of the Federation and the State Duma are immediately notified and a draft Federal Law is submitted to the State Duma. If the State Duma rejects the draft Federal Law, the operation of the international treaty of the RF is subject to immediate reinstatement.

The 1995 Law is silent with respect to how immediate reinstatement may occur. The phrase 'subject to' implies that further action must be taken, either by the President by way of withdrawing his suspension or by the State Duma in the form of adopting a Federal Law rejecting suspension or reinstating the treaty.

CIS

The CIS treaty laws do not contain a provision equivalent to this.

Russia

5 The termination or suspension of interdepartmental international treaties of the RF is effectuated, as a rule, by the federal agencies of executive power in whose name those treaties were concluded by agreement with the Ministry of Foreign Affairs and also with other interested federal agencies of executive power or agencies of State power of the respective subjects of the RF, on condition of obtaining the authorization of the Government. The 1995 Law does not lay down the procedure for obtaining the authorization of the Government in such instances, but one may assume that the procedure is analogous to that used for obtaining the decision to conclude the treaty. Such decisions are concluded in the form of a regulation by the Government.

CIS

Several CIS treaty laws contain provisions concerning the termination and suspension of interdepartmental treaties.

One group of treaty laws provides that the termination of interdepartmental treaties is regulated by special normative acts of the Government: *Armenia* (Article 26), *Ukraine* (Article 24[7]), and *Uzbekistan* (Article 42).

A second group vests the Government of the respective Independent State with the right to terminate interdepartmental treaties: *Kazakhstan* (Article 34), *Kyrgyzstan* (Article 36[4]).

Russia

6 If the matters regulated by an interdepartmental international treaty of the RF are deemed to be of important significance for the State interests of the RF, the Government may itself adopt the decision to terminate or suspend the operation of such an international treaty of the RF. The decision is adopted in the form of a regulation.

CIS

The CIS treaty laws do not contain a provision equivalent to this point of the 1995 Law.

Russia

7 The dissolution of the former Soviet Union did not automatically affect the bindingness of those treaties concluded by the USSR upon

the RF by reason of the principle set out in Article 1(3) of the 1995 Law: that the RF considered itself to be the legal-continuer of the former Soviet Union. Although the terminology of legal-continuer was not used by the Government of the RSFSR and later by the Soviet Government with respect to treaties concluded by Russia before 26 October 1917, the position taken was very similar.[243] As the legal-continuer of the former Soviet Union, the RF also is the legal-continuer of the Russian Empire treaty relations which survived the Soviet era.

The 1995 Law has proceeded from the principle, following the 1993 Constitution, that decisions concerning termination and suspension of international treaties of the RF are to be taken by agencies of State power of the RF in accordance with their competence. Proposals and drafts to this end are submitted in accordance with Article 36 of the 1995 Law (see Gloss on Article 36, above). However, the State structure of the RF is in many key respects quite different from that of the former Soviet Union; many matters within the competence of the Government of the USSR are under the 1993 Constitution now within the competence of the President of the RF or the Federal Assembly.

Where the competence of the agencies of the former Soviet Union and the RF coincides, decisions concerning termination and suspension of treaties to which the RF is a party by virtue of being the legal-continuer of the USSR are adopted as previously. The Government of the RF therefore adopted the decision to terminate the Soviet–American Agreement on Cooperation in the Domain of Agriculture.[244] Insofar as possible necessary adjustments are made to comply with Article 36 of the 1995 Law. Citizenship under the 1993 Constitution is no longer within the jurisdiction of the Government; accordingly the President of the RF submitted to the State Duma the Proposal and draft Federal Law to terminate the Soviet–Hungarian Convention on dual citizenship.[245] The Government submitted to the State Duma the Proposal to denounce the Soviet–Finnish Agreement on fishing and sealing.[246]

In some cases the RF has entered into comprehensive negotiations with other States in order to determine globally what the legal status is of treaties concluded during the Soviet era. An example of such direct consultations and the results produced is the Agreement in the Form of an Exchange of Letters between the Government of the RF and the Government of Bulgaria relating to the results of inventorying inter-State

[243] See the Note of the Soviet Government to the Director of the Institute of International Law, The Hague, 2 April 1924, reproduced below as an annex.

[244] Decree of 7 March 1995, No. 234. *СЗ РФ* (1995), no. 11, item 994.

[245] Regulation of 1 November 1995, No. 489-рп. *СЗ РФ* (1995), no. 45, item 4310.

[246] Decree of 31 July 1995, No. 776. *СЗ РФ* (1995), no. 32, item 3320.

and intergovernmental treaties and agreements concluded between the USSR and Bulgaria from 1945–91.[247]

The Commentary stresses that the termination or suspension of international treaties to which the RF is a party in its capacity as the legal-continuer of the former USSR does not pre-decide whether that treaty remains in force in relations between the foreign party concerned and other Independent States which were former union republics of the USSR.[248] The formula used to express the position that a treaty of the former USSR which is terminated at the initiative of the RF but may remain in force between the foreign party and other Independent States is that the treaty is terminated 'in relations of the RF and the respective country'.[249] This position is consolidated in the Memorandum of Understanding Regarding the Question of Legal Succession in Respect of Treaties of the Former USSR of Mutual Interest, signed 6 July 1992.

The Memorandum of Understanding observed that 'virtually all multilateral international treaties of the former USSR are of common interest for member-States of the Commonwealth. However, these treaties do not require joint decisions or actions of member-States of the Commonwealth. The question of participation in these treaties shall be decided in accordance with the principles and norms of international law by each member-State of the Commonwealth autonomously, depending upon the specific nature of each concrete instance and the character and content of the particular treaty.'

As regards bilateral treaties affecting the interests of two or more (but not all) member-States of the Commonwealth, they required the adoption of decisions or actions on the part of those member-States to which such treaties are applicable. As for those bilateral treaties that affected the interests of all Independent States, such as treaties on boundaries and the regime thereof, they remained in force but only those member-States of the Commonwealth whose frontiers were adjacent to the interested foreign States would remain parties to them.[250]

CIS

The CIS treaty laws do not contain a provision regulating the matters in this point of the 1995 Law.

247 *БМД*, no. 10 (1996), pp. 66–79.

248 Osminin, Commentary, p. 115.

249 This formula is used in the Federal Law of the RF terminating the Soviet–Hungarian Convention on dual citizenship. *СЗ РФ* (1996), no. 1, item 8.

250 The text of the Memorandum appears in Iu. M. Kolosov and E. S. Krivchikova (comps.), *Действующее международное право в трех томах* [Prevailing International Law in Three Volumes] (M., izd-vo Moskovskogo nezavisimogo instituta mezhdunarodnogo prava, 1996), I, pp. 492–3.

Article 38 Consequences of Termination of International Treaty of Russian Federation

The termination of an international treaty of the Russian Federation, unless provided otherwise by the treaty or there is another arrangement with its other participants, shall relieve the Russian Federation from any obligation to fulfil the treaty thereafter and shall not influence the rights, obligations, or legal status of the Russian Federation which arose as a result of the fulfilment of the treaty before the termination thereof.

Russia

This Article of the 1995 Law incorporates the provisions of Article 70(1) of the 1969 Vienna Convention. A treaty may itself provide particular consequences in the event of termination or the parties to the treaty may agree as to what these consequences should be. Commercial treaties, for example, sometimes continue to operate with respect to transactions concluded during the period of its operation but not completed at the moment of termination, or foreign investment treaties, with respect to privileges and exemptions or other protections accorded to investments made while the treaty was in force.

Termination of a treaty does not extinguish the existence of the norms of the treaty, as doctrinal writings sometimes suggest, but rather, in the language of the 1969 Vienna Convention, relieves the RF of the obligation to fulfil the treaty with respect to the former Contracting Party(ies). That treaty norms cease to be part of the legal system of Russia is true with respect to treaties having direct effect. Legislation enacted in pursuance of treaty obligations, however, has an autonomous existence in the Russian legal system and would survive the termination of the treaty unless repealed or unless such legislation expressly provides otherwise.

Termination of a treaty does not have retroactive effect in the sense of eliminating the rights, duties, or legal consequences which came into being during the operation of the treaty. The Agreement in the Form of an Exchange of Notes between the RF and Poland concerning the termination of the operation of military agreements signed by them on 20 and 22 May 1992 expressly stipulated: 'The termination of the operation of the aforesaid documents shall not affect the legal consequences which arose as a result of the operation of these treaties.'[251]

CIS

The CIS treaty laws contain variations on the formulation of this Article of the 1995 Law.

The first group follows the formulation of the 1995 Law: *Georgia* (Article 38), *Kyrgyzstan* (Article 37), and *Uzbekistan* (Article 39). The *Tadzhikistan* (Article 26) treaty law provides that denunciation of a treaty, unless the treaty provides otherwise, 'relieves the Republic Tadzhikistan from the obligation to fulfil the treaty thereafter'.

Some CIS treaty laws contain no provisions concerning the consequences of termination or denunciation: *Armenia, Azerbaidzhan, Belarus, Kazakhstan, Moldova, Ukraine*.

[251] *БМД*, no. 10 (1996), p. 64.

Article 39 Consequences of Suspension of Operation of International Treaty of Russian Federation

1. The suspension of the operation of an international treaty of the Russian Federation, unless provided otherwise by the treaty or there is another arrangement with its other participants, shall relieve the Russian Federation from the obligation to fulfil the treaty during the period of suspension in its relations with those of its participants with whom the operation of the treaty is suspended and shall not influence for the others the legal relations of the Russian Federation established by the treaty with its other participants.

2. In the period of suspension of the operation of an international treaty of the Russian Federation the agencies of State power of the Russian Federation of the respective subjects of the Russian Federation shall refrain from actions which might impede renewal of the operation of the treaty.

Russia

1 Point one of this Article is based on Article 72(1) of the 1969 Vienna Convention. Suspension is a temporary termination of the operation of a treaty and always admissible by agreement of the parties or in accordance with the provisions of the respective treaty. Under Article 60 of the 1969 Vienna Convention, material breach of a treaty also is grounds for suspension of its operation. Suspension may operate, in a multilateral treaty, with respect to individual parties thereto instead of all of the parties.

The implications of suspension of a treaty have yet to be fully explored in Russian Law. Where a treaty is of direct effect in the RF, one may presume that the suspension of its operation operates not only between the parties to the treaty, but also within the Russian legal system with respect to those who may claim directly the rights and protections of the treaty. Where, however, a treaty has required internal legislation to give effect to its provisions, it does not follow that suspension of the operation of the treaty should necessarily affect the implementing legislation adopted further to the treaty but having an autonomous legal foundation. The Commentary suggests that suspension generally give rise to 'respective changes . . . in the legal system of Russia. Norms of the suspended treaty are not excluded from the system, but suspends their operation and are not subject to application.'[252] While the last is undoubtedly the case, this should not necessarily extend to Russian legislation adopted on the basis of the treaty.

CIS

The CIS treaty laws fall into two categories with respect to the consequences of suspension of the operation of a treaty. The first group determines the consequences just as the 1995 Law: *Belarus* (Article 24), *Georgia* (Article 39[1]), and *Kyrgyzstan* (Article 38[1]).

In the second group the treaty laws of *Tadzhikistan* (Article 26), and *Uzbekistan* (Article 41), in common with most in the first group and unlike the 1995 Law, speak only of the obligation to suspend fulfilment of the treaty. No reference is made to influencing for the others the legal relations established by the treaty with other participants.

The third group contains no provisions on the consequences of suspension: *Armenia, Azerbaidzhan, Moldova, Ukraine.*

Russia

2 Point two of this Article follows Article 72(2) of the 1969 Vienna Convention. In accordance with the principle of good faith, suspension should not become a pretext for termination of the operation of a treaty. The 1995 Law translates these general requirements of the 1969 Vienna Convention into a specific obligation for agencies of State power of the RF and of the respective subjects of the RF.

CIS

The treaty laws of *Belarus* (Article 24), *Georgia* (Article 39[2]), and *Kyrgyzstan* (Article 38[2]) contain a like provision.

[252] Lukashuk, Commentary, p. 117.

Article 40 Official Communications Concerning Termination or Suspension of Operation of International Treaties of Russian Federation

Official communications of the Ministry of Foreign Affairs of the Russian Federation concerning the termination or suspension of the operation of international treaties of the Russian Federation concluded in the name of the Russian Federation and in the name of the Government of the Russian Federation shall be published in the procedure provided for by Article 30 of the present Federal Law.

Russia

This Article links communications concerning the termination or suspension of international treaties of the RF with the procedure for the publication of treaties of the RF laid down in Article 30 of the 1995 Law. Accordingly, such communications of the Ministry of Foreign Affairs are subject to publication in the *СЗ РФ* if the decision to terminate or suspend was adopted in the form of a Federal Law. If the treaties were concluded in the name of the RF or in the name of the Government, the official communications of the Ministry also are to be published in the *БМД*.

No provision is made in the 1995 Law for communications concerning the termination or suspension of interdepartmental treaties.

CIS

Several CIS treaty laws contain analogous provisions: *Georgia* (Article 40[1]), *Kyrgyzstan* (Article 39), *Tadzhikistan* (Article 27), and *Uzbekistan* (Article 43).

In addition to official publication, the *Georgian* (Article 40[2]) treaty law requires that the Ministry of Foreign Affairs of Georgia officially shall notify the party participating in the treaty or depositary about the suspension or termination of the operation of an international treaty of Georgia.

Some CIS treaty laws do not contain a provision on the subject: *Armenia, Azerbaidzhan, Belarus, Kazakhstan, Moldova*, and *Ukraine*.

Section VI

Concluding Provisions

Article 41 Entry of Present Federal Law into Force

The present Federal Law shall enter into force from the date of its official publication.

Russia

In accordance with the Federal Law 'On the Procedure for the Publication and Entry into Force of Federal Constitutional Laws, Federal Laws, and Acts of Chambers of the Federal Assembly',[253] the date of official publication is considered to be the date on which the full text of a Federal Law is published in one of the two official gazettes, either *СЗ РФ* or the newspaper *Российская газета*. Publication occurred in *Российская газета* on 21 July 1995 and in the *СЗ РФ* bearing the cover date of 17 July 1995.

The Constitutional Court of the RF has ruled on the date of official publication of laws. In determining whether publication first occurred in *Российская газета* or the *СЗ РФ*, the Constitutional Court noted that the cover date of the last is not decisive but rather the date on which the issue was signed to press (which is indicated on the last page of each issue together with other issue data). The date of signing to press, which can be days or weeks after the cover date, must be compared with the newspaper date to determine which first appeared.[254]

CIS

The treaty laws of the CIS countries fall into two groups. The first group, following the model of the 1995 Law, regulates the entry into force of the treaty law in the law itself, in the form of a concluding provision. The second group adopted a separate decree concerning the entry into force of the respective treaty law.

253 *СЗ РФ* (1994), no. 8, item 801.
254 See W. E. Butler, *Russian Law* (Oxford, Oxford University Press, 1999), pp. 101–2.

Within the first group are the treaty laws of: *Georgia* (Article 41), *Kazakhstan* (Article 35), and *Kyrgyzstan* (Article 40).

The second group consists of the treaty laws of: *Armenia, Azerbaidzhan, Belarus, Moldova, Tadzhikistan* (Decree No. 909, 11 December 1999), *Turkmenistan, Ukraine,* and *Uzbekistan* (22 December 1995).

The precise formulation for entry into force varies and is sometimes indefinite. The Tadzhikistan formulation provides, for example, that the treaty law enters into force 'after its official publication'. But how long after? And the Georgian treaty law stipulates 'upon publication' without requiring 'official' publication.

Annexes

UNION OF SOVIET SOCIALIST REPUBLICS

Letter of the Soviet Government to the Director of the Institute of International Law, the Hague

[Dated 2 April 1924]

Decree I, adopted by the Second Congress of Soviets on 26 October (8 November) 1917 announced the invalidity of all secret political treaties concluded by the former government 'for the benefit of landowners and capitalists'. The attitude of the Soviet Government towards other treaties and agreements depends upon a number of conditions. The unusually prolonged break of political relations with all countries of the world, which followed the Revolution of 1917, and changes which occurred in the entire totality of international circumstances, do not permit all treaties of the old Russian Government to be simply and unreservedly re-established. It is doubtful whether any of these actually might be fulfilled without contradicting the most modern regulation of these questions that has ensued since 1917 without the participation of one of the parties to such treaty.

Therefore, in its Note of 8 February 1924 to the British Government the Government of the Soviet Union expressed a readiness to conclude an agreement 'concerning the question of replacement of treaties which lost force as a result of events of the wartime and postwar period.' This question must be resolved in each individual instance at the discretion of the respective governments. It is clear from the Note of 8 February 1924 that no category of treaties may be placed in another position, except those which were mentioned in the Decree of 26 October 1917.

The Soviet Government has never declared a general renunciation of all treaties concluded by Russia under the Tsarist regime or under the Provisional Government. But it does not follow from this that all treaties obligatorily must be re-concluded. The present question must be considered from the viewpoint of the *rebus sic stantibus* clause for each State and each treaty individually.

All that has been said relates to treaties and agreements in the literal sense of the word and does not affect financial obligations of the former Russian Governments.

Decree on the Procedure for the Conclusion, Ratification (or Confirmation), and Denunciation (or Declaration Concerning Termination of Operation) of International Treaties of the USSR

[Adopted by the Central Executive Committee of the USSR, 21 May 1925, as amended 15 June 1927. *C3 CCCP* (1925), no. 35, item 258; (1927), no. 40, item 393]

In development of Article 1(a) and (f) of the Constitution (Fundamental Law) of the USSR, the first session of the Central Executive Committee of the USSR, third convocation, decrees:

Article 1 International treaties and agreements of the USSR which are subject to ratification in accordance with Article 2 of the present Decree shall be concluded in the name of the Congress of Soviets of the USSR, if a decree concerning the conclusion thereof has been adopted by the Congress of Soviets of the USSR, and in the name of the Central Executive Committee of the USSR in remaining instances.

International treaties and agreements which do not require ratification shall be concluded in the name of the Council of People's Commissars of the USSR.

Article 2 Treaties and agreements concerning the conclusion of peace and changes of borders of the USSR, as well as treaties requiring ratification according to the laws of the country with whom the treaty is concluded, shall be subject to ratification.

Article 3 International treaties and agreements which are ratified by the Central Executive Committee of the USSR, or which have been ratified prior to the formation of the USSR by the central executive committees of union republics, shall be subject to denunciation by the Central Executive Committee of the USSR.

International treaties and agreements which are confirmed by the Council of People's Commissars of the USSR, or which have been confirmed prior to the formation of the USSR by councils of people's commissars of union republics, shall be denounced by the Council of People's Commissars of the USSR [Article 3 was added by Decree of 15 June 1927. *C3 CCCP* (1927), no. 40, item 393].

Decree on the Procedure for the Submission of International Treaties and Agreements Concluded in the Name of the USSR for Approval, Confirmation, and Ratification of the Government of the USSR

[Adopted by the Central Executive Committee and Council of People's Commissars of the USSR, 2 October 1925. *C3 CCCP* (1925), no. 68, item 503]

The Central Executive Committee and Council of People's Commissars of the USSR decree:

Article 1 Treaties and agreements concluded with foreign States, prior to being signed in the name of the USSR, shall be submitted by the People's Commissariat of Foreign Affairs for preliminary approval of the Council of People's Commissars of the USSR.

Article 2 Preliminary approval (Article 1) shall be made in the following procedure:

(a) in those instances when plenipotentiaries of the USSR propose to advance their own draft of a treaty or agreement, such draft or the basic provisions thereof shall be submitted by the People's Commissariat of Foreign Affairs to the Council of People's Commissars of the USSR even prior to the beginning of formal negotiations with plenipotentiaries or delegates of the appropriate States;

(b) in those instances when, having entered negotiations, plenipotentiaries of the USSR do not propose to set forth their own draft, the draft of the basic provisions thereof submitted by the plenipotentiaries of the other Contracting Party shall be submitted to the Council of People's Commissars, with appropriate notations thereon of the plenipotentiaries of the USSR, or a counter-draft or counter-provision of the plenipotentiaries of the USSR;

(c) after a draft treaty or agreement has been finally agreed upon with plenipotentiaries of the other party, such agreed draft shall be sent by the plenipotentiaries of the USSR to the People's Commissariat of Foreign Affairs. The last, after consideration of the document, shall either notify the plenipotentiaries of the USSR of the possibility of signing the text as drawn up, or, if in the process of discussion of the draft essential changes have been made in the text or basic provisions approved by the Council of People's Commissars, the final text shall be submitted for a second consideration and approval of the Council of People's Commissars of the USSR.

Article 3 Treaties and agreements with foreign States signed by plenipotentiaries of the USSR shall be submitted by the People's Commissariat of Foreign Affairs to the Council of People's Commissars of the USSR, for the purposes of:
(a) informing the Council of People's Commissars of the signing of acts which enter into force by virtue of the very fact of their signature;
(b) consideration of treaties and agreements with governments of foreign States, as well as confirmation of those which do not require ratification;
(c) consideration by the Council of People's Commissars of the USSR and subsequent sending for ratification to the Congress of Soviets of the USSR, the Central Executive Committee of the USSR, or its Presidium, of documents which require ratification (Article 2, Decree of the Central Executive Committee of the USSR of 21 May 1925, 'On the Procedure for the Conclusion and Ratification of International Treaties of the USSR' (*C3 CCCP* (1925), no. 35, item 258).

Article 4 Articles 1 and 2 of the present Decree shall not apply in those instances when treaties and agreements are concluded in the name of the USSR by persons having unlimited authority from the Government of the USSR.

Article 5 In the event of the necessity of adherence of the USSR to prevailing international treaties or agreements, the right of adherence to which has been accorded to all States, the draft decree of adherence shall be brought by the People's Commissariat for Foreign Affairs to the Council of People's Commissars of the USSR in the usual procedure. Upon confirmation of the draft, the appropriate decree shall be published in the Collected Laws and Orders of the Worker-Peasant Government of the USSR.

Law on the Procedure for the Ratification and Denunciation of International Treaties of the USSR

[Adopted by the Supreme Soviet of the USSR, 20 August 1938. *Ведомости СССР* (1938), no. 11]

Article 1 In accordance with Article 49(1) of the Constitution (Fundamental Law) of the Union of Soviet Socialist Republics, ratification of international treaties shall be made by the Presidium of the Supreme Soviet of the USSR.

Article 2 Peace treaties, treaties concerning mutual defence against aggression, and treaties of mutual nonaggression concluded by the Union of Soviet Socialist Republics shall be subject to ratification.

Moreover, international treaties upon the conclusion of which the parties have agreed to a subsequent ratification shall be subject to ratification.

Article 3 Denunciation of ratified international treaties shall be made on the basis of edicts of the Presidium of the Supreme Soviet of the USSR.

Edict on Decrees of the TsIK SSSR Which Have Lost the Force of Law in Connection with the Adoption by the Supreme Soviet of the USSR of the Law 'on the Procedure for the Ratification and Denunciation of International Treaties of the USSR'

[Adopted by the Presidium of the Supreme Soviet of the USSR, 26 April 1940. *Ведомости СССР* (1940), no. 14]

In connection with the adoption by the Supreme Soviet of the USSR of the Law 'On the Procedure for the Ratification and Denunciation of International Treaties of the USSR', the following Law shall be considered to have lost its force:

the Decree of the Central Executive Committee of the USSR of 21 May 1925 'On the Procedure for the Conclusion and Ratification of International Treaties of the USSR' (*СЗ СССР* (1925), no. 35, item 258), with subsequent additions and changes (*СЗ СССР* (1927), no. 40, item 393; (1928), no. 24, item 214).

Law on the Procedure for the Conclusion, Performance, and Denunciation of International Treaties of the USSR

[Adopted by the Supreme Soviet of the USSR, 6 July 1978. *Ведомости СССР* (1978), no. 28, item 439]

International treaties of the Union of Soviet Socialist Republics are an important means for conducting the Leninist policy of peace and for consolidating the security of peoples and extensive international cooperation.

The Union of Soviet Socialist Republics shall conclude and perform international treaties by proceeding from the constitutional bases of foreign policy in accordance with generally-recognized principles and norms of international law.

True to the principle of compliance with international treaties by the participants thereof, the USSR strictly and conscientiously shall fulfil its international obligations.

I General Provisions

Article 1 Tasks of the Law

The present Law shall establish the procedure for the conclusion, performance, and denunciation of international treaties of the USSR, being called upon to further the realization of the purposes and principles of USSR foreign policy which are proclaimed and consolidated by the USSR Constitution.

The procedure for the conclusion, performance, and denunciation of international treaties of the USSR – inter-State, intergovernmental, and interdepartmental – established by the present Law shall apply with respect to all international treaties of the USSR irrespective of their form and appellation (treaty, agreement, convention, covenant, protocol, exchange of letters or notes, or other forms and appellations of international treaties).

Article 2 International Treaties of the USSR

The conclusion, and also the denunciation, of international treaties shall be subject to the jurisdiction of the Union of Soviet Socialist Republics.

International treaties of the USSR shall be concluded with foreign States, and also with international organizations, in the name of:

the Union of Soviet Socialist Republics;

the Presidium of the USSR Supreme Soviet;

the Government of the USSR;

the ministries, State committees, and departments of the USSR.

II Conclusion of International Treaties of the USSR

Article 3 Proposals Concerning the Conclusion of International Treaties of the USSR

Proposals concerning the conclusion of international treaties of the USSR shall be submitted in the established procedure to the USSR Council of Ministers by the USSR Ministry of Foreign Affairs.

Other ministries, and also State committees and departments of the USSR, shall submit proposals to the USSR Council of Ministers concerning the conclusion of international treaties of the USSR jointly with the USSR Ministry of Foreign Affairs or by agreement therewith, and independently, only in the instances provided for by Article 4 of the present Law.

Article 4 Proposals Concerning the Conclusion of International Treaties of the USSR Relating to Questions of Foreign Trade, Other Types of Foreign Economic Activity, and Scientific–Technical Cooperation

Proposals concerning the conclusion of international treaties of the USSR relating to questions of foreign trade, including questions of trade–economic and industrial cooperation, relating to questions of economic cooperation and rendering technical assistance, and relating to questions of scientific–technical cooperation shall be submitted to the USSR

Council of Ministers respectively by the USSR Ministry of Foreign Trade, the State Committee of the USSR for Foreign Economic Relations, and the State Committee of the USSR for Science and Technology autonomously or jointly with the USSR Ministry of Foreign Affairs or by agreement therewith.

Proposals concerning the conclusion of international treaties of the USSR relating to questions connected with the realization of socialist economic integration shall be submitted to the USSR Council of Ministers by the ministries, State committees, and departments of the USSR within whose competence the questions being regulated by the treaties is, by agreement with the interested ministries, State committees, and departments of the USSR.

Article 5 Proposals Concerning the Conclusion of International Treaties of the USSR of an Interdepartmental Character

The procedure for submitting proposals concerning the conclusion by ministries, State committees, and departments of the USSR of international treaties of the USSR of an interdepartmental character shall be determined by the USSR Council of Ministers.

Article 6 Proposals Concerning the Conclusion of International Treaties of the USSR Subject to Agreement with the USSR Ministry of Justice

Proposals concerning the conclusion of international treaties of the USSR establishing rules other than those which are contained in Soviet legislation shall be submitted to the USSR Council of Ministers by agreement with the USSR Ministry of Justice.

Article 7 Proposals of the Union Republics Concerning the Conclusion of International Treaties of the USSR

Proposals concerning the conclusion of international treaties of the USSR may be submitted by union republics in the person of their highest agencies of State power and administration.

Article 8 Decision to Conduct Negotiations and Sign International Treaties of the USSR

Decisions to conduct negotiations and sign international treaties of the USSR shall be adopted with respect to:

(1) treaties concluded in the name of the Union of Soviet Socialist Republics: by the Presidium of the USSR Supreme Soviet; and with respect to treaties concluded in the name of the Union of Soviet Socialist Republics relating to questions appertaining to the jurisdiction of the Government of the USSR: by the USSR Council of Ministers;
(2) treaties concluded in the name of the Presidium of the USSR Supreme Soviet: by the Presidium of the USSR Supreme Soviet;
(3) treaties concluded in the name of the Government of the USSR: by the USSR Council of Ministers.

Decisions to conduct negotiations and to sign international treaties of the USSR of an interdepartmental character shall be adopted in the procedure determined by the USSR Council of Ministers.

Article 9 Powers to Conduct Negotiations and Sign International Treaties of the USSR

Powers to conduct negotiations and sign international treaties of the USSR shall be issued with respect to:

(1) treaties concluded in the name of the Union of Soviet Socialist Republics: by the Presidium of the USSR Supreme Soviet; and with respect to treaties concluded in the name of the Union of Soviet Socialist Republics relating to questions appertaining to the jurisdiction of the Government of the USSR: by the USSR Council of Ministers. Powers to conduct negotiations and sign the said treaties also may be issued in the name of the Presidium of the USSR Supreme Soviet or the Government of the USSR by the Ministry of Foreign Affairs of the USSR;
(2) treaties concluded in the name of the Presidium of the USSR Supreme Soviet: by the Presidium of the USSR Supreme Soviet or by the USSR Ministry of Foreign Affairs in the name of the Presidium of the USSR Supreme Soviet;
(3) treaties concluded in the name of the Government of the USSR: by the USSR Council of Ministers or by the USSR Ministry of Foreign Affairs in the name of the Government of the USSR;
(4) treaties of an interdepartmental character: by the respective ministry, State committee, or department of the USSR.

Article 10 Conducting Negotiations and Signing International Treaties of the USSR Without Special Powers

The Chairman of the Presidium of the USSR Supreme Soviet, the Chairman of the USSR Council of Ministers, and the Minister of Foreign Affairs of the USSR shall have the right to conduct negotiations and to sign international treaties of the USSR without special powers.

The head of a diplomatic representation of the USSR in a foreign State or the head of a representation of the USSR attached to an international organization shall have the right to conduct, without special powers, negotiations concerning the conclusion of international treaties of the USSR respectively with the receiving State or within the framework of the particular international organization.

A minister of the USSR, chairman of a State committee of the USSR, and director of a department of the USSR shall, within the limits of his competence, have the right to conduct negotiations and to sign international treaties of the USSR of an interdepartmental character without special powers.

Article 11 Ratification of International Treaties of the USSR

In accordance with the USSR Constitution, the international treaties of the USSR shall be ratified by the Presidium of the USSR Supreme Soviet.

Article 12 International Treaties of the USSR Subject to Ratification

International treaties of the USSR on friendship, cooperation, and mutual assistance, treaties on the mutual renunciation of the use or threat of force, peace treaties, treaties on the territorial delimitation of the USSR with other States, and treaties establishing rules other than those which are contained in legislative acts of the USSR shall be subject to ratification.

International treaties of the USSR during the conclusion of which the Parties have stipulated subsequent ratification also shall be subject to ratification.

The Presidium of the USSR Supreme Soviet may also ratify other international treaties of the USSR.

Article 13 Proposals Concerning Approval and Concerning Ratification of International Treaties of the USSR

Proposals concerning the approval by the USSR Council of Ministers of international treaties of the USSR and concerning their ratification shall be submitted to the USSR Council of Ministers by the USSR Ministry of Foreign Affairs autonomously or jointly or by agreement with other ministries, State committees, and departments of the USSR.

The USSR Council of Ministers shall consider proposals concerning the approval of treaties and concerning their submission to the Presidium of the USSR Supreme Soviet for ratification and shall adopt an appropriate decree.

Article 14 Preliminary Consideration of International Treaties of the USSR in Permanent Commissions of Chambers of the USSR Supreme Soviet

On behalf of the Presidium of the USSR Supreme Soviet, the commissions for foreign affairs of the Soviet of the Union and of the Soviet of Nationalities of the USSR Supreme Soviet shall consider in advance the international treaties of the USSR submitted for ratification and shall give a respective opinion.

Article 15 Adoption of Decisions on the Ratification of International Treaties of the USSR

The Presidium of the USSR Supreme Soviet shall consider international treaties of the USSR submitted by the USSR Council of Ministers for ratification and shall render a respective decision.

A decision of the Presidium of the USSR Supreme Soviet concerning ratification of an international treaty of the USSR shall be adopted in the form of an edict. The instrument of ratification shall be signed on the basis of the edict concerning the ratification.

Article 16 Exchange of Instruments of Ratification and Handing Them Over for Keeping

The exchange of instruments of ratification and handing the instruments concerning ratification of international treaties of the USSR over for keeping to depositaries shall be carried out by the USSR Ministry of Foreign Affairs or on its behalf by the diplomatic representation of the USSR or by the representation of the USSR attached to an international organization.

Article 17 Confirmation of International Treaties of the USSR Which Are Not Subject to Ratification

Confirmation (or adoption) of international treaties of the USSR which are not subject to ratification but provide for their confirmation (or adoption) shall be carried out with respect to:

(1) treaties concluded in the name of the Union of Soviet Socialist Republics: by the Presidium of the USSR Supreme Soviet; and with respect to treaties concluded in the name of the Union of Soviet Socialist Republics relating to questions appertaining to the jurisdiction of the Government of the USSR: by the USSR Council of Ministers;

(2) treaties concluded in the name of the Presidium of the USSR Supreme Soviet: by the Presidium of the USSR Supreme Soviet;

(3) treaties concluded in the name of the Government of the USSR: by the USSR Council of Ministers.

Confirmation (or adoption) of international treaties of the USSR of an interdepartmental character shall be carried out in the procedure determined by the USSR Council of Ministers.

Article 18 Accession to International Treaties

Decisions concerning accession of the Union of Soviet Socialist Republics to international treaties shall be adopted with respect to:

(1) treaties subject to ratification by the Presidium of the USSR Supreme Soviet;

(2) treaties not subject to ratification, accession to which shall be made in the name of the Union of Soviet Socialist Republics: by the Presidium of the USSR Supreme Soviet; and with respect to treaties not subject to ratification, accession to which shall be made in the name of the Union of Soviet Socialist Republics relating to questions appertaining

to the jurisdiction of the Government of the USSR: by the USSR Council of Ministers;

(3) treaties not subject to ratification, accession to which shall be made in the name of the Presidium of the USSR Supreme Soviet: by the Presidium of the USSR Supreme Soviet;

(4) treaties not subject to ratification, accession to which shall be made in the name of the Government of the USSR: by the USSR Council of Ministers.

Decisions concerning accession to international treaties of an interdepartmental character shall be adopted in the procedure determined by the USSR Council of Ministers.

III Performance of International Treaties of the USSR

Article 19 Compliance with International Treaties of the USSR

International treaties of the USSR shall be subject to strict compliance by the Union of Soviet Socialist Republics in accordance with norms of international law.

In accordance with the principle of compliance in good faith of international treaties, the Union of Soviet Socialist Republics favours that other participants of bilateral and multilateral international treaties in which the USSR participates strictly fulfil their obligations arising from such treaties.

Article 20 Ensuring the Fulfilment of International Treaties of the USSR

In accordance with the USSR Constitution, the USSR Council of Ministers shall take measures to ensure the fulfilment of international treaties of the USSR.

Article 21 Fulfilment of Obligations Under International Treaties of the USSR

Ministries, State committees, and departments of the USSR, union republic councils of ministers, and other State agencies in whose competence are the questions being regulated by international treaties of the USSR shall ensure the fulfilment of the obligations accepted under treaties by the Soviet party and supervise the realization of the rights belonging to the Soviet party which arise from such treaties and over the fulfilment by the other participants of treaties of their obligations.

Article 22 General Supervision Over the Performance of International Treaties of the USSR

General supervision over the performance of international treaties of the USSR shall be carried out by the USSR Ministry of Foreign Affairs.

Article 23 Measures Taken in Event of Breach of International Treaty of the USSR by Other Participants Thereof

In the event of a breach of obligations under an international treaty of the USSR by the other participants thereof, the USSR Ministry of Foreign Affairs and other ministries, State committees, and departments of the USSR shall, by agreement with the USSR Ministry of Foreign Affairs, submit proposals to the USSR Council of Ministers concerning the taking of measures in accordance with norms of international law.

In the event of a material violation of an international treaty of the USSR by other participants thereof, and also in other instances provided for by norms of international law, this treaty may be terminated in the procedure established by Articles 27–30 of the present Law.

Article 24 Proposals on Making Changes in and Additions to Soviet Legislation in Connection with the Conclusion of an International Treaty of the USSR

In instances when, with a view to fulfilling an international treaty of the USSR, the promulgation of a law of the USSR, an edict, or a decree of the Presidium of the USSR Supreme Soviet, or the adoption of a decree or regulation of the USSR Council of Ministers is necessary, the interested ministries, State committees, and departments of the USSR shall, by agreement with the USSR Ministry of Justice in the established procedure, submit proposals concerning the adoption of the proper act.

IV Publication and Registration of International Treaties of the USSR

Article 25 Publication of International Treaties of the USSR

International treaties concluded in the name of the USSR which have entered into force for the USSR, decisions concerning the signature of which have been adopted by the Presidium of the USSR Supreme Soviet, international treaties of the USSR concluded in the name of the Presidium of the USSR Supreme Soviet, ratified treaties, and treaties, the accession to which is carried out on the basis of decisions of the Presidium of the USSR Supreme Soviet, shall be published upon the recommendation of the USSR Ministry of Foreign Affairs in the *Ведомости Верховного Совета СССР*.

International treaties concluded in the name of the USSR which have entered into force for the USSR, decisions concerning the signature of which were adopted by the USSR Council of Ministers, treaties concluded in the name of the Government of the USSR and not subject to ratification, and treaties, the accession to which was carried out on the basis of decisions of the USSR Council of Ministers, shall be published upon the recommendation of the USSR Ministry of Foreign Affairs in the *Собрание постановлений правительства СССР*.

International treaties of the USSR, the authentic texts of which were drawn up in foreign languages, shall be published in one of these languages with an official translation into the Russian language.

The procedure for the publication of international treaties of the USSR of an interdepartmental character shall be determined by the USSR Council of Ministers.

Article 26 Registration of International Treaties of the USSR

The registration of international treaties of the USSR at the Secretariat of the United Nations and in respective organs of other international organizations shall be carried out by the USSR Ministry of Foreign Affairs.

The procedure for the registration of international treaties of the USSR of an interdepartmental character shall be determined by the USSR Council of Ministers.

V Denunciation of International Treaties of the USSR

Article 27 Proposals Concerning Denunciation of International Treaties of the USSR

Proposals concerning the denunciation of international treaties of the USSR shall be submitted in the established procedure by the USSR Ministry of Foreign Affairs to the USSR Council of Ministers autonomously or jointly or by agreement with other ministries, State committees, and departments of the USSR.

Article 28 Denunciation of International Treaties of the USSR by the Presidium of the USSR Supreme Soviet

The denunciation of international treaties of the USSR concluded in the name of the Union of Soviet Socialist Republics, decisions concerning the signature of which were adopted by the Presidium of the USSR Supreme Soviet, of international treaties of the USSR concluded in the name of the Presidium of the USSR Supreme Soviet, of ratified treaties, and of treaties, accession to which was carried out on the basis of decisions of the Presidium of the USSR Supreme Soviet, shall be by the Presidium of the USSR Supreme Soviet.

Article 29 Preliminary Consideration of Proposals Concerning Denunciation of International Treaties of the USSR in Permanent Commissions of Chambers of the USSR Supreme Soviet

On behalf of the Presidium of the USSR Supreme Soviet, the commissions for foreign affairs of the Soviet of the Union and of the Soviet of Nationalities of the USSR Supreme Soviet shall consider in advance international treaties of the USSR submitted for denunciation and shall give appropriate opinions.

Article 30 Denunciation of International Treaties of the USSR by the USSR Council of Ministers

The denunciation of international treaties of the USSR concluded in the name of the Union of Soviet Socialist Republics, the decisions concerning the signature of which were adopted by the USSR Council of Ministers, treaties concluded in the name of the Government of the USSR and not subject to ratification, and treaties, accession to which was carried out on the basis of decisions of the USSR Council of Ministers, shall be by the USSR Council of Ministers.

Denunciation of international treaties of the USSR of an interdepartmental character shall be in the procedure determined by the USSR Council of Ministers.

RUSSIA

Decree on Peace

[Adopted 8 November 1917. *СУ РСФСР* (1918), no. 1 item 2] [Excerpt]

The Government abolishes secret diplomacy and, on its part, expresses its firm intention to carry on all negotiations completely before all the people only, and is acting immediately to publish in full the secret treaties confirmed or concluded by the Government of landowners and capitalists from February to 25 October 1917. The Government announces that unconditional and immediate abrogation of the entire content of these secret treaties, inasmuch as they were directed, in the majority of instances, to giving advantage and privileges to Russian landowners and capitalists, and to retaining and increasing annexations of Great Russians.

Note on Legal Succession of Russian Federation to Obligations Arising Out of Prevailing International Treaties Concluded by the USSR

[Note of Ministry of Foreign Affairs of RF, 13 January 1992,
No. 11/Угп. *Дипломатический вестник*,
no. 2–3 (1992), pp. 34]

City of Moscow 13 January 1992

The Ministry of Foreign Affairs of the Russian Federation attests to its respect to the Heads of Diplomatic Representations in Moscow and has the honour to request that the following be brought to the information of the Governments of accredited States.

The Russian Federation continues to effectuate the rights and fulfil the obligations arising from international treaties concluded by the Union of Soviet Socialist Republics.

Accordingly the Government of the Russian Federation will fulfil in place of the USSR the functions of depositary under respective multilateral treaties.

In this connection the Ministry requests that the Russian Federation be regarded as the Party of all prevailing international treaties in place of the USSR.

The Ministry takes advantage of this occasion to assure the Heads of Diplomatic Representations of its highest respect.

Questions of Submitting to the State Duma International Treaties Temporarily Being Applied by Russian Federation

[Regulation of the President of the Russian Federation, No. 370-рп, 7 August 1995. *Российская газета*, 16 August 1995, p. 5, cols. 5-8]

1. The Ministry of Foreign Affairs of Russia and other federal agencies of executive power jointly with the Ministry of Foreign Affairs of Russia or by agreement with it shall submit respectively to the President of the Russian Federation or to the Government of the Russian Federation proposals for submitting to the State Duma according to Article 23(2) of the Federal Law on International Treaties of the Russian Federation within a 6-month period from the date of entry of international treaties into force by virtue of this Law, the decision concerning consent to the bindingness for the Russian Federation of which is subject to adoption in the form of a federal law and the provisional application of which by the Russian Federation has commenced before the entry into force of the said Law.

2. Control over the fulfilment of the present Regulation shall be entrusted to the Government of the Russian Federation and the Administration of the President of the Russian Federation.

3. The present Regulation shall enter into force from the date of signature thereof.

Federal Law on Coordination of International and Foreign Economic Relations of Subjects of Russian Federation

[Adopted 4 January 1999, No. 4-ФЗ. *СЗ РФ* (1999), no. 2, item 231]

The present Federal Law shall in accordance with Article 72 of the Constitution of the Russian Federation establish the general procedure for the coordination of international and foreign economic relations of subjects of the Russian Federation and contains legal guarantees for ensuring the rights and legal interests of subjects of the Russian Federation when establishing and developing international and foreign economic relations.

Article 1 Right of Subjects of Russian Federation for Effectuation of International and Foreign Economic Relations

1. Subjects of the Russian Federation shall within the limits of powers granted to them by the Constitution of the Russian Federation and by federal legislation and treaties between the agencies of State power of the Russian Federation and agencies of State power of subjects of the Russian Federation concerning the delimitation of subjects of jurisdiction and powers possess the right to the effectuation of international and foreign economic relations with subjects of foreign federated States, administrative – territorial formations of foreign States, and also to participate in the activity of international organizations within the framework of agencies created specially for this purpose. Subjects of the Russian Federation may with the consent of the Government of the Russian Federation effectuate such relations also with agencies of State power of foreign States.

2. For the purposes of the present Federal Law, international and foreign economic relations of subjects of the Russian Federation shall be understood as relations to be effectuated in the trade and economic,

scientific – technical, ecological, humanitarian, cultural, and other domains with the foreign partners specified in point 1 of the present Article.

Article 2 Right of Agencies of State Power of Subject of Russian Federation to Conduct Negotiations and Conclude Agreements Concerning Effectuation of International and Foreign Economic Relations

1. Agencies of State power of a subject of the Russian Federation shall within the limits of the powers granted by the Constitution of the Russian Federation, federal legislation, and legislation of subjects of the Russian Federation have the right to conduct negotiations with foreign partners specified in Article 1(1) of the present Federal Law, and also to conclude agreements with them concerning the effectuation of international and foreign economic relations.

2. Agreements concerning the effectuation of international and foreign economic relations concluded by agencies of State power of a subject of the Russian Federation may not contain provisions contrary to the Constitution of the Russian Federation, generally-recognized principles and norms of international law, international treaties of the Russian Federation, federal legislation, treaties between agencies of State power of the Russian Federation and agencies of State power of subjects of the Russian Federation concerning the delimitation of subjects of jurisdiction and powers, and also provisions impinging on the legal interests of another subject of the Russian Federation.

Article 3 Conclusion by Agencies of State Power of Subject of Russian Federation of Agreements Concerning Effectuation of International and Foreign Economic Relations

1. Agencies of State power of a subject of the Russian Federation shall inform in good time the respective federal agencies of executive power concerning the entry into negotiations about the conclusion of an agreement concerning the effectuation of international and foreign economic relations.

2. Agencies of State power of a subject of the Russian Federation shall determine the procedure for the conclusion of agreements concerning

the effectuation of international and foreign economic relations, taking into account the necessity for agreeing draft agreements.

Article 4 Agreeing Draft Agreements Concerning Effectuation of International and Foreign Economic Relations

1. A draft agreement concerning the effectuation of international and foreign economic relations to be concluded by agencies of State power of a subject of the Russian Federation shall not later than a month before signature be submitted for agreement to the Ministry of Foreign Affairs of the Russian Federation and, when necessary, also to other federal agencies of executive power.

2. The Ministry of Foreign Affairs of the Russian Federation and other federal agencies of executive power shall inform the agency of State power of the subject of the Russian Federation about the results of consideration of a draft agreement concerning the effectuation of international and foreign economic relations, as a rule, not later than 20 days after receipt of the draft of the said agreement.

3. In the event disagreements arise between federal agencies of executive power and agencies of State power of a subject of the Russian Federation with respect to the draft agreement concerning the effectuation of international and foreign economic relations, the conciliation procedures shall apply in accordance with legislation of the Russian Federation.

Article 5 Registration of Agreements Concerning Effectuation of International and Foreign Economic Relations

Agreements concerning the effectuation of international and foreign economic relations concluded by agencies of State power of a subject of the Russian Federation shall be registered in the procedure established by the Government of the Russian Federation.

Article 6 Publication of Agreements Concerning Effectuation of International and Foreign Economic Relations

1. The texts of agreements concerning the effectuation of international and foreign economic relations concluded by agencies of State

power of a subject of the Russian Federation shall be subject to publication.

2. The procedure for the publication of agreements concerning the effectuation of international and foreign economic relations shall be established by laws and other normative legal acts of subjects of the Russian Federation.

Article 7 Status of Agreements Concerning Effectuation of International and Foreign Economic Relations

Agreements concerning the effectuation of international and foreign economic relations concluded by agencies of State power of a subject of the Russian Federation shall, irrespective of form, name, and content, not be international treaties.

Article 8 Responsibility of Federal Agencies of State Power for Agreements Concerning Effectuation of International and Foreign Economic Relations

Federal agencies of State power shall not bear responsibility for agreements concerning the effectuation of international and foreign economic relations concluded by agencies of State power of subjects of the Russian Federation, except for instances when the said agreements have been concluded with agencies of State power of foreign States with the consent of the Government of the Russian Federation or with regard to a specific agreement of a subject of the Russian Federation have official guarantees of the Government of the Russian Federation.

Article 9 Assistance of Federal Agencies of State Power to Agencies of State Power of Subject of Russian Federation in Effectuation of International and Foreign Economic Relations

Federal agencies of State power shall render to agencies of State power of subjects of the Russian Federation necessary legal and expert-consultation assistance in the development of international and foreign economic relations, in the organization and conducting of negotiations, in working out the texts of agreements concerning the effectuation of international and foreign economic relations to be concluded by agencies of State power of subjects of the Russian Federation, in the fulfilment of the said agreements, and also ensure defence of the rights and legal interests of subjects of the Russian Federation in foreign States.

Article 10 Right of Subjects of Russian Federation to Have Their Representations on Territories of Foreign States

1. Subjects of the Russian Federation shall for the purpose of the realization of agreements concerning the effectuation of international and foreign economic relations by agreement with the Ministry of Foreign Affairs of the Russian Federation enjoy the right to open their representations beyond the limits of the Russian Federation.

2. Agencies of State power of a subject of the Russian Federation shall have the right by agreement with the Ministry of Foreign Affairs of the Russian Federation to give authorization to open on the territory of the said subject the representations of subjects of foreign federated States and administrative – territorial formations of foreign States.

3. The opening of representations of subjects of the Russian Federation on the territories of foreign States, and likewise the opening of foreign representations on the territory of a subject of the Russian Federation, shall be on the basis of an agreement between the respective agency of State power of a subject of the Russian Federation and empowered agency of a subject of a foreign federated State or empowered agency of an administrative – territorial formation of a foreign State.

4. Representations of subjects of the Russian Federation on the territories of foreign States, and likewise foreign representations on the territory of a subject of the Russian Federation specified in point 2 of the present Article, shall not possess the status of diplomatic representations and consular or diplomatic functions may not be placed on them. Workers of the said representations shall not enjoy diplomatic privileges and immunities.

5. Representations of subjects of the Russian Federation beyond the limits of the Russian Federation shall be headed by citizens of the Russian Federation.

Article 11 Federal Agencies of State Power Effectuating Coordination of International and Foreign Economic Relations of Subjects of Russian Federation

1. The coordination of international and foreign economic relations of subjects of the Russian Federation shall be placed on federal agencies of executive power in the procedure established by the President of the Russian Federation upon the proposal of the Government of the Russian Federation.

2. Respective federal agencies of executive power shall have the right to receive from agencies of State power of subjects of the Russian Federation information concerning measures to be conducted by subjects of the Russian Federation with regard to the effectuation of international and foreign economic relations and to give to agencies of State power of subjects of the Russian Federation their proposals and recommendations.

Article 12 Settlement of Disputes With Respect to Agreements Concerning Effectuation of International and Foreign Economic Relations

1. In the event disagreements arise between agencies of State power of the Russian Federation and agencies of State power of subjects of the Russian Federation, and also between agencies of State power of subjects of the Russian Federation with respect to agreements concerning the effectuation of international and foreign economic relations to be concluded by agencies of State power of subjects of the Russian Federation, the conciliation procedures shall apply in accordance with the Constitution of the Russian Federation and legislation of the Russian Federation.

2. If an agreement concerning the effectuation of international and foreign economic relations concluded by an agency of State power of a subject of the Russian Federation is contrary to the Constitution of the Russian Federation, federal laws, generally-recognized principles and norms of international law, and international treaties of the Russian Federation, impinges the legal interests of another subject of the Russian Federation, or violates the procedure established by the present Federal Law, such agreement may be contested in a judicial proceeding.

3. The operation of agreements concerning the effectuation of international and foreign economic relations concluded by agencies of executive power of subjects of the Russian Federation and containing provisions which are contrary to the Constitution of the Russian Federation, federal laws, generally-recognized principles and norms of international law, and international treaties of the Russian Federation may in accordance with Article 85, paragraph two, of the Constitution of the Russian Federation be suspended until a resolution of this question by a respective court.

Article 13 On the Entry of the Present Federal Law into Force

The present Federal Law shall enter into force from the day of official publication thereof.

Article 14 Bringing of Normative Legal Acts into Conformity with Present Federal Law

The President of the Russian Federation, Government of the Russian Federation, and agencies of State power of subjects of the Russian Federation shall bring their normative legal acts into conformity with the present Federal Law.

Decree of the Government of Russian Federation on the Adoption by the Government of the Russian Federation of Decisions Concerning Consent for the Effectuation by Subjects of Russian Federation of International and Foreign Economic Relations with Agencies of State Power of Foreign States

[Adopted 1 February 2000, No. 91. *СЗ РФ* (2000), no. 6, item 771]

In execution of Article 1(1) of the Federal Law on the Coordination of International and Foreign Economic Relations of Subjects of Russian Federation, the Government of the Russian Federation decrees:

A decision of the Government of the Russian Federation concerning its consent to the effectuation by subjects of the Russian Federation of international and foreign economic relations with agencies of State power of foreign States shall be adopted on the basis of recourse of agencies of executive power of subjects of the Russian Federation containing a substantiation of the necessity for the effectuation of such relations when there is a positive opinion of the Ministry of Foreign Affairs of the Russian Federation, Ministry of Justice of the Russian Federation, and other federal agencies of executive power in accordance with their competence.

ARMENIA

Law on the Conclusion, Ratification, and Denunciation of International Treaties of the Republic Armenia

[Adopted 6 June 1992]

Chapter I General Provisions

Article 1 The present Law establishes the procedure for the conclusion, ratification, performance, and denunciation of international treaties of the Republic Armenia – inter-State, intergovernmental, and interdepartmental – and shall apply with respect to all international treaties of the Republic Armenia, irrespective of the names and forms thereof.

Article 2 International treaties of the Republic Armenia with foreign States and international organizations shall be concluded in the name of:

– the Republic Armenia;
– the Government of the Republic Armenia;
– the republic agencies of State administration and departments of the Republic Armenia.

When concluding, ratifying, performing, and denouncing international treaties, the Republic Armenia shall be guided by generally-recognized norms of international law and by legislation of the Republic Armenia.

Chapter II Procedure for Conclusion of International Treaties of Republic Armenia

Article 3 Proposals concerning the conclusion of international treaties of the Republic Armenia shall be submitted to the President of the Republic Armenia or to the Government of the Republic Armenia by the Ministry of Foreign Affairs of the Republic Armenia, and also by other republic agencies of State administration and departments of the Republic Armenia after agreement with the Ministry of Foreign Affairs of the Republic Armenia.

Article 4 Decisions concerning the conducting of negotiations and conclusion of international treaties shall be adopted by:

– the President of the Republic Armenia: with respect to treaties to be concluded in the name of the Republic Armenia;

– the Government of the Republic Armenia: with respect to treaties to be concluded in the name of the Government of the Republic Armenia.

The procedure for conducting negotiations and the conclusion of international interdepartmental treaties of the Republic Armenia shall be established by the Government of the Republic Armenia.

Article 5 The President of the Republic Armenia, the Prime Minister of the Republic Armenia, and the Minister of Foreign Affairs of the Republic Armenia shall have the right to conduct negotiations and to sign international treaties of the Republic Armenia without special powers.

The heads of Republic agencies of State administration and departments of the Republic Armenia shall within the limits of their powers have the right to conduct negotiations and to sign international interdepartmental treaties of the Republic Armenia without special powers.

Article 6 Special powers for conducting negotiations in order to conclude international treaties of the Republic Armenia shall be issued by:

– the President of the Republic Armenia: with respect to treaties to be concluded in the name of the Republic Armenia;

– the Government of the Republic Armenia: with respect to treaties to be concluded in the name of the Government of the Republic Armenia;

– respective Republic agency of State administration or department of the Republic Armenia: with respect to treaties to be concluded in the name of the Republic agency of State administration or department of the Republic Armenia.

Article 7 Special powers for the signature of international treaties of the Republic Armenia shall be issued by:

– the President of the Republic Armenia: with respect to treaties to be concluded in the name of the Republic Armenia;

– the Government of the Republic Armenia: with respect to treaties to be concluded in the name of the Government of the Republic Armenia;

– respective Republic agency of State administration or department of the Republic Armenia: with respect to treaties to be concluded in the name of the Republic agency of State administration or department of the Republic Armenia.

Chapter III Ratification of International Treaties of Republic Armenia

Article 8 International treaties of the Republic Armenia shall be ratified by the Supreme Soviet of the Republic Armenia.

Article 9 Treaties concerning cooperation and mutual assistance; defence, mutual renunciation of the use or threat of force; territorial delimitation; peace; regulation of trade; relating to international organizations; imposing obligations on finances of the State; treaties concerning a change of provisions of law relating to the status of the individual shall be subject to ratification.

International treaties of the Republic Armenia during the conclusion of which the parties have stipulated the subsequent ratification thereof also shall be subject to ratification.

The Supreme Soviet of the Republic Armenia may render a decision concerning the necessity of ratification of other international treaties of the Republic Armenia.

Article 10 International treaties of the Republic Armenia shall be submitted for ratification of the Supreme Soviet of the Republic Armenia by:

– to be concluded in the name of the Republic Armenia: the President of the Republic Armenia;

– to be concluded in the name of the Government of the Republic Armenia and Republic agencies of State administration and departments of the Republic Armenia: the Government of the Republic Armenia.

Article 11 The Supreme Soviet of the Republic Armenia shall consider an international treaty submitted for ratification by taking into account the opinion of the permanent commission for questions of foreign relations of the Supreme Soviet of the Republic Armenia. The Supreme Soviet of the Republic Armenia shall adopt a decree concerning ratification of an international treaty of the Supreme Soviet.

On the basis of a decree adopted by the Supreme Soviet of the Republic Armenia concerning the ratification of an international treaty of the

Republic Armenia, the President of the Republic Armenia shall sign the instrument of ratification, which shall be affixed with the State seal of the Republic Armenia and the signature of the Minister of Foreign Affairs of the Republic Armenia.

An international treaty not ratified by the Supreme Soviet of the Republic Armenia may be submitted for a second ratification in compliance with the entire procedure for the submission of a document and the consideration thereof in full. An international treaty not ratified by the Supreme Soviet of the Republic Armenia after a second submission and nonratification shall not be subject to further consideration and ratification by the Supreme Soviet unless the Supreme Soviet adopts a decision otherwise.

Article 12 The exchange of instruments of ratification for international treaties of the Republic Armenia and the giving thereof for keeping to depositaries shall be done by the Ministry of Foreign Affairs of the Republic Armenia either on its behalf by the diplomatic representation of the Republic Armenia or by the representation of the Republic Armenia attached to an international organization, or by a person specially empowered by the President of the Republic Armenia.

International treaties ratified by the Supreme Soviet of the Republic Armenia shall enter into force from the moment of the exchange of instruments of ratification unless another procedure has been established by the treaty.

Article 13 International treaties of the Republic Armenia not subject to ratification but the confirmation of which is provided for shall enter into force after confirmation by the President of the Republic Armenia or by the Government of the Republic Armenia.

The procedure for the confirmation of international interdepartmental treaties of such a character shall be established by the Government of the Republic Armenia.

Article 14 Decisions concerning the accession of the Republic Armenia to international treaties shall be adopted by:

– the Supreme Soviet of the Republic Armenia: upon the submission of the President of the Republic Armenia – with respect to treaties subject to ratification;

– the President of the Republic Armenia: with respect to those treaties not subject to ratification, accession to which is in the name of the Republic Armenia;

– the Government of the Republic Armenia: with respect to intergovernmental and interdepartmental treaties not subject to ratification.

Chapter IV Performance of International Treaties of Republic Armenia

Article 15 International treaties of the Republic Armenia shall be subject to undeviating performance by the Republic Armenia. In the event an international treaty of the Republic Armenia is contrary to legislation of the Republic Armenia, the legal norm established by the international treaty shall be given priority.

Article 16 The President of the Republic Armenia and the Government of the Republic Armenia shall effectuate measures relating to ensuring the performance of international treaties of the Republic Armenia.

Article 17 Republic agencies of State administration, departments, and other State agencies of the Republic Armenia within whose competence are questions regulated by international treaties of the Republic Armenia shall ensure the fulfilment of obligations of the Republic Armenia with regard to treaties, and watch over the effectuation of rights of the Republic Armenia and the fulfilment by other Contracting Parties of the obligations arising from these treaties.

General supervision over the performance of international treaties of the Republic Armenia shall be effectuated by the Ministry of Foreign Affairs of the Republic Armenia.

Article 18 In the event of a violation of obligations provided for by an international treaty of the Republic Armenia by other participants of the treaty, the Ministry of Foreign Affairs, Republic and other agencies of State administration and departments of the Republic Armenia shall, by agreement with the Government of the Republic Armenia, submit to the President of the Republic Armenia proposals concerning the effectuation of necessary measures.

In the event of a material violation of obligations provided for by an international treaty of the Republic Armenia by the other participants thereof, and also in other instances provided for by norms of international law, a treaty may be declared to be invalid in the procedure established by Articles 22–26 of the present Law.

Chapter V Publication, Registration, and Giving for Keeping of International Treaties of Republic Armenia

Article 19 Inter-State and intergovernmental treaties of the Republic Armenia which have entered into force shall upon the recommendation of the Ministry of Foreign Affairs of the Republic Armenia be published respectively in the *Ведомости Верховного Совета Республики Армения* and the *Сборник постановлений Правительства Республики Армения.*

Article 20 The originals of international treaties of the Republic Armenia shall within a two-week period after the signature thereof be handed over for keeping to the Ministry of Foreign Affairs of the Republic Armenia unless provided otherwise by the treaty. The Ministry of Foreign Affairs of the Republic Armenia shall send copies of the treaties to the permanent commission for questions of foreign relations of the Supreme Soviet of the Republic Armenia and respective Republic agencies of State administration and departments of the Republic Armenia.

Article 21 International treaties of the Republic Armenia shall be registered in the Secretariat of the United Nations by the Ministry of Foreign Affairs of Republic Armenia.

The procedure for the registration of international interdepartmental treaties of the Republic Armenia shall be established by the Government of the Republic Armenia.

Chapter VI Denunciation of International Treaties of Republic Armenia

Article 22 Proposals concerning the necessity to denounce international treaties of the Republic Armenia and the substantiating documents shall be submitted to the President of the Republic Armenia by the Ministry of Foreign Affairs of the Republic Armenia by agreement with the Government of the Republic Armenia.

Article 23 Proposals concerning the denunciation of international treaties of the Republic Armenia shall be submitted to the Supreme Soviet of the Republic Armenia by the President of the Republic Armenia.

Article 24 International treaties of the Republic Armenia concluded in the name of the Republic Armenia, and also ratified or confirmed international treaties, shall be denounced by the Supreme Soviet of the Republic Armenia.

The Supreme Soviet of the Republic Armenia shall adopt a decree concerning the denunciation of international treaties.

In the event of the failure of the Supreme Soviet of the Republic Armenia to denounce an international treaty of the Republic Armenia, the President of the Republic Armenia shall have the right to submit his proposal anew to the Supreme Soviet of the Republic Armenia.

Article 25 The permanent commission for questions of foreign relations of the Supreme Soviet of the Republic Armenia shall consider in advance an international treaty submitted for denunciation to the Supreme Soviet of the Republic Armenia and the proposal concerning denunciation and give a respective opinion.

Article 26 International treaties of the Republic Armenia concluded in the name of the Government of the Republic Armenia and not regulated by Article 24 of the present Law shall be denounced by the President of the Republic Armenia, upon the recommendation of the Government.

The procedure for the denunciation of international interdepartmental treaties of the Republic Armenia shall be established by the Government of the Republic Armenia.

AZERBAIDZHAN

Law on the Procedure for the Conclusion, Performance, and Denunciation of International Treaties of the Azerbaidzhan Republic

[Signed 13 June 1995, No. 1057]

Chapter I General Provisions

Article 1 Tasks of the Law

The present Law in accordance with the Constitution of the Azerbaidzhan Republic and generally-recognized principles and norms of international law shall determine the procedure for the conclusion, performance, and denunciation of all written international treaties of the Azerbaidzhan Republic irrespective of their name (treaty, agreement, convention, covenant, protocol, exchange of letters or notes, and other names of international treaties).

Irrespective of the name, an international treaty of the Azerbaidzhan Republic shall be an agreement of the Azerbaidzhan Republic with foreign States and international organizations concluded in written form in the procedure determined by the present Law.

Article 2 International Treaties of Azerbaidzhan Republic

International treaties of the Azerbaidzhan Republic shall be concluded with foreign States and international organizations in the name of:

– the Azerbaidzhan Republic;

– the Government of the Azerbaidzhan Republic;

– the ministries, State committees, and departments of the Azerbaidzhan Republic.

The procedure for the conclusion, execution, and denunciation of international treaties of the Azerbaidzhan Republic of an interdepartmental character shall be established by the President of the Azerbaidzhan Republic.

Article 3 Means of Expression of Consent to Bindingness of International Treaties for Azerbaidzhan Republic

Consent to the bindingness for it of international treaties of the Azerbaidzhan Republic shall be expressed by means of the signature of the treaty, exchange of documents comprising the treaty, ratification thereof, acceptance, confirmation, accession thereto, and any other means stipulated by the contracting parties.

Chapter II Conclusion of International Treaties of Azerbaidzhan Republic

Article 4 Conclusion of International Treaties of Azerbaidzhan Republic

Proposals concerning the conclusion of international treaties of the Azerbaidzhan Republic shall be submitted to the President of the Azerbaidzhan Republic by the Cabinet of Ministers and the Ministry of Foreign Affairs of the Azerbaidzhan Republic.

Ministries, State committees, and departments of the Azerbaidzhan Republic shall submit to the Cabinet of Ministers of the Azerbaidzhan Republic proposals concerning the conclusion of international treaties of the Azerbaidzhan Republic jointly with the Ministry of Foreign Affairs or by agreement with it in the established procedure.

The Cabinet of Ministers of the Azerbaidzhan Republic shall consider the proposals submitted and submit them with a respective opinion to the President of the Azerbaidzhan Republic.

When submitting a proposal concerning the conclusion of an international treaty of the Azerbaidzhan Republic, the need for the conclusion thereof shall be substantiated, its proposed political, economic, legal, material, and financial consequences shall be determined, the executors of the international treaty shall be indicated, and the composition of the delegation or representative of the Azerbaidzhan Republic shall be proposed to conduct negotiations, adopt the text of the international treaty, or establish the conformity thereof to the original.

Proposals concerning the conclusion of international treaties of the

Azerbaidzhan Republic establishing other rules than those which are contained in legislation of the Azerbaidzhan Republic shall be submitted to the President of the Azerbaidzhan Republic by agreement with the Ministry of Justice of the Azerbaidzhan Republic and with the respective expert opinion appended.

Article 5 Adoption of Decisions Concerning Conducting of International Negotiations and Signature of International Treaties of Azerbaidzhan Republic

Decisions concerning the conducting of international negotiations and the signature of international treaties of the Azerbaidzhan Republic shall be adopted with respect to:

(1) treaties to be concluded in the name of the Azerbaidzhan Republic – by the President of the Azerbaidzhan Republic;

(2) treaties to be concluded in the name of the Government of the Azerbaidzhan Republic – by the President of the Azerbaidzhan Republic or upon the proposal of the Cabinet of Ministers of the Azerbaidzhan Republic or Ministry of Foreign Affairs of the Azerbaidzhan Republic by the President of the Azerbaidzhan Republic.

Article 6 Powers to Conduct International Negotiations and for Signature of International Treaties of Azerbaidzhan Republic

The powers to conduct international negotiations and for the signature of international treaties of the Azerbaidzhan Republic shall be issued with respect to treaties:

(1) to be concluded in the name of the Azerbaidzhan Republic – by the President of the Azerbaidzhan Republic;

(2) to be concluded in the name of the Government of the Azerbaidzhan Republic – by the President of the Azerbaidzhan Republic.

Article 7 Conducting of International Negotiations and Signature of International Treaties of Azerbaidzhan Republic without Special Powers

The President of the Azerbaidzhan Republic shall have the right to conduct negotiations with respect to all international treaties of the

Azerbaidzhan Republic and to sign them, and the Prime Minister of the Azerbaidzhan Republic and the Minister of Foreign Affairs of the Azerbaidzhan Republic – with respect to other international treaties of the Azerbaidzhan Republic, except for those specified in Article 8, paragraph one, of the present Law.

Powers to conduct negotiations with respect to international treaties of the Azerbaidzhan Republic specified in Article 8, paragraph two, of the present Law, and to sign them, the President of the Azerbaidzhan Republic may grant to the Prime Minister of the Azerbaidzhan Republic, Minister of Foreign Affairs of the Azerbaidzhan Republic, and also to the heads of the respective central agencies of executive power. In so doing the subject of negotiations and necessary actions relating to the performance thereof, shall be specified.

The head of a diplomatic representation of the Azerbaidzhan Republic in a foreign State or the head of a representation of the Azerbaidzhan Republic at an international conference, attached to an international organization, or one of the organs thereof shall have the right to conduct negotiations without special powers concerning the conclusion of international treaties of the Azerbaidzhan Republic respectively with the receiving State or within the framework of the particular conference, organization, or one of the organs thereof.

Article 8 Ratification of International Treaties of Azerbaidzhan Republic

In accordance with the Constitution of the Azerbaidzhan Republic, international treaties of the Azerbaidzhan Republic shall be ratified by the Supreme Soviet of the Azerbaidzhan Republic. International treaties of the Azerbaidzhan Republic must be submitted within a month to the Supreme Soviet of the Azerbaidzhan Republic for ratification.

There shall be relegated to international treaties of the Azerbaidzhan Republic subject to ratification:

(1) treaties concerning friendship, cooperation, and mutual assistance (or solidarity) and treaties establishing principles of inter-State relations;
(2) peace treaties;
(3) treaties of the Azerbaidzhan Republic with other States in regard to territorial and frontier questions and questions of the separation or alienation of territories and clarification of boundaries;
(4) treaties of a defence character and with regard to military cooperation;
(5) treaties concerning legal assistance;

(6) treaties concerning the entry of the Azerbaidzhan Republic into international organizations of a universal and regional character;
(7) multilateral and long-term economic treaties;
(8) treaties establishing other rules than those which are contained in laws of the Azerbaidzhan Republic;
(9) treaties whose ratification is provided for by laws or international treaties of the Azerbaidzhan Republic;
(10) treaties with regard to questions of receiving credits;
(11) treaties concerning participation in inter-State unions and other inter-State associations;
(12) treaties concerning the despatch of a contingent of the Armed Forces of the Azerbaidzhan Republic to other countries or admittance of a contingent of armed forces of other States to the territory of the Azerbaidzhan Republic.

Other international treaties of the Azerbaidzhan Republic also may be submitted by decision of the President of the Azerbaidzhan Republic for ratification by the Supreme Soviet of the Azerbaidzhan Republic.

Article 9 Proposals Concerning Approval and Ratification of International Treaties of Azerbaidzhan Republic

Proposals concerning approval by the President of the Azerbaidzhan Republic of international treaties of the Azerbaidzhan Republic and the ratification thereof shall be submitted by the Ministry of Foreign Affairs of the Azerbaidzhan Republic autonomously or jointly or by agreement with other ministries, State committees, and departments of the Azerbaidzhan Republic.

The President of the Azerbaidzhan Republic shall consider the said proposals and adopt a respective decision.

The Supreme Soviet of the Azerbaidzhan Republic may decide the question of the ratification of any international treaty with the participation of the Azerbaidzhan Republic which is not subject to ratification.

Article 10 Preliminary Consideration of Proposals Concerning Ratification of International Treaties of Azerbaidzhan Republic

The respective commissions of the Supreme Soviet of the Azerbaidzhan Republic shall consider preliminarily international treaties of the

Azerbaidzhan Republic submitted by the President of the Azerbaidzhan Republic for ratification to the Supreme Soviet and give opinions.

Article 11 Adoption of Decisions Concerning Ratification of International Treaties of Azerbaidzhan Republic

The Supreme Soviet of the Azerbaidzhan Republic shall consider international treaties of the Azerbaidzhan Republic submitted by the President of the Azerbaidzhan Republic for ratification and render respective decisions.

International treaties submitted for ratification must be in the State language. In the absence of official texts in the State language international treaties must be translated into the State language with a document appended confirming the conformity of the translation to the official text.

On the basis of a decree of the Supreme Soviet of the Azerbaidzhan Republic concerning the ratification of international treaties of the Azerbaidzhan Republic the President of the Azerbaidzhan Republic shall sign the instrument of ratification.

Article 12 Exchange of Instruments of Ratification and Handing Them Over for Keeping

Instruments of ratification shall be exchanged and the instruments concerning ratification of international treaties of the Azerbaidzhan Republic shall be handed over for keeping to depositaries by the Ministry of Foreign Affairs of the Azerbaidzhan Republic or on its behalf by the diplomatic representation of the Azerbaidzhan Republic in the respective State or by the representation of the Azerbaidzhan Republic at an international conference, attached to an international organization, or one of the organs thereof.

Article 13 Confirmation or Adoption of International Treaties of Azerbaidzhan Republic Not Subject to Ratification

International treaties of the Azerbaidzhan Republic which are not subject to ratification shall be confirmed or adopted with respect to:

(1) treaties to be concluded in the name of the Azerbaidzhan Republic – by the President of the Azerbaidzhan Republic;
(2) treaties to be concluded in the name of the Government of the Azerbaidzhan Republic – by the President of the Azerbaidzhan Republic or on his behalf by the Cabinet of Ministers of the Azerbaidzhan Republic or Ministry of Foreign Affairs of the Azerbaidzhan Republic.

The President of the Azerbaidzhan Republic, Cabinet of Ministers of the Azerbaidzhan Republic, and Ministry of Foreign Affairs of the Azerbaidzhan Republic shall inform the Supreme Soviet of the Azerbaidzhan Republic concerning the conclusion of international treaties of the Azerbaidzhan Republic which are not subject to ratification.

Article 14 Accession to International Treaties

Decisions concerning accession of the Azerbaidzhan Republic to international treaties shall be adopted with respect to:
(1) treaties subject to ratification – by the Supreme Soviet of the Azerbaidzhan Republic;
(2) treaties not subject to ratification, the accession to which is in the name of the Azerbaidzhan Republic – by the President of the Azerbaidzhan Republic;
(3) treaties not subject to ratification, the accession to which is in the name of the Government of the Azerbaidzhan Republic – by the President of the Azerbaidzhan Republic or by his decision by the Cabinet of Ministers of the Azerbaidzhan Republic or Ministry of Foreign Affairs of the Azerbaidzhan Republic.

Chapter III Performance of International Treaties of Azerbaidzhan Republic

Article 15 Compliance with International Treaties of Azerbaidzhan Republic

International treaties of the Azerbaidzhan Republic shall be subject to undeviating compliance by the Azerbaidzhan Republic in accordance with the norms of international law.

In accordance with the principle of compliance in good faith with international treaties the Azerbaidzhan Republic shall make efforts so that other participants of bilateral and multilateral international treaties in which the Azerbaidzhan Republic participates have fulfilled their obligations arising from these treaties.

Article 16 Ensuring Fulfilment of International Treaties of Azerbaidzhan Republic

The President of the Azerbaidzhan Republic shall ensure the fulfilment of international treaties of the Azerbaidzhan Republic.

Article 17 Fulfilment of Obligation Under International Treaties of Azerbaidzhan Republic

The Cabinet of Ministers, ministries, State committees, departments, and other State agencies of the Azerbaidzhan Republic within whose competence are questions regulated by international treaties of the Azerbaidzhan Republic shall ensure the fulfilment of obligations accepted under treaties of the Azerbaidzhan Republic.

The Ministry of Foreign Affairs of the Azerbaidzhan Republic regularly shall inform the President of the Azerbaidzhan Republic concerning the fulfilment of obligations under international treaties both by the Azerbaidzhan Republic and also by other participants of the said treaties.

Article 18 General Observation Over Performance of International Treaties of Azerbaidzhan Republic

General observation over the performance of international treaties of the Azerbaidzhan Republic shall be effectuated by the Ministry of Foreign Affairs of the Azerbaidzhan Republic.

Article 19 Measures to be Adopted in Event of Violation of International Treaty of Azerbaidzhan Republic by Other Participants Thereof

In the event of a violation of obligations under an international treaty of the Azerbaidzhan Republic by other participants thereof the Cabinet of

Ministers of the Azerbaidzhan Republic, Ministry of Foreign Affairs, and other ministries, State committees, and departments of the Azerbaidzhan Republic jointly or by agreement with the Ministry of Foreign Affairs shall submit to the President of the Azerbaidzhan Republic proposals concerning the adoption of necessary measures in accordance with norms of international law.

In the event of a material violation of an international treaty of the Azerbaidzhan Republic by other participants thereof, and also in other instances provided for by norms of international law, such treaty shall be terminated in the procedure established by Articles 21–24 of the present Law.

Article 20 Proposals Concerning Making of Changes in Legislation of Azerbaidzhan Republic in Connection with Conclusion of International Treaties of Azerbaidzhan Republic

In instances when for the purposes of the fulfilment of international treaties of the Azerbaidzhan Republic the adoption of laws of the Azerbaidzhan Republic and decrees of the Supreme Soviet of the Azerbaidzhan Republic and the issuance of edicts and regulations of the President of the Azerbaidzhan Republic and decrees and regulations of the Cabinet of Ministers of the Azerbaidzhan Republic, the interested ministries, State committees, and departments by agreement with the Ministry of Justice of the Azerbaidzhan Republic shall submit proposals in the procedure established by legislation concerning the adoption of the appropriate act.

Chapter IV Denunciation of International Treaties of Azerbaidzhan Republic

Article 21 Proposals Concerning Denunciation of International Treaties of Azerbaidzhan Republic

Proposals concerning the denunciation of international treaties of the Azerbaidzhan Republic shall be submitted in the established procedure by the Cabinet of Ministers of the Azerbaidzhan Republic, and also by the Ministry of Foreign Affairs of the Azerbaidzhan Republic, to the President of the Azerbaidzhan Republic autonomously or jointly or by agreement with other ministries, State committees, and departments.

Article 22 Denunciation of International Treaties of Azerbaidzhan Republic by Supreme Soviet of Azerbaidzhan Republic

International treaties of the Azerbaidzhan Republic concluded and ratified in the name of the Azerbaidzhan Republic shall be denounced by the Supreme Soviet of the Azerbaidzhan Republic upon the proposal of the President of the Azerbaidzhan Republic.

International treaties of the Azerbaidzhan Republic shall be denounced in the procedure specified in paragraph one of the present Article, and also in the instances provided for by Article 8, paragraphs two and three, of the present Law.

Article 23 Preliminary Consideration of Proposals Concerning Denunciation of International Treaties of Azerbaidzhan Republic

The respective commissions of the Supreme Soviet of the Azerbaidzhan Republic shall consider in advance proposals concerning the denunciation of international treaties of the Azerbaidzhan Republic to be denounced in accordance with Article 22 of the present Law and give opinions.

Article 24 Denunciation of International Treaties of Azerbaidzhan Republic by President of Azerbaidzhan Republic

Denunciation of international treaties of the Azerbaidzhan Republic concluded in the name of the Azerbaidzhan Republic and in the name of the Government of the Azerbaidzhan Republic and not subject to ratification shall be by the President of the Azerbaidzhan Republic.

Chapter V Concluding Provisions

Article 25 Publication of International Treaties of Azerbaidzhan Republic

International treaties of the Azerbaidzhan Republic ratified, and also confirmed or accepted in accordance with the present Law, or international treaties to which the Azerbaidzhan Republic has acceded, shall be published upon the recommendation of the Ministry of Foreign Affairs of the Azerbaidzhan Republic in the *Ведомости Верховного Совета Азербайджанской Республики* and in the official State newspaper of the Azerbaidzhan Republic.

International treaties of the Azerbaidzhan Republic whose authentic texts have been drawn up in foreign languages shall be published in one of these languages with an official translation into the Azerbaidzhan language.

Article 26 Official Registration of International Treaties of Azerbaidzhan Republic

All international treaties of the Azerbaidzhan Republic shall be registered by the Ministry of Foreign Affairs of the Azerbaidzhan Republic in the register of international treaties of the Azerbaidzhan Republic.

The registration of all international treaties of the Azerbaidzhan Republic in the Secretariat of the United Nations or in respective organs of other international organizations shall be effectuated by the Ministry of Foreign Affairs of the Azerbaidzhan Republic.

BELARUS

Law on International Treaties of the Republic Belarus

[Adopted by the Supreme Soviet of the Republic Belarus, 23 October 1991, as amended 26 November 1992 and 8 July 1998. *Ведомости Верховного Совета Белорусской ССР* (1991), no. 32, item 584; *Ведомости Национального собрания Республики Беларусь* (1992), no. 32, item 519; (1998), no. 29-30, item 469]

The Republic Belarus shall conclude and perform international treaties in accordance with the Constitution and other legislation of the Republic Belarus, and also with generally-recognized principles and norms of international law, including the Vienna Convention on the Law of Treaties of 23 May 1969.

The conclusion of international treaties which are contrary to the Constitution of the Republic Belarus shall not be permitted.

Article 1 Sphere of Application of Present Law

The present Law shall establish the procedure for the conclusion, performance, and termination of the operation of international treaties of the Republic Belarus applicable with respect to all inter-State and intergovernmental treaties of the Republic Belarus.

The procedure for the conclusion, performance, and termination of the operation of international treaties of the Republic Belarus of an interdepartmental character concluded by State agencies of the Republic Belarus, except those specified in paragraph three of the present article, shall be determined by the President of the Republic Belarus.

The procedure for the conclusion, performance, and termination of the operation of international treaties of the Republic Belarus of an interdepartmental character concluded by Republic agencies of State administration subordinate to the Council of Ministers of the Republic Belarus shall be determined by the Council of Ministers of the Republic Belarus.

Procedural questions of the conclusion of international treaties of the Republic Belarus shall be determined by the President of the Republic Belarus.

Article 2 Basic Terms Used in Present Law

The following terms and their definitions shall be used in the present Law:

international treaty of Republic Belarus – inter-State or intergovernmental treaty concluded in written form with a foreign State or States, with the Government of a foreign State or governments of foreign States, or with an international organization or international organizations which are regulated by international law irrespective of whether the treaty is contained in one document or in several related documents, and also irrespective of the specific name thereof and means of conclusion (treaty, agreement, convention, decision, covenant, protocol, exchange of letters or notes, and others);

inter-State treaty of the Republic Belarus – international treaty concluded in the name of the Republic Belarus with a foreign State or States or with an international organization or international organizations;

intergovernmental treaty of Republic Belarus – international treaty concluded in the name of the Council of Ministers of the Republic Belarus with the government of a foreign State or governments of foreign States or with an international organization or international organizations;

bilateral international treaty – international treaty concluded by two contracting parties;

multilateral international treaty – international treaty concluded by several contracting parties;

conclusion of international treaty of Republic Belarus – sequence of stages and legal actions with regard to the formation of a treaty (putting forward the treaty initiative, conducting negotiations, drawing up and adopting the text of the treaty, establishment of authenticity thereof, signature, expression of consent to obligatoriness of treaty);

signature – stage of conclusion of treaty or means of expression of consent of Republic Belarus to obligatoriness of international treaty for it;

powers – document emanating from the President of the Republic Belarus or Council of Ministers of the Republic Belarus and formalized by the Ministry of Foreign Affairs of the Republic Belarus by means of which one or several persons are appointed to represent the Republic Belarus for the purpose of conducting negotiations, signature of the treaty, expression of consent of the Republic Belarus to the obligatoriness of the treaty for it or for the purpose of formalizing any other act relating to the treaty;

reservation – unilateral statement in any formulation and under any name by means of which in accordance with international law the wish is expressed to exclude or change the legal operation of determined provisions of a treaty in their application to the Republic Belarus;

international organization – inter-State (or intergovernmental) organization created for the fulfilment of determined tasks of an international character in accordance with the constitutive act of this organization;

contracting party – the State, government, or international organization which has expressed consent to the obligatoriness of a treaty for it irrespective of whether it has entered into force or not;

participant – State, government, or international organization which has expressed consent to the obligatoriness of a treaty for it and for which the treaty is in force;

depositary – State, government, international organization or chief executive official thereof to whom the original of an international treaty is handed over for keeping and who fulfils with respect to this treaty the functions provided for by international law.

Article 3 Expression of Consent of Republic Belarus to Bindingness of International Treaty for It

The consent of the Republic Belarus to the bindingness of an international treaty for it may be expressed by means of signature of the treaty, exchange of documents, letters, or notes forming the treaty, ratification of the treaty, confirmation of the treaty, accession to the treaty, or by any other means which the contracting parties have stipulated.

The decision concerning consent to the bindingness for the Republic Belarus of international treaties shall be adopted by the President of the Republic Belarus, National Assembly of the Republic Belarus, and

Council of Ministers of the Republic Belarus in accordance with their competence determined by the Constitution of the Republic Belarus, the present Law, other laws of the Republic Belarus, and decrees and edicts of the President of the Republic Belarus.

Article 4 Decisions Concerning Conducting of Negotiations With Regard to Draft International Treaties of Republic Belarus

Proposals concerning the conducting of negotiations with regard to draft international treaties of the Republic Belarus shall by agreement with the Ministry of Foreign Affairs of the Republic Belarus and the Ministry of Justice of the Republic Belarus, be submitted to the Council of Ministers of the Republic Belarus by republic agencies of State administration and other State agencies of the Republic Belarus with regard to questions within their competence.

Proposals concerning the conducting of negotiations must contain:

the draft international treaty or basic provisions of the position in negotiations;

the draft of the respective decision of the President of the Republic Belarus or Council of Ministers of the Republic Belarus;

the substantiation of the advisability of concluding the international treaty;

the opinion of the respective State agencies of the Republic Belarus within whose competence the questions contained in the draft international treaty are relegated;

the opinion of the Ministry of Foreign Affairs of the Republic Belarus concerning the conformity of the draft international treaty to international obligations of the Republic Belarus;

the opinion of the Ministry of Justice of the Republic Belarus concerning the conformity of the draft international treaty to the Constitution and other legislation of the Republic Belarus;

the list of norms of laws of the Republic Belarus, acts of the President of the Republic Belarus, and Government of the Republic Belarus subject to change, addition, repeal, or adoption in connection with the conclusion of the international treaty;

the proposals concerning the working out of acts of legislation of the Republic Belarus necessary for the realization of the international treaty;

the list of persons who have taken part in working out the draft international treaty and proposed for participation in the negotiation process;

the financial–economic substantiation of the expenditures proposed which are connected with the realization of the international treaty.

The Council of Ministers of the Republic Belarus shall consider the proposals submitted and adopt a decision concerning the conducting of negotiations with regard to draft intergovernmental treaties of the Republic Belarus, and shall submit proposals to the President of the Republic Belarus with regard to draft international treaties, who shall adopt a decision concerning the conducting of negotiations.

Article 5 Decision Concerning Signature of International Treaties of Republic Belarus

Proposals concerning the signature of international treaties of the Republic Belarus shall by agreement with the Ministry of Foreign Affairs of the Republic Belarus and the Ministry of Justice of the Republic Belarus be submitted to the Council of Ministers of the Republic Belarus by republic agencies of State administration and other State agencies of the Republic Belarus.

Proposals concerning the signature of international treaties of the Republic Belarus must contain materials provided for by Article 4, paragraph two, of the present Law.

Decisions concerning the signature of international treaties of the Republic Belarus shall be adopted with respect to:

inter-State treaties of the Republic Belarus – by the President of the Republic Belarus;

intergovernmental treaties of the Republic Belarus – by the Council of Ministers of the Republic Belarus.

Article 6 Powers for Conducting of Negotiations and for Signature of International Treaties of Republic Belarus

Powers for the conducting of negotiations and signature of international treaties of the Republic Belarus shall be issued with respect to:

inter-State treaties of the Republic Belarus – by the President of the Republic Belarus;

intergovernmental treaties of the Republic Belarus – by the Council of Ministers of the Republic Belarus.

Powers for the conducting of negotiations and signature of international treaties shall be formalized by the Ministry of Foreign Affairs of the Republic Belarus for a specific person(s).

Article 7 Submission of Proposals With Regard to Fulfilment of Intra-State Procedures

After the signature of an international treaty of the Republic Belarus, except for that entering into force from the day of signature, proposals with regard to the fulfilment of intra-State procedures necessary for the expression of consent of the Republic Belarus to the obligatoriness of an international treaty for it, by agreement with the Ministry of Foreign Affairs of the Republic Belarus and the Ministry of Justice of the Republic Belarus shall be submitted in the established procedure to the Council of Ministers of the Republic Belarus by republic agencies of State administration and other State agencies of the Republic Belarus within whose competence are the questions regulated by this treaty.

Article 8 International Treaties of Republic Belarus Subject to Ratification

International treaties of the Republic Belarus subject to ratification by the National Assembly of the Republic Belarus shall be:

during the signature of which the parties have agreed about ratification;

establishing other rules than those which are contained in laws of the Republic Belarus, decrets, and edicts of the President of the Republic Belarus;

the subject of which are questions relegated only to the sphere of legislative regulation but are not regulated by laws of the Republic Belarus, decrets, and edicts of the President of the Republic Belarus;

concerning the territorial delimitation of the Republic Belarus with other States;

concerning the participation of the Republic Belarus in inter-State formations.

Article 9 Ratification of International Treaties of Republic Belarus

Proposals relative to the ratification of an international treaty of the Republic Belarus by agreement with the Ministry of Foreign Affairs of the Republic Belarus shall be submitted to the Council of Ministers of the Republic Belarus within a three-month period from the day of signature of the international treaty by republic agencies of State administration and by other State agencies of the Republic Belarus within whose competence are the questions regulated by this treaty.

Proposals concerning the ratification of an international treaty of the Republic Belarus must contain:

the draft law on ratification of the international treaty of the Republic Belarus;

a copy of the international treaty of the Republic Belarus;

a substantiation of the need for ratification of the international treaty of the Republic Belarus;

the opinion of the Ministry of Justice of the Republic Belarus concerning the conformity of the international treaty of the Republic Belarus to the Constitution and other legislation of the Republic Belarus;

a list of norms of laws of the Republic Belarus, acts of the President of the Republic Belarus and Government of the Republic Belarus subject to change, addition, repeal, or adoption for the purposes of performance of the international treaty of the Republic Belarus;

other opinions of interested State agencies;

a financial–economic substantiation of the proposed expenditures in connection with the realization of the international treaty of the Republic Belarus submitted for ratification;

a list of persons who took part in working out this international treaty.

The Council of Ministers of the Republic Belarus shall consider the proposals received and submit the inter-State treaties of the Republic Belarus to the President of the Republic Belarus, and intergovernmental treaties of the Republic Belarus for ratification to the National Assembly of the Republic Belarus.

The President of the Republic Belarus or on his behalf the Council of Ministers of the Republic Belarus shall submit inter-State treaties of the Republic Belarus for ratification to the National Assembly of the Republic Belarus.

The ratification of an international treaty of the Republic Belarus shall be effectuated in the form of a law of the Republic Belarus.

Article 10 Confirmation of International Treaties of Republic Belarus

International treaties of the Republic Belarus not subject to ratification and not entering into force from the day of signature shall be subject to confirmation. Inter-State treaties of the Republic Belarus shall be confirmed by the President of the Republic Belarus, and intergovernmental treaties of the Republic Belarus, by the Council of Ministers of the Republic Belarus.

Proposals relative to the confirmation of an international treaty of the Republic Belarus by agreement with the Ministry of Foreign Affairs of the Republic Belarus shall be submitted to the Council of Ministers within a three-month period from the day of signature thereof by republic agencies of State administration and other State agencies of the Republic Belarus within whose competence are the questions regulated by this treaty.

Proposals concerning the confirmation of an international treaty of the Republic Belarus must contain:

- the draft decision concerning confirmation of the international treaty of the Republic Belarus;
- a copy of the international treaty of the Republic Belarus;
- a substantiation of the need for confirmation of the international treaty of the Republic Belarus;
- the opinion of the Ministry of Justice of the Republic Belarus concerning the conformity of the international treaty of the Republic Belarus to the Constitution and other legislation of the Republic Belarus;
- a list of norms of laws of the Republic Belarus, acts of the President of the Republic Belarus and Government of the Republic Belarus subject to change, addition, repeal, or adoption for the purposes of performance of the international treaty of the Republic Belarus;
- other opinions of interested State agencies, remarks, and proposals with regard to the particular international treaty, if there are any;
- a financial–economic substantiation of the proposed expenditures in connection with the realization of the international treaty of the Republic Belarus submitted for confirmation;
- a list of persons who took part in working out this international treaty.

Article 11 Accession of Republic Belarus to International Treaties

The Republic Belarus may accede to international treaties in accordance with the conditions of the international treaty, and also in other instances provided for by international law.

Proposals concerning accession of the Republic Belarus to international treaties shall be submitted in the procedure provided for by Article 4 of the present Law.

Decisions concerning the accession of the Republic Belarus to international treaties shall be adopted with respect to:

inter-State and intergovernmental treaties subject to ratification – by the National Assembly of the Republic Belarus in the form of a law of the Republic Belarus concerning accession to the international treaty;

inter-State treaties not subject to ratification – by the President of the Republic Belarus in the form of an edict of the President of the Republic Belarus;

intergovernmental treaties not subject to ratification – by the Council of Ministers of the Republic Belarus in the form of a decree of the Council of Ministers of the Republic Belarus.

Article 12 Entry into Force of International Treaties of Republic Belarus

International treaties shall enter into force for the Republic Belarus after the expression of consent of the Republic Belarus to the bindingness for it of the international treaty in accordance with the present Law in the procedure and within the periods provided for in the treaty or otherwise agreed between the Contracting Parties.

Article 13 Reservations to International Treaties of Republic Belarus

When signing, ratifying, and confirming international treaties of the Republic Belarus or of acceding to them reservations may be made according to the conditions of the treaty and respective norms of international law.

Unless provided otherwise by an international treaty of the Republic Belarus, reservations may be removed at any time in the same procedure by which they were made.

The adoption of a reservation to an international treaty of the Republic Belarus made by the other Contracting Party or objection with respect to such reservation shall be effectuated in accordance with the conditions of the treaty itself and the norms of international law.

Article 14 Provisional Application of International Treaty by Republic Belarus

An international treaty or part of an international treaty may before entry into force be applied by the Republic Belarus provisionally if an arrangement concerning this was reached by the parties who have signed the treaty. Provisional application of the treaty or part thereof shall be possible on condition that it as a whole or part thereof does not contain provisions establishing other rules than those which are contained in laws of the Republic Belarus, acts of the President of the Republic Belarus, or provisions not regulated by laws of the Republic Belarus and acts of the President of the Republic Belarus.

The decision concerning the provisional application of an international treaty by the Republic Belarus or part thereof shall be adopted with respect to:

inter-State treaties of the Republic Belarus – by the President of the Republic Belarus;

intergovernmental treaties of the Republic Belarus – by the Council of Ministers of the Republic Belarus.

Unless provided otherwise in an international treaty or the Contracting Parties have not agreed otherwise, provisional application of a treaty or part thereof by the Republic Belarus shall terminate after notification by the Contracting Party(ies) temporarily applying the treaty of the intention of the Republic Belarus not to participate in the treaty.

Article 15 Performance of International Treaties of Republic Belarus

International treaties of the Republic Belarus shall be subject to good-faith performance by the Republic Belarus in accordance with the norms of international law.

Generally-recognized principles of international law and norms of international treaties of the Republic Belarus which have entered into force shall be part of the law operating on the territory of the Republic Belarus.

[paragraph three is omitted for failure to enter into force by reason of objections of the President of the Republic Belarus submitted in accordance with Article 100, paragraph eight, of the 1994 Constitution of the Republic Belarus, as amended]

The Ministry of Foreign Affairs of the Republic Belarus shall effectuate general supervision over the performance of international treaties of the Republic Belarus and render assistance to State agencies of the Republic Belarus within the limits of its competence in the performance of international treaties.

Article 16 Fulfilment of Obligations Under International Treaties of Republic Belarus

The President of the Republic Belarus, National Assembly of the Republic Belarus, and Council of Ministers of the Republic Belarus shall adopt measures to ensure the performance of international treaties of the Republic Belarus by means of adoption of the respective decisions. Such decisions shall, as a rule, contain:

the determination of the State agency (or official) responsible for performance of the international treaty or coordinating performance of the international treaty;

the commission to the competent State agency to make proposals concerning the bringing of legislation of the Republic Belarus into conformity with the international treaty which has entered into force.

Republic agencies of State administration and other State agencies of the Republic Belarus within whose competence are questions regulated by international treaties of the Republic Belarus, ensure the fulfilment of obligations accepted with regard to these treaties of the Republic Belarus, observe the effectuation of the rights belonging to the Republic Belarus which arise from international treaties and over the fulfilment by other participants of the treaties of their obligations.

Article 17 Measures to be Taken in Event of Violation of Obligations With Regard to International Treaty of Republic Belarus

In the event of a violation of obligations under an international treaty of the Republic Belarus by other participants thereof, republic agencies of State administration and other State agencies of the Republic Belarus by agreement with the Ministry of Foreign Affairs of the Republic Belarus shall submit to the Council of Ministers of the Republic Belarus proposals concerning the taking of necessary measures in accordance with the norms of international law.

Article 18 Keeping of Texts of International Treaties of Republic Belarus

The originals of international treaties of the Republic Belarus shall within a month from the day of signature, certified copies thereof, or official translations be transferred for keeping to the Ministry of Foreign Affairs of the Republic Belarus.

Article 19 Effectuation of Functions of Depositary

The Ministry of Foreign Affairs of the Republic Belarus shall effectuate the functions of depositary of multilateral international treaties if in accordance with the conditions of these treaties such functions have been placed on the Republic Belarus or the Government of the Republic Belarus.

Correspondence with agencies of foreign States, international organizations, or the chief executive officials thereof who are performing the functions of depositary of multilateral international treaties shall be effectuated by the Ministry of Foreign Affairs of the Republic Belarus.

Article 20 Publication of International Treaties of Republic Belarus

Ratified international treaties of the Republic Belarus shall be published in the *Ведомости Национального Собрания Республики Беларусь*, and those not subject to ratification and which have entered into force, in an annex to the *Собрание декретов, указов Президента и постановлений Правительства Республики Беларусь.*

Article 21 Registration of International Treaties of Republic Belarus

The registration of international treaties of the Republic Belarus at the Secretariat of the United Nations or in the respective agencies of other international organizations shall be effectuated by the Ministry of Foreign Affairs of the Republic Belarus.

Article 22 Termination or Suspension of Operation of International Treaties of Republic Belarus

Termination, including denunciation, or suspension of the operation of an international treaty of the Republic Belarus shall be effectuated in accordance with the conditions of the treaty itself and norms of international law by the agency within whose competence is the adoption of the decision concerning consent to the bindingness of the international treaty for the Republic Belarus.

Proposals concerning termination, including denunciation, or suspension of the operation of international treaties of the Republic Belarus shall be submitted in the procedure provided for by Article 4 of the present Law.

The President of the Republic Belarus shall consider proposals concerning termination, including denunciation, or suspension of the operation of inter-State treaties of the Republic Belarus, except for those specified in paragraph four of the present Article, and adopt a decision in the form of an edict of the President of the Republic Belarus.

[paragraph four is omitted for failure to enter into force by reason of objections of the President of the Republic Belarus submitted in accordance with Article 100, paragraph eight, of the 1994 Constitution of the Republic Belarus, as amended]

The Council of Ministers of the Republic Belarus shall consider proposals concerning the termination, including denunciation, or suspension of the operation of an intergovernmental treaty of the Republic Belarus, except for those specified in paragraph four of the present Article, and adopt a decision in the form of a decree of the Council of Ministers of the Republic Belarus.

Article 23

[Article 23 is omitted for failure to enter into force by reason of objections of the President of the Republic Belarus submitted in accordance with Article 100, paragraph eight, of the 1994 Constitution of the Republic Belarus, as amended]

Article 24 Consequences of Suspension of Operation of International Treaty of Republic Belarus

The suspension of the operation of an international treaty of the Republic Belarus, unless provided otherwise by this treaty or there is another arrangement with the participant(s), shall relieve the Republic Belarus from the obligation to perform the treaty during the period for which the operation thereof was suspended, and State agencies of the Republic Belarus shall refrain from actions which might obstruct the renewal of the operation of this treaty.

GEORGIA

Law on International Treaties of Georgia

[Adopted 16 October 1997]

Chapter I General Provisions

Article 1 Tasks of the Law

The present Law shall determine the procedure for the conclusion, fulfilment, and termination of the operation of an international treaty of Georgia. An international treaty of Georgia shall be concluded, fulfilled, and terminated in accordance with generally-accepted principles and norms of international law, the Constitution of Georgia, international treaties, and the present Law.

Article 2 Sphere of Operation of Law

1. The present Law shall apply with respect to all international (inter-State, intergovernmental, and interdepartmental character) treaties which are regulated by norms of international law irrespective of the type and name thereof (treaty, agreement, convention, covenant, protocol, exchange of letters, and international treaties of other types and names).

2. The provisions of the present Law shall also extend to those international treaties of the former USSR with regard to which Georgia has declared itself to be a legal successor.

Article 3 Interpretation of Terms

The terms used in the present Law shall have the following meanings:

(a) international treaty – an agreement concluded by Georgia in written form with a foreign State(s) or international organization(s) which are regulated by norms of international law notwithstanding the specific name thereof and whether represented by one or by several related documents;

(b) contracting party – the State which has expressed consent to deeming an international treaty to be binding for performance notwithstanding the entry of the treaty into operation;

(c) State-participant – a State which has expressed consent to deeming an international treaty to be obligatory for performance and for which the treaty has entered into operation;

(d) conclusion of treaty – all actions which Georgia effectuates with respect to a treaty at the international level, including the conducting of negotiations, signature of the treaty, and including the deeming thereof to be binding;

(e) signature – stage of conclusion of a treaty or form of expression by Georgia of consent to deeming treaty to be binding for performance;

(f) ratification, confirmation, accession – form of expression of consent on the part of Georgia to deeming a treaty to be binding for performance;

(g) powers – document issued by competent agency of Georgia on the basis of which one person or several persons are appointed as representatives of the Georgian side in order to conduct negotiations, adopt the text of the treaty, or establish the authenticity thereof, or for the purpose of the effectuation of any other acts connected with the treaty;

(h) reservation – unilateral statement made when signing a treaty, ratification, confirmation, or during accession thereto which expresses the wish to change or exclude the legal operation of determined provisions of the treaty with respect to Georgia;

(i) international organization – international inter-State or intergovernmental organization;

(j) depositary – State or international organization or chief executive official thereof which keeps the original international treaty and fulfils other functions connected with it provided for by norms of international law;

(k) denunciation – form of unilateral termination of the operation of an international treaty which according to the provisions of the treaty signifies the termination of the operation of the treaty;

(l) abrogation (annulment) – form of unilateral termination of operation of international treaty which signifies the termination of the operation of the treaty in the event of a material violation thereof by another participating party or in accordance with other norms of international law.

Article 4 International Treaty of Georgia

1. An international treaty of Georgia with a foreign State and international organization shall be concluded in the name of:
(a) Georgia – inter-State treaty;
(b) executive power of Georgia – intergovernmental treaty;
(c) central agencies of executive power of Georgia – international treaty of an interdepartmental character.

2. An international treaty shall be concluded in the name of Georgia to which by agreement of the parties an inter-State character is imparted, and also a treaty concerning:
(a) territorial questions and questions of peace;
(b) rights and freedoms of man;
(c) citizenship;
(d) participation of Georgia in inter-State unions and other inter-State associations (or organizations);
(e) military questions;
(f) use of the territory of Georgia and natural resources;
(g) taking and issuing of loan by the State, and issuance of State guarantee.

3. All international treaties not concerning questions enumerated in point (2) of the present Article or with regard to which by agreement of the parties an intergovernmental character is imparted shall be concluded in the name of executive power.

4. An international treaty of an interdepartmental character with regard to questions relegated to their competence shall be concluded in the name of central agencies of executive power of Georgia.

Article 5 Competence of Territorial Entities of Georgia

The competence of the Abkhazian and Adzharian autonomous republics and other territorial entities with respect to international treaties shall be determined after the establishment of the territorial State system of Georgia.

Article 6 International Treaty in Legislation of Georgia

1. An international treaty of Georgia is an integral part of the legislation of Georgia.

2. An international treaty of Georgia, unless it is contrary to the Constitution of Georgia, shall have preferential legal force with respect to municipal normative acts.

3. The provisions of officially published international treaties of Georgia establishing rights and duties of a specific character and not requiring the adoption of municipal clarifying normative acts shall operate in Georgia directly.

Article 7 Consent of Georgia to Deeming International Treaty Binding for Performance

1. The consent of Georgia to deeming an international treaty to be binding for performance may be expressed by:
(a) signature of the treaty;
(b) exchange of documents (or notes) comprising the treaty;
(c) ratification of the treaty;
(d) accession to the treaty;
(e) use of any other mutually-agreed means of consent to the treaty.

2. The decision concerning the giving of consent to deeming an international treaty to be binding for performance shall be adopted by agencies of State power of Georgia according to the competence established by the Constitution of Georgia and the present Law.

Chapter II Conclusion of International Treaty

Article 8 Recommendations Concerning Conclusion of International Treaty

1. The Parliament of Georgia shall submit its recommendations concerning the conclusion of an international treaty to the President of Georgia.

2. Recommendations concerning their competence may also be submitted by the Supreme Court of Georgia and the People's Defender.

3. Recommendations concerning the conclusion of an international treaty of Georgia must contain a substantiation of the advisability of concluding the treaty.

4. In the event of approval of the recommendation the President of Georgia shall within a period of up to two months from the day of receipt

thereof charge the Ministry of Foreign Affairs of Georgia to prepare a proposal concerning the conclusion of the said treaty.

Article 9 Proposals With Regard to Conclusion of International Treaty

1. A proposal concerning the conclusion of an international treaty provided for by Article 8(4) shall be submitted to the President of Georgia by the Ministry of Foreign Affairs of Georgia within a period of not later than 6 months from the day of adoption of the respective decision.

2. The Ministry of Foreign Affairs of Georgia shall submit its proposal concerning the conclusion of an international treaty to the President of Georgia according to the procedure established by the present Article.

3. Central agencies of executive power of Georgia shall submit their proposals concerning the conclusion of an international treaty to the Ministry of Foreign Affairs of Georgia.

4. The proposals of central agencies of executive power of Georgia must contain the text of the international treaty in the Georgian language (when there is an authentic text in a foreign language it shall be necessary to also submit a Georgian translation), a substantiation of the advisability of the conclusion of an international treaty and its political, legal, economic, financial, and other possible results. When necessary, a draft must be attached to the proposal concerning the making of changes in and additions to normative acts of Georgia, and the State agency responsible for performance of the treaty and the need to effectuate other measures also must be determined.

5. A proposal provided for by the present Article the Ministry of Foreign Affairs of Georgia shall submit for the opinion of the Ministry of Justice of Georgia concerning conformity to legislation of Georgia and possible legal consequences, the Ministry of Finances of Georgia concerning possible financial–economic consequences, and also respective central agency of executive power of Georgia.

6. The proposals of central agencies of executive power of Georgia concerning the conclusion of inter-State and intergovernmental international treaties and the opinions noted in point (5) of the present Article shall be submitted to the President of Georgia with the opinion of the Ministry of Foreign Affairs of Georgia.

7. A proposal concerning the conclusion of an international treaty submitted to the President of Georgia must contain: the draft treaty (in the Georgian language), opinions of the Ministry of Justice of Georgia concerning possible legal consequences and the conformity thereof to

legislation of Georgia, of the Ministry of Finances of Georgia concerning possible financial–economic consequences of the conclusion of the aid treaty, and opinions of the respective central agency of executive power of Georgia and Ministry of Foreign Affairs of Georgia concerning possible foreign policy consequences of conclusion of the treaty. When necessary, a draft must be attached to the proposal concerning the making of changes in and additions to normative acts of Georgia.

8. A proposal concerning the conclusion of an international treaty of an interdepartmental character requiring the making of changes in and additions to normative acts of Georgia the Ministry of Foreign Affairs of Georgia shall submit to the President of Georgia.

9. A proposal of a foreign State or international organization concerning the conclusion of an international treaty the Ministry of Foreign Affairs of Georgia shall submit to the President of Georgia in the procedure established by the present Article.

Article 10 Intention Concerning Participation of Georgia in International Treaty

1. If participation in an international treaty requires the prior consent of another State (or international organization) participating in the treaty, the Ministry of Foreign Affairs of Georgia shall in accordance with the procedure established by Article 9 submit the proposal to the President of Georgia concerning the intention to participate in the international treaty.

2. The decision concerning the intention of Georgia to participate in an international treaty the President of Georgia shall adopt in the form of an edict.

3. The Ministry of Foreign Affairs of Georgia shall notify the depositary of the respective international treaty or other participating State about the intention of Georgia to participate in an international treaty.

Article 11 Decision Concerning Conducting of Negotiations and Signature of International Treaty

1. The decision concerning the conducting of negotiations concerning inter-State and intergovernmental treaties and the signature thereof shall be adopted by the President of Georgia in the form of a regulation.

2. The decision concerning the conducting of negotiations concerning an international treaty of an interdepartmental character and the signature thereof shall be adopted, by agreement with the respective

department, by the Ministry of Foreign Affairs of Georgia in the form of an order.

Article 12 Effectuation of Actions Connected with Conclusion of International Treaty Without Presentation of Powers

1. The President of Georgia and the Minister of Foreign Affairs of Georgia shall have the right to effectuate all types of actions connected with the conclusion of an international treaty without the presentation of powers.

2. The head of the diplomatic representation of Georgia and chief of the representation of Georgia in an international organization shall have the right for the purpose of the adoption of a text of an international treaty to conduct negotiations without the presentation of powers to the respective receiving State or within the limits of the particular international organizations.

Article 13 Power to Effectuate Actions Connected With Conclusion of International Treaty

1. The power must determine the object of the agreements and limits of the competence of a person.

2. The power in connection with the conclusion of inter-State and intergovernmental treaties shall be granted by the President of Georgia by an edict and formalized by the Ministry of Foreign Affairs of Georgia.

Article 14 International Treaty, Consent to Deeming Bindingness of Which is Expressed by Parliament of Georgia

1. The Parliament of Georgia shall express consent to the deeming of an international treaty to be binding upon Georgia by means of ratification (or accession thereto).

2. In addition to a treaty which provides for ratification, the ratification (or accession thereto) of such an international treaty also shall be necessary which:

(a) provides for the entry of Georgia into an international organization or inter-State union;
(b) is of a military character;

(c) affects the territorial integrity of the State or a change of State boundaries;
(d) is connected with the receipt or issuing of a State loan;
(e) requires a change of municipal legislation or adoption in performance of international obligations assumed of necessary laws and acts having the force of a law;
(f) requires ratification according to other legislative acts of Georgia.

Article 15 Submission of International Treaty to Parliament of Georgia

1. An international treaty whose consent to deeming the bindingness of which is expressed by the Parliament of Georgia shall be submitted to the Parliament of Georgia for ratification (or accession thereto) only by the President of Georgia.

2. An international treaty must be submitted for ratification (or accession) in the Georgian language (if there is an authentic text in a foreign language, it must be submitted together with an officially attested Georgian translation). To the treaty must be appended the opinions of the Ministry of Justice of Georgia concerning the conformity thereof to legislation of Georgia and possible legal consequences, the Ministry of Finances of Georgia concerning possible financial–economic consequences of the conclusion of the particular treaty, and the opinion of the respective central agency of executive power of Georgia and Ministry of Foreign Affairs of Georgia concerning possible foreign policy consequences.

3. The Georgian translation of foreign-language texts of international treaties and the official attesting of the translation shall be effectuated by the State Chancellery of Georgia.

4. The President together with the international treaty submitted for ratification (or accession thereto) shall, when necessary, submit to the Parliament of Georgia a draft law on making changes in and additions to the respective legislative act of Georgia.

Article 16 Preliminary Consideration of International Treaty Presented for Ratification

An international treaty submitted for ratification to the Parliament of Georgia, and also the draft law provided for by Article 15(4), the Committee for foreign relations shall consider in advance and, when necessary, jointly with other committees of the Parliament of Georgia and render a respective opinion.

Article 17 Adoption of Decision Concerning Ratification (or Accession Thereto) of International Treaty of Georgia

1. An international treaty submitted for ratification (or accession thereto) by the President of Georgia shall be considered by the Parliament of Georgia and a respective decision adopted in the form of a decree by a majority of the full composition.

2. On the basis of the adopted decree concerning ratification (or accession thereto) of an international treaty, the Ministry of Foreign Affairs of Georgia shall issue an instrument of ratification which the President of Georgia shall sign and the Ministry of Foreign Affairs of Georgia shall certify.

Article 18 Confirmation (or Accession Thereto) of International Treaty of Georgia Not Subject to Ratification

The President of Georgia shall adopt by an edict a decision concerning the confirmation (or accession thereto) of an international treaty not subject to ratification (or accession thereto) by the Parliament of Georgia and for the introduction into operation of the required effectuation of municipal procedures.

Article 19 Making of Changes in and Additions to Normative Acts of Georgia Arising from International Treaty

1. The Parliament of Georgia before deciding the question concerning the deeming of an international treaty to be binding shall, when necessary, consider within the limits of its competence and adopt a decision concerning the making of changes in and additions to the respective normative act of Georgia.

2. The President of Georgia before deciding the questions concerning the deeming of an international treaty to be binding shall, when necessary,

consider and within the limits of his competence adopt a decision concerning the making of changes in and additions to the respective normative act of Georgia.

Article 20 Provisional Application of International Treaty by Georgia

If an international treaty provided for provisional application of a treaty as a whole or certain provisions thereof, or agreement has been reached concerning this between the parties, Georgia shall apply such treaty from the moment of the entry thereof into force.

Article 21 Conformity of International Treaty to Constitution of Georgia

1. In the event a constitutional suit is brought by an empowered subject before an international treaty is deemed by Georgia to be binding, the Constitutional Court of Georgia shall adopt a decision concerning the constitutionality of the international treaty.
2. In the event of the bringing of a constitutional suit to the Constitutional Court of Georgia, consideration of the question of deeming the respective international treaty to be binding upon Georgia before the rendering of a decision by the Constitutional Court shall not be permitted.
3. In the event the Constitutional Court establishes the nonconformity of an international treaty to the Constitution of Georgia, the deeming of a treaty to be binding upon Georgia shall be permitted only after respective changes are made in the Constitution in the established procedure.

Article 22 Reservation to International Treaty of Georgia

1. In the event of the signature, ratification, and confirmation of an international treaty or accession thereto, a reservation may be made thereto in compliance with the conditions of the treaty and according to norms of international law. It shall not be permitted to make a reservation to an international treaty of Georgia if the international treaty prohibits such action and if this is contrary to the object and purposes of the treaty.
2. A reservation made when signing, ratifying, and confirming an international treaty or while acceding to the treaty shall be formalized in writing, the depositary or other contracting party being notified thereof.

3. Unless provided otherwise by an international treaty of Georgia, to retract a reservation made by Georgia shall be possible at any time in the same procedure in which the reservation was made.

4. The recognition by another Contracting State of a reservation to an international treaty made by Georgia, or the expression of a protest with respect to it in compliance with the conditions of the international treaty and according to norms of international law shall be effectuated by the State agency deciding the question of deeming an international treaty to be binding upon Georgia.

Article 23 Notification Concerning Deeming by Georgia of International Treaty to be Binding for Performance

The Ministry of Foreign Affairs of Georgia or on its behalf the diplomatic representation of Georgia or representation of Georgia at an international organization shall effectuate all necessary measures for the purpose of notifying the Contracting Parties or depositary concerning the deeming by Georgia of an international treaty to be binding for performance.

Article 24 Entry into Force of International Treaty of Georgia

1. An international treaty shall enter into force for Georgia in that procedure and within that period which is provided for in the international treaty or agreed between the parties and in accordance with the present Law.

2. If legislation of Georgia requires for the entry of an international treaty into force the fulfilment of any municipal procedure, such treaty shall enter into force for Georgia only after the fulfilment of the respective procedure.

Article 25 Informing President of Georgia and Parliament of Georgia About International Treaty

The Ministry of Foreign Affairs of Georgia immediately shall inform the President of Georgia and the Parliament of Georgia about the conclusion of an international treaty of Georgia, and also the termination or suspension of the operation thereof.

Chapter III Registration of International Treaty of Georgia, Keeping of Text, and Official Publication

Article 26 Unified State Register of Registration of International Treaties of Georgia

1. The Ministry of Foreign Affairs of Georgia shall effectuate the recording and registration of international treaties of Georgia.
2. The text of an international treaty shall within a ten-day period from the day of entry into force be transferred to the Ministry of Justice of Georgia for entry in the State register and conferment of a registration code.

Article 27 Registration of International Treaty of Georgia in International Organizations

The Ministry of Foreign Affairs of Georgia shall ensure the registration of an international treaty which has entered into force for Georgia at the Secretariat of the United Nations and other agencies of international organizations.

Article 28 Keeping of Text of International Treaty of Georgia

1. The original of an international treaty of Georgia (or attested copy, official translation) shall be transferred to the Ministry of Foreign Affairs of Georgia for keeping within 15 days from the day of signature.
2. To the original of the treaty must be appended information concerning the persons who signed it and, when necessary, documents confirming their powers.

Article 29 Effectuation of Functions of Depositary and Mutual Relations with Other Depositaries

1. When according to an international treaty the function of depositary is placed on Georgia, the Ministry of Foreign Affairs of Georgia shall effectuate this function.

2. The Ministry of Foreign Affairs of Georgia shall effectuate correspondence with agencies of foreign States, international organizations, or their highest officials effectuating the functions of depositary with respect to multilateral treaties.

Article 30 Official Publication of International Treaty of Georgia

1. An international treaty of Georgia, consent to the deeming of the bindingness of which for Georgia was expressed by the Parliament of Georgia, shall after entry of the treaty into force be published officially upon the recommendation of the Ministry of Foreign Affairs of Georgia in the *Парламентис уцкубани*.

2. An international treaty of Georgia, consent to the deeming of the bindingness of which for Georgia was expressed by the President of Georgia, shall after entry of the treaty into force be published officially upon the recommendation of the Ministry of Foreign Affairs of Georgia in the *Сборник указов и распоряжений Президенма Грузии*.

3. An international treaty of Georgia, the deeming of the bindingness of which for Georgia does not require consent on the part of the Parliament of Georgia and the President of Georgia, shall be published officially in accordance with the provisions of the Law of Georgia on Normative Acts.

4. The publication of all international treaties of Georgia in the *Сборник международных договоров Грузии* shall be obligatory.

5. When one of the authentic texts of an international treaty of Georgia is drawn up in the Georgian language, the treaty shall be published in the Georgian language.

6. An international treaty of Georgia whose authentic text is drawn up only in foreign languages shall be published in one of these languages with an official Georgian translation appended.

Chapter IV Performance of International Treaty of Georgia

Article 31 Performance of International Treaty of Georgia

1. An international treaty of Georgia shall be subject to performance in good faith in accordance with the conditions of this treaty themselves, norms of international law, the Constitution of Georgia, the present Law, and other normative acts of Georgia.

2. Georgia shall until the entry into force of an international treaty for it refrain from acts, taking into account norms of international law, destroying the object and purposes of the treaty.

3. Georgia shall perform an international treaty from the moment of the entry into force thereof for Georgia.

Article 32 Ensuring Performance of International Treaty of Georgia

1. The President of Georgia and the Parliament of Georgia shall take measures with regard to ensuring the performance of an international treaty of Georgia.

2. Central agencies of executive power of Georgia to whose competence questions have been relegated to be determined by an international treaty of Georgia shall ensure the performance of the obligations assumed by Georgia under the international treaty and shall watch over compliance with the rights of Georgia and performance by other parties to the treaty of their obligations arising from the treaty.

3. Central agencies of executive power of Georgia shall be obliged to provide to the Ministry of Foreign Affairs of Georgia information affecting the performance of an international treaty of Georgia.

Article 33 Supervision Over Performance of International Treaty of Georgia

1. General supervision over the performance of an international treaty of Georgia shall be effectuated by the Ministry of Foreign Affairs of Georgia.

2. Central agencies of executive power of Georgia shall be obliged to provide to the Ministry of Foreign Affairs of Georgia full information concerning the performance of an international treaty.

3. Central agencies of executive power shall in the event of a violation of their duties by other parties to an international treaty of Georgia be obliged immediately to inform the Ministry of Foreign Affairs of Georgia about such facts.

Article 34 Measures to be Effectuated in Event of Violation of International Treaty of Georgia by Other Participants of Treaty

In the event of a violation by other participants of an international treaty of Georgia of their obligations, the Ministry of Foreign Affairs of Georgia or other central agencies of executive power of Georgia shall, by agreement with the Ministry of Foreign Affairs of Georgia, submit to the President of Georgia proposals concerning the effectuation of necessary measures in accordance with norms of international law and the treaty itself.

Chapter V Termination or Suspension of Operation of International Treaty of Georgia

Article 35 Proposals Concerning Termination or Suspension of Operation of International Treaty of Georgia

1. Central agencies of executive power of Georgia shall submit their substantiated proposals concerning the suspension or termination of the operation of an international treaty to the Ministry of Foreign Affairs of Georgia.

2. The Ministry of Foreign Affairs of Georgia shall submit to the President of Georgia a proposal provided for by the present Article concerning the suspension or termination of the operation of an international treaty, consent to deeming the obligatoriness of which for Georgia was expressed by the President of Georgia or Parliament of Georgia.

3. The proposal of a foreign State or international organization concerning the suspension or termination of the operation of an international

treaty of Georgia shall be submitted by the Ministry of Foreign Affairs of Georgia to the President of Georgia in the form of a proposal in the procedure established by the present Article.

4. Proposals concerning the suspension or termination of an international treaty of Georgia, consent to the deeming of the bindingness of which for Georgia was expressed by the Parliament of Georgia, the President of Georgia shall submit to the Parliament of Georgia.

5. A proposal concerning the suspension or termination of an international treaty must contain an attested copy of the original of the treaty (in the Georgian language), opinions of the Ministry of Foreign Affairs of Georgia concerning possible foreign policy consequences of the suspension or termination thereof, Ministry of Justice of Georgia concerning the legal consequences, Ministry of Finances of Georgia concerning possible financial–economic consequences of suspension or termination of the present treaty, and also the opinion of a respective central agency of executive power of Georgia.

Article 36 Preliminary Consideration of International Treaty Submitted to Parliament of Georgia for Purpose of Termination or Suspension of Operation

An international treaty submitted to the Parliament of Georgia for the purpose of the termination or suspension of operation shall be considered preliminarily by the Committee for foreign relations of the Parliament of Georgia, and, when necessary, jointly with other committees of the Parliament of Georgia and render a respective opinion.

Article 37 Decision Concerning Suspension or Termination of Operation of International Treaty of Georgia

1. The Parliament of Georgia shall by a majority of the full composition in the form of a decree adopt a decision concerning the suspension or termination of the international treaty, the deeming of the bindingness of which for Georgia it expressed consent.

2. The President of Georgia in the form of an edict shall adopt a decision concerning the suspension or termination of the operation of an

international treaty, the deeming of the bindingness of which for Georgia he expressed consent.

3. The Minister of Foreign Affairs of Georgia shall in the form of an order adopt a decision concerning the suspension or termination of an international treaty, the deeming of the bindingness of which for Georgia he expressed consent.

Article 38 Results of Termination of Operation of International Treaty of Georgia

According to norms of international law, unless provided otherwise by the treaty or agreement otherwise is reached between the parties to the treaty, the termination of the operation of an international treaty shall relieve Georgia from any obligation to fulfil the treaty and shall not influence the rights, duties, and legal status created as a result of the fulfilment of the treaty before the termination of the operation thereof.

Article 39 Results of Suspension of Operation of International Treaty of Georgia

1. According to norms of international law, the suspension of the operation of an international treaty shall, unless provided otherwise by the treaty or other agreement between the parties, relieve Georgia from the obligations to fulfil the international treaty in mutual relations with those participating parties with respect to which the operation of the treaty is suspended and shall not influence those legal relations which have been determined by the treaty between Georgia and other participating persons.

2. During the period of suspension of the operation of an international treaty Georgia shall refrain from acts which may obstruct the renewal of the operation of the treaty.

Article 40 Official Notification Concerning Suspension or Termination of Operation of International Treaty of Georgia

1. A decision concerning the suspension or termination of the operation of an international treaty of Georgia shall be published in the procedure provided for by Article 30.

2. The Ministry of Foreign Affairs of Georgia officially shall notify the party participating in the treaty or depositary about the suspension or termination of the operation of an international treaty of Georgia.

Chapter VI Concluding Provisions

Article 41 Introduction of Law into Operation

1. The present Law shall be introduced into operation upon publication.

2. From the moment of the introduction of the present Law into operation, to consider to have lost force the Law of the Republic Georgia 'On the Conclusion, Ratification, Performance, and Denunciation of International Treaties of the Republic Georgia' of 11 February 1993 (*Ведомости Парламента Грузии* (1993), no. 4, item 22).

KAZAKHSTAN

Edict of the President of the Republic Kazakhstan Having the Force of a Law on the Procedure for the Conclusion, Performance, and Denunciation of International Treaties of the Republic Kazakhstan

[Adopted 12 December 1995, No. 2679.
Ведомости Верховного Совета Республики Казахстан
(1995), no. 23, item 144]

In accordance with Article 1 of the Law of the Republic Kazakhstan of 10 December 1993 'On the Temporary Delegation to the President of the Republic Kazakhstan and Heads of Local Administrations of Additional Powers' and for the purpose of realizing the provisions of the Constitution of the Republic Kazakhstan, determining a unified procedure for the conclusion, performance, and denunciation of international treaties of the Republic Kazakhstan, and called upon to promote the effectuation of the purposes and principles of the foreign policy of the Republic Kazakhstan, I issue the present Edict.

Chapter I General Provisions

Article 1 Sphere of Application of Edict

1. The procedure for the conclusion, performance, and denunciation of international treaties of the Republic Kazakhstan established by the present Edict shall apply with respect to international treaties of the Republic Kazakhstan irrespective of their form and name (treaty, agreement, convention, pact, protocol, exchange of letters or notes, or other forms and names of the international treaties).

2. The operation of the present Edict shall extend to international treaties to be concluded with foreign States and international

organizations by the President of the Republic Kazakhstan, Government of the Republic Kazakhstan, ministries, State committees, and other central executive agencies of the Republic Kazakhstan which are directly subordinate and accountable to the President of the Republic Kazakhstan.

3. The President of the Republic Kazakhstan shall have the right with respect to international treaties relegated to the jurisdiction of State agencies directly subordinate and accountable to him to establish a different procedure for their conclusion, performance, and denunciation than that which is provided for by the present Edict.

Article 2 Basic Concepts Used in Present Edict

The concepts used in the present Edict shall mean the following:

(1) '*international treaty of Republic Kazakhstan*' – an international agreement concluded by the Republic Kazakhstan with a foreign State(s) or with an international organization in writing and regulated by international law irrespective of whether such agreement is contained in one document or in several interrelated documents, and also irrespective of its specific name;

(2) '*conclusion*' – the expression of consent of the Republic Kazakhstan to the obligatoriness of an international treaty for it;

(3) '*signature*' – the means of expressing consent of the Republic Kazakhstan to the obligatoriness of an international treaty for it unless it is thereafter subject to ratification or confirmation;

(4) '*ratification*' – the means of expressing consent of the Republic Kazakhstan to the obligatoriness of an international treaty for it by means of confirmation thereof by the Parliament of the Republic Kazakhstan;

(5) '*confirmation (or adoption)*' – the means of expressing consent of the Republic Kazakhstan to the obligatoriness of an international treaty for it, which is not subject to ratification, by the Government of the Republic Kazakhstan;

(6) '*accession*' – the means of expressing consent of the Republic Kazakhstan to the obligatoriness for it of an international treaty, in the conclusion of which it did not participate;

(7) '*exchange of instruments of ratification, documents concerning confirmation (or adoption) or accession*' – the means of expressing consent of the Republic Kazakhstan to the obligatoriness for it of an international treaty from the moment of the exchange (or notification) of such instruments (or documents) of States which participated in the treaty or the depositary;

(8) '*powers*' – a document emanating from the competent agency of the Republic Kazakhstan by means of which one person or several persons are appointed to represent the Republic Kazakhstan for the purpose of concluding an international treaty;
(9) '*international organization*' – an interstate or intergovernmental organization;
(10) '*depositary*' – a State or international organization or its chief executive official to whom the original of an international treaty is handed over for keeping and who fulfils the functions provided for by international law;
(11) '*denunciation*' – the properly formalized renunciation of the Republic Kazakhstan of an international treaty concluded by it;
(12) '*authentic text of treaty*' – the text of an international treaty regarded by the Contracting Parties as the basic (or reliable) [text].

Article 3 Types of International Treaties

1. International treaties of the Republic Kazakhstan shall be concluded with foreign States in the name of:
(1) the Republic Kazakhstan (interstate treaties);
(2) the Government of the Republic Kazakhstan (intergovernmental treaties);
(3) ministries, State committees, and other central executive agencies of the Republic Kazakhstan, and also State agencies directly subordinate and accountable to the President of the Republic Kazakhstan (interdepartmental treaties).

2. International treaties of the Republic Kazakhstan shall be concluded with international organizations in the name of the Republic Kazakhstan, the Government of the Republic Kazakhstan, ministries, State committees, and other central executive agencies of the Republic Kazakhstan, and also State agencies directly subordinate and accountable to the President of the Republic Kazakhstan.

Chapter II Conclusion of International Treaties

Article 4 Proposals Concerning Conclusion of International Treaties

1. Proposals concerning the conclusion of international treaties of the Republic Kazakhstan of an inter-State character shall be submitted to

the President of the Republic Kazakhstan by the Government of the Republic Kazakhstan or by the Ministry of Foreign Affairs of the Republic Kazakhstan.

2. Ministries, State committees, and other central executive agencies of the Republic Kazakhstan, and also State agencies directly subordinate and accountable to the President of the Republic Kazakhstan, shall jointly with the Ministry of Foreign Affairs of the Republic Kazakhstan or by agreement with them submit to the Government of the Republic Kazakhstan with regard to questions of its competence proposals concerning the conclusion of the treaties specified in point 1 of the present Article.

3. The Government of the Republic Kazakhstan shall consider the proposals concerning the conclusion of treaties specified in point 2 of the present Article and submit them to the President of the Republic Kazakhstan.

4. Proposals concerning the conclusion of international treaties of the Republic Kazakhstan with regard to questions relegated to the jurisdiction of the Government shall be submitted to the Government of the Republic Kazakhstan by the Ministry of Foreign Affairs of the Republic Kazakhstan.

5. Ministries, State committees, and other central executive agencies of the Republic Kazakhstan, and also State agencies directly subordinate and accountable to the President of the Republic Kazakhstan, shall jointly with the Ministry of Foreign Affairs of the Republic Kazakhstan or by agreement with it submit to the Government of the Republic Kazakhstan with regard to questions of its competence proposals concerning the conclusion of treaties specified in point 4 of the present Article.

6. Proposals concerning the conclusion of international treaties of an interdepartmental character shall be submitted by the respective ministries, State committees, and other central executive agencies of the Republic Kazakhstan, and also State agencies directly subordinate and accountable to the President of the Republic Kazakhstan, to the Government of the Republic Kazakhstan by agreement with the Ministry of Foreign Affairs of the Republic Kazakhstan.

Article 5 Language of International Treaties

1. Bilateral international treaties shall be concluded, as a rule, in the State languages of the Contracting Parties.

2. Multilateral international treaties shall be concluded in the languages determined by consent of the participants of the treaties.

Article 6 Legal Expert Examination of Draft International Treaties

1. Draft international treaties of the Republic Kazakhstan shall, after preliminary agreement with the interested ministries, State committees, and other central executive agencies of the Republic Kazakhstan, and also State agencies directly subordinate and accountable to the President of the Republic Kazakhstan, be subject to obligatory legal expert examination in the Ministry of Justice of the Republic Kazakhstan.

2. Draft international treaties which have undergone legal expert examination shall be subject to agreement in the Ministry of Foreign Affairs of the Republic Kazakhstan.

Article 7 Decisions Concerning Conducting of Negotiations and Signature of International Treaties

Decisions concerning the conducting of negotiations and signature of international treaties of the Republic Kazakhstan shall be adopted by:

(1) the President of the Republic Kazakhstan – with respect to international treaties of an inter-State character, and also with respect to international treaties with regard to questions relegated to the jurisdiction of the Government of the Republic Kazakhstan if this is called for by necessity;

(2) the Government of the Republic Kazakhstan – with respect to international treaties with regard to questions relegated to the jurisdiction of the Government;

(3) ministers, chairmen of State committees and directors of other central executive agencies of the Republic Kazakhstan, and also directors of State agencies directly subordinate and accountable to the President of the Republic Kazakhstan – with respect to international treaties of an interdepartmental character by agreement with the Government of the Republic Kazakhstan.

Article 8 Powers to Conduct Negotiations and Sign International Treaties

1. Powers to conduct negotiations and to sign international treaties of the Republic Kazakhstan of an interstate character shall be issued by

the President of the Republic Kazakhstan, and with regard to questions relegated to the jurisdiction of the Government of the Republic Kazakhstan, by the Government of the Republic Kazakhstan.

2. Powers to conduct negotiations and to sign international treaties or treaties relegated to the jurisdiction of the Government of the Republic Kazakhstan may be issued on behalf of the President of the Republic Kazakhstan or of the Government of the Republic Kazakhstan by the Ministry of Foreign Affairs of the Republic Kazakhstan.

3. Powers to conduct negotiations and to sign international treaties of an interdepartmental character shall be issued by the minister, chairman of the State committee, or director of other central executive agency of the Republic Kazakhstan, and also by the director of the State agency directly subordinate and accountable to the President of the Republic Kazakhstan.

Article 9 Conducting Negotiations and Signature of International Treaties Without Special Powers

1. The President of the Republic Kazakhstan, Prime Minister of the Republic Kazakhstan, and Minister of Foreign Affairs of the Republic Kazakhstan shall have the right to conduct negotiations and to sign international treaties of the Republic Kazakhstan without special powers.

2. The head of a diplomatic representation of the Republic Kazakhstan in a foreign State or the head of a representation of the Republic Kazakhstan attached to an international organization shall have the right without special powers to conduct negotiations concerning the conclusion of an international treaty of the Republic Kazakhstan respectively with the receiving State or within the framework of the particular international organization.

3. The head of a diplomatic representation of the Republic Kazakhstan in a foreign State or the head of a representation of the Republic Kazakhstan attached to an international organization shall have the right to sign international treaties of the Republic Kazakhstan only when there are special powers.

4. A minister, chairman of a State committee, or director of another central executive organ of the Republic Kazakhstan, and also the director of the State agency directly subordinate and accountable to the President of the Republic Kazakhstan, shall have the right with regard to

questions of his competence to conduct negotiations and to sign international treaties of an interdepartmental character without special powers.

Article 10 Ratification of International Treaties

1. The ratification of international treaties of the Republic Kazakhstan shall be performed by the Parliament of the Republic Kazakhstan.

2. International treaties ratified by the Republic Kazakhstan shall have priority over its laws and shall apply directly except for instances when it follows from the international treaty that the issuance of a law is required in order to apply it.

Article 11 International Treaties Subject to Ratification

1. International treaties of the Republic Kazakhstan shall be subject to ratification:

(1) the performance of which requires a change of prevailing or the adoption of new laws, and also establishing other rules not provided for by laws of the Republic Kazakhstan;

(2) concerning territorial demarcation of the Republic Kazakhstan with other States, including treaties concerning the course of the State boundary of the Republic Kazakhstan, and also the demarcation of the exclusive economic zone and continental shelf of the Republic Kazakhstan;

(3) concerning the fundamental principles of interstate relations, regarding questions of disarmament or international control over armaments, ensuring international peace and security, and also peace treaties and treaties concerning collective security;

(4) concerning the participation of the Republic Kazakhstan in interstate unions, international organizations, and other associations if such treaties provide for the transfer to them of the effectuating of part of the sovereign rights of the Republic Kazakhstan or establish the legal obligatoriness of decisions of their organs for the Republic Kazakhstan;

(5) concerning State loans and the rendering of economic and other assistance by the Republic Kazakhstan.

2. International treaties of the Republic Kazakhstan, during the conclusion of which the Contracting Parties have stipulated the subsequent ratification thereof, shall be subject to ratification.

Article 12 Consideration Before Ratification of International Treaties for Their Conformity to Constitution of the Republic Kazakhstan

1. The Constitutional Council shall, upon the application of the President of the Republic Kazakhstan, Chairman of the Senate, Chairman of the Mazhilis, not less than one-fifth of the total number of deputies of Parliament, or the Prime Minister, consider before ratification international treaties of the Republic Kazakhstan for their conformity to the Constitution.

2. In the event of an application to the Constitutional Council with regard to the questions specified in point 1 of the present Article, the running of the periods for the ratification of international treaties shall be suspended.

3. International treaties deemed not to conform to the Constitution of the Republic Kazakhstan may not be ratified and introduced into operation.

Article 13 Proposals Concerning Ratification of International Treaties

1. Proposals concerning the ratification of international treaties of the Republic Kazakhstan of an interstate character shall be submitted to the President of the Republic Kazakhstan by the Government of the Republic Kazakhstan upon the proposal of the Ministry of Foreign Affairs of the Republic Kazakhstan.

2. Ministries, State committees, and other central executive agencies of the Republic Kazakhstan, and also State agencies directly subordinate and accountable to the President of the Republic Kazakhstan, shall jointly with the Ministry of Foreign Affairs of the Republic Kazakhstan or by agreement with it submit to the Government of the Republic Kazakhstan with regard to questions of its competence proposals concerning the ratification of the treaties specified in point 1 of the present Article.

3. The Government of the Republic Kazakhstan shall consider proposals concerning ratification of international treaties specified in point 2 of the present Article and submit them to the President of the Republic Kazakhstan.

4. The President shall consider proposals concerning the ratification of the treaties specified in points 1 and 3 of the present Article and submit these treaties to the Parliament of the Republic Kazakhstan for ratification.

5. The Ministry of Foreign Affairs of the Republic Kazakhstan shall submit to the Government of the Republic Kazakhstan proposals concerning the ratification of international treaties subject to the said procedure with regard to the questions relegated to the jurisdiction of the Government of the Republic Kazakhstan.

6. Ministries, State committees, and other central executive agencies of the Republic Kazakhstan, and also State agencies directly subordinate and accountable to the President of the Republic Kazakhstan, shall jointly with the Ministry of Foreign Affairs of the Republic Kazakhstan or by agreement with it submit to the Government of the Republic Kazakhstan with regard to questions of its competence proposals concerning the ratification of the international treaties specified in point 5 of the present Article.

7. The Government shall consider proposals concerning the ratification of the treaties specified in points 5 and 6 of the present Article and shall submit these treaties for ratification to the Parliament of the Republic Kazakhstan.

Article 14 Adoption of Decisions Concerning Ratification of International Treaties

1. The Parliament of the Republic Kazakhstan in a separate session of the Chambers beginning in the Mazhilis and then in the Senate shall consider the international treaties submitted for ratification by the President of the Republic Kazakhstan or the Government of the Republic Kazakhstan and adopt the respective law.

2. After the signature and promulgation of the law on the ratification of an international treaty of the Republic Kazakhstan, the President of the Republic Kazakhstan shall sign the instrument of ratification.

Article 15 Exchange of Instruments of Ratification and Documents Concerning Confirmation or Accession

The exchange of instruments of ratification and documents concerning the confirmation of or accession of the Republic Kazakhstan to multilateral international treaties and the handing over of the instruments concerning the ratification of multilateral international treaties for keeping to depositaries shall be performed by the Ministry of Foreign Affairs of the Republic Kazakhstan or on its behalf by the diplomatic representation of the Republic Kazakhstan or by the representation of the Republic Kazakhstan attached to an international organization.

Article 16 Confirmation (or Adoption) of International Treaties Not Subject to Ratification

1. The confirmation (or adoption) of international treaties of the Republic Kazakhstan which are not subject to ratification but have provided for the confirmation (or adoption) thereof shall be performed by:
(1) with respect to international treaties of an interstate character – the President of the Republic Kazakhstan;
(2) with respect to international treaties of an intergovernmental character – the Government of the Republic Kazakhstan.

2. The confirmation (or adoption) of international treaties of an interdepartmental character shall be performed by the Government of the Republic Kazakhstan upon the recommendation of the respective ministries, State committees, or other central executive agencies of the Republic Kazakhstan, and also State agencies directly subordinate and accountable to the President of the Republic Kazakhstan.

Article 17 Proposals Concerning Accession to International Treaties

1. The Government of the Republic Kazakhstan shall upon the recommendation of the Ministry of Foreign Affairs of the Republic Kazakhstan submit to the President of the Republic Kazakhstan proposals concerning accession to international treaties of an interstate character.

2. The Ministry of Foreign Affairs of the Republic Kazakhstan shall submit to the Government of the Republic Kazakhstan proposals concerning accession to intergovernmental treaties.

3. Ministries, State committees, and other central executive agencies of the Republic Kazakhstan, and also State agencies directly subordinate and accountable to the President of the Republic Kazakhstan shall, jointly with the Ministry of Foreign Affairs of the Republic Kazakhstan or by agreement with it, submit to the Government of the Republic Kazakhstan with regard to questions of its competence proposals concerning accession to treaties specified in points 1 and 2 of the present Article.

4. The respective ministries, State committees, and other central executive agencies of the Republic Kazakhstan, and also State agencies directly subordinate and accountable to the President of the Republic

Kazakhstan, by agreement with the Ministry of Foreign Affairs of the Republic Kazakhstan shall submit to the Government of the Republic Kazakhstan proposals concerning accession to international treaties of an interdepartmental character.

Article 18 Accession to International Treaties

1. Decisions concerning accession of the Republic Kazakhstan to international treaties shall be adopted by:

(1) with respect to international treaties of an inter-State character submitted by the President of the Republic Kazakhstan, and also with respect to international treaties submitted by the Government of the Republic Kazakhstan and subject to ratification with regard to questions relegated to the jurisdiction of the Government – the Parliament of the Republic Kazakhstan;

(2) with respect to international treaties relegated to the jurisdiction of the Government of the Republic Kazakhstan and not subject to ratification – the Government of the Republic Kazakhstan.

2. Decisions concerning accession to international treaties of an interdepartmental character shall be adopted by the Government of the Republic Kazakhstan.

Article 19 Proposals Concerning Suspension of Operation of International Treaties

1. The Government of the Republic Kazakhstan shall upon the recommendation of the Ministry of Foreign Affairs of the Republic Kazakhstan submit to the President of the Republic Kazakhstan proposals concerning the suspension of the operation of international treaties of the Republic Kazakhstan of an inter-State character.

2. The Ministry of Foreign Affairs of the Republic Kazakhstan shall submit to the Government of the Republic Kazakhstan proposals concerning the suspension of the operation of international treaties of the Republic Kazakhstan with regard to questions relegated to the jurisdiction of the Government.

3. The ministries, State committees, and other central executive agencies of the Republic Kazakhstan, and also State agencies directly subordinate and accountable to the President of the Republic Kazakhstan shall, jointly with the Ministry of Foreign Affairs of the Republic Kazakhstan or by agreement with it, submit to the Government of the Republic Kazakhstan with regard to questions of its competence proposals

concerning the suspension of the operation of international treaties specified in points 1 and 2 of the present Article.

4. The respective ministries, State committees, and other central executive agencies of the Republic Kazakhstan, and also State agencies directly subordinate and accountable to the President of the Republic Kazakhstan, shall by agreement with the Ministry of Foreign Affairs of the Republic Kazakhstan submit to the Government of the Republic Kazakhstan proposals concerning the suspension of international treaties of an interdepartmental character.

Article 20 Suspension of Operation of International Treaties

1. Decisions concerning the suspension of the operation of international treaties of the Republic Kazakhstan shall be adopted by the Parliament of the Republic Kazakhstan:

(1) with respect to international treaties of an inter-State character which are subject to ratification;

(2) with respect to international treaties of an intergovernmental character specified in Article 11 of the present Edict.

2. Decisions concerning the suspension of the operation of international treaties of an inter-State character which are not subject to ratification shall be adopted by the President of the Republic Kazakhstan.

3. Decisions concerning the suspension of the operation of international treaties relegated to the jurisdiction of the Government shall be adopted by the Government of the Republic Kazakhstan except for treaties specified in Article 11 of the present Edict.

4. Decisions concerning the suspension of the operation of international treaties of an interdepartmental character shall be adopted by the Government of the Republic Kazakhstan.

Chapter III Performance of International Treaties of the Republic Kazakhstan

Article 21 Compliance with and Ensuring Fulfilment of International Treaties of Republic Kazakhstan

1. In accordance with the Constitution of the Republic Kazakhstan, the present Edict, other normative acts of the Republic Kazakhstan, and

norms of international law, international treaties shall be subject to absolute compliance by the Republic Kazakhstan.

2. The President of the Republic Kazakhstan shall ensure compliance with treaties concluded by the Republic and obligations adopted by it.

3. The Government of the Republic Kazakhstan shall adopt measures with regard to ensuring the fulfilment of international treaties of the Republic Kazakhstan which have entered into force.

Article 22 Fulfilment of Obligations Under International Treaties

The Government of the Republic Kazakhstan, respective ministries, State committees, and other central executive agencies of the Republic Kazakhstan, and also State agencies directly subordinate and accountable to the President of the Republic Kazakhstan within whose competence are the questions regulated by international treaties of the Republic Kazakhstan shall ensure the fulfilment of the obligations adopted under treaties by the Kazakhstan party, observe the effectuation of the rights belonging to the Kazakhstan party arising from such treaties and over the fulfilment by other participants of the treaties of their obligations.

Article 23 General Observation Over Performance of International Treaties

General observation over the performance of international treaties of the Republic Kazakhstan shall be effectuated by the Ministry of Foreign Affairs of the Republic Kazakhstan.

Article 24 Measures Adopted in Event of Violation of International Treaty of Republic Kazakhstan by its Other Participants

1. In the event of a violation of obligations under an international treaty of the Republic Kazakhstan by its other participants, the Ministry of Foreign Affairs of the Republic Kazakhstan shall submit to the Government of the Republic Kazakhstan a proposal concerning the adoption of necessary measures in accordance with the norms of international law and the conditions of the treaty itself.

2. In the event of a violation of obligations under an international treaty of the Republic Kazakhstan by its other participants, the ministries, State committees, and other central executive agencies of the Republic Kazakhstan, and also State agencies directly subordinate and accountable to the President of the Republic Kazakhstan, shall jointly with the Ministry of Foreign Affairs of the Republic Kazakhstan or by agreement with it submit to the Government of the Republic Kazakhstan with regard to questions of its competence proposals concerning the adoption of necessary measures in accordance with the norms of international law and the conditions of the treaty itself.

3. In the event of a material violation of an international treaty of the Republic Kazakhstan by its other participants, and also in other instances provided for by norms of international law, such treaty may be terminated in the procedure established by Articles 33 and 34 of the present Edict.

Article 25 Interpretation of International Treaties

The interpretation of international treaties of the Republic Kazakhstan shall be performed in accordance with the Constitution of the Republic Kazakhstan and norms of international law.

Article 26 Proposals Concerning Making of Changes in and Additions to Legislation of Republic Kazakhstan in Connection with Conclusion of International Treaty

1. In instances when for the purpose of the fulfilment of an international treaty of the Republic Kazakhstan the adoption of a law or other normative legal act of the Parliament of the Republic Kazakhstan, or the issuance of an Edict of the President of the Republic Kazakhstan, or the issuance of a decree of the Government of the Republic Kazakhstan is necessary, the interested ministries, State committees, and other central executive agencies of the Republic Kazakhstan, and also State agencies directly subordinate and accountable to the President of the Republic Kazakhstan shall, by agreement with the Ministry of Justice of the Republic Kazakhstan and the Ministry of Foreign Affairs of the Republic Kazakhstan, submit in the established procedure proposals concerning the adoption of the proper law or other normative legal act to the President of the Republic Kazakhstan or to the Government of the Republic Kazakhstan.

2. The repeal of normative legal acts of the Republic Kazakhstan adopted in performance of international treaties of the Republic Kazakhstan shall be permitted only after their denunciation, change, or termination of operation.

Article 27 Entry into Force of International Treaties of Republic Kazakhstan

International treaties shall enter into force for the Republic Kazakhstan in the procedure and within the periods provided for in the treaty or agreed between the Contracting Parties.

Chapter IV Publication, Registration, and Keeping of International Treaties of Republic Kazakhstan

Article 28 Publication of International Treaties

1. Inter-State and intergovernmental treaties which have entered into force for the Republic Kazakhstan and undergone in accordance with the present Edict ratification in the Parliament of the Republic Kazakhstan shall be published in official publications of the Parliament.

2. Inter-State and intergovernmental treaties which have entered into force for the Republic Kazakhstan and are not subject to ratification, and also intergovernmental treaties, the accession to which by the Republic Kazakhstan is effectuated in the procedure established by the present Edict, shall be published in the *Собрание актов Президента Республики Казахстан и Правительства Республики Казахстан*.

3. International treaties which have entered into force for the Republic Kazakhstan, including interdepartmental, and also treaties, accession to which by the Republic Kazakhstan is effectuated in the procedure established by the present Edict, shall be published in the *Бюллетень международных договоров, соглашений и отдельных законодательных актов Республики Казахстан*.

4. International treaties of the Republic Kazakhstan whose authentic texts have been drawn up in foreign languages shall be published in one of these languages with an official translation into the Kazakh and Russian languages.

Article 29 Unified State System of Registration and Recording of International Treaties

The unified State system of registration and recording of international treaties of the Republic Kazakhstan shall be within the jurisdiction of the Ministry of Foreign Affairs of the Republic Kazakhstan.

Article 30 Registration and Keeping of Texts of International Treaties

1. The registration of international treaties of the Republic Kazakhstan shall be effectuated by the Ministry of Foreign Affairs of the Republic Kazakhstan at the Secretariat of the United Nations and in respective organs of other international organizations.

2. The originals (or attested copies, official translations) of international treaties of the Republic Kazakhstan concluded in the name of the Republic Kazakhstan and in the name of the Government of the Republic Kazakhstan shall be handed over for keeping to the Ministry of Foreign Affairs of the Republic Kazakhstan within a two-week period from the date of their signature (or receipt from the depositary of attested copies, official translations), and copies of the treaties shall be circulated within a two-week period from the date of their entry into force by the Ministry of Foreign Affairs of the Republic Kazakhstan to the respective State agencies.

3. The originals of interdepartmental treaties of the Republic Kazakhstan shall be kept in the archives of the respective ministries and departments, and attested copies of these treaties shall be sent within a two-week period from the date of signature (or receipt of attested copies or official translations from the depositary) to the Ministry of Foreign Affairs of the Republic Kazakhstan.

Article 31 Effectuation of Functions of Depositary

1. The Ministry of Foreign Affairs of the Republic Kazakhstan shall effectuate the functions of depositary of multilateral international treaties if in accordance with the conditions of these treaties such functions have been placed on the Republic Kazakhstan.

2. Correspondence with the agencies of foreign States, international organizations, or their chief executive officials fulfilling the functions of depositary of multilateral international treaties shall be effectuated by the Ministry of Foreign Affairs of the Republic Kazakhstan.

Chapter V Denunciation of International Treaties of the Republic Kazakhstan

Article 32 Proposals Concerning Denunciation of International Treaties

1. The Government of the Republic Kazakhstan upon the recommendation of the Ministry of Foreign Affairs of the Republic Kazakhstan shall submit to the President of the Republic Kazakhstan proposals concerning the denunciation of international treaties of the Republic Kazakhstan of an inter-State character.

2. The Ministry of Foreign Affairs of the Republic Kazakhstan shall submit to the Government of the Republic Kazakhstan proposals concerning the denunciation of international treaties of the Republic Kazakhstan with regard to questions relegated to the jurisdiction of the Government.

3. Ministries, State committees, and other central executive agencies of the Republic Kazakhstan, and also State agencies directly subordinate and accountable to the President of the Republic Kazakhstan shall, jointly with the Ministry of Foreign Affairs of the Republic Kazakhstan or by agreement with it, submit to the Government of the Republic Kazakhstan with regard to questions of its competence proposals concerning the denunciation of international treaties specified in points 1 and 2 of the present Article.

4. The respective ministries, State committees, and other central executive agencies of the Republic Kazakhstan, and also State agencies directly subordinate and accountable to the President of the Republic Kazakhstan, shall, by agreement with the Ministry of Foreign Affairs of the Republic Kazakhstan, submit to the Government of the Republic Kazakhstan proposals concerning the denunciation of international treaties of an interdepartmental character.

Article 33 Denunciation of International Treaties by Parliament of Republic Kazakhstan

The Parliament of the Republic Kazakhstan in a separate session of the Chambers by means of consecutive consideration of the questions, first in the Mazhilis and then in the Senate, shall denounce:

(1) international treaties of the Republic Kazakhstan of an inter-State character ratified and not subject to ratification upon the recommendation of the President of the Republic Kazakhstan;

(2) international treaties of the Republic Kazakhstan relegated to the jurisdiction of the Government, and also international treaties of the Republic Kazakhstan accession to which was effectuated on the basis of decisions of the Government of the Republic Kazakhstan upon the recommendation of the Government of the Republic Kazakhstan.

Article 34 Denunciation of International Treaties by Government of Republic Kazakhstan

The Government of the Republic Kazakhstan shall denounce international treaties of the Republic Kazakhstan of an interdepartmental character upon the recommendation of the respective ministries, State committees, and other central executive agencies of the Republic Kazakhstan, and also State agencies directly subordinate and accountable to the President of the Republic Kazakhstan, by agreement with the Ministry of Foreign Affairs of the Republic Kazakhstan.

Chapter VI Concluding Provisions

Article 35 Procedure for Entry into Force of Present Edict

1. The Government of the Republic Kazakhstan shall:

(1) submit to the President of the Republic Kazakhstan a proposal with regard to bringing prevailing legislation of the Republic Kazakhstan into conformity with the present Edict;

(2) bring decisions of the Government of the Republic Kazakhstan into conformity with the present Edict.

2. To deem to have lost force point 5 of the Edict of the President of the Republic Kazakhstan of 16 June 1993, No. 1228 'On Measures Relating to Increasing the Effectiveness of Legal Reform in the Republic Kazakhstan' (*САПП Республики Казахстан.* (1993), no. 19, item 230).

3. The present Edict shall enter into from the day of publication.

KYRGYZSTAN

Law on International Treaties of the Kyrgyz Republic

[Adopted by the Zhogorku Kenesh, 22 June 1999; signed by the President of Kyrgyzstan, 21 July 1999, No. 89]

International treaties are the legal foundation of international relations of the Kyrgyz Republic.

International treaties of the Kyrgyz Republic shall in accordance with the Constitution of the Kyrgyz Republic, be an integral and directly operating part of the legislation of the Kyrgyz Republic.

The Kyrgyz Republic favours undeviating compliance with the norms of international law and affirms its adherence to the fundamental principle of international law – the principle of the fulfilment of international obligations in good faith.

I General Provisions

Article 1 Tasks and Sphere of Application of Present Law

1. The present Law shall establish the procedure for the conclusion, performance, termination, suspension, and denunciation of international treaties of the Kyrgyz Republic.

International treaties of the Kyrgyz Republic shall be concluded, performed, terminated, suspended, and denounced in accordance with generally-recognized principles and norms of international law, the Constitution of the Kyrgyz Republic, and also by the present Law and the provisions of the treaty itself.

2. The procedure for the conclusion, performance, termination, suspension, and denunciation of international treaties of the Kyrgyz Republic established by the present Law shall be applied with respect to all international treaties of the Kyrgyz Republic irrespective of their type, form, and name.

Article 2 Use of Terms

For the purposes of the present Law the following terms shall be used:

international treaty of Kyrgyz Republic – equal and voluntary agreement of the Kyrgyz Republic with one or several States, international organizations, or other subjects of international law relating to the rights and duties in the domain of international relations;

conclusion shall mean the expression of consent of the Kyrgyz Republic to the bindingness of the international treaty for it;

signature shall mean either the stage of conclusion of a treaty, or the means of the expression of consent of the Kyrgyz Republic to the bindingness of the international treaty for it, unless it is subject to ratification or confirmation thereafter;

municipal procedures shall mean ratification or confirmation of an international treaty;

ratification, confirmation, and accession shall mean, depending upon the instance, the form of the expression of consent of the Kyrgyz Republic to the bindingness of an international treaty for it;

powers shall mean the document which emanates from the competent agency of the Kyrgyz Republic and by means of which one person or several persons are appointed to represent the Kyrgyz Republic for the purposes of conducting negotiations, adoption of the text of a treaty, or the establishment of its authenticity, expression of consent of the Kyrgyz Republic to the bindingness of the treaty for it or for the purposes of the performance of any other act relating to the treaty;

initialling shall mean certification of the final agreement of the text of an international treaty by the parties expressed in the placing by the plenipotentiaries of the Contracting States of their initials on the text of the treaty;

authentic texts shall mean the texts of the same international treaty drawn up in different languages but having identical legal force;

reservation shall mean a unilateral statement by empowered persons or competent agencies of a state made when signing, ratifying, accepting, or confirming a treaty or accession thereto by means of which the wish is expressed to exclude or change the legal operation of determined provisions of the treaty in their application to the particular State;

international organization shall mean an inter-State or intergovernmental organization;

depositary shall mean the State, international organization, or its chief executive official to whom the original of an international treaty is handed over for keeping and who fulfils with respect to this treaty the functions provided for by international law;

denunciation shall mean the renunciation by the Kyrgyz Republic of an international treaty concluded by it with a warning made in the procedure and within the periods provided for in the treaty itself;

instrument of ratification – a special document testifying to the consideration of the international treaty by the Zhogorku Kenesh of the Kyrgyz Republic and expressing the consent to the bindingness of the international treaty for the Kyrgyz Republic.

Article 3 Names and Types of International Treaties

1. International treaties may be named and concluded in the form of a treaty, agreement, convention, protocol, memorandum, exchange of letters and notes, and also have other names.

2. According to the number of subjects participating therein, international treaties shall be subdivided into bilateral and multilateral. By content international treaties may be: economic, political, financial, legal, and also concluded with regard to other questions. By periods treaties are subdivided into fixed-term and in perpetuity. International treaties may also be concluded in other forms.

3. International treaties of the Kyrgyz Republic shall be concluded with foreign States, and also with international organizations in the name of:

– the Kyrgyz Republic (inter-State treaties);

– the Government of the Kyrgyz Republic (intergovernmental treaties);

– the Zhogorku Kenesh of the Kyrgyz Republic (interparliamentary treaties);

– ministries, State committees, and administrative departments of the Kyrgyz Republic (interdepartmental treaties).

Article 4 Language and Form of International Treaty

The Kyrgyz language shall be the language of an international treaty of the Kyrgyz Republic, and in certain instances the Russian language and language of the other contracting party(ies).

By agreement with the other party to an international treaty, another language may be selected as the language of the treaty.

The language in which the text of an international treaty is drawn up shall be specified in the text of the particular treaty, where the authenticity and official nature thereof shall be determined.

International treaties shall be concluded in written form.

Article 5 Expression of Consent of Kyrgyz Republic to Bindingness of International Treaty for It

1. The consent of the Kyrgyz Republic to the bindingness of an international treaty for it may be expressed by means of:

– signature of the treaty;
– exchange of notes or letters forming the treaty;
– ratification of the treaty;
– confirmation of the treaty;
– accession to the treaty;
– use of any other means of expression of consent which the Contracting Parties have stipulated.

2. Decisions concerning consent to the bindingness of international treaties for the Kyrgyz Republic shall be adopted by agencies of State power of the Kyrgyz Republic in accordance with their competence established by the Constitution of the Kyrgyz Republic, the present Law, and other normative legal acts of the Kyrgyz Republic.

II Procedure for Conclusion and Entry into Force of International Treaties of Kyrgyz Republic

Section I Proposals Concerning Conclusion of International Treaties, Conducting of Negotiations, and Signature of International Treaties

Article 6 Proposals Concerning Conclusion of International Treaties

1. Proposals concerning the conclusion of international treaties in the name of the Kyrgyz Republic shall be submitted to the President of the

Kyrgyz Republic, and proposals concerning the conclusion of international treaties in the name of the Kyrgyz Republic with regard to questions relegated to the jurisdiction of the Government of the Kyrgyz Republic, to the Government of the Kyrgyz Republic.

2. Proposals concerning the conclusion of international treaties in the name of the Kyrgyz Republic shall be submitted to the President of the Kyrgyz Republic by the Ministry of Foreign Affairs of the Kyrgyz Republic.

Other ministries, State committees, and administrative departments shall submit to the President of the Kyrgyz Republic proposals concerning the conclusion of international treaties in the name of the Kyrgyz Republic with regard to questions within their competence by agreement with the Ministry of Foreign Affairs of the Kyrgyz Republic.

3. Proposals concerning the conclusion of interparliamentary treaties shall be submitted by the Torag of the Legislative Assembly, the Torag of the Assembly of People's Representatives of the Zhogorku Kenesh of the Kyrgyz Republic or by deputies of the Zhogorku Kenesh of the Kyrgyz Republic for consideration of the chambers of the Zhogorku Kenesh of the Kyrgyz Republic.

4. Proposals concerning the conclusion of international treaties of the Kyrgyz Republic in the name of the Government of the Kyrgyz Republic shall be submitted to the Government of the Kyrgyz Republic by the Ministry of Foreign Affairs of the Kyrgyz Republic.

Other ministries, State committees, and administrative departments shall submit to the Government of the Kyrgyz Republic proposals concerning the conclusion of international treaties in the name of the Government of the Kyrgyz Republic by agreement with the Ministry of Foreign Affairs of the Kyrgyz Republic.

5. Proposals concerning the conclusion of international treaties of the Kyrgyz Republic of an interdepartmental character shall be submitted for agreement to the Government of the Kyrgyz Republic by ministries, State committees, and administrative departments with regard to questions within their competence by agreement with the Ministry of Foreign Affairs of the Kyrgyz Republic.

6. The draft treaty, substantiation of the advisability of the conclusion thereof, mechanism for realization of the treaty, opinion concerning the conformity of the draft treaty to legislation of the Kyrgyz Republic, and also an assessment of the respective ministries, State committees, and administrative departments of the Kyrgyz Republic concerning the possible financial–economic and other consequences of conclusion of the treaty, must be appended to the proposals concerning the conclusion of international treaties.

Article 7 Agreement of Proposals Concerning Conclusion of International Treaties With Respective Ministries, State Committees, and Administrative Departments

1. Proposals concerning the conclusion of international treaties of the Kyrgyz Republic shall before the submission thereof to the President of the Kyrgyz Republic or to the Government of the Kyrgyz Republic be agreed with the interested ministries, State committees, and administrative departments.

Drafts of treaties subject to ratification by the Zhogorku Kenesh of the Kyrgyz Republic shall be sent for agreement to the respective committees of the Legislative Assembly of the Zhogorku Kenesh of the Kyrgyz Republic.

Draft treaties shall undergo expert examination in the Ministry of Justice of the Kyrgyz Republic with regard to questions of their conformity to legislation of the Republic, in the Ministry of Finances of the Kyrgyz Republic in the part of financial obligations arising from the draft treaties, and agreed with the Ministry of Foreign Affairs of the Kyrgyz Republic.

2. Ministries, State committees, and administrative departments of the Kyrgyz Republic shall have the right to conduct by agreement with the Ministry of Foreign Affairs of the Kyrgyz Republic consultations with the respective agencies of foreign States or international organizations with regard to the preparation of draft international treaties for submission in the procedure established by Article 6 of the present Law and the present Article of proposals concerning the conclusion thereof to the President of the Kyrgyz Republic or to the Government of the Kyrgyz Republic.

Article 8 Decisions Concerning Signature of International Treaties

1. Decisions concerning the signature of international treaties of the Kyrgyz Republic shall be adopted with respect to:

(a) treaties to be concluded in the name of the Kyrgyz Republic, by the President of the Kyrgyz Republic, and with respect to treaties to be concluded in the name of the Kyrgyz Republic with regard to questions relegated to the jurisdiction of the Government of the Kyrgyz Republic, by the Government of the Kyrgyz Republic;

(b) treaties to be concluded in the name of the Government of the Kyrgyz Republic, by the Government of the Kyrgyz Republic.

2. Decisions concerning the signature of interparliamentary treaties of the Kyrgyz Republic shall be adopted by the chambers of the Zhogorku Kenesh of the Kyrgyz Republic.

3. Decisions concerning the signature of interdepartmental treaties shall be adopted by ministries, State committees, and administrative departments of the Kyrgyz Republic within whose competence are the questions to be regulated by such treaties, by agreement with the Government of the Kyrgyz Republic.

4. Decisions concerning the signature of international treaties of an interdepartmental character, if the respective questions have significance for the State interests of the Kyrgyz Republic, shall be adopted by the Government of the Kyrgyz Republic.

Article 9 Conducting of Negotiations and Signature of International Treaties of Kyrgyz Republic Without Special Powers

1. The President of the Kyrgyz Republic as the Head of State shall represent the Kyrgyz Republic in international relations and in accordance with international law and the Constitution of the Kyrgyz Republic conduct negotiations and sign international treaties of the Kyrgyz Republic without special powers.

2. The Toraga of the Legislative Assembly and the Toraga of the Assembly of People's Representatives of the Zhogorku Kenesh of the Kyrgyz Republic shall have the right to conduct negotiations and sign in the name of the Zhogorku Kenesh of the Kyrgyz Republic international treaties of the Kyrgyz Republic without special powers.

3. The Prime Minister of the Kyrgyz Republic as the Head of Government of the Kyrgyz Republic shall in accordance with international law conduct negotiations and sign international treaties of the Kyrgyz Republic without special powers.

4. The Minister of Foreign Affairs of the Kyrgyz Republic shall by virtue of his powers and in accordance with international law conduct negotiations and sign international treaties of the Kyrgyz Republic without special powers.

5. The head of a diplomatic representation of the Kyrgyz Republic in a foreign State or the head of representation of the Kyrgyz Republic attached to an international organization shall have the right to conduct negotiations concerning the conclusion of an international treaty of the Kyrgyz Republic with the receiving State or within the framework of the particular international organization without special powers on the basis of instructions of the Ministry of Foreign Affairs of the Kyrgyz Republic.

6. A minister, chairman of a State committee, or head of an administrative department shall within the limits of his competence have the right to conduct negotiations and sign international treaties of an interdepartmental character without special powers.

Article 10 Powers to Conduct Negotiations and to Sign International Treaties of Kyrgyz Republic

The powers to conduct negotiations and sign international treaties of the Kyrgyz Republic shall be issued with respect to:

– treaties to be concluded in the name of the Kyrgyz Republic, by the President of the Kyrgyz Republic, and with respect to treaties to be concluded in the name of the Kyrgyz Republic with regard to questions relegated to the jurisdiction of the Government of the Kyrgyz Republic, by the Government of the Kyrgyz Republic. Powers to conduct negotiations and to sign the said treaties shall be formalized and issued on the basis of the adopted decision of the President of the Kyrgyz Republic or Government of the Kyrgyz Republic by the Ministry of Foreign Affairs of the Kyrgyz Republic;

– treaties to be concluded in the name of the Zhogorku Kenesh of the Kyrgyz Republic, the Toraga of the Legislative Assembly or the Toraga of the Assembly of People's Representatives of the Zhogorku Kenesh of the Kyrgyz Republic;

– treaties to be concluded in the name of the Government of the Kyrgyz Republic, by the Government of the Kyrgyz Republic. The powers to conduct negotiations and to sign the said treaties shall be formalized in the name of the Government of the Kyrgyz Republic by the Ministry of Foreign Affairs of the Kyrgyz Republic;

– interdepartmental treaties, by the minister, chairman of the State committee, or head of the administrative department of the Kyrgyz Republic.

Section 2 Municipal Procedures of Kyrgyz Republic

Article 11 International Treaties of Kyrgyz Republic Subject to Ratification

1. There shall be subject to ratification:

– international treaties of the Kyrgyz Republic concerning friendship, cooperation, and mutual assistance and treaties concerning the foundations of inter-State relations;

– treaties with regard to questions touching upon the defence capability of the country;

– treaties with regard to questions of disarmament;

– treaties with regard to questions of ensuring international peace and security;

– treaties concerning collective security;

– treaties concerning the boundary and territorial delimitation of the Kyrgyz Republic with other States;

– treaties concerning the granting by the Kyrgyz Republic of state loans and economic and other assistance to foreign States;

– treaties concerning investments;

– treaties, the subject of which are the basic rights and freedoms of man and citizen;

– treaties concerning the participation of the Kyrgyz Republic in inter-State alliances, international organizations, and other inter-State associations if such treaties provide for the transfer to them of the effectuation of part of the powers of the Kyrgyz Republic or establish the legal obligatoriness of decisions of their organs for the Kyrgyz Republic;

– treaties concerning the use of natural resources by other subjects of international law and foreign companies;

– treaties with regard to the granting of credits to the Kyrgyz Republic and treaties providing for financial obligations of the Kyrgyz Republic;

– treaties establishing other rules than those which are contained in legislation of the Kyrgyz Republic.

2. International treaties of the Kyrgyz Republic, during the conclusion of which the parties have stipulated subsequent ratification, likewise shall be subject to ratification.

3. The President of the Kyrgyz Republic shall ratify financial treaties and credit agreements signed on his behalf by the Prime Minister of the Kyrgyz Republic, members of the Government, or other officials.

Article 12 Proposals Concerning Ratification of International Treaties of Kyrgyz Republic

1. Proposals concerning the ratification of international treaties, the decisions concerning the signature of which were adopted by the President of the Kyrgyz Republic shall be submitted to the Zhogorku Kenesh of the Kyrgyz Republic for ratification by the President of the Kyrgyz Republic.

2. Proposals concerning the ratification of international treaties of the Kyrgyz Republic, decisions concerning the signature of which were adopted by the Government of the Kyrgyz Republic, shall be submitted to

the Legislative Assembly of the Zhogorku Kenesh of the Kyrgyz Republic for ratification by the Government of the Kyrgyz Republic.

3. Proposals concerning the ratification of international financial treaties and credit agreements shall be submitted to the President of the Kyrgyz Republic by the Government of the Kyrgyz Republic in accordance with the Constitution of the Kyrgyz Republic.

4. Proposals concerning the submission for ratification of international treaties of the Kyrgyz Republic shall be submitted respectively to the President of the Kyrgyz Republic or to the Government of the Kyrgyz Republic by ministries, State committees, and administrative departments with regard to treaties within their competence by agreement with the Ministry of Foreign Affairs of the Republic Kyrgyzstan.

International treaties subject to presentation to the President of the Kyrgyz Republic for submission for ratification, the fulfilment of which requires preliminary consideration thereof by the Government of the Kyrgyz Republic, shall be submitted to the Government of the Kyrgyz Republic.

A proposal concerning ratification of an international treaty must contain an attested copy of the official text of the international treaty, substantiation of the advisability of the ratification thereof, agreement with interested ministries, State committees, and administrative departments, and also an evaluation of the possible and financial–economic and other consequences of ratification, in particular entailing a change of legislation of the Kyrgyz Republic.

5. Decisions of the Government of the Kyrgyz Republic concerning approval and submission for ratification of international treaties shall be adopted in the form of a decree.

Article 13 Decision Concerning Ratification of International Treaties of Kyrgyz Republic

1. A decision concerning the ratification of international treaties of the Kyrgyz Republic (including financial treaties and credit agreements) shall be adopted by the Legislative Assembly of the Zhogorku Kenesh of the Kyrgyz Republic in the form of a law, which shall be approved by the Assembly of People's Representatives of the Zhogorku Kenesh of the Kyrgyz Republic and shall be signed by the President of the Kyrgyz Republic.

2. A decision concerning the ratification of financial treaties and credit agreements of the Kyrgyz Republic shall be adopted by the President of the Kyrgyz Republic in the form of an edict only in the event of the transfer of the powers to him for the signature thereof.

Article 14 Instrument of Ratification

On the basis of a law concerning the ratification of an international treaty the President of the Kyrgyz Republic shall sign the instrument of ratification, which shall be sealed with the seal thereof and the signature of the Minister of Foreign Affairs of the Kyrgyz Republic.

Article 15 Exchange of Instruments of Ratification and Handing Over Thereof for Keeping

The exchange of instruments of ratification and handing over instruments concerning ratification of international treaties of the Kyrgyz Republic for keeping to depositaries shall be by the Ministry of Foreign Affairs of the Kyrgyz Republic or on its behalf by the diplomatic representation of the Kyrgyz Republic or permanent representation of the Kyrgyz Republic attached to an international organization.

Article 16 Confirmation of International Treaties of Kyrgyz Republic not Subject to Ratification

1. International treaties of the Kyrgyz Republic not subject to ratification but providing for the confirmation thereof shall be confirmed with respect to:

(a) treaties to be concluded in the name of the Kyrgyz Republic – by the President of the Kyrgyz Republic in the form of an edict, and with respect to treaties to be concluded in the name of the Kyrgyz Republic with regard to questions relegated to the jurisdiction of the Government of the Kyrgyz Republic, by the Government of the Kyrgyz Republic in the form of a decree;

(b) treaties to be concluded in the name of the Government of the Kyrgyz Republic, by the Government of the Kyrgyz Republic in the form of a decree;

(c) interdepartmental treaties providing for the entry thereof into force after confirmation, by the ministry, State committee, or administrative department in whose name such treaties have been signed, in the form of a regulation.

2. Proposals concerning the confirmation of international treaties of the Kyrgyz Republic shall be submitted in the procedure established by Article 6 of the present Law.

Article 17 Accession of Kyrgyz Republic to International Treaties

1. A decision concerning the accession of the Kyrgyz Republic to international treaties shall be adopted with respect to:
(a) treaties subject to ratification – by the Zhogorku Kenesh of the Kyrgyz Republic in the procedure established by Article 12 of the present Law;
(b) treaties not subject to ratification, accession to which is in the name of the Kyrgyz Republic – by the President of the Kyrgyz Republic, and with respect to treaties not subject to ratification, accession to which is in the name of the Kyrgyz Republic with regard to questions relegated to the jurisdiction of the Government of the Kyrgyz Republic – by the Government of the Kyrgyz Republic;
(c) treaties, accession to which is in the name of the Government of the Kyrgyz Republic – by the Government of the Kyrgyz Republic.

2. Decisions concerning accession to interparliamentary treaties shall be adopted by the Legislative Assembly and Assembly of People's Representatives of the Zhogorku Kenesh of the Kyrgyz Republic.

3. Accession to international treaties of an interdepartmental character shall be effectuated in the procedure established by Article 8(3) and (4) of the present Law.

4. Proposals concerning accession to international treaties to be effectuated in the form of a law shall be submitted in the procedure established by Article 12 of the present Law, and in the remaining instances, in the procedure provided for by Articles 6, 7, and 16 of the present Law.

Article 18 Proposals Concerning the Making of Changes in and Additions to Legislation of the Kyrgyz Republic in Connection with the Conclusion of International Treaty of Kyrgyz Republic

In instances when it is necessary to eliminate contradictions which have arisen between norms of an international treaty and legislation of the Republic or for the purposes of the fulfilment of the international treaty of the Kyrgyz Republic the adoption of a law or other act is necessary, the interested ministries, State committees, and administrative departments of the Kyrgyz Republic shall in the established procedure submit necessary draft normative legal acts to the President of the Kyrgyz Republic or Government of the Kyrgyz Republic.

Article 19 Special Procedure for Expression of Consent to Obligatoriness of International Treaties for Kyrgyz Republic

If an international treaty contains rules requiring changes of individual provisions of the Constitution of the Kyrgyz Republic, the decision concerning consent to the obligatoriness thereof for the Kyrgyz Republic shall be possible in the form of a law only after the making of respective amendments to the Constitution of the Kyrgyz Republic or review of its provisions in the established procedure.

Article 20 Provisional Application of International Treaty by Kyrgyz Republic

1. An international treaty or part of a treaty may until its entry into force be applied by the Kyrgyz Republic provisionally if this has been provided for in the contract or an arrangement was reached concerning this with the parties who have signed the contract.

2. A decision concerning the temporary application by the Kyrgyz Republic of an international treaty or part thereof shall be adopted by the agency which adopted the decision concerning the signature of the international treaty.

Article 21 Entry into Force and Period of Operation of International Treaties of Kyrgyz Republic

1. International treaties shall enter into force for the Kyrgyz Republic in accordance with the present Law in the procedure and within the periods provided for in the treaty or agreed between the Contracting Parties.

2. Official communications of the Ministry of Foreign Affairs of the Kyrgyz Republic concerning the entry into force of international treaties of the Kyrgyz Republic concluded in the name of the Kyrgyz Republic and in the name of the Government of the Kyrgyz Republic shall be published in the procedure provided for by Article 23 of the present Law.

Article 22 Reservations to International Treaties of Kyrgyz Republic

1. When signing, ratifying, confirming (or accepting) international treaties of the Kyrgyz Republic or acceding to treaties reservations may be made in compliance with the conditions of the treaty and respective norms of international law.

2. Reservations may be removed at any time in the same procedure by which they were made.

3. The acceptance of a reservation made by another Contracting State to an international treaty of the Kyrgyz Republic or objections against it shall be effectuated in accordance with the conditions of the treaty itself and norms of international law by the agency adopting the decision concerning consent to the obligatoriness of the international treaty for the Kyrgyz Republic.

Proposals concerning the acceptance of reservations to international treaties requiring ratification shall be submitted in the procedure established by Article 12 of the present Law, and in the remaining instances, in the procedure provided for by Article 6 of the present Law.

III Publication and Registration of International Treaties of Kyrgyz Republic

Article 23 Publication of International Treaties of Kyrgyz Republic

1. International treaties which have entered into force for the Kyrgyz Republic (except for treaties of an interdepartmental character) shall be published officially in the *Ведомости Жогорку Кенеша Кыргызской Республики*, collection of acts and laws of the President of the Kyrgyz Republic, and official publications of the Government of the Kyrgyz Republic in accordance with laws of the Kyrgyz Republic 'On Normative Legal Acts of the Kyrgyz Republic' and 'On the Procedure for the Publication of Laws of the Kyrgyz Republic'.

2. International treaties of the Kyrgyz Republic of an interdepartmental character shall be published by decision of the respective ministries, State committees, and administrative departments in whose name such treaties have been concluded in the official publications of these agencies or in official publications of the Government of the Kyrgyz Republic.

3. International treaties of the Kyrgyz Republic whose authentic texts have been drawn up in foreign languages shall be published in the State language. International treaties of the Kyrgyz Republic may also be published in other languages.

Article 24 Unified State System of Registration and Recording of International Treaties of Kyrgyz Republic

The unified State system of registration and recording of international treaties of the Kyrgyz Republic shall be effectuated by the Ministry of Foreign Affairs of the Kyrgyz Republic.

Article 25 Registration of International Treaties of Kyrgyz Republic in International Organizations

The registration of international treaties of the Kyrgyz Republic at the Secretariat of the United Nations and in respective agencies of other international organizations shall be effectuated by the Ministry of Foreign Affairs of the Kyrgyz Republic.

Article 26 Keeping of Texts of International Treaties of Kyrgyz Republic

1. The originals (or attested copies, official translations) of international treaties of the Kyrgyz Republic concluded in the name of the Kyrgyz Republic and in the name of the Government of the Kyrgyz Republic shall be handed over for keeping to the Ministry of Foreign Affairs of the Kyrgyz Republic within a two-week period from the day of signature thereof (or receipt of attested copies from depositary, official translations), and copies of these treaties within a two-week period from the day of their entry into force shall be circulated to the respective ministries, State committees, and administrative departments.

2. The originals of international interdepartmental treaties of the Kyrgyz Republic shall be kept in archives of the respective ministries, State committees, and administrative departments of the Kyrgyz Republic, and attested copies of these treaties within a two-week period from the day of their signature (or receipt from the depositary of attested copies, official translations) shall be sent to the Ministry of Foreign Affairs of the Kyrgyz Republic.

3. The procedure for keeping originals of international treaties of the Kyrgyz Republic shall be confirmed by the Minister of Foreign Affairs of the Kyrgyz Republic.

Article 27 Effectuation of Functions of Depositary

1. The Ministry of Foreign Affairs of the Kyrgyz Republic shall effectuate the functions of depositary of multilateral international treaties if in accordance with the conditions of these treaties such functions have been placed on the Kyrgyz Republic.

2. Correspondence with agencies of foreign States, international organizations, or their chief executive officials fulfilling the functions of depositary of multilateral international treaties shall be effectuated by the Ministry of Foreign Affairs of the Kyrgyz Republic.

IV Performance of International Treaties of Kyrgyz Republic

Article 28 Compliance with International Treaties of Kyrgyz Republic

1. International treaties of the Kyrgyz Republic shall be subject to undeviating and obligatory compliance by the Kyrgyz Republic in accordance with norms of international law and legislation of the Kyrgyz Republic.

2. An international treaty shall be subject to fulfilment by the Kyrgyz Republic from the moment of entry into force for the Kyrgyz Republic. The Kyrgyz Republic shall until the entry into force of an international treaty for it refrain from actions, taking into account the respective norms of international law, which would deprive the treaty of its object and purpose.

Article 29 Fulfilment of Obligations With Regard to International Treaties of Kyrgyz Republic

1. The President of the Kyrgyz Republic shall in accordance with the Constitution of the Kyrgyz Constitution ensure compliance with treaties concluded by the Republic and obligations accepted by it.

2. The Government of the Kyrgyz Republic shall work out measures relating to the fulfilment of international treaties of the Kyrgyz Republic

and determine the ministries, State committees, and administrative departments and officials on which responsibility for the performance of obligations shall be placed with regard to international treaties of the Kyrgyz Republic.

3. The Government of the Kyrgyz Republic, ministries, State committees, and administrative departments, and other State agencies within whose competence are questions to be regulated by international treaties of the Kyrgyz Republic shall ensure the fulfilment of obligations accepted with regard to the treaty on the part of the Kyrgyz Republic, watch over the effectuation of rights arising from such treaties which belong to the Kyrgyz Republic, and over the fulfilment by other participants of the treaties of their obligations.

4. The Government of the Kyrgyz Republic shall effectuate control over the fulfilment of obligations with regard to international treaties of the Kyrgyz Republic.

Article 30 Observation Over Performance of International Treaties of Kyrgyz Republic

1. General observation over the performance of international treaties of the Kyrgyz Republic shall be effectuated by the Ministry of Foreign Affairs of the Kyrgyz Republic.

2. General observation over the performance of international financial treaties of the Kyrgyz Republic, credit agreements, and agreements concerning a grant shall be effectuated by the Ministry of Finances of the Kyrgyz Republic.

Article 31 Measures to be Adopted in Event of Violation of International Treaty of Kyrgyz Republic by Other Participants Thereof

In the event of a violation of obligations under an international treaty of the Kyrgyz Republic by other participants thereof the Ministry of Foreign Affairs of the Kyrgyz Republic or other interested ministries, State committees, and administrative departments shall by agreement with the Ministry of Foreign Affairs of the Kyrgyz Republic submit to the President of the Kyrgyz Republic or to the Government of the Kyrgyz Republic proposals concerning the taking of necessary measures in accordance with norms of international law and the conditions of the treaty itself.

V Invalidity, Termination, Denunciation, and Suspension of International Treaties of Kyrgyz Republic

Article 32 Invalidity of International Treaties of Kyrgyz Republic

1. An international treaty of the Kyrgyz Republic may be deemed to be invalid in accordance with the norms of international law.

2. If there are grounds provided for by norms of international law for deeming an international treaty to be invalid, the Ministry of Foreign Affairs of the Kyrgyz Republic or other interested ministries, State committees, and administrative departments shall by agreement with the Ministry of Foreign Affairs of the Kyrgyz Republic submit to the President of the Kyrgyz Republic (with regard to inter-State treaties) or to the Government of the Kyrgyz Republic (with regard to intergovernmental treaties) proposals concerning the deeming of a treaty to be invalid.

Article 33 Termination of International Treaty or Withdrawal Therefrom

Termination of an international treaty or withdrawal therefrom by the Kyrgyz Republic may occur:

(a) in accordance with the provisions of the treaty;

(b) at any time on the basis of consultations with other participants of the treaty.

Article 34 Denunciation of International Treaty of Kyrgyz Republic

1. Proposals concerning the denunciation of international treaties of the Kyrgyz Republic concluded in the name of the Kyrgyz Republic and in the name of the Government of the Kyrgyz Republic shall be submitted, depending upon who adopted the decision concerning consent to the obligatoriness of the treaty for the Kyrgyz Republic, to the President of the Kyrgyz Republic or to the Government of the Kyrgyz Republic by the Ministry of Foreign Affairs of the Kyrgyz Republic autonomously or by agreement with other ministries, State committee, and administrative departments of the Kyrgyz Republic.

2. Proposals concerning the denunciation of international treaties of the Kyrgyz Republic, decisions concerning consent to the obligatoriness of which for the Kyrgyz Republic were adopted in the form of a law shall be submitted to the Zhogorku Kenesh of the Kyrgyz Republic by the President of the Kyrgyz Republic or by the Government of the Kyrgyz Republic depending upon who submitted the proposal on the basis of which ratification of the international treaty by the Kyrgyz Republic occurred.

3. The Government of the Kyrgyz Republic shall have the right, when necessary, to submit to the President of the Kyrgyz Republic a proposal concerning the submission of proposal to the Zhogorku Kenesh of the Kyrgyz Republic on the denunciation of an international treaty of the Kyrgyz Republic, the decision concerning consent to the obligatoriness of which for the Kyrgyz Republic was adopted in the form of a law on the basis of a submission of the Government of the Kyrgyz Republic.

4. Proposals concerning the denunciation of international treaties of the Kyrgyz Republic must contain an attested copy of the official text of the international treaty, a substantiation of the advisability of the denunciation thereof, and also an evaluation of possible financial–economic or other consequences of the termination of the operation of an international treaty.

Article 35 Suspension of Operation of International Treaty of Kyrgyz Republic

1. Suspension of the operation of an international treaty of the Kyrgyz Republic with respect to all participants of the treaty or with respect to an individual participant of the treaty shall be possible:

(a) in accordance with the provisions of the treaty;

(b) at any time on the basis of consultations with other participants of the treaty.

2. Proposals concerning the suspension of an international treaty of the Kyrgyz Republic shall be submitted in accordance with Article 34 of the present Law.

Article 36 Termination and Suspension of Operation of International Treaties of Kyrgyz Republic

1. The termination and suspension of the operation of international treaties of the Kyrgyz Republic shall be effectuated in accordance with the conditions of the treaty itself and norms of international law by the

agency which adopted the decision concerning consent to the bindingness of the international treaty for the Kyrgyz Republic.

2. Proposals concerning the suspension of the operation of an international treaty shall be submitted by the Ministry of Foreign Affairs of the Kyrgyz Republic with respect to inter-State treaties to the President of the Kyrgyz Republic, and with respect to intergovernmental treaties, to the Government of the Kyrgyz Republic.

Proposals concerning the suspension of international treaties of the Kyrgyz Republic, decisions concerning consent to the bindingness of which for the Kyrgyz Republic were adopted in the form of a law shall be submitted to the Zhogorku Kenesh of the Kyrgyz Republic by the President of the Kyrgyz Republic or by the Government of the Kyrgyz Republic, depending upon which submitted the proposal on the basis of which ratification of the international treaty by the Zhogorku Kenesh of the Kyrgyz Republic occurred.

3. Termination and suspension of the operation of international interdepartmental treaties of the Kyrgyz Republic shall be by ministries, State committees, and administrative departments in whose name such treaties were concluded by agreement with the Ministry of Foreign Affairs of the Kyrgyz Republic, other interested State agencies of the Kyrgyz Republic, and with the authorization of the Government of the Kyrgyz Republic.

Article 37 Consequences of Termination of International Treaty of Kyrgyz Republic

Termination of an international treaty of the Kyrgyz Republic, unless provided otherwise by the treaty or there is another arrangement with other participants thereof, shall release the Kyrgyz Republic from any obligation to fulfil the treaty thereafter and shall not affect the rights, obligations, or legal position of the Kyrgyz Republic which arose as a result of the fulfilment of the treaty before the termination thereof.

Article 38 Consequences of Suspension of Operation of International Treaty

1. The suspension of the operation of an international treaty of the Kyrgyz Republic, unless provided otherwise by the treaty or there is another arrangement of the participants thereof, shall release the Kyrgyz

Republic from the obligation to fulfil provisions of the treaty during the period of suspension of the treaty in its relations with those of its participants with which the operation of the treaty is suspended and shall not affect the remaining legal relations of the Kyrgyz Republic established by the treaty with other participants thereof.

2. In the period of suspension of the operation of an international treaty of the Kyrgyz Republic agencies of State power of the Kyrgyz Republic shall refrain from actions which may impede the renewal of the operation of the treaty.

Article 39 Official Communications Concerning Termination or Suspension of Operation of International Treaties

Official communications of the Ministry of Foreign Affairs of the Kyrgyz Republic concerning the termination or suspension of the operation of international treaties of the Kyrgyz Republic to be concluded in the name of the Kyrgyz Republic and in the name of the Government of the Kyrgyz Republic shall be published in the procedure provided for by Article 23 of the present Law.

VI Concluding Provisions

Article 40 Entry of Present Law into Force

1. The present Law shall enter into force from the day of publication.

2. To deem to have lost force:

the Law of the Kyrgyz Republic 'On the Conclusion, Ratification, Performance, and Denunciation of International Treaties of the Kyrgyz Republic' (*Ведомости Жогорку Кенеша Кыргызской Республики* (1994), no. 7, item 320);

the Law of the Kyrgyz Republic 'On Making Changes in and Additions to the Law of the Kyrgyz Republic' (of 7 September 1996, no. 54).

3. The Government of the Kyrgyz Republic shall bring its decisions into conformity with the present Law.

MOLDOVA

Law on the Procedure for the Conclusion, Application, Ratification, and Denunciation of International Treaties, Conventions, and Agreements

[Adopted 4 August 1992, No. 1137-XII]

Article 1 The Republic Moldova shall undertake necessary actions for the conducting of negotiations and conclusion of international treaties, conventions, and agreements (hereinafter: treaties) in the domain of politics, security, economy, culture, science, technology, and other domains by proceeding from its fundamental interests and in accordance with existing international rules and practice.

Article 2 The President of the Republic, Prime Minister and Minister of Foreign Affairs shall represent the State in international relations and in this capacity shall conclude treaties in the name of the Republic Moldova. The President of the Republic may empower members of the Government to conclude treaties.

On the basis of powers given by the President of the Republic, the Government shall take measures for the commencement and conducting of negotiations with regard to the conclusion of treaties in the name of the Republic Moldova.

Article 3 The Government may conduct negotiations and conclude intergovernmental treaties.

The Government shall confirm interdepartmental treaties concluded.

Article 4 The conducting of negotiations and conclusion of treaties in the name of the Republic Moldova shall be effectuated by delegations confirmed by the President of the Republic on the basis of powers received in accordance with the provisions of Article 2.

The conducting of negotiations and conclusion of intergovernmental and interdepartmental treaties shall be effectuated on the basis of the powers by delegations confirmed for this purpose.

Article 5 The President of the Republic, Prime Minister, and Minister of Foreign Affairs shall conduct negotiations and conclude treaties without the presentation of powers.

In other instances the powers for signature of intergovernmental treaties shall be consolidated by a document issued by the Ministry of Foreign Affairs in accordance with norms of international law and international practice.

Article 6 Parliament shall ratify:

(a) treaties concluded in the name of the Republic Moldova;

(b) intergovernmental treaties concerning political and military cooperation;

(c) intergovernmental treaties requiring the adoption of new laws or the revision of prevailing ones;

(d) intergovernmental treaties which:

presuppose the fulfilment of political and financial obligations;

relate to:

- the political regimes of States;
- the territory of the Republic Moldova;
- the status of persons, the rights and freedoms of man and citizen, and the status of national minorities;

determine the participation of the Republic Moldova in international organizations;

(e) any treaty whose ratification is specially provided for by the Parliament.

Article 7 The provisions of Article 6 also shall apply in the event of the accession of the Republic Moldova to treaties.

Article 8 Treaties which are not subject to ratification shall be relegated to the competence of the Government. After conclusion they shall be confirmed by the Government.

The Government shall inform the Parliament and President of the Republic about the conclusion of any treaties not subject to ratification.

Article 9 Treaties of a technical character concluded by the Ministry of Foreign Affairs or by other ministries and departments by means of the exchange of notes or letters may enter into force from the day of exchange thereof without their ratification or subsequent confirmation.

Article 10 The initiative in conducting negotiations and concluding treaties in the name of the Republic Moldova or the Government in accordance with the provisions of Article 4 shall belong to the Ministry of Foreign Affairs.

Other ministries and departments having external functions and respective powers may take the initiative with regard to conducting negotiations for the conclusion of treaties only on the basis of powers and with the cooperation of the Ministry of Foreign Affairs.

The Ministry of Foreign Affairs autonomously or when necessary jointly with other ministries and departments shall submit to the Government proposals with regard to the conclusion, ratification, and confirmation of treaties, accession thereto, or the denunciation thereof.

Article 11 Treaties shall be denounced in the same procedure as their ratification.

Article 12 The ratification of treaties concluded in the name of the Republic Moldova, accession thereto, or the denunciation thereof shall be consolidated by respective documents over the signature of the President of the Republic and sealed with the sealing-wax seal of the State and the signature of the Minister of Foreign Affairs.

The aforesaid documents shall be subject to exchange between the Contracting Parties or handed over for keeping to the depositary in accordance with the norms of international law and international practice.

Approval of intergovernmental treaties shall be brought by diplomatic means to the information of the other Contracting Party or depositary.

Article 13 The Government shall undertake necessary measures for the application of treaties and control the performance thereof.

The Government periodically shall inform the Parliament and the President of the Republic about problems arising in connection with the application of treaties for the purpose of an operational settlement in full conformity with the norms of international law and the interests of the Republic Moldova.

Article 14 Decrees concerning ratification of treaties, and also the full texts thereof, shall be published in official publications of the Parliament and the Government. The Ministry of Foreign Affairs shall ensure the publication of information concerning the course of the fulfilment of basic treaties, one of the parties to which is the Republic Moldova, and also the registration thereof in the United Nations.

Article 15 In the process of conducting negotiations the initiator of the conclusion of a treaty shall request a written opinion with regard to the political, legal, economic, and other aspects from ministries and departments which may be interested in the realization thereof.

The said ministries and departments shall be obliged within a 30-day period from the day of recourse to them to submit a written opinion to the initiator.

Article 16 The originals of the texts of treaties signed by empowered representatives of the Republic Moldova shall be transferred within a 15-day period from the day of ratification or confirmation for registration and keeping in the archive of treaties of the Ministry of Foreign Affairs.

Attested copies of treaties, one of the parties to which is the Republic Moldova, shall be registered and kept in the archive of treaties of the Ministry of Foreign Affairs.

Article 17 The Ministry of Foreign Affairs autonomously or jointly with other ministries and departments shall within a 30-day period from the day of accession of the Republic Moldova to a treaty be obliged to come to Parliament with proposals concerning the bringing of legislation into conformity with the provisions of the treaty.

Article 18 The Methods Instruction for the Conclusion, Application, Ratification, and Denunciation of International Treaties, Conventions, and Agreements is appended.

Annex: Methods Instruction for the Conclusion, Application, Ratification, and Denunciation of International Treaties, Conventions, and Agreements

I Stages of Conclusion of Treaty

1. The conducting of negotiations encompasses the activity of the representatives of States relating to the establishment of the clause of the treaty. Negotiations are conducted between governments through external and internal State agencies for international relations. In international practice negotiations are conducted usually by diplomatic means, specially empowered persons, at international conferences and congresses, and in international organizations.

2. The working out of the text is a process taking into account the fact that the text must have a determined structure consisting of a preamble, basic part, content or essence, concluding part or concluding clause, conclusion or protocol part, specification in which languages of the treaty are set out, and also the annexes.

3. The signature of a treaty is the stage which determines the treaties which must according to the will of the parties receive obligatory legal force only through the subsequent procedure of ratification and is distinguished from signature and treaties which according to the will of the parties receive legal force through the signature thereof.

4. Ratification is effectuated by means of a written document called an instrument of ratification, the form of which is regulated by internal law. By means of ratification a State becomes one of the parties to a treaty if it entered into force or enters into force as a consequence of ratification.

5. Acceptance or accession is used in international practice analogously to ratification. This occurs especially when States participating in the working out of a treaty have not signed or have signed a treaty only *ad referendum* or acceded to a treaty open for signature.

6. A reservation to a treaty is a problem which arises only in the event of the conclusion of multilateral treaties. The existence of a reservation in a bilateral treaty is equivalent to a new proposal with regard to the conducting of negotiations between these two States.

II Initiative for Concluding Treaty

1. A government, Ministry of Foreign Affairs, other ministries and departments which in accordance with their duties effectuate activity linked with the activity of the government and have contacts with official foreign partners enjoy the rights of initiative to conclude bilateral intergovernmental treaties within the limits of the competence established by a law.

2. The initiative of concluding such contracts is manifested in accordance with the policy of the Republic Moldova in the need to defend and support its interests, by decisions of the Parliament, President of the Republic, and Government, by arrangements reached at meetings on a high level, and also with international practice.

3. At the preliminary stage it is necessary to receive the consent in principle of the partner relative to the conclusion of such treaties as an expression of joint political will to develop bilateral relations. Consent in principle may emanate from direct contacts between the interested institutions of the two countries or it is possible to receive it through

political – diplomatic channels by means of diplomatic representations in the respective capitals.

III Working Out Draft Treaty

1. After receiving the consent in principle, the partners commence to work out the draft treaty, proceeding from the interests of the Republic Moldova in the respective domain, international practice, knowledge of the positions of principle of the government of the country with which negotiations are being conducted.

2. The text of the draft treaty shall be drawn up in the State language and submitted for the opinion of interested government institutions.

3. After receiving the opinion within the period established by a law the initiator-institution shall give a final form to the draft treaty. In the event of a divergence of opinions, working groups shall be formed in order to agree the texts. The results of the debates shall be entered in a protocol to be signed by the participants thereof empowered by the leadership of the institutions which they represent.

4. The text shall be translated into one of the generally-accepted international languages in which the negotiations will be conducted.

5. The draft treaty officially is sent to the partner either directly or through politico-diplomatic channels. Sending by international post shall be avoided. Certain texts may be transmitted by telefax.

6. If the initiative belongs to the partner who submits the draft treaty, the responsible governmental institution of the Republic Moldova shall before conducting negotiations submit a counter draft worked out in accordance with the aforesaid criteria. It is recommended that the negotiations be conducted with two texts submitted in good time by both sides.

IV Negotiations

1. It is recommended that negotiations proceed between the delegations of experts (as a rule, be led by ministers and directors of the initiating institutions).

2. The delegation of the Republic Moldova will be guided by a mandate confirmed by the competent agencies which compares the own draft with the counter draft of the partner.

3. Before the negotiations commence, the delegation of the Republic Moldova shall be thoroughly informed both with respect to own positions and interests and with respect to the official positions, interests, and practice of the partner.

4. Negotiations shall be conducted, as a rule, in not less than two rounds in the capitals of the States. It is recommended that the first round take place in the capital of the initiating country, which allows discussions to be conducted on the basis of the draft text proposed by the receiving country.

5. The delegation must display flexibility so as to further the movement of negotiations without conceding, however, on questions of principle and insisting on the basic interests of the Republic Moldova.

6. If the parties have different points of view which obstruct the completion of the text, one should apply for additional instructions. It is possible to agree *ad referendum* with certain formulations which do not coincide with but are not contrary to own positions; certain formulations insistently proposed by the partners may be included in square brackets for the purpose of receiving explanations with regard to them for the next round of negotiations; it is recommended that the delegation conducting the negotiations endeavour to achieve a balance between the formulations proposed by both partners and adopted *ad referendum* or included in square brackets.

7. Throughout the entire period of conducting negotiations one should have in view the attainment of equilibrium in the rights and obligations assumed by the parties so that compliance with the principle of sovereign equality of States is ensured.

8. Special attention should be devoted to the concluding clauses:

(a) the introduction into operation of the agreed text of the treaty (as a rule, after the last notification concerning the confirmation or ratification thereof by competent agencies of each State);

(b) the language of the official texts of the treaty; the texts are drawn up, as a rule, in two examples of the originals, each in the State language of the Republic Moldova and in the language of the partner State, and also in one further example in one of the generally-accepted international languages (in which the negotiations were conducted); in the event of a different interpretation, the text drawn up in the international language shall govern; responsibility for the original translations into the State language of the Republic Moldova and into the language of the partner State shall be borne by each of the parties;

(c) duration of operation; treaties are concluded, as a rule, for a determined period stipulated in the agreed text (from a year up to 20 years, depending on the situation); with a clause relating to the automatic extension of the period (tacit renewal) or agreed extension for one period, and also with special clauses affecting the termination of operation (as a rule, by means of unilateral notification of not less than 6 months before the termination of operation).

9. After the agreeing and drawing up of the final texts, they are printed on paper specially intended for treaties in the stipulated languages; each party ensures the printing in its own language of two examples of the originals; the printing in the international language is effectuated, by arrangement, by one of the parties.

10. Both original texts are alternating (not identical in the sense that the text of each of the parties each time as the need arises commences with the names of the respective country).

For example:

'The Government of the Republic Moldova and the Government of Romania, wishing . . . ' (for the variant of the Republic Moldova);

'The Government of Romania and the Government of the Republic Moldova, wishing . . . ' (for the variant of Romania).

The signature on the variant of each of the parties is placed on the left side of the last page.

V Initialling and Signature

1. After agreeing of the text and the printing thereof in the aforesaid manner we pass to preparation for initialling and signature, which means:

(a) verification of the texts printed by the parties against the starting text on the subject of conformity;

(b) binding of the texts of the treaty in special leather or cardboard folders with the national symbols of both parties;

(c) sealing of the texts of the treaty with the State seals of both partners.

2. The initialling shall be done by the heads of the Contracting delegations (or at a higher level) within the framework of the ceremony when each of the pages of the agreed text is signed only by the initials on the lower corner of the sheet being initialled.

3. Signature may occur later, in an official setting, at a higher level or at once upon the completion of negotiations if there is no need for initialling.

VI Introduction into Operation. Extension of Period of Operation. Termination of Operation or Denunciation

1. An agreed treaty shall enter into force according to the concluding clauses in one of the following situations:

(a) after the exchange of instruments of ratification if the treaty by reason of its significance requires ratification by legislative agencies; the exchange of instruments of ratification is made, as a rule, within the framework of a ceremony in the second participant country of the treaty and not in the country in which the signature occurred;

(b) after an exchange of *notes verbales* by which each of the parties announces confirmation of the treaty by competent agencies of its country.

2. After entry into force of the treaty the initiating institution of the Republic Moldova shall inform all ministries and departments thereof and, when necessary, shall make proposals to Parliament concerning a change of and addition to legislation in the respective domain.

3. The original of the text of the treaty is handed over to the archive of treaties of the Ministry of Foreign Affairs for registration and keeping.

4. Extension of the operation of a treaty is made either by tacit renewal or by agreement between the parties.

5. Possible denunciation of a treaty is made in special instances when the partner deliberately violates obligations assumed and its good faith is subject to doubt or when the partner violates basic, generally-accepted principles of international law and inter-State relations.

As a rule, States-participants fulfil treaty clauses in good faith under the principle *Pacta sunt servanta* (treaties must be complied with).

TADZHIKISTAN

Law on the Procedure for the Conclusion, Ratification, Performance, and Denunciation of Treaties in the Republic Tadzhikistan

[Adopted 25 June 1993. *Ведомости Верховного Совета Республики таджикистан* (1993), no. 17, item 375; repealed: *Ахбори Маджлиси Олий Республики Таджикистан* (2000), no. 6, item 359]

The Republic Tadzhikistan shall conclude and perform international treaties in accordance with the Constitution of the Republic Tadzhikistan and generally-recognized norms of international law.

True to the principle of the obligatoriness of complying with each international treaty by participants thereof, the Republic Tadzhikistan shall undeviatingly and voluntarily fulfil its international obligations.

I General Provisions

Article 1 Tasks of the Law

The present Law shall establish the procedure for the conclusion, ratification, performance, and denunciation of international, inter-State, and intergovernmental treaties of the Republic Tadzhikistan which apply with respect to all international treaties of the Republic Tadzhikistan irrespective of their form and name (treaty, agreement, convention, pact, charter, protocol, declaration, communiqué, exchange of letters or notes, other forms, and names of international treaties).

The procedure for the signature, performance, and denunciation of international treaties of the Republic Tadzhikistan of an interdepartmental character shall be determined by the Council of Ministers of the Republic Tadzhikistan.

Article 2 International Treaties of Republic Tadzhikistan

International treaties of the Republic Tadzhikistan shall be concluded with foreign States, their respective agencies, and also international organizations in the name of the Republic Tadzhikistan or the Government of the Republic Tadzhikistan.

Article 3 Means of Expressing Consent of Republic Tadzhikistan to Bindingness of International Treaties

The consent of the Republic Tadzhikistan to the bindingness on it of an international treaty may be expressed by the signature of the treaty, exchange of documents forming the treaty, ratification of the treaty, adoption, confirmation thereof, accession thereto, or by any other means stipulated by the Contracting Parties.

II Conclusion of International Treaties of Republic Tadzhikistan

Article 4 Proposals Concerning Conclusion of International Treaties of Republic Tadzhikistan

Proposals concerning the conclusion of international treaties of the Republic Tadzhikistan shall be submitted to the Council of Ministers of the Republic Tadzhikistan by the Ministry of Foreign Affairs of the Republic Tadzhikistan.

Other ministries, State committees, and departments of the Republic Tadzhikistan shall submit to the Council of Ministers of the Republic Tadzhikistan proposals concerning the conclusion of international treaties of the Republic Tadzhikistan jointly with the Ministry of Foreign Affairs of the Republic Tadzhikistan.

Proposals concerning the conclusion of international treaties of the Republic Tadzhikistan establishing other rules than those which are contained in republic legislation shall be submitted by the Ministry of Foreign Affairs of the Republic Tadzhikistan by agreement with the Ministry of Justice of the Republic Tadzhikistan.

Article 5 Decisions Concerning the Conducting of Negotiations and Signature of International Treaties of the Republic Tadzhikistan

Decisions concerning the conducting of negotiations and signature of international treaties of the Republic Tadzhikistan shall be adopted:

(1) with respect to treaties concluded in the name of the Republic Tadzhikistan: by the Supreme Soviet of the Republic Tadzhikistan;

(2) with respect to treaties concluded in the name of the Republic Tadzhikistan with regard to questions relegated to the jurisdiction of the Government of the Republic Tadzhikistan: by the Council of Ministers of the Republic Tadzhikistan;

(3) with respect to treaties concluded in the name of the Government of the Republic Tadzhikistan: by the Council of Ministers of the Republic Tadzhikistan.

Article 6 Powers to Conduct Negotiations and to Sign International Treaties of Republic Tadzhikistan

Powers to conduct negotiations and to sign international treaties of the Republic Tadzhikistan shall be issued:

(1) with respect to treaties concluded in the name of the Republic Tadzhikistan, by the Supreme Soviet of the Republic Tadzhikistan;

(2) with respect to treaties concluded in the name of the Republic Tadzhikistan in respect of questions relegated to the jurisdiction of the Government of the Republic Tadzhikistan, by the Council of Ministers of the Republic Tadzhikistan;

(3) with respect to treaties concluded in the name of the Government of the Republic Tadzhikistan, by the Council of Ministers of the Republic Tadzhikistan.

Article 7 Conducting Negotiations and Signature of International Treaties of Republic Tadzhikistan Without Special Powers

The Chairman of the Supreme Soviet of the Republic Tadzhikistan, Chairman of the Council of Ministers of the Republic Tadzhikistan, and the Minister of Foreign Affairs of the Republic Tadzhikistan shall have the right to conduct negotiations and sign international treaties of the Republic Tadzhikistan without special powers.

The head of a diplomatic representation of the Republic Tadzhikistan in a foreign State, chief of the representation of the Republic Tadzhikistan attached to an international organization shall have the right to conduct negotiations without special powers concerning the conclusion of an international treaty of the Republic Tadzhikistan respectively with the receiving State or within the framework of the particular international organization.

III Ratification of International Treaties of Republic Tadzhikistan

Article 8 Ratification of International Treaties of Republic Tadzhikistan

In accordance with the Constitution of the Republic Tadzhikistan, international treaties of the Republic Tadzhikistan shall be ratified by the Supreme Soviet of the Republic Tadzhikistan.

Article 9 International Treaties of the Republic Tadzhikistan Subject to Ratification

International treaties of the Republic Tadzhikistan on friendship, cooperation and mutual assistance, treaties on the mutual renunciation of the use or threat of force, peace treaties, treaties on the territorial delimitation of the Republic Tadzhikistan with other States, treaties establishing other rules than those which are contained in legislative acts of the Republic Tadzhikistan shall be subject to ratification.

International treaties of the Republic Tadzhikistan, during the conclusion of which the Parties have stipulated subsequent ratification also shall be subject to ratification.

The Supreme Soviet of the Republic Tadzhikistan may also ratify other international treaties of the Republic Tadzhikistan.

Article 10 Submission of International Treaties of Republic Tadzhikistan for Ratification

International treaties of the Republic Tadzhikistan not later than a month from the day of signature shall be submitted for ratification to the

Supreme Soviet of the Republic Tadzhikistan by the Council of Ministers of the Republic Tadzhikistan upon the recommendation of the Ministry of Foreign Affairs of the Republic Tadzhikistan autonomously or jointly with other ministries, State committees, and departments of the Republic Tadzhikistan.

Article 11 Preliminary Consideration of International Treaties of Republic Tadzhikistan

The preliminary consideration of international treaties of the Republic Tadzhikistan submitted for ratification shall be done by the respective committees of the Supreme Soviet of the Republic Tadzhikistan, which shall give an opinion with regard to them.

Article 12 Adoption of Decisions on Ratification of International Treaties of Republic Tadzhikistan

The Supreme Soviet of the Republic Tadzhikistan shall consider international treaties of the Republic Tadzhikistan submitted for ratification and render a respective decision.

The decision of the Supreme Soviet of the Republic Tadzhikistan on the ratification of an international treaty of the Republic Tadzhikistan shall be adopted in the form of a decree. On the basis of the decree adopted concerning the ratification, the instrument of ratification shall be signed by the Chairman of the Supreme Soviet of the Republic Tadzhikistan.

Article 13 Exchange of Instruments of Ratification and Giving Thereof for Keeping

Instruments of ratification shall be exchanged and the instruments concerning the ratification of international treaties of the Republic Tadzhikistan given for keeping to depositaries by the Ministry of Foreign Affairs of the Republic Tadzhikistan or on its behalf by the diplomatic representation of the Republic Tadzhikistan or representation of the Republic Tadzhikistan attached to an international organization.

Article 14 Adoption or Confirmation of International Treaties of Republic Tadzhikistan Not Subject to Ratification

The adoption or confirmation of international treaties of the Republic Tadzhikistan which are not subject to ratification but which provide for their adoption or confirmation shall be performed:

(1) with respect to treaties to be concluded in the name of the Republic Tadzhikistan: by the Supreme Soviet of the Republic Tadzhikistan;
(2) with respect to treaties to be concluded in the name of the Republic Tadzhikistan with regard to questions relegated to the jurisdiction of the Government of the Republic Tadzhikistan: by the Council of Ministers of the Republic Tadzhikistan;
(3) with respect to treaties to be concluded in the name of the Government of the Republic Tadzhikistan: by the Council of Ministers of the Republic Tadzhikistan.

Article 15 Accession to International Treaties

Decisions concerning the accession of the Republic Tadzhikistan to international treaties shall be adopted by:

(1) with respect to treaties subject to ratification: by the Supreme Soviet of the Republic Tadzhikistan;
(2) with respect to treaties not subject to ratification, accession to which is performed in the name of the Republic Tadzhikistan: by the Supreme Soviet of the Republic Tadzhikistan;
(3) with respect to treaties not subject to ratification, accession to which is performed in the name of the Republic Tadzhikistan with regard to questions relegated to the jurisdiction of the Government of the Republic Tadzhikistan: by the Council of Ministers of the Republic Tadzhikistan;
(4) with respect to treaties not subject to ratification, accession to which is performed in the name of the Government of the Republic Tadzhikistan: by the Council of Ministers of the Republic Tadzhikistan.

IV Performance of International Treaties of Republic Tadzhikistan

Article 16 Compliance with International Treaties of Republic Tadzhikistan

International treaties of the Republic Tadzhikistan shall be subject to undeviating compliance by the Republic Tadzhikistan in accordance with norms of international law.

Article 17 Ensuring Fulfilment of International Treaties

The Council of Ministers of the Republic Tadzhikistan shall adopt measures to ensure the fulfilment of international treaties of the Republic Tadzhikistan.

Article 18 Fulfilment of Obligations with Regard to International Treaties

Ministries, State committees, departments, and other State agencies within whose competence are questions regulated by international treaties of the Republic Tadzhikistan shall ensure the fulfilment of obligations accepted under these treaties of the Republic Tadzhikistan, observe the effectuation of rights arising from the treaties belonging to the Republic Tadzhikistan, and over the fulfilment by other participants of the treaties of their obligations.

Article 19 General Observation Over Performance of Treaties of Republic Tadzhikistan

General observation over the performance of international treaties of the Republic Tadzhikistan shall be effectuated by the Ministry of Foreign Affairs of the Republic Tadzhikistan.

The Ministry of Foreign Affairs of the Republic Tadzhikistan shall ensure the recording and keeping of the originals or authentic texts of international treaties of the Republic Tadzhikistan.

Article 20 Violation of Obligations by Other Participants of International Treaty of Republic Tadzhikistan

In the event of a violation of obligations under an international treaty of the Republic Tadzhikistan by other participants thereof, the Ministry of Foreign Affairs of the Republic Tadzhikistan and other ministries, State committees, and departments of the Republic Tadzhikistan, jointly with the Ministry of Foreign Affairs of the Republic Tadzhikistan, shall submit proposals to the Council of Ministers of the Republic Tadzhikistan concerning the adoption of necessary measures in accordance with norms of international law.

In the event of a material violation of an international treaty of the Republic Tadzhikistan by other participants thereof, and also in other instances provided for by norms of international law, such treaty may be terminated in the procedure established by Articles 24–27 of the present Law.

Article 21 Proposals Concerning Making of Changes in and Additions to Republic Legislation in Connection with Conclusion of International Treaty of Republic Tadzhikistan

In instances when for the purpose of the fulfilment of an international treaty of the Republic Tadzhikistan the issuance of a law of the Republic Tadzhikistan of a decree of the Supreme Soviet of the Republic Tadzhikistan is necessary, or the adoption of a decree or regulation of the Council of Ministers of the Republic Tadzhikistan, the interested ministries, state committees, and departments of the Republic Tadzhikistan, by agreement with the Ministry of Justice of the Republic Tadzhikistan, shall submit proposals in the established procedure concerning the adoption of the proper act.

V Publication and Registration of International Treaties of Republic Tadzhikistan

Article 22 Publication of International Treaties of Republic Tadzhikistan

International treaties of the Republic Tadzhikistan which have entered into force, additions, amendments, protocols and annexes thereto concluded in the name of the Republic Tadzhikistan, ratified treaties and treaties the accession to which was effectuated on the basis of decisions of the Supreme Soviet of the Republic Tadzhikistan, and also treaties not subject to ratification, shall be published in the *Ведомости Верховного Совета Республики Таджикистан*.

*International treaties of the Republic Tadzhikistan which have entered into force, additions, amendments, protocols and annexes thereto concluded in the name of the Republic Tadzhikistan, ratified treaties and treaties . . . .

Article 23 Registration of International Treaties of Republic Tadzhikistan

The registration of international treaties of the Republic Tadzhikistan at the Secretariat of the United Nations or respective agencies of other international organizations shall be effectuated by the Ministry of Foreign Affairs of the Republic Tadzhikistan.

VI Denunciation of International Treaties of Republic Tadzhikistan

Article 24 Proposals Concerning Denunciation of International Treaties of Republic Tadzhikistan

Proposals concerning the denunciation of international treaties of the Republic Tadzhikistan shall be submitted to the Supreme Soviet of the

Republic Tadzhikistan by the Council of Ministers of the Republic Tadzhikistan upon the recommendation of the Ministry of Foreign Affairs of the Republic Tadzhikistan autonomously or jointly with other ministries, State committees, and departments of the Republic Tadzhikistan.

Article 25 Preliminary Consideration of Proposals Concerning Denunciation of International Treaties of Republic Tadzhikistan

The preliminary consideration of proposals concerning the denunciation of international treaties of the Republic Tadzhikistan shall be done by the respective committees of the Supreme Soviet of the Republic Tadzhikistan, which shall give opinions with regard to them.

Article 26 Denunciation of International Treaties of Republic Tadzhikistan

Denunciation of international treaties of the Republic Tadzhikistan concluded in the name of the Republic Tadzhikistan, decisions concerning the signature of which were adopted by the Supreme Soviet of the Republic Tadzhikistan, ratified treaties, and also treaties the accession to which was effectuated on the basis of decisions of the Supreme Soviet of the Republic Tadzhikistan, shall be done by the Supreme Soviet of the Republic Tadzhikistan.

Article 27 Denunciation of International Treaties of Republic Tadzhikistan by Council of Ministers of Republic Tadzhikistan

Denunciation of international treaties of the Republic Tadzhikistan concluded in the name of the Republic Tadzhikistan, decisions concerning the signature of which were adopted by the Council of Ministers of the Republic Tadzhikistan, treaties concluded in the name of the Government of the Republic Tadzhikistan and not subject to ratification, and of treaties the accession to which was effectuated on the basis of decisions of the Council of Ministers of the Republic Tadzhikistan, shall be done by the Council of Ministers of the Republic Tadzhikistan.

Law on International Treaties of The Republic Tadzhikistan

[Adopted 11 December 1999. *Ахбори Маджлиси Олий Республики Таджикистан* (1999), no. –, item 348]

International treaties form the legal foundation of international relations and promote the maintenance of peace and security and development of international cooperation in accordance with the purposes and principles of the United Nations Charter. An important role belongs to international treaties in defence of the basic rights and freedoms of man and in ensuring the legal interests of States.

The Republic Tadzhikistan favours undeviating compliance with international treaties and affirms its adherence to the principle of good-faith fulfilment of international obligations.

Chapter I General Provision

Article 1 Tasks of Law and Sphere of its Application

The present Law determines the procedure for the conclusion, ratification, adoption, confirmation, registration, publication, fulfilment, denunciation, and suspension of international treaties of the Republic Tadzhikistan.

International treaties of the Republic Tadzhikistan shall be concluded, fulfilled, and denounced in accordance with the Constitution of the Republic Tadzhikistan, generally-recognized principles and norms of international law, the provisions of the treaty itself, and the present Law.

The operation of the present Law shall extend with respect to international treaties of the Republic Tadzhikistan, irrespective of the character thereof (inter-State, intergovernmental, and interdepartmental) and name (treaty, agreement, convention, protocol, covenant, exchange of letters or notes, and others) with foreign States and international organizations.

Article 2 Means of Expression of Consent of Republic Tadzhikistan to Bindingness of International Treaty for It

The consent of the Republic Tadzhikistan to the bindingness for it of an international treaty shall be expressed by means of signature of the treaty, its ratification, adoption, confirmation, accession thereto, exchange of documents comprising the treaty, or by other means concerning which the parties have agreed.

Article 3 Meanings of Terms

For the purposes of the present Law the following terms shall mean:

(1) 'international treaty of Republic Tadzhikistan' – an agreement concluded in the name of the Republic Tadzhikistan (inter-State treaty), of the Government of the Republic Tadzhikistan (intergovernmental treaty), or of a ministry, State committee, or other agency of State administration (interdepartmental treaty) with foreign States or international organizations in written form irrespective of whether such agreement is contained in one document or in several interrelated documents;

(2) 'signature' – the stage of conclusion of a treaty or means of consent of the Republic Tadzhikistan to the bindingness of an international treaty if such has been provided for by the treaty itself or by arrangement of the parties or by the intention of the Republic Tadzhikistan to impart such force to the signature;

(3) ratification, confirmation, adoption, and accession – these are means of expression of consent of the Republic Tadzhikistan to the bindingness for it of an international treaty signed by its empowered representative:

  (a) 'ratification' – the means of expression of the consent of the Republic Tadzhikistan to the bindingness of an international treaty signed by its empowered representative;

  (b) 'adoption' – the means of expression of the consent of the Republic Tadzhikistan to the bindingness of an international treaty signed by its empowered representative, but which has not entered into legal force;

  (c) 'confirmation' – the means of expression of the consent of the Republic Tadzhikistan to the bindingness of an international treaty

which is not subject to ratification but provides for another means of additional approval besides the signature thereof;
(d) 'accession' – the means of expression of the consent of the Republic Tadzhikistan to the bindingness of an international treaty which has entered into force but was not signed by its empowered representative;

(4) 'powers' – the document confirming the representation by a person or several persons of the Republic Tadzhikistan to conduct negotiations, adopt the text of a treaty, or establish its authenticity, and expression of the consent of the Republic Tadzhikistan to the bindingness of the treaty and conclusion of any other act relegated to a treaty;
(5) 'reservation' – a unilateral statement uttering or expressing the consent of the Republic Tadzhikistan to the bindingness of an international treaty for the purpose of excluding or changing the legal operation of individual provisions of the international treaty in their application to the Republic Tadzhikistan;
(6) 'denunciation' – a unilateral statement duly formalized for the purpose of termination of the legal operation of an international treaty or individual provisions thereof in their application with respect to the Republic Tadzhikistan;
(7) 'international organization' – inter-State, intergovernmental organization;
(8) 'depositary' – State, international organization, or chief executive organ or official thereof on which is placed the fulfilment of the functions provided for by international law with respect to an international treaty.

Article 4 Place of International Treaties of Republic Tadzhikistan in Legal System of Republic Tadzhikistan

International treaties recognized by Tadzhikistan in accordance with the Constitution of the Republic Tadzhikistan shall be an integral part of its legal system.

In the event of the failure of laws of the Republic to conform to recognized international legal acts, the norms of the international treaty shall apply.

Norms of officially published international treaties of the Republic Tadzhikistan which do not require the adoption of laws in order to apply them shall operate in the Republic Tadzhikistan directly. Respective normative acts shall be adopted for the application of other provisions of international treaties of the Republic Tadzhikistan.

Chapter II Conclusion of International Treaties of Republic Tadzhikistan

Article 5 Proposals Concerning Conclusion of International Treaties of Republic Tadzhikistan

Proposals concerning the conclusion of international treaties of the Republic Tadzhikistan shall be submitted to the President of the Republic Tadzhikistan, and proposals concerning the conclusion of international treaties in the name of the Government of the Republic Tadzhikistan shall be submitted to the Government of the Republic Tadzhikistan by the Ministry of Foreign Affairs of the Republic Tadzhikistan.

Other ministries and departments of the Republic Tadzhikistan shall submit to the Government of the Republic Tadzhikistan proposals concerning the conclusion of international treaties with regard to questions within their competence by agreement with the Ministry of Foreign Affairs of the Republic Tadzhikistan.

Proposals concerning the conclusion of international treaties of the Republic Tadzhikistan must contain:

– the draft treaty;

– the substantiation of the advisability of concluding it;

– the opinion of the Ministry of Justice concerning its conformity to laws of the Republic Tadzhikistan;

– an assessment of political, financial – economic, and other consequences of conclusion of the treaty.

Article 6 Decisions Concerning Conducting of Negotiations on Conclusion and on Signature of International Treaties of Republic Tadzhikistan

Decisions concerning the conducting of negotiations on the conclusion and signature of inter-State and intergovernmental treaties to be concluded in the name of the Republic Tadzhikistan and concerning the granting of powers to the effectuation thereof shall be adopted respectively by the President of the Republic Tadzhikistan and Government of the Republic Tadzhikistan.

Decisions concerning the conducting of negotiations on the conclusion and signature of interdepartmental international treaties of the Republic Tadzhikistan and granting of powers for the effectuation thereof shall be adopted by the Government of the Republic Tadzhikistan.

The following persons by virtue of their functions and without the necessity of presenting powers shall be considered to be representing the Republic Tadzhikistan:

(a) the President of the Republic Tadzhikistan, the Chairman of the Government of the Republic Tadzhikistan, and the Minister of Foreign Affairs of the Republic Tadzhikistan – for the purposes of all acts relating to the conclusion of the treaty;

(b) the head of a diplomatic representation of the Republic Tadzhikistan in a foreign State or head of a representation of the Republic Tadzhikistan attached to an international organization – for the purposes of conducting negotiations for the adoption of the text of a treaty respectively with the receiving State or within the framework of the particular international organization.

Chapter III Ratification, Adoption, and Confirmation of International Treaties of the Republic Tadzhikistan and Accession Thereto

Article 7 Ratifications of International Treaties of Republic Tadzhikistan

International treaties of the Republic Tadzhikistan shall be ratified by the Madzhlisi Namoiandagon.

Article 8 International Treaties of Republic Tadzhikistan Subject to Ratification

The following international treaties of the Republic Tadzhikistan shall be subject to ratification:

(1) those establishing other rules than provided for by laws of the Republic Tadzhikistan;
(2) those the subject of which are the basic rights and freedoms of man;
(3) those concerning the territorial delimitation of the Republic Tadzhikistan with other States and the course of the State boundary;
(4) those concerning the foundations of inter-State relations, peace, and friendship;
(5) those with regard to questions affecting the defence capability of the Republic Tadzhikistan, disarmament or international control over armaments, ensuring international peace and security, and also peace treaties and treaties concerning collective security;
(6) those concerning participation of the Republic Tadzhikistan in international unions, international organizations, and other international associations, if such treaties provide for the transfer to them of part of the powers of the Republic Tadzhikistan or establish the legal bindingness of decisions of their organs for the Republic Tadzhikistan.

International treaties of the Republic Tadzhikistan during the conclusion of which the parties have stipulated subsequent ratification also shall be subject to ratification.

Article 9 Submission of International Treaties of Republic Tadzhikistan for Ratification

International treaties of the Republic Tadzhikistan shall be submitted for ratification to the Madzhlisi Namoiandagon by the President of the Republic Tadzhikistan.

Proposals concerning the submission for ratification of international treaties of the Republic Tadzhikistan to the President of the Republic Tadzhikistan shall be submitted by the Ministry of Foreign Affairs of the Republic Tadzhikistan autonomously or by agreement with other State agencies if the treaty affects questions within their competence.

A proposal concerning the ratification of an international treaty of the Republic Tadzhikistan must contain:

– a certified copy of the official text of the international treaty (or official translation thereof);

– substantiation of the advisability of ratification thereof;

– opinion of the Ministry of Justice of the Republic Tadzhikistan concerning the conformity of the treaty to laws of the Republic Tadzhikistan.

Article 10 Preparation of Instrument Concerning Ratification of International Treaty of Republic Tadzhikistan

On the basis of a decree of the Madzhlisi Namoiandagon concerning ratification of the international treaty of the Republic Tadzhikistan, the President of the Republic Tadzhikistan shall sign the instrument concerning ratification, which shall be affixed with his seal and the signature of the Minister of Foreign Affairs of the Republic Tadzhikistan.

Article 11 Exchange of Instruments of Ratification and Handing Them Over for Keeping by Depositaries

The exchange of instruments of ratification and handing them over for keeping to depositaries shall be performed in the absence of an arrangement otherwise by the Ministry of Foreign Affairs of the Republic Tadzhikistan or on its behalf by the diplomatic representation of the Republic Tadzhikistan in the foreign State or by the representation of the Republic Tadzhikistan attached to an international organization.

Article 12 Confirmation of International Treaties of Republic Tadzhikistan

International treaties of the Republic Tadzhikistan shall be confirmed:

(1) with respect to treaties to be concluded in the name of the Republic Tadzhikistan – by the President of the Republic Tadzhikistan;

(2) with respect to treaties to be concluded in the name of the Government of the Republic Tadzhikistan, and also with respect to interdepartmental international treaties of the Republic Tadzhikistan – by the Government of the Republic Tadzhikistan.

Article 13 Adoption of International Treaties of Republic Tadzhikistan and Accession Thereto

The adoption of international treaties of the Republic Tadzhikistan and accession thereto shall be effectuated:

(1) with respect to the treaties specified in Article 8 of the present Law in the procedure provided for the ratification of international treaties;
(2) with respect to international treaties to be concluded in the name of the Republic Tadzhikistan, except for treaties specified in Article 8 of the present Law – by the President of the Republic Tadzhikistan;
(3) with respect to other international treaties – by the Government of the Republic Tadzhikistan.

Article 14 Proposals Concerning Confirmation and Adoption of International Treaties of Republic Tadzhikistan and Accession Thereto

Proposals concerning the confirmation and adoption of international treaties of the Republic Tadzhikistan and accession thereto shall be submitted to the President of the Republic Tadzhikistan and to the Government of the Republic Tadzhikistan by the Ministry of Foreign Affairs of the Republic Tadzhikistan in compliance with the requirements provided for by Article 5 of the present Law.

Article 15 Entry of International Treaties of Republic Tadzhikistan into Force

International treaties of the Republic Tadzhikistan shall enter into force for the Republic Tadzhikistan in the procedure and within the periods provided for by the treaty itself and by laws of the Republic Tadzhikistan.

Article 16 Reservations to International Treaties of Republic Tadzhikistan

Reservations may be made when signing, ratifying, confirming, and adopting an international treaty or acceding thereto in accordance with the provisions of the treaty itself and norms of international law.

The declaration of a reservation incompatible with the object and purpose of an international treaty shall not be permitted.

Unless an international treaty provides otherwise, reservations may be removed at any time in the same procedure in which they were made.

The acceptance of reservations made by other parties of an international treaty or objections against them shall be effectuated in accordance with the conditions of the treaty itself and norms of international law by the agency which adopted the decision concerning consent to the bindingness of the international treaty for the Republic Tadzhikistan.

Chapter IV Registration and Publication of International Treaties of Republic Tadzhikistan

Article 17 Recording and Registration of International Treaties of Republic Tadzhikistan

The Ministry of Foreign Affairs of the Republic Tadzhikistan shall effectuate the recording and registration of international treaties of the Republic Tadzhikistan.

Copies of international treaties of the Republic Tadzhikistan shall be sent to the Ministry of Justice of the Republic Tadzhikistan for inclusion in the State Register of Legal Acts.

Article 18 Registration of International Treaties of Republic Tadzhikistan in International Organizations

The registration of international treaties of the Republic Tadzhikistan at the Secretariat of the United Nations and in respective organs of other international organizations shall be effectuated by the Ministry of Foreign Affairs of the Republic Tadzhikistan.

Article 19 Keeping of Originals of International Treaties of Republic Tadzhikistan

The originals (or certified copies, official translations) of international treaties of the Republic Tadzhikistan concluded in the name of the Republic Tadzhikistan and in the name of the Government of the Republic Tadzhikistan shall be handed over for keeping to the Ministry of Foreign Affairs of the Republic Tadzhikistan within a two-week period from the day after the signature thereof (or receipt of the certified copy, official translation).

The originals of interdepartmental international treaties of the Republic Tadzhikistan shall be kept in the archives of the respective State agencies, and certified copies thereof within a two-week period from the day of signature (or receipt of the certified copy from the depositary, official translation) shall be sent to the Ministry of Foreign Affairs of the Republic Tadzhikistan.

Article 20 Effectuation of Functions of Depositary

The functions of depositary of multilateral international treaties, in the event of their being placed by these treaties on the Republic Tadzhikistan, shall be effectuated by the Ministry of Foreign Affairs of the Republic Tadzhikistan.

Article 21 Official Publication of International Treaties of Republic Tadzhikistan Which have Entered into Force

Ratified international treaties which have entered into force for the Republic Tadzhikistan, and also other international treaties of the Republic Tadzhikistan, except for interdepartmental, shall be published in the Digest of Laws of the Republic Tadzhikistan. International interdepartmental treaties of the Republic Tadzhikistan shall be published in the official printed publications of the respective agencies.

Chapter V Fulfilment of International Treaties of Republic Tadzhikistan

Article 22 Principles of Fulfilment of International Treaties of Republic Tadzhikistan

International treaties of the Republic Tadzhikistan shall be subject to fulfilment in good faith from the moment of their entry into force for the Republic Tadzhikistan.

Until the entry of an international treaty into force, the Republic Tadzhikistan shall in accordance with norms of international law, refrain from actions which deprive the treaty of its object and purposes.

Article 23 Organization of Fulfilment of International Treaties of Republic Tadzhikistan

The President of the Republic Tadzhikistan and the Government of the Republic Tadzhikistan shall take measures directed towards ensuring the fulfilment of international treaties of the Republic Tadzhikistan and determine the official or department on which control is placed over the course of the realization of international treaties of the Republic Tadzhikistan.

General observance over the fulfilment of international treaties of the Republic Tadzhikistan, including by the foreign party, shall be effectuated by the Ministry of Foreign Affairs of the Republic Tadzhikistan.

Article 24 Measures to be Adopted in Event of Violation of International Treaty of Republic Tadzhikistan by Other Participants Thereof

In the event of a violation of obligations under an international treaty of the Republic Tadzhikistan by other participants thereof, the Ministry of Foreign Affairs of the Republic Tadzhikistan autonomously, or jointly with interested State agencies, shall submit to the President of the Republic Tadzhikistan or to the Government of the Republic Tadzhikistan proposals concerning the adoption of necessary measures in accordance with norms of international law and the treaty itself.

Chapter VI Denunciation and Suspension of Operation of International Treaties of Republic Tadzhikistan

Article 25 Proposals Concerning Denunciation or Suspension of Operation of International Treaties of Republic Tadzhikistan

Proposals concerning the denunciation or suspension of the operation of ratified international treaties of the Republic Tadzhikistan shall be submitted to the Madzhlisi Namoiandagon by the President of the Republic Tadzhikistan.

Proposals concerning the denunciation or suspension of the operation of other international treaties of the Republic Tadzhikistan shall be submitted, depending upon who adopted the decision concerning consent to the bindingness of the treaty for the Republic Tadzhikistan, to the President of the Republic Tadzhikistan or to the Government of the Republic Tadzhikistan by the Ministry of Foreign Affairs of the Republic Tadzhikistan autonomously or by agreement with the respective State agencies.

Proposals concerning denunciation or suspension of the operation of an international treaty of the Republic Tadzhikistan must contain:

(a) a certified copy of the official text of the international treaty;
(b) a substantiation of the advisability of denunciation or suspension of the operation of the treaty;
(c) an assessment of the financial – economic and other consequences of denunciation or suspension of the treaty.

Article 26 Denunciation and Suspension of Operation of International Treaties of Republic Tadzhikistan

Denunciation and suspension of the operation of international treaties of the Republic Tadzhikistan shall be effectuated in accordance with the conditions of the treaty itself and norms of international law by the agency which adopted the decision concerning consent to the bindingness of the international treaty for the Republic Tadzhikistan.

Denunciation of an international treaty of the Republic Tadzhikistan, unless provided otherwise by the treaty, shall relieve the Republic Tadzhikistan from the obligation to fulfil the treaty thereafter.

Suspension of the operation of an international treaty of the Republic Tadzhikistan, unless provided otherwise by the treaty, shall relieve the Republic Tadzhikistan from the obligation to fulfil the treaty during the period of suspension.

Article 27 Official Notice Concerning Denunciation or Suspension of Operation of International Treaties of Republic Tadzhikistan

Official notice concerning denunciation or suspension of the operation of international treaties of the Republic Tadzhikistan shall be published in the procedure provided for by Article 21 of the present Law.

Decree on the Introduction into Operation of the Law of the Republic Tadzhikistan 'On International Treaties of the Republic Tadzhikistan'

[Decree of the Madzhlisi Oli of the Republic Tadzhikistan, No. 909, 11 December 1999. *Ахбори Маджлиси Олий Республики Таджикистан* (1999), no. –, item 349]

The Madzhlisi Oli of the Republic Tadzhikistan decrees:

1. To introduce into operation the Law of the Republic Tadzhikistan 'On International Treaties of the Republic Tadzhikistan' after its official publication.

2. The Government of the Republic Tadzhikistan shall:

– submit to the Madzhlisi Oli of the Republic Tadzhikistan proposals concerning the bringing of laws of the Republic Tadzhikistan into conformity with the Law of the Republic Tadzhikistan 'On International Treaties of the Republic Tadzhikistan';

– to bring its decisions into conformity with the present Law.

TURKMENISTAN

Law on the Procedure for the Conclusion, Performance, and Denunciation of International Treaties of Turkmenistan

[Adopted 15 June 1995. *Ведомости Меджлиса Туркменистана* (1995), no. 2, item 14]

The present Law shall establish the procedure for the conclusion, performance, and denunciation of international treaties of Turkmenistan, being called upon to further the effectuation of the purposes and principles of the foreign policy of Turkmenistan proclaimed and consolidated in the Constitution of Turkmenistan.

The procedure established by the present Law for the conclusion, performance, and denunciation of international treaties of Turkmenistan shall apply with respect to all international treaties of Turkmenistan irrespective of the form and names thereof (treaty, agreement, convention, covenant, protocol, exchange of letters or notes, and other forms and names of international treaties).

I General Provisions

Article 1 International Treaties of Turkmenistan

Treaties with foreign States and international organizations concluded by it with regard to various questions of their mutual international relations establishing international rights and duties for the participants thereof shall be international treaties of Turkmenistan.

International treaties of Turkmenistan shall be concluded in the name of:

Turkmenistan – inter-State;

Cabinet of Ministers (Government) of Turkmenistan – intergovernmental;

ministries and departments – interdepartmental.

Article 2 Means of Expression of Consent of Turkmenistan to Bindingness of International Treaties

The consent of Turkmenistan to the bindingness of an international treaty for it may be expressed by the signature of the treaty, exchange of documents forming the treaty, ratification of the treaty, confirmation thereof, accession thereto, or by any other means concerning which the Contracting Parties have stipulated.

Article 3 Correlation of Generally-Recognized Norms of International Law, International Treaties of Turkmenistan, and Legislation of Turkmenistan

When concluding and performing international treaties, Turkmenistan shall be guided by generally-recognized principles and norms of international law.

If other rules have been established with an international treaty of Turkmenistan than are provided for by legislation of Turkmenistan, the provisions of the international treaty shall apply.

II Conclusion of International Treaties of Turkmenistan

Article 4 Proposals Concerning Conclusion of International Treaties of Turkmenistan

Proposals concerning the conclusion of international treaties of Turkmenistan at the inter-State and intergovernmental levels shall be submitted by the Ministry of Foreign Affairs of Turkmenistan respectively to the President of Turkmenistan or to the Cabinet of Ministers of Turkmenistan.

Proposals concerning the conclusion of international treaties of Turkmenistan of an interdepartmental character shall be submitted to the Cabinet of Ministers of Turkmenistan by ministries and departments of Turkmenistan jointly with the Ministry of Foreign Affairs of Turkmenistan or by agreement with them.

International treaties of Turkmenistan establishing other rules than those which are contained in legislation of Turkmenistan shall be submitted to the President of Turkmenistan or to the Cabinet of Ministers of Turkmenistan by agreement with the Ministry of Justice of Turkmenistan.

Article 5 Decisions Concerning Conducting of Negotiations and Signature of International Treaties of Turkmenistan

Decisions concerning the conducting of negotiations and the signature of international treaties of Turkmenistan shall be adopted by the:

President of Turkmenistan – with respect to inter-State and intergovernmental treaties; Cabinet of Ministers of Turkmenistan – with respect to treaties of an interdepartmental character.

Article 6 Powers to Conduct Negotiations and Sign International Treaties of Turkmenistan

Powers to conduct negotiations and sign international treaties of Turkmenistan shall be issued by the:

President of Turkmenistan – with respect to inter-State and intergovernmental treaties;

Cabinet of Ministers of Turkmenistan – with respect to treaties of an interdepartmental character.

Powers to conduct negotiations and sign international treaties of Turkmenistan may be issued to the:

Chairman of the Medzhlis of Turkmenistan – with respect to inter-State treaties;

deputy chairmen of the Cabinet of Ministers of Turkmenistan – with respect to intergovernmental treaties;

ministers and leaders of departments – with respect to treaties of an interdepartmental character.

Powers to conduct negotiations and sign international treaties of Turkmenistan shall be formalized by acts of the President of Turkmenistan or Cabinet of Ministers of Turkmenistan in accordance with their competence.

Article 7 Conducting Negotiations and Signature of International Treaties of Turkmenistan Without Special Powers

The President of Turkmenistan shall conduct negotiations and sign international treaties of Turkmenistan without special powers.

The Minister of Foreign Affairs of Turkmenistan, being guided by the fundamental principles of foreign policy of the State and in accordance with generally-recognized norms of international law, shall have the right to conduct negotiations and to sign international treaties of Turkmenistan without special powers.

The head of a diplomatic representation of Turkmenistan in a foreign State or the head of a representation of Turkmenistan attached to an international organization shall have the right to conduct negotiations without special powers concerning the conclusion of an international treaty of Turkmenistan respectively with the receiving State or within the framework of the particular international organization.

Article 8 Language of International Treaties of Turkmenistan

Bilateral international treaties of Turkmenistan shall be drawn up in two examples in the languages of the Contracting Parties, both texts being deemed to be of equal significance (authentic). By arrangement of the parties, an international treaty may be drawn up additionally also in another language or only in one language.

Multilateral treaties with the participation of Turkmenistan shall be drawn up either in the languages of the Contracting Parties or by arrangement, in one language.

Article 9 Ratification of International Treaties of Turkmenistan

International treaties of Turkmenistan shall be ratified by the Halk Maslakhaty of Turkmenistan and by the Medzhlis of Turkmenistan.

International treaties of Turkmenistan concerning inter-State unions and other formations shall be subject to ratification of the Halk Maslakhaty of Turkmenistan.

International treaties of Turkmenistan shall be subject to obligatory ratification by the Medzhlis of Turkmenistan:

(1) concerning friendship, cooperation, and mutual assistance;
(2) mutual renunciation of the use or threat of force;
(3) peace treaties;
(4) territorial delimitation of Turkmenistan with other States;
(5) providing for the need to adopt, change, or repeal laws of Turkmenistan or establish other rules than those which are contained in the legislation of Turkmenistan;
(6) connected with the defence and security of the State;
(7) multilateral or long-term treaties of an economic character.

International treaties of Turkmenistan during the conclusion of which the parties have stipulated their subsequent ratification shall also be subject to ratification.

Article 10 Proposals Concerning Ratification of International Treaties of Turkmenistan

Proposals concerning the ratification of international treaties of Turkmenistan shall be submitted to the President of Turkmenistan by the Ministry of Foreign Affairs of Turkmenistan autonomously or jointly or by agreement with other ministries and departments.

The President of Turkmenistan shall adopt decisions concerning the submission of international treaties of Turkmenistan for ratification respectively to the Halk Maslakhaty of Turkmenistan or to the Medzhlis of Turkmenistan.

Article 11 Adoption of Decisions Concerning Ratification of International Treaties of Turkmenistan

The Halk Maslakhaty or Medzhlis of Turkmenistan shall consider international treaties of Turkmenistan submitted for ratification and render decisions with regard to them.

Decisions of the Halk Maslakhaty and Medzhlis of Turkmenistan concerning ratification of an international treaty of Turkmenistan shall be adopted respectively in the form of a decision and decree. On the basis of a decision or decree concerning ratification, the President of Turkmenistan shall sign the instrument of ratification.

The form of the instrument of ratification shall be confirmed by the President of Turkmenistan.

Article 12 Exchange of Instruments of Ratification and Giving Them Over for Keeping

The exchange of instruments of ratification and handing over of instruments concerning ratification of international treaties of Turkmenistan for keeping to depositaries shall be by the Ministry of Foreign Affairs of Turkmenistan or on its behalf by the head of the diplomatic representation of Turkmenistan in the State of accreditation or head of representation of Turkmenistan attached to an international organization or by a person specially empowered by the President of Turkmenistan.

Article 13 Confirmation of International Treaties of Turkmenistan Not Subject to Ratification

Inter-State and intergovernmental treaties of Turkmenistan not subject to ratification but providing for their confirmation shall be confirmed by the President of Turkmenistan.

International treaties of Turkmenistan of an interdepartmental character shall be confirmed by the Cabinet of Ministers of Turkmenistan.

International treaties of Turkmenistan concluded by the Ministry of Foreign Affairs of Turkmenistan or by other ministries and departments of Turkmenistan by means of an exchange of notes or letters shall enter into force from the day of the exchange thereof without the ratification or subsequent confirmation thereof.

Article 14 Accession to International Treaties

A decision concerning the accession of Turkmenistan to international treaties shall be adopted with respect to treaties:

requiring ratification – by the Halk Maslakhaty or the Medzhlis of Turkmenistan upon the recommendation of the President of Turkmenistan;

not requiring ratification, and accession to which is made in the name of Turkmenistan, the Cabinet of Ministers (Government) of Turkmenistan – by the President of Turkmenistan;

of an interdepartmental character – by the Cabinet of Ministers of Turkmenistan.

III Performance of International Treaties

Article 15 Compliance with International Treaties

International treaties of Turkmenistan shall be subject to undeviating compliance by Turkmenistan in the person of its State agencies in accordance with norms of international law.

In accordance with the principle of good-faith compliance with international treaties, Turkmenistan shall act so that the other participants of bilateral and multilateral international treaties in which Turkmenistan participates have undeviatingly fulfilled their obligations arising from these treaties.

Article 16 Ensuring Fulfilment of International Treaties of Turkmenistan

The President of Turkmenistan and Cabinet of Ministers of Turkmenistan shall take measures to ensure the fulfilment of international treaties of Turkmenistan.

Article 17 Fulfilment of Obligations With Regard to International Treaties of Turkmenistan

State agencies of Turkmenistan within whose competence are questions regulated by international treaties of Turkmenistan shall ensure the fulfilment of obligations accepted with regard to these treaties, watch over the effectuation of rights arising from the treaties which belong to Turkmenistan, and also over the fulfilment by other participants of the treaties of their obligations.

Article 18 General Observation Over Performance of International Treaties of Turkmenistan

General observation over the performance of international treaties of Turkmenistan shall be effectuated by the Ministry of Foreign Affairs of Turkmenistan.

The Cabinet of Ministers of Turkmenistan shall be the depositary of inter-State and intergovernmental treaties of Turkmenistan, and the Ministry of Foreign Affairs of Turkmenistan, the depositary of treaties of Turkmenistan of an interdepartmental character.

Article 19 Measures to be Taken in Event of Violation of International Treaty of Turkmenistan by Other Participants Thereof

In the event of a violation of obligations with regard to an international treaty of Turkmenistan by the other participants thereof, the Ministry of Foreign Affairs of Turkmenistan, State agencies of Turkmenistan jointly or by agreement with the Ministry of Foreign Affairs of Turkmenistan, shall submit to the Cabinet of Ministers of Turkmenistan proposals concerning the taking of necessary measures in accordance with norms of international law.

In the event of a material violation of an international treaty of Turkmenistan by other participants thereof, and also in other instances provided for by norms of international law, such treaty may be terminated in the procedure established by Articles 23 and 24 of the present Law.

Article 20 Proposals Concerning the Making of Changes in and Additions to Legislation in Connection with Conclusion of International Treaty of Turkmenistan

In instances when for the purpose of the fulfilment of an international treaty of Turkmenistan it is necessary to adopt a law of Turkmenistan, acts of the President of Turkmenistan, or decrees of the Medzhlis of Turkmenistan, the interested ministries and departments by agreement with the Ministry of Justice and the Ministry of Foreign Affairs of Turkmenistan shall submit in the established procedure to the Cabinet of Ministers of Turkmenistan a proposal concerning the adoption of such normative acts or proposals concerning the making of changes in and additions to legislation of Turkmenistan.

IV Publication and Registration of International Treaties of Turkmenistan

Article 21 Publication of International Treaties of Turkmenistan

International treaties which have entered into force for Turkmenistan that were concluded in the name of Turkmenistan and international treaties, accession to which is effectuated on the basis of decisions of the Halk Maslakhaty of Turkmenistan or decrees of the Medzhlis of Turkmenistan shall be published in the *Ведомости Меджлиса Туркменистана*, and also in the newspapers *Туркменистан* and *Туркменская искра*.

International treaties which have entered into force for Turkmenistan that were concluded in the name of Turkmenistan and the Cabinet of Ministers of Turkmenistan and are not subject to ratification shall be published in the *Собрание актов Президента Туркменистана и постановлений Кабинета министров Туркменистана*.

International treaties of Turkmenistan, the authentic texts of which have been drawn up in foreign languages, shall be published in one of these languages with an official translation into the Turkmen language.

International treaties of Turkmenistan of an interdepartmental character shall be published in departmental publications of ministries and departments of Turkmenistan in whose name such treaties were concluded.

Article 22 Registration of International Treaties of Turkmenistan

The registration of international treaties of Turkmenistan in the Secretariat of the United Nations or in respective organs of other international organizations shall be effectuated by the Ministry of Foreign Affairs of Turkmenistan.

V Denunciation of International Treaties of Turkmenistan

Article 23 Proposals Concerning Denunciation of International Treaties of Turkmenistan

Proposals concerning the denunciation of international treaties of Turkmenistan shall be submitted by the Ministry of Foreign Affairs of Turkmenistan and by other ministries and departments to the Cabinet of Ministers of Turkmenistan in accordance with the procedure established by Article 4 of the present Law for the making of proposals concerning the conclusion of an international treaty.

The Cabinet of Ministers of Turkmenistan shall submit the respective proposals to the President of Turkmenistan.

Article 24 Denunciation of International Treaties of Turkmenistan

The denunciation of international treaties of Turkmenistan of ratified treaties and treaties the accession to which was effectuated on the basis of decisions of the Halk Maslakhaty or decrees of the Government of the Medzhlis of Turkmenistan upon the recommendation of the President of Turkmenistan or Cabinet of Ministers of Turkmenistan shall be effectuated respectively by the Halk Maslakhaty or the Medzhlis of Turkmenistan.

Inter-State and intergovernmental treaties of Turkmenistan not requiring ratification shall be denounced by the President of Turkmenistan.

International treaties of an interdepartmental character shall be denounced by the Cabinet of Ministers of Turkmenistan.

UKRAINE

Law on the Operation of International Treaties on the Territory of Ukraine

[Adopted 10 December 1991. *Ведомости Верховной Рады Украины* (1992), no. 10, item 137]

Proceeding from the priority of general humanitarian values and generally-recognized principles of international law, endeavouring to ensure the inviolability of the rights and freedoms of man and to be included in the system of legal relations between States on the basis of mutual respect for State sovereignty and democratic principles of international cooperation, the Supreme Soviet of Ukraine decrees:

To establish that international treaties concluded and duly ratified by Ukraine shall constitute an integral part of the national legislation of Ukraine and be applied in the procedure provided for norms of national legislation.

Law on International Treaties of Ukraine

[Adopted 22 December 1993. *Ведомости Верховной Рады Украины* (1994), no. 10, item 45]

The present Law establishes the procedure for the conclusion, fulfilment, and denunciation of international treaties of Ukraine for the purpose of the proper ensuring of national interests and effectuation of the purposes, tasks and principles of foreign policy of Ukraine consolidated in the Constitution of Ukraine.

I General Provisions

Article 1 Sphere of Application of Law

1. The present Law shall apply to all international treaties of Ukraine – inter-State, intergovernmental, and interdepartmental – regulated by norms of international law, irrespective of the form and name thereof (treaty, agreement, convention, covenant, protocol, exchange of letters or notes, and other forms and names of international treaties).

2. For the purposes of the present Law the concept 'conclusion of an international treaty of Ukraine' shall encompass the conducting of negotiations for the purpose of the preparation of the text of an international treaty, adoption of the text of an international treaty or the establishment of the authenticity thereof, and the expression of consent to the obligatoriness of the international treaty for Ukraine.

Article 2 International Treaties of Ukraine

1. International treaties of Ukraine shall be concluded with foreign States and international organizations in the name of:

Ukraine;

the Government;

ministries and other central agencies of State executive power.

2. In the name of Ukraine international treaties shall be concluded:
(a) political, territorial, peace;
(b) concerning the rights and freedoms of man;
(c) concerning citizenship;
(d) concerning the participation of Ukraine in inter-State unions and other inter-State associations (or organizations) and collective security systems;
(e) concerning military assistance and relative to sending a contingent of the Armed Forces of Ukraine to another country or admitting the armed forces of foreign States to the territory of Ukraine;
(f) concerning the use of the territory and natural resources of Ukraine;
(g) to which with the consent of the Parties an inter-State character is imparted.

3. In the name of the Government shall be concluded international treaties with regard to economic, trade, scientific–technical, and other questions relegated to the competence thereof.

4. In the name of ministries and other central agencies of State executive power of Ukraine shall be concluded international treaties with regard to questions relegated to the competence thereof.

II Conclusion of International Treaties of Ukraine

Article 3 Proposals with Regard to Conclusion of International Treaties

1. Proposals with regard to the conclusion of international treaties of Ukraine shall be submitted to the Government of Ukraine by the Ministry of Foreign Affairs of Ukraine.

2. Other ministries and central agencies of State executive power shall submit proposals to the Government of Ukraine with regard to the conclusion of international treaties of Ukraine jointly with the Ministry of Foreign Affairs of Ukraine or by agreement with it.

3. The procedure for the submission of proposals concerning the conclusion of international treaties of an interdepartmental character by ministries and other central agencies of State executive power shall be determined by the Government of Ukraine.

4. In the proposals shall be substantiated the necessity for the conclusion of an international treaty, the possible political, legal, material, and financial consequences of the conclusion thereof determined, and the composition of the delegation or representative of Ukraine to conduct

the negotiations, adopt the text of the international treaty, or establish the authenticity thereof specified. The draft international treaty shall be appended thereto and, when necessary, the draft recommendation to the delegation or representative of Ukraine.

5. The Government of Ukraine shall consider the proposals submitted and not later than within a ten-day period shall submit them together with the respective opinions to the President of Ukraine, and with regard to treaties to be concluded in the name of the Government of Ukraine, shall adopt a decision concerning the conclusion of such treaty of Ukraine.

6. Proposals with regard to the conclusion of international treaties of Ukraine may be submitted by the Republic Crimea in the person of its highest agencies of legislative and executive power.

7. Proposals with regard to the conclusion of international treaties of Ukraine which establish other rules than those are contained in legislation of Ukraine shall be submitted to the Government of Ukraine by agreement with the Ministry of Justice of Ukraine.

Article 4 Decisions Concerning Conducting of Negotiations and Signing of International Treaties of Ukraine

Decisions concerning the conducting of negotiations and signing of international treaties of Ukraine shall be adopted:

(a) with respect to treaties to be concluded in the name of Ukraine: by the President of Ukraine;

(b) with respect to treaties to be concluded in the name of the Government of Ukraine: by the Government of Ukraine;

(c) with respect to treaties to be concluded in the name of ministries and other central agencies of State executive power of Ukraine: in the procedure established by the Government of Ukraine.

Article 5 Powers to Conclude International Treaty of Ukraine

1. The conducting of negotiations concerning the preparation of the text of an international treaty, adoption of the text of an international treaty, or establishment of the authenticity thereof and signing an international treaty of Ukraine shall be effectuated only by empowered persons.

2. The President of Ukraine, the Prime Minister of Ukraine, and the Minister of Foreign Affairs of Ukraine shall have the right to conduct negotiations and sign international treaties of Ukraine without special powers.

3. The head of a diplomatic representation of Ukraine in a foreign State or the head of a representation of Ukraine attached to an international organization shall have the right to conduct negotiations without special powers concerning the conclusion of an international treaty of Ukraine respectively with the receiving State or within the framework of the respective international organization.

4. The powers to conduct negotiations and sign international treaties of Ukraine shall be granted to:

(a) with respect to treaties concluded in the name of Ukraine: by the President of Ukraine;
(b) with respect to treaties concluded in the name of the Government of Ukraine: by the Government of Ukraine or on its behalf, by the Minister of Foreign Affairs of Ukraine;
(c) with respect to treaties of an interdepartmental character: by the respective ministry or other central agency of State executive power jointly with the Ministry of Foreign Affairs of Ukraine.

Article 6 Delegation or Representative of Ukraine to Conclude International Treaty of Ukraine

1. A delegation or representative of Ukraine endowed with powers in accordance with Article 5(1) and (4) of the present Law shall be obliged to conduct negotiations or effectuate other actions in accordance with the powers granted to them and taking into account the recommendations of the Ministry of Foreign Affairs of Ukraine.

2. A delegation or representative of Ukraine shall by agreement with the Ministry of Foreign Affairs of Ukraine submit to the President of Ukraine or to the Government of Ukraine a report concerning the fulfilment of the recommendations given to them. The report must contain opinions concerning the subsequent actions of Ukraine relative to the conclusion of the international treaty.

Article 7 Ratification of International Treaties of Ukraine

1. The ratification of international treaties of Ukraine shall be effectuated by the Supreme Rada of Ukraine by means of the adoption of a

special Law on ratification, which shall be signed by the Chairman of the Supreme Rada of Ukraine.

2. International treaties of Ukraine shall be subject to ratification:

(a) political (concerning friendship, mutual assistance, and cooperation, neutrality), general economic (concerning economic and scientific – technical cooperation), general financial questions, questions of loans and credits, territorial, and peace;
(b) affecting the rights and freedoms of man and citizen;
(c) concerning citizenship;
(d) concerning participation in inter-State unions and other inter-State associations (or organizations), and collective security systems;
(e) concerning military assistance and relative to sending a contingent of the Armed Forces of Ukraine to another country or admitting the armed forces of foreign States to the territory of Ukraine;
(f) concerning the historical and cultural heritage of the people of Ukraine;
(g) the fulfilment of which is conditioned by the change of prevailing or the adoption of new laws of Ukraine;
(h) other international treaties whose ratification is provided for by a law or by the international treaty itself.

3. Territorial international treaties of Ukraine and international treaties of Ukraine provided for by point 2(c) and (d) of the present Article shall be ratified by a Law of Ukraine adopted by two-thirds of the votes of people's deputies of the actual number of people's deputies of Ukraine whose powers have been recognized and not terminated before time in the procedure established by legislation.

4. Proposals concerning the approval by the President of Ukraine or by the Government of Ukraine of international treaties of Ukraine and the ratification thereof shall be submitted to the President of Ukraine or to the Government of Ukraine by the Ministry of Foreign Affairs of Ukraine autonomously or jointly or by agreement with other ministries and central agencies of State executive power.

5. The President of Ukraine or Government of Ukraine shall consider proposals concerning the approval of contracts and adopt respective decisions concerning the submission thereof to the Supreme Rada of Ukraine for ratification.

6. International treaties of Ukraine submitted for ratification shall be considered in advance by the Permanent Commission of the Supreme Rada of Ukraine for Foreign Affairs and, when necessary, by other permanent commissions of the Supreme Rada of Ukraine.

7. If the Permanent Commission of the Supreme Rada of Ukraine for Foreign Affairs or other permanent commissions of the Supreme Rada of

Ukraine establishes the existence of divergencies between the treaty submitted for ratification and the Constitution of Ukraine, the treaty shall be sent to the Constitutional Court of Ukraine in order to receive an opinion concerning the conformity thereof to the Constitution of Ukraine.

8. If an international treaty has been submitted for ratification, the fulfilment of which requires the adoption of new laws of Ukraine, the draft laws concerning ratification and concerning changes in legislative acts shall be submitted for consideration of the Supreme Rada of Ukraine together and shall be adopted simultaneously.

9. If an international treaty of Ukraine contains provisions which are contrary to the Constitution of Ukraine, the ratification thereof shall be possible after making the respective changes in the Constitution of Ukraine.

10. The Supreme Rada of Ukraine, taking into account the opinions of the respective permanent commissions, shall consider the international treaties of Ukraine submitted for ratification by the President of Ukraine or Government of Ukraine and adopt the respective decisions.

11. On the basis of the decision concerning ratification, the Chairman of the Supreme Rada of Ukraine shall sign the instrument of ratification, which shall be certified by the signature of the Minister of Foreign Affairs of Ukraine.

Article 8 Exchange of Instruments of Ratification

The exchange of instruments of ratification and transfer of the instruments concerning ratification of international treaties of Ukraine for keeping to the depositaries shall be effectuated by the Ministry of Foreign Affairs of Ukraine or on behalf thereof by the diplomatic representation of Ukraine or representation of Ukraine attached to an international organization.

Article 9 Confirmation of International Treaties of Ukraine Not Requiring Ratification

1. The confirmation of international treaties of Ukraine not requiring ratification, but requiring confirmation, shall be effectuated by:

(a) with respect to treaties concluded in the name of Ukraine: the President of Ukraine. The decision of the President of Ukraine concerning confirmation of an international treaty of Ukraine shall be adopted in the form of an edict;

(b) with respect to treaties concluded in the name of the Government of Ukraine: the Government of Ukraine. The decision of the Government of Ukraine concerning the confirmation of an international treaty of Ukraine shall be adopted in the form of a decree.

2. International treaties of Ukraine of an interdepartmental character shall be confirmed in the procedure determined by the Government of Ukraine.

Article 10 Accession to International Treaties or Adoption Thereof

1. Decisions concerning the accession of Ukraine to international treaties and the adoption thereof shall be adopted by:

(a) with respect to treaties requiring ratification: the Supreme Rada of Ukraine in the form of a Law;

(b) with respect to treaties not requiring ratification, and accession to which or the adoption of which is in the name of Ukraine: the President of Ukraine in the form of an edict;

(c) with respect to treaties not subject to ratification and accession to which or the adoption of which is in the name of the Government of Ukraine: the Government of Ukraine in the form of a decree.

2. Decisions concerning accession to international treaties of an interdepartmental character or the adoption thereof shall be adopted in the procedure determined by the Government of Ukraine.

Article 11 Signing of International Treaties of Ukraine

When an international treaty enters into force from the moment of signature thereof, consent to the obligatory character of its provisions shall be expressed in the form of signing the international treaty by an empowered person in accordance with Article 5 of the present Law.

III Fulfilment of International Treaties of Ukraine

Article 12 Compliance with International Treaties of Ukraine

1. International treaties of Ukraine shall be subject to undeviating compliance by Ukraine in accordance with the norms of international law.

2. According to the principle of good-faith compliance of international treaties Ukraine shall act so that the other participants of bilateral and multilateral international treaties in which Ukraine participants also have undeviatingly fulfilled their obligations arising from these treaties.

Article 13 Ensuring Fulfilment of International Treaties of Ukraine

The President of Ukraine and the Government of Ukraine shall take measures with regard to ensuring the fulfilment of international treaties of Ukraine.

Article 14 Fulfilment of Obligations with Regard to International Treaties of Ukraine

1. Ministries and other central agencies of State executive power of Ukraine, the Government of the Republic Crimea, other State agencies to whose competence questions are relegated regulated by international treaties of Ukraine shall ensure the fulfilment of obligations assumed under international treaties by the Ukrainian Party and over the fulfilment by other participants of international treaties of their obligations.

2. The said State agencies, and also enterprises, institutions, and organizations, shall be obliged to grant to the Ministry of Foreign Affairs of Ukraine information affecting the fulfilment of international treaties of Ukraine.

Article 15 General Supervision Over Fulfilment of International Treaties of Ukraine

1. General supervision over the fulfilment of international treaties of Ukraine shall be effectuated by the Ministry of Foreign Affairs of Ukraine.

2. Upon the demand of agencies applying international treaties of Ukraine, the Ministry of Foreign Affairs of Ukraine must provide official information relative to questions arising in connection with the fulfilment of the international treaty of Ukraine.

3. In the event of the improper fulfilment of obligations assumed under international treaties by the Ukrainian Party, the Ministry of Foreign Affairs of Ukraine shall inform the President of Ukraine or the Government of Ukraine thereof for the taking of necessary measures.

Article 16 Measures to be Taken in Event of Violation of International Treaty of Ukraine by Other Participants Thereof

1. In the event of a violation of obligations under an international treaty of Ukraine by the other participants thereof, the Ministry of Foreign Affairs of Ukraine, other central agencies of State executive power of Ukraine, and the Government of the Republic Crimea by agreement with the Ministry of Foreign Affairs of Ukraine shall submit to the President of Ukraine or to the Government of Ukraine proposals concerning the taking of necessary measures in accordance with norms of international law.

2. In the event of a material violation of an international treaty of Ukraine by other participants thereof, and also in other instances provided for by norms of international law, such treaty may be denounced in the procedure established by Articles 23 and 24 of the present Law.

Article 17 Operation of International Treaties of Ukraine on Territory of Ukraine

1. International treaties of Ukraine concluded and duly ratified shall constitute an integral part of the national legislation of Ukraine and shall be applied in the procedure provided for norms of national legislation.

2. If other rules have been established by an international treaty of Ukraine whose conclusion has occurred in the form of a law than those which have been provided for by legislation of Ukraine, the rules of the international treaty of Ukraine shall apply.

Article 18 Proposals Concerning the Making of Changes in and Additions to Legislation of Ukraine in Connection with Conclusion of International Treaty of Ukraine

In instances when in order to fulfil an international treaty of Ukraine it is necessary to adopt a law of Ukraine or decree of the Supreme Rada of Ukraine, edict of the President of Ukraine, or decree of the Government of Ukraine the interested ministries, other central agencies of State executive power of Ukraine, and the Government of Ukraine by agreement with the Ministry of Justice of Ukraine shall submit proposals in the established procedure concerning the adoption of the respective act.

Article 19 Prolongation of International Treaty of Ukraine

An international treaty of Ukraine may be prolonged in accordance with the conditions determined by the international treaty itself.

IV Publication, Registration, and Keeping of Texts of International Treaties of Ukraine

Article 20 Publication of International Treaties of Ukraine

1. Treaties which have entered into force for Ukraine – ratified treaties and treaties whose confirmation or adoption, or accession to which, is effectuated in the basis of decisions respectively of the Supreme Rada of Ukraine or President of Ukraine and treaties which have entered into force from the moment of their signature by the President of Ukraine, shall be published in the *Ведомости Верховного Совета Украины* and in the *Собрание действующих международных договоров Украины.*

2. Treaties which have entered into force for Ukraine, international treaties not requiring ratification, confirmation, adoption, or accession respectively by the Supreme Rada of Ukraine or by the President of Ukraine, and also treaties, the adoption or accession to which was effectuated on the basis of decisions of the Government of Ukraine, shall be published in the *Собрание постановлений Правительства Украины* and in the newspaper of the Government of Ukraine.

3. The procedure for publication of international treaties of Ukraine of an interdepartmental character which have entered into force shall be determined by the Government of Ukraine.

4. If an international treaty of Ukraine has an authentic text in the State language of Ukraine, the authentic text shall be published in the State language of Ukraine.

5. When an international treaty of Ukraine does not have an authentic text in the State language of Ukraine, one of the authentic texts in a foreign language shall be published, and also an official translation into the State language of Ukraine effectuated by the Ministry of Foreign Affairs of Ukraine.

Article 21 Registration of International Treaties of Ukraine

The registration of international treaties which have entered into force for Ukraine shall be effectuated by the Ministry of Foreign Affairs of Ukraine at the Secretariat of the United Nations and respective organs of other international organizations.

Article 22 Keeping of Texts of International Treaties of Ukraine

1. The originals of texts of international treaties of Ukraine shall be kept by the Ministry of Foreign Affairs of Ukraine.
2. The procedure for keeping international treaties of Ukraine of an interdepartmental character shall be determined by the Government of Ukraine.

V Denunciation of International Treaties of Ukraine

Article 23 Proposals Concerning Denunciation of International Treaties of Ukraine

1. Proposals concerning the denunciation of international treaties of Ukraine shall be submitted by the Ministry of Foreign Affairs of Ukraine and by other ministries and departments to the Government of Ukraine in accordance with the procedure established by Article 3 of the present Law for the making of proposals concerning the conclusion of an international treaty.
2. The Government of Ukraine shall make respective proposals to the President of Ukraine or to the Supreme Rada of Ukraine.

Article 24 Denunciation of International Treaties of Ukraine

1. The denunciation of international treaties of Ukraine shall be effectuated by a Law of Ukraine, edict of the President of Ukraine, and decree of the Government of Ukraine.

2. The denunciation of international treaties of Ukraine ratified by the Supreme Rada of Ukraine, and treaties adopted or accession to which was effectuated on the basis of decisions of the Supreme Rada of Ukraine, shall be effectuated by the Supreme Rada of Ukraine.

3. Territorial international treaties of Ukraine and international treaties of Ukraine provided for by Article 7(2)(c) and (d) of the present Law shall be denounced by a Law of Ukraine which is adopted by two-thirds of the votes of the people's deputies of the actual number of people's deputies of Ukraine whose powers have been recognized and not terminated before time in the procedure established by legislation.

4. The Permanent Commission of the Supreme Rada of Ukraine for Foreign Affairs, and when necessary also other permanent commissions of the Supreme Rada of Ukraine, shall consider preliminarily the international treaties of Ukraine submitted for denunciation and give respective opinions.

5. The denunciation of international treaties of Ukraine concluded by the President of Ukraine not requiring ratification, adoption, or accession by the Supreme Rada of Ukraine shall be done by the President of Ukraine in the form of an edict.

6. The denunciation of international treaties concluded by the Government of Ukraine and not requiring ratification, adoption, or accession by the Supreme Rada of Ukraine shall be done by the Government of Ukraine.

7. The denunciation of international treaties of Ukraine of an interdepartmental character shall be done in the procedure determined by the Government of Ukraine.

Article 25 Informing Supreme Rada of Ukraine Relative to International Treaties

The Supreme Rada of Ukraine must within thirty days be informed about the conclusion and termination of international treaties of Ukraine with respect to which ratification or denunciation has not been provided for.

UZBEKISTAN

Law on International Treaties of the Republic Uzbekistan

[Adopted by the Olii Mazhlis of the Republic Uzbekistan, 22 December 1995. *Ведомости Олий Мажлиса Республики Узбекистан* (1995), no. 12, item 262]

I General Provisions

Article 1 Tasks of the Law

The present Law shall establish the procedure for the conclusion, performance, termination, suspension, and denunciation of international treaties of the Republic Uzbekistan.

Article 2 Legislation on International Treaties

International treaties of the Republic Uzbekistan shall be concluded, performed, terminated, suspended, and denounced in accordance with generally-recognized principles and norms of international law, the Constitution of the Republic Uzbekistan, and also the present Law and the provisions of the treaty itself.

The procedure for the conclusion, performance, termination, suspension, and denunciation of international treaties of the Republic Uzbekistan established by the present Law shall apply with respect to all international treaties of Uzbekistan irrespective of their type, form, and name.

In instances when for the purpose of performing an international treaty of the Republic Uzbekistan the adoption of a law of the Republic Uzbekistan or decree of the Olii Mazhlis or the issuance of an Edict, decree, or regulation of the President Uzbekistan, or decree or regulation of the Government of the Republic Uzbekistan is necessary, the interested ministries and departments shall, upon agreement with the Ministry of

Justice and the Ministry of Foreign Affairs, submit proposals in the established procedure concerning the adoption of the proper act.

Article 3 Concept of International Treaty

An international treaty of the Republic Uzbekistan is an equal and voluntary agreement of the Republic with one or several States, international organizations, or other subjects of international law relating to rights and duties in the domain of international relations.

Article 4 Name and Types of International Treaties

International treaties may be named and concluded in the form of: a treaty, agreement, convention, protocol, memorandum, declaration, exchange of letters and notes, and also have other names.

According to the quantity of subjects participating therein international treaties shall be subdivided into bilateral and multilateral. According to content international treaties may be: economic, political, legal, and also concluded with regard to other questions. According to periods treaties may be subdivided into fixed-term and in perpetuity. International treaties also may be concluded in other types.

Article 5 Language and Form of International Treaty

The State language of the Republic Uzbekistan and the language of the other Contracting Party(ies) shall be the language of an international treaty of the Republic Uzbekistan.

By agreement of the subjects of the international treaty another language may be selected as the language of the treaty. The language in which the text of the international treaty is drawn up shall be specified in the text of the particular treaty, where the authenticity and official nature thereof shall be determined.

International treaties shall be concluded, as a rule, in writing.

Article 6 Object of International Treaty

Political, economic, scientific–technical, cultural, legal, and other spheres of activity of a State may be the object of an international treaty of the Republic Uzbekistan.

Article 7 Right to Conclude International Treaties

The right to conclude international treaties of the Republic Uzbekistan shall belong to the State.

International treaties of the Republic Uzbekistan shall be concluded in the name of:

the Republic Uzbekistan – interstate;

the Government of the Republic Uzbekistan – intergovernmental;

the ministries and departments of the Republic Uzbekistan – interdepartmental.

II Procedure for Conclusion and Entry into Force of International Treaties of Republic Uzbekistan

Article 8 Proposals Concerning Conclusion of International Treaties

Proposals concerning the conclusion of international treaties in the name of the Republic Uzbekistan shall be submitted to the President of the Republic Uzbekistan, and proposals concerning the conclusion of international treaties in the name of the Republic Uzbekistan with regard to questions relegated to the jurisdiction of the Government of the Republic Uzbekistan, to the Government of the Republic Uzbekistan.

Proposals concerning the conclusion of international treaties in the name of the Republic Uzbekistan shall be submitted to the President of the Republic Uzbekistan by the Ministry of Foreign Affairs. Other ministries and departments shall submit to the President of the Republic Uzbekistan proposals concerning the conclusion of international treaties in the name of the Republic Uzbekistan with regard to questions within the competence thereof jointly with the Ministry of Foreign Affairs or by agreement with it.

Proposals concerning the conclusion of international treaties of the Republic Uzbekistan in the name of the Government of the Republic Uzbekistan shall be submitted to the Government of the Republic Uzbekistan by the Ministry of Foreign Affairs.

Other ministries and departments shall submit to the Government of the Republic Uzbekistan proposals concerning the conclusion of international treaties of the Republic Uzbekistan jointly with the Ministry of Foreign Affairs or by agreement with it, and autonomously, only in the instances provided for by the present Law.

The procedure for submitting proposals concerning the conclusion by ministries and departments of interdepartmental treaties shall be determined by the Government of the Republic Uzbekistan.

Proposals concerning the conclusion of international treaties of the Republic Uzbekistan before their submission to the President of the Republic Uzbekistan or to the Government of the Republic Uzbekistan shall be agreed with the Ministry of Justice, and also with other interested ministries and departments.

A proposal concerning the conclusion of an international treaty must contain the draft treaty or its basic provisions, a substantiation of the advisability of concluding it, and also, when necessary, an evaluation of the possible financial – economic consequences of concluding the treaty.

When necessary a commission of representatives of the interested ministries and departments, specialists, and independent experts shall be created in order to draw up or consider a draft international treaty.

Article 9 Proposals Concerning Conclusion of International Treaties Regarding Questions of Foreign Economic Activity

A proposal concerning the conclusion of international treaties of the Republic Uzbekistan regarding questions of foreign economic activity, including questions of trade and economic cooperation and rendering technical assistance, shall be submitted to the Government of the Republic Uzbekistan by the Ministry of Foreign Economic Relations autonomously with the simultaneous notification of the Ministry of Foreign Affairs.

Other ministries and departments shall submit to the Government of the Republic Uzbekistan proposals concerning the conclusion of international treaties regarding questions of foreign economic activity jointly with the Ministry of Foreign Economic Relations or by agreement with it.

Article 10 Procedure for Consideration of Proposal Concerning Conclusion of International Treaty of Republic Uzbekistan

A proposal concerning the conclusion of an international treaty of the Republic Uzbekistan shall be considered by the President of the Republic Uzbekistan or by the Government of the Republic Uzbekistan when the opinions are present of the respective ministries and departments.

Article 11 Decisions Concerning the Conducting of Negotiations and the Signature of International Treaties of the Republic Uzbekistan

Decisions concerning the conducting of negotiations and the signature of international treaties of the Republic Uzbekistan shall be adopted:

(1) with respect to treaties to be concluded in the name of the Republic Uzbekistan – by the President of the Republic Uzbekistan, and with respect to treaties to be concluded in the name of the Republic Uzbekistan with regard to questions relegated to the jurisdiction of the Government of the Republic Uzbekistan – by the Government of the Republic Uzbekistan;

(2) with respect to treaties to be concluded in the name of the Government of the Republic Uzbekistan – by the Government of the Republic Uzbekistan;

(3) with respect to interdepartmental treaties – in the procedure determined by the Government of the Republic Uzbekistan.

Article 12 Powers to Conduct Negotiations and to Sign International Treaties of Republic Uzbekistan

Powers to conduct negotiations and to sign international treaties of the Republic Uzbekistan shall be issued:

(1) with respect to treaties to be concluded in the name of the Republic Uzbekistan, by the President of the Republic Uzbekistan, and with respect to treaties to be concluded in the name of the Republic Uzbekistan with regard to questions relegated to the jurisdiction of the Government of the Republic Uzbekistan, by the Government of the Republic Uzbekistan;

(2) with respect to treaties to be concluded in the name of the Government of the Republic Uzbekistan – by the Government of the Republic Uzbekistan;

(3) with respect to interdepartmental treaties – in the procedure determined by the Government of the Republic Uzbekistan.

Powers to conduct negotiations and to sign international treaties of the Republic Uzbekistan shall be issued according to the established written form.

Article 13 Conduct of Negotiations and Signature of International Treaties of Republic Uzbekistan Without Special Powers

The President of the Republic Uzbekistan as the head of State shall represent the Republic Uzbekistan in international relations and in accordance with international law and the Constitution of the Republic Uzbekistan shall conduct negotiations and sign international treaties of the Republic Uzbekistan without special powers.

The Minister of Foreign Affairs also shall have the right to conduct negotiations and to sign international treaties of the Republic Uzbekistan without special powers.

The head of a diplomatic representation of the Republic Uzbekistan in a foreign State, or the head of a representation of the Republic Uzbekistan attached to an international organization or conference, shall have the right to conduct negotiations concerning the conclusion of an international treaty of the Republic Uzbekistan with the receiving State or within the framework of the particular international organization or conference without special powers.

The minister or head of a department shall have the right within the limits of his competence to conduct negotiations and to sign interdepartmental treaties without special powers.

Article 14 International Treaties of Republic Uzbekistan Subject to Ratification

In accordance with the Constitution of the Republic Uzbekistan the Olii Mazhlis shall perform the ratification of international treaties of the Republic Uzbekistan.

There shall be subject to ratification: international treaties of the Republic Uzbekistan concerning cooperation and mutual assistance; treaties concerning the fundamental principles of interstate relations; treaties with regard to questions affecting the defence capability of the Republic Uzbekistan; treaties concerning the mutual renunciation of the use or threat of force; peace treaties and treaties concerning collective security; treaties concerning the territorial demarcation of the Republic Uzbekistan with other States; treaties concerning the participation of the Republic Uzbekistan in interstate unions, international organizations, and other associations; treaties whose performance requires a change of prevailing or the adopting of new laws, and also establishing other rules than those which are contained in legislative acts of the Republic Uzbekistan.

Likewise subject to ratification shall be international treaties of the Republic Uzbekistan during the conclusion of which the parties have stipulated subsequent ratification.

The Olii Mazhlis may also ratify other international treaties of the Republic Uzbekistan.

International loan and guarantee treaties of the Republic Uzbekistan concluded by the Government of the Republic Uzbekistan or agencies empowered by it with international financial institutions shall not be subject to ratification and shall enter into force for the Republic Uzbekistan from the moment of signature.

Article 15 Proposals Concerning Ratification of International Treaties of Republic Uzbekistan

Proposals concerning the ratification of international treaties, decisions concerning the signature of which were adopted by the President of the Republic Uzbekistan shall be submitted to the Olii Mazhlis by the President of the Republic Uzbekistan.

Proposals concerning the ratification of international treaties of the Republic Uzbekistan, decisions concerning the signature of which were adopted by the Government of the Republic Uzbekistan shall be submitted to the Olii Mazhlis by the representation of the Republic Uzbekistan, concerning which a respective decree shall be adopted.

Proposals concerning the submission for ratification of international treaties of the Republic Uzbekistan shall be submitted respectively to the President of the Republic Uzbekistan or to the Government of the Republic Uzbekistan by the Ministry of Foreign Affairs autonomously or by agreement with other ministries and departments if the treaties affect questions within their competence.

Article 16 Decision of Olii Mazhlis Concerning Ratification of International Treaties of Republic Uzbekistan

The decision of the Olii Mazhlis concerning the ratification of an international treaty of the Republic Uzbekistan shall be adopted in the form of a decree.

Article 17 Instrument of Ratification

An instrument of ratification is a special document certifying the consideration of an international treaty by the Olii Mazhlis and expressing consent to the obligatoriness of the international treaty for the Republic Uzbekistan.

The form of an instrument of ratification shall be established by the President of the Republic Uzbekistan upon the recommendation of the Ministry of Foreign Affairs.

Article 18 Signature of Instrument of Ratification

On the basis of a decree of the Olii Mazhlis concerning the ratification of an international treaty by the President of the Republic Uzbekistan the instrument of ratification shall be signed, which shall be affixed with the seal thereof and the signature of the Minister of Foreign Affairs.

Article 19 Exchange of Instruments of Ratification and Giving Thereof for Keeping

The exchange of instruments of ratification and the giving of the instruments of ratification of international treaties of the Republic Uzbekistan for keeping to depositaries shall be performed by the Ministry of Foreign Affairs or on its behalf by the diplomatic representation of the Republic Uzbekistan or representation of the Republic Uzbekistan attached to an international organization.

Article 20 Confirmation (or Adoption) of International Treaties of the Republic Uzbekistan Not Subject to Ratification

The confirmation (or adoption) of international treaties of the Republic Uzbekistan which are not subject to ratification but provide therein for confirmation (or adoption) shall be performed:

(1) with respect to treaties to be concluded in the name of the Republic Uzbekistan – by the President of the Republic Uzbekistan, and with respect to treaties to be concluded in the name of the Republic

Uzbekistan with regard to questions relegated to the jurisdiction of the Government of the Republic Uzbekistan, by the Government of the Republic Uzbekistan;

(2) with respect to treaties to be concluded in the name of the Government of the Republic Uzbekistan, by the Government of the Republic Uzbekistan;

(3) with respect to intergovernmental treaties, in the procedure determined by the Government of the Republic Uzbekistan.

Article 21 Accession to International Treaties

A decision concerning accession of the Republic Uzbekistan to international treaties shall be adopted by:

(1) with respect to treaties subject to ratification – the Olii Mazhlis;

(2) with respect to treaties not subject to ratification, accession to which is performed in the name of the Republic Uzbekistan – the President of the Republic Uzbekistan, and with respect to treaties not subject to ratification, accession to which is performed in the name of the Republic Uzbekistan with regard to questions relegated to the jurisdiction of the Government of the Republic Uzbekistan, the Government of the Republic Uzbekistan;

(3) with respect to treaties not subject to ratification, accession to which is performed in the name of the Government of the Republic Uzbekistan, the Government of the Republic Uzbekistan;

(4) with respect to interdepartmental treaties – in the procedure determined by the Government of the Republic Uzbekistan.

Article 22 Provisional Application by Republic Uzbekistan of International Treaty

An international treaty or part of a treaty may, before the entry thereof into force, be applied by the Republic Uzbekistan provisionally if this is provided for in the treaty or an arrangement has been reached concerning this with the parties who have signed the treaty.

A decision concerning the provisional application by the Republic Uzbekistan of an international treaty or part thereof shall be adopted by the agency which adopted the decision concerning signature of the international treaty.

Article 23 Entry into Force and Period of Operation of International Treaties of Republic Uzbekistan

International treaties shall enter into force for the Republic Uzbekistan in accordance with the present Law in the procedure and periods provided for in the treaty or agreed between the Contracting Parties.

Article 24 Reservations to International Treaties of Republic Uzbekistan

When signing, ratifying, confirming, or adopting international treaties of the Republic Uzbekistan or acceding to treaties, reservations may be made while complying with the conditions of the treaty and respective norms of international law.

Reservations may be removed at any time in the same procedure in which they were made.

III Publication and Registration of International Treaties of Republic Uzbekistan

Article 25 Publication of International Treaties of Republic Uzbekistan

The procedure for the publication of international treaties of the Republic Uzbekistan shall be determined by the Government of the Republic Uzbekistan.

International treaties of the Republic Uzbekistan, the authentic texts of which have been drawn up in foreign languages, shall be published in the State language. International treaties of the Republic Uzbekistan may also be published in other languages.

Article 26 Registration of International Treaties of Republic Uzbekistan

The registration of international treaties of the Republic Uzbekistan at the Secretariat of the United Nations and respective organs of other international organizations shall be effectuated by the Ministry of Foreign Affairs.

IV Performance of International Treaties of Republic Uzbekistan

Article 27 Compliance with International Treaties of Republic Uzbekistan

International treaties of the Republic Uzbekistan shall be subject to absolute and obligatory compliance by the Republic Uzbekistan in accordance with the norms of international law.

Article 28 Fulfilment of Obligations Under International Treaties of Republic Uzbekistan

The President of the Republic Uzbekistan shall, in accordance with the Constitution of the Republic Uzbekistan, ensure compliance with treaties and agreements concluded by the Republic, and obligations adopted by it.

The Government of the Republic Uzbekistan shall work out measures with regard to the fulfilment of international treaties of the Republic Uzbekistan and determine the ministries, departments, and officials on which responsibility for the performance of obligations under international treaties of the Republic Uzbekistan is placed.

The Government of the Republic Uzbekistan, ministries and departments, and other State agencies within whose competence questions being regulated by international treaties of the Republic Uzbekistan are, shall ensure the fulfilment of obligations adopted under the treaty on the part of Uzbekistan, and watch over the effectuation of the rights arising from such treaties which belong to the Republic Uzbekistan and over the fulfilment by other participants of the treaties of their obligations.

The Government of the Republic Uzbekistan shall effectuate control over the fulfilment of obligations under international treaties of the Republic Uzbekistan.

Article 29 Watching Over Performance of International Treaties of Republic Uzbekistan

The Ministry of Foreign Affairs shall watch over the performance of international treaties of the Republic Uzbekistan.

Article 30 Keeping of Texts of International Treaties of Republic Uzbekistan and Effectuation of Functions of Depositary

The originals (or attested copies, official translations) of international treaties of the Republic Uzbekistan concluded in the name of the Republic Uzbekistan and in the name of the Government of the Republic Uzbekistan shall be handed over for keeping to the Ministry of Foreign Affairs within a two-week period from the date of their signature (or receipt from the depositary of attested copies, official translations), and the copies of these documents shall within a two-week period from the date of their entry into force be circulated by the Ministry of Foreign Affairs to the respective ministries and departments.

The procedure for keeping originals of international treaties of the Republic Uzbekistan shall be confirmed by the Ministry of Foreign Affairs.

The originals of interdepartmental treaties shall be kept in the archives of the respective ministries and departments, and attested copies of these treaties shall within a two-week period from the date of their signature (or receipt from the depositary of attested copies, official translations) be sent to the Ministry of Foreign Affairs.

The Ministry of Foreign Affairs shall effectuate the functions of depositary of multilateral international treaties if in accordance with the conditions of these treaties such functions are placed on the Republic Uzbekistan.

Correspondence with agencies of foreign States, international organizations, or their chief executive officials fulfilling the functions of depositary of multilateral international treaties shall be effectuated by the Ministry of Foreign Affairs.

Article 31 Measures to be Adopted in Event of Violation of International Treaty of Republic Uzbekistan by Other Participants Thereof

In the event of a violation of obligations under an international treaty of the Republic Uzbekistan by other participants thereof the Ministry of Foreign Affairs or other interested ministries and departments jointly with the Ministry of Foreign Affairs shall submit to the President of the Republic Uzbekistan or to the Government of the Republic Uzbekistan proposals concerning the adoption of necessary measures in accordance with the norms of international law.

In the event of a material violation of an international treaty of the Republic Uzbekistan by the other participants thereof, and also in other instances provided for by norms of international law, such treaty may be terminated in the procedure established by Articles 38–43 of the present Law.

V Invalidity, Termination, Denunciation, and Suspension of Actions of International Treaties of Republic Uzbekistan

Article 32 Invalidity of International Treaties of Republic Uzbekistan

International treaties of the Republic Uzbekistan may be considered to be invalid in the instances provided for by norms of international law.

Article 33 Termination of International Treaty or Withdrawal Therefrom

The termination of an international treaty of the Republic Uzbekistan or withdrawal therefrom may occur:
(1) in accordance with the provisions of the treaty;
(2) at any time on the basis of consultations with other participants of the treaty.

Article 34 Denunciation of International Treaty of Republic Uzbekistan or Withdrawal from Treaty Not Containing Provisions Concerning Termination Thereof

An international treaty of the Republic Uzbekistan which does not contain provisions concerning its termination and which does not provide for denunciation or withdrawal therefrom shall not be subject to denunciation and withdrawal therefrom shall not be permitted unless:
(1) it is established that the participants of the international treaty intended to permit the possibility of denunciation or withdrawal;

(2) the character of the treaty assumes the right of denunciation or withdrawal therefrom.

The Republic Uzbekistan shall notify not less than twelve months beforehand its intention to denounce a treaty or withdraw therefrom.

Article 35 Suspension of International Treaty of Republic Uzbekistan

The suspension of the operation of an international treaty of the Republic Uzbekistan with respect to all participants of the treaty or with respect to an individual treaty shall be possible:

(1) in accordance with the provisions of the treaty;
(2) at any time on the basis of consultations with other participants of the treaty.

Article 36 Termination or Suspension of Operation of International Treaty of Republic Uzbekistan Arising from Conclusion of Subsequent Treaty

An international treaty of the Republic Uzbekistan shall be considered to be terminated if all of the participants thereof have concluded a subsequent treaty with regard to the same question and:

(1) from the subsequent treaty it arises or otherwise is established that the particular question is regulated by this treaty;
(2) the provisions of the subsequent treaty of the Republic Uzbekistan are not compatible with the provisions of the preceding treaty and both treaties are impossible to apply simultaneously.

The operation of the preceding treaty of the Republic Uzbekistan shall be considered only to be suspended if from the subsequent treaty it arises or is otherwise established that such was the intention of the participants thereof.

Article 37 Termination or Suspension of International Treaty of Republic Uzbekistan as Consequence of Violation Thereof

The material violation of an international treaty of the Republic Uzbekistan by one of the participants of the treaty shall give the Republic

Uzbekistan the right to refer to such violation as the grounds for termination of the treaty or for suspension of its operation as a whole or in part.

A material violation of an international treaty shall consist of:

(1) renunciation of a treaty which is not permitted by norms of international law;

(2) violation of a provision having material significance for effectuating of the object and purposes of the treaty.

Article 38 Proposals Concerning Termination, Denunciation, or Suspension of International Treaties of Republic Uzbekistan

Proposals concerning termination, denunciation, or suspension of the operation of international treaties of the Republic Uzbekistan concluded in the name of the Republic Uzbekistan or in the name of the Government of the Republic Uzbekistan shall be submitted by the Ministry of Foreign Affairs autonomously or upon agreement with other ministries and departments respectively to the President of the Republic Uzbekistan or to the Government of the Republic Uzbekistan. The Ministry of Foreign Economic Relations shall have the right to submit proposals concerning the termination, denunciation, or suspension of the operation of international treaties of the Republic Uzbekistan with regard to questions of foreign economic activity to the Government of the Republic Uzbekistan, simultaneously notifying the Ministry of Foreign Affairs of the Republic Uzbekistan. Other ministries and departments shall submit proposals concerning termination, denunciation, or suspension of the operation of international treaties to the Ministry of Foreign Affairs.

Article 39 Termination or Denunciation of International Treaties of the Republic Uzbekistan by the Olii Mazhlis

The termination or denunciation of international treaties of the Republic Uzbekistan concluded in the name of the Republic Uzbekistan shall be performed by the Olii Mazhlis upon the recommendation of the President of the Republic Uzbekistan, and treaties concluded in the name of the Republic Uzbekistan with regard to questions relegated to the jurisdiction of the Government of the Republic Uzbekistan, upon the recommendation of the Government of the Republic Uzbekistan.

The termination and denunciation of ratified international treaties of the Republic Uzbekistan concluded in the name of the Government of the Republic Uzbekistan shall be performed by the Olii Mazhlis upon the recommendation of the Government of the Republic Uzbekistan.

The termination and denunciation of an international treaty of the Republic Uzbekistan, unless provided otherwise by the treaty and there is no other arrangement with the other participants thereof, shall relieve the Republic Uzbekistan from the obligation to fulfil the treaty and shall not influence the rights and duties of the Republic Uzbekistan which arose in the period of its operation.

Article 40 Termination and Denunciation of International Treaties of Republic Uzbekistan by Government of Republic Uzbekistan

The termination and denunciation of international treaties of the Republic Uzbekistan concluded in the name of the Government of the Republic Uzbekistan and not subject to ratification, and also treaties the accession to which was effectuated on the basis of decisions of the Government, shall be performed by the Government of the Republic Uzbekistan.

Article 41 Suspension of Operation of International Treaties of Republic Uzbekistan

The suspension of the operation of international treaties of the Republic Uzbekistan shall be effectuated in accordance with the conditions of the treaty itself and the norms of international law by the agency which adopted the decision concerning consent to the obligatoriness of the international treaty for the Republic Uzbekistan.

The suspension of the operation of an international treaty of the Republic Uzbekistan, unless the treaty provides otherwise or there is another arrangement with the other participants thereof, shall relieve the Republic Uzbekistan from the obligation to fulfil the treaty during the period of suspension.

Article 42 Termination and Suspension of Operation of Interdepartmental Treaties of Republic Uzbekistan

The termination and suspension of the operation of interdepartmental treaties shall be performed in the procedure determined by the Government of the Republic Uzbekistan.

Article 43 Communications Concerning Termination, Denunciation, or Suspension of Operation of International Treaties of Republic Uzbekistan

Official communications concerning the termination, denunciation, or suspension of the operation of international treaties concluded in the name of the Republic Uzbekistan and in the name of the Government of the Republic Uzbekistan shall be published in the procedure provided for by Article 25 of the present Law.

Decree on the Introduction into Operation of the Law on International Treaties of the Republic Uzbekistan

[Adopted by the Olii Mazhlis of the Republic Uzbekistan, 22 December 1995. *Ведомости Олий Мажлиса Республики Узбекистан* (1995), no. 12, item 263]

The Olii Mazhlis of the Republic Uzbekistan decrees:

1. To introduce the Law on International Treaties of the Republic Uzbekistan into operation from the date of publication.

2. The Cabinet of Ministers of the Republic Uzbekistan shall bring decisions of the Government into accordance with the Law on International Treaties of the Republic Uzbekistan and ensure the review and repeal by ministries and departments of the Republic of their normative acts which are contrary to the said Law.

ECONOMIC COURT OF THE COMMONWEALTH OF INDEPENDENT STATES

Advisory Opinion of the Economic Court of the Commonwealth of Independent States at the Request of the Inter-State Economic Committee of the Economic Union [on Reservations to Certain CIS Agreements]

[15 May 1996. *Решения экономического суда Содружества независимых государств (1996 г.)* (Minsk, 1997), pp. 80–93]

The Inter-State Economic Committee of the Economic Union has applied to the Economic Court of the Commonwealth of Independent States with a request to give a legal opinion on the conformity of certain agreements adopted within the framework of the Commonwealth to which reservations have been made to the provisions of the 1969 Vienna Convention on the Law of Treaties.

The Economic Court has analysed the international legal documents adopted within the framework of the Commonwealth during 1991–95 to which reservations were made by states on the subject of their conformity to the Vienna Convention and offers the following opinion.

Reservations were used most frequently by Ukraine, the Republic Moldova, and the Azerbaidzhan Republic both when decisions were adopted by the Council of the Heads of Governments and also when signing and acceding to multilateral agreements concluded within the framework of the Commonwealth.

Agreements adopted within the framework of the Commonwealth, and also decisions and memorandums of the Heads of States and Governments to which reservations were made, may be classified by object into the following types:

agreements of a constitutive character: the Agreement of the Council of Heads of States-Participants of the Commonwealth of Independent States on the Armed Forces and Border Forces of 30 December 1991; the Agreement on Interaction in the Domain of Hydrometeorology of 8 February 1992; the Agreement Between States-Participants of the Commonwealth of Independent States on the Status of Strategic Forces of 14 February 1992; the Agreement Between the Republic Armenia, Republic Belarus, Republic Kazakhstan, Republic Kyrgyzstan, Russian Federation, Republic Tadzhikistan, Turkmenistan, and Republic Uzbekistan on Forces of General Designation for Transition Period of 14 February 1992; the Agreement on the Powers of the Highest Organs of the Commonwealth of Independent States on Questions of Defence of 20 March 1992; the Agreement on the Protection of State Boundaries and Maritime Economic Zones of States-Participants of the Commonwealth of Independent States of 20 March 1992; the Agreement on the Creation of the Advisory Economic Working Commission attached to the Council of the Heads of States and the Council of Heads of Governments of the Commonwealth of Independent States of 9 October 1992; the Agreement on the Creation of the inter-State Teleradio Company of 9 October 1992; the Agreement on Interaction of States-Participants of the Commonwealth in the Domain of Geodesy, Cartography, Cadastre, and Distance Probing of the Earth of 9 October 1992; the Statement of the Council of Heads of States-Participants of the CIS of 22 January 1993; the Charter of the Commonwealth of Independent States of 22 January 1993; the Agreement of Intergovernmental Courier Communications of 22 January 1993 with the appended Statute on the Procedure for the Activity of Intergovernmental Courier Communications; the Decision of the Council of the Heads of States of the Commonwealth on the Executive Secretariat of the Commonwealth of Independent States of 14 May 1993 with the appended Statute on the Executive Secretariat of the Commonwealth of Independent States; the Decision of the Council of Heads of States of the Commonwealth on the Permanent Powers of Representatives of States-Participants of the Commonwealth of Independent States of 24 September 1993; the Agreement on the Creation of the inter-State Euroasian Coal and Metal Association of 24 September 1993; the Constitutive Treaty on the Creation of the Fund for Assistance to the Republic Tadzhikistan of 15 April 1994; the Agreement on the Creation of the inter-State Economic Committee of the Economic Union of 21 October 1994 with appended the Statute on the inter-State Economic Committee of the Economic Union; and the Agreement on the Creation of the Unified System of Anti-Aircraft Defence of States-Participants of the Commonwealth of Independent States of 10 February 1995 with appended the Statute on the Unified System of Anti-Aircraft Defence of States-Participants of the Commonwealth of Independent States;

agreements of an economic character: the Agreement Between States-Participants of the Commonwealth of Independent States on Forming a Unified Defence Budget and the Procedure for Financing the Armed Forces of the States of the Commonwealth of 14 February

1992; the Agreement on the Regulation of Mutual Relations of the Commonwealth in the Domain of Trade and Economic Cooperation in 1992 of 14 February 1992; the Agreement on the Principles of Provision of the Armed Forces of States-Participants of the Commonwealth with Armaments, Technology, Material Means, and Organization of Production Activity of Repair Enterprises, Scientific-Research, and Experimental-Construction Design Work of 14 February 1992; the Agreement on the Principles of Customs Policy of 13 March 1992; the Agreement on the Principles and Procedure for the Fulfilment of Military Carriages of 15 May 1992; the Decision of the Council of the Heads of Government of the Commonwealth on the Draft Agreement on Defence of the Interests of States of the Ruble Zone in the Event of the Introduction of a National Currency by Individual States of 26 June 1992; the Agreement on Coordination of Work on Questions of Export Control of Raw Material, Materials, Equipment, Technology and Services Which May Be Used for Creation of Weapons of Mass Destruction and Missile Means of Delivery Thereof of 26 June 1992; the Agreement on Mutual Recognition of Rights and Regulation of Relations of Ownership of 9 October 1992; the Agreement on Cooperation with Regard to Ensuring Uniformity in Measurements of Time and Frequencies of 9 October 1992; the Agreement on Multilateral inter-State Production Specialization and Deliveries of High-Grade and Hybrid Seed for Agricultural Crops of 9 October 1992; the Agreement on the Procedure for Financing Joint Activity Relating to the Research and Use of Outer Space of 13 November 1992; the Agreement on the Organization of Work Relating to inter-State Standardization of the Armed Forces and Military Technology of 13 November 1992; the Declaration of the Heads of States-Participants of the Commonwealth of Independent States of 14 May 1993; the Treaty on Conducting an Agreed Anti-Monopoly Policy of 23 December 1993; the Agreement on Cooperation in the Domain of Investment Activity of 24 December 1993; the Agreement on the Accession of Ukraine to the Economic Union with the Rights of an Associate Member of 15 April 1994; the Agreement on Cooperation in the Domain of Mobilized Preparation of the Economy of 15 April 1994; the Decision of the Heads of Governments of the Commonwealth on the Draft Agreement on the Creation of a Free Trade Zone of 15 April 1994; the Decision of the Council of Heads of States of the Commonwealth on the Memorandum of the Council of the Heads of States of the Commonwealth of Independent States 'Basic Orientations of Integration Activity of Commonwealth of Independent States' and Long-Term Plan for Integration Development of Commonwealth of Independent States of 21 October 1994; the Agreement on the Creation of the Payments Union of States-Participants of the Commonwealth of Independent States of 21 October 1994; the Decision of the Council of Heads of States of the Commonwealth of Independent States of 10 February 1995; the Agreement on the Creation of the inter-State Currency Committee of 26 May 1995; the Decision of the Council of Heads of Governments of the Commonwealth on the Necessity to Settle inter-State Accounts With Regard to Results of Trade–Economic Relations of States-Participants of Commonwealth of Independent States for 1992–1993 of 26 May 1995; the Decision of the Council of Heads of Governments of the Commonwealth on the Draft Agreement on the Creation of the inter-State Currency Committee of 26 May 1995; the Agreement on Carriages of Special Cargoes and Products of Military Designation of 26 May 1995; the Agreement on the Creation of Common Scientific–Technological Space of States-Participants of Commonwealth of Independent States of 3 November 1995; and the Agreement on Conducting an Agreed Policy in the Domain of Transit of Natural Gas of 3 November 1995;

agreements with regard to social questions: the Agreement between States-Participants of the Commonwealth of Independent States on Social and Legal Guarantees of Military Servicemen, Persons Discharged from Military Service, and Members of Their Families of 14 February 1992; the Agreement on Guarantees of Rights of Citizens of States-Participants of the Commonwealth of Independent States in the Domain of Pension Security of 13 March 1992; the Agreement on the Principles of Bringing Up to Strength the Border Forces of the Commonwealth and Undergoing Military Service Therein of 15 May 1992; the Agreement on the Procedure for Pension Security of Military Servicemen of the Border Guards, Members of Their Families, and State Insurance of Military Servicemen of the Border Forces of States-Participants of the Commonwealth of Independent States of 15 May 1992; the Agreement on the Organization of Medical Provision for Military Servicemen and Members of Their Families and Workers and Employees of the Armed Forces of States-Participants of the Commonwealth and the Unified Armed Forces of the Commonwealth of Independent States of 15 May 1992; and the Agreement on the Training of Military Cadres of 13 November 1992;

agreements of a political character: the Agreement Between States-Participants of the Commonwealth of Independent States With Regard to Strategic Forces of 30 December 1991; the Agreement on the Principles and Procedure for Fulfilment of the Treaty on Conventional Armed Forces in Europe of 15 May 1992; the Agreement on Joint Measures Relating to the Prevention and Averting of Blockade of 24 September

1993; and the Memorandum on the Maintenance of Peace and Stability in the Commonwealth of Independent States of 10 February 1995;

agreements with regard to special questions: the Agreement on Joint Activity With Regard to Research and Use of Outer Space of 30 December 1991; the Agreement on Interaction in the Domain of Ecology and Protection of the Natural Environment of 8 February 1992; the Agreement on the Use of Airspace of 15 May 1992; the Agreement on Interaction in the Domain of the Prevention and Liquidation of the Consequences of Extraordinary Situations of a Natural and Technogenic Character of 22 January 1993; and the Agreement on Cooperation in the Domain of Veterinary Medicine of 12 March 1993;

agreements with regard to humanitarian questions: the Agreement on Cooperation in the Domain of Information of 9 October 1992; the Agreement on Joint Activity With Regard to the Search for and Release of Citizens of the Former USSR Who Were Imprisoned or Missing in the War in Afghanistan and Military Conflicts in Other Countries of 28 April 1993; the Agreement on Assistance to Refugees and Forced Resettlers of 24 September 1993; the Convention on Ensuring the Rights of Persons Belonging to National Minorities of 21 October 1994; the Decision of the Council of Heads of Governments of the Commonwealth on the Creation of the Inter-State Fund for Assistance to Refugees and Forced Resettlers of 9 October 1994; the Decision of the Council of Heads of Governments of the Commonwealth of 10 February 1995 on the draft Protocol to the Agreement on Assistance to Refugees and Forced Resettlers of 24 September 1993 and Decision on the Creation of the inter-State Fund for Assistance to Refugees and Forced Resettlers; the Protocol of 10 February 1995 to the Agreement on Assistance to Refugees and Forced Resettlers of 24 September 1993; and the Decision of the Council of Heads of States of the Commonwealth on the Creation of the inter-State Fund for Assistance to Refugees and Forced Resettlers of 10 February 1995.

In accordance with the provisions of the Vienna Convention (Article 31) for the purposes of interpretation of a treaty there are used not only the text thereof, but also any agreement relevant to the treaty if it was reached between the participants of the treaty, and also any document drawn up by the participants of the treaty and accepted as a document relating to the treaty. Basing ourselves on these provisions, one may draw the conclusion that there shall be relegated to **international agreements:**

decisions of the Heads of States and Governments,

approving draft agreements and annexes thereto (for example, the Decision of the Council of Heads of Governments of the Commonwealth on the draft Agreement on the Creation of the inter-State Currency Committee of 26 May 1995);

founding organs provided for an international agreement (for example, the Decision of the Council of Heads of States of the Commonwealth on the Executive Secretariat of the Commonwealth of Independent States of 14 May 1993 with the annex – the Statute on the Executive Secretariat of the Commonwealth of Independent States);

statements of the Heads of States and Governments if they are an annex to a treaty (for example, the Statement of the Council of Heads of States-Participants of the CIS of 22 January 1993 as an Annex to the Charter of the Commonwealth of Independent States of 22 January 1993);

memorandums and declarations of Heads of States and Governments, if they have the respective attributes of international agreements (for example, the Memorandum on the Maintenance of Peace and Stability in the Commonwealth of Independent States of 10 February 1995).

Decisions of organs of the Commonwealth affecting budgetary questions and Statutes on the personnel of organizations or establishing auxiliary organs of organizations are the **internal law of international organizations**.

In accordance with the Vienna Convention (Article 23[2]), a reservation made when signing a treaty subject to ratification must be officially confirmed by the State which made the reservation when expressing its consent to the obligatoriness of that treaty for it.

Being guided by the said norm, one should deem **invalid reservations to a number of agreements** by virtue of the absence on the part of States which made the reservation of the act of ratification required under the conditions of the said agreements. Among their number are relegated the reservations of:

Republic Belarus to the Decision of the Council of the Heads of Governments of the Commonwealth of 10 February 1995 on the draft Protocol to the Agreement on Assistance to Refugees and Forced Resettlers of 24 September 1993 and draft Decision on the Creation of the Inter-State Fund for Assistance to Refugees and Forced Resettlers;

Kyrgyz Republic to the Agreement on Mutual Recognition of Rights and Regulation of Relations of Ownership of 9 October 1992;

Ukraine to the Agreement on Joint Measures Relating to the Prevention and Averting of Blockade of 24 September 1993; Agreement on the Creation of the Inter-State Eurasian Coal and Metal Association of 24 September 1993; the Treaty on Conducting an Agreed Anti-Monopoly Policy of 23 December 1993; the Agreement on Cooperation in the Domain of Investment Activity of 24 December 1993; the Agreement on the Accession of Ukraine to the Economic Union with the Rights of an Associate Member of 15 April 1994; the Constitutive Treaty on the Creation of the Fund for Assistance to the Republic Tadzhikistan of 15 April 1994; the Agreement on Cooperation in the Domain of Mobilized Preparation of the Economy of 15 April 1994; and the Agreement on the Creation of the inter-State Currency Committee of 26 May 1995;

Azerbaidzhan Republic and *Ukraine* to the Convention on Ensuring the Rights of Persons Belonging to National Minorities of 21 October 1994; the Agreement on the Creation of Common Scientific–Technological Space of States-Participants of the Commonwealth of Independent States of 3 November 1995;

Republic Uzbekistan and *Ukraine* to the Agreement on Carriages of Special Cargoes and Products of Military Designation of 26 May 1995;

Azerbaidzhan Republic, Republic Georgia, and *Republic Uzbekistan* to the Agreement on Conducting an Agreed Policy in the Domain of the Transit of Natural Gas of 3 November 1995;

Azerbaidzhan Republic, Republic Kazakhstan, and *Ukraine* to the Agreement Between States-Participants of the Commonwealth of Independent States on the Status of Strategic Forces of 14 February 1992;

Republic Armenia, Republic Moldova, and *Turkmenistan* to the Agreement on the Principles of Customs Policy of 13 March 1992.

Violations of procedural norms of the Vienna Convention relative to reservations concern the forms of declaring reservations (for example, reservations of: the *Kyrgyz Republic* – to the Agreement on Mutual Recognition of the Rights and Regulation of Relations of Ownership of 9 October 1992; *Ukraine* – to the Agreement on Joint Measures Relating to the Prevention and Averting of Blockade of 24 September 1993). Certain reservations were written illegibly and are difficult to read (for example: reservations of: *Ukraine* – to the Agreement on the Use of Airspace of 15 May 1992; *Turkmenistan* – to the Agreement on the Interaction of

States-Participants of the Commonwealth in the Domain of Geodesy, Cartography, Cadastre, and Distance Probing of Earth of 9 October 1992).

Violations of material norms of the Vienna Convention relative to reservations are manifest in the following:

reservations are formulated as a demand concerning a change of, addition to, or exclusion of articles addressed to all participants of the treaty. Illustrative in this respect is the dissenting opinion of the *Republic Belarus* to the Agreement on the Creation of a Unified System of Air Defence of States-Participants of the Commonwealth of Independent States of 10 February 1995 containing the formulation: 'Article 1: to add to the first paragraph ... to set out paragraph two as follows ... Article 2: to change paragraph one ... Article 5: to remove paragraph one';

a reservation relating to the entire treaty, being a condition of signature thereof on the part of the State declaring the reservation. For example, the reservation of the *Republic Moldova* to the Agreement on the Principles of Provision of the Armed Forces of States-Participants of the Commonwealth With Armament, Technology, Material Means, and Organization of Production Activity of Repair Enterprises, Scientific-Research, and Experimental-Construction Design Work of 14 February 1992 provides: 'Questions set out in the present treaty the Republic Moldova shall decide only on a bilateral basis.' The reservation of *Ukraine* to the Decision of the Council of Heads of Governments of the Commonwealth on the draft Agreement on the Creation of the inter-State Currency Committee of 26 May 1995 provides that Ukraine 'supports the creation of such a committee and will accede thereto after the introduction of a new national currency'.

reservations incompatible with the objects and purposes of the agreement. Such are reservations of the *Republic Kazakhstan* and *Republic Uzbekistan* to the Agreement on the Principles of Bringing up to Strength the Border Forces of the Commonwealth and Undergoing Military Service of 15 May 1992, consolidating that 'the officers of the Border Forces of the Commonwealth shall be appointed to and relieved from their posts in accordance with legislation of the States-Participants of the Commonwealth'. This is contrary to Article 1 of the Agreement, according to which States-Participants are obliged to effectuate agreed measures directed towards ensuring a uniform procedure for the call-up, bringing up to strength, and undergoing of military service;

reservations violating generally-recognized principles and norms of international law. Such is the reservation of the *Republic Armenia* to the Memorandum on the Maintenance of Peace and Stability in the Commonwealth of Independent States of 10 February 1995 excluding points 7 and 8 of the Memorandum obliging States to undertake measures with regard to the suppression of any manifestations of separatism, nationalism, chauvinism, and fascism, not support separatist movements, and not permit the use by them of territories and communications of States-Participants of the Commonwealth.

Incompatible with procedural and material norms of the Vienna Convention are those reservations of:

Republic Moldova to the Statement of the Council of Heads of States-Participants of the CIS of 22 January 1993 (reservation contrary to object and purpose);

Ukraine to the Statute on the Executive Secretariat of the Commonwealth of Independent States of 14 May 1993 (reservation formulated as an amendment to the agreement); the Agreement on Joint Measures With Regard to Prevention and Averting of Blockade of 24 September 1993 and Decision of the Council of Heads of State of the Commonwealth on Permanent Powers of Representatives of States-Participants of the Commonwealth of Independent States of 24 September 1993 (reservations with violation of form of declaration of reservations); the Treaty on Conducting an Agreed Anti-Monopoly Policy of 23 December 1993 (reservation formulated as demand to all participants of treaty); the Agreement on Cooperation in the Domain of Investment Activity of 24 December 1993 (reservations contrary to purposes of agreement); the Decision of the Council of Heads of Government of the Commonwealth on the draft Agreement on the Creation of a Free Trade Zone of 15 April 1994 (reservation incompatible by virtue of prohibition of reservations to said Agreement); the Decision of the Council of Heads of Governments of Commonwealth on the Creation of the inter-State Fund for Assistance to Refugees and Forced Resettlers of 9 December 1994, and also the Convention on Ensuring the Rights of Persons Belonging to National Minorities of 21 October 1994 (reservations relate in essence to the entire text of the Agreement as a condition of recognition of its legal force); in addition, the reservation to the Convention is contrary to generally-recognized principles of international law, the priority of which is proclaimed in legislation of Ukraine)[1]; the Decision of the Council of Heads of States of the Commonwealth on the Fundamental Principles of Customs Legislation of States-Participants of the Commonwealth of Independent

States of 10 February 1995 (reservation does not correspond to the form of declaring reservations and is contrary to the purposes of the Agreement).[1]

In the view of the Economic Court, the failure of the reservations made by States to conform to the material and procedural norms of the Vienna Convention cannot be explained by the improper work of the depositary. The depositary in the person of the Ministry of Foreign Affairs of the Republic Belarus has fulfilled its functions, sending respective copies of the agreements with reservations thereto to the States-Participants of the Agreements. No State, except for the Republic Armenia, which objected to the reservation of the Azerbaidzhan Republic to the Convention on Ensuring the Rights of Persons Belonging to National Minorities (Note of 1 November 1995), has made any statements of objections.

One may illustrate the proper work of the depositary with regard to familiarizing States-Participants of Agreements with reservations thereto with the example of the diplomatic correspondence of the Ministry of Foreign Affairs of the Republic Belarus, as the former depositary of documents of the Commonwealth, with States-Participants of the Commonwealth on the subject of consent or objection to reservations made by the Azerbaidzhan Republic to the Agreement on the Creation of the inter-State Economic Committee of the Economic Union of 21 October 1994, the Convention on Ensuring the Rights of Persons Belonging to National Minorities of 21 October 1994, and also the Decision of the Council of Heads of States of the Commonwealth on the Memorandum of the Council of the Heads of States of the Commonwealth of Independent States 'Basic Orientations of the Integration Development of the Commonwealth of Independent States' and the Long-Term Plan for Integration Development of the Commonwealth of Independent States of 21 October 1994 (Issue No. 12/9174-H of 6 October 1995, Issue No. 12/2120-H of 7 March 1995, Issue No. 12/4634-H of 24 May 1995). It should be stressed that the depositary in the Note sent to the Ministry of Foreign Affairs of the Azerbaidzhan Republic pointed out with full substantiation the failure of the reservations made by the Azerbaidzhan Republic to conform to the provisions of the Vienna Convention (Issue No. 12/2120-H of 7 March 1995). Thus, the reservations of the Azerbaidzhan Republic to the Agreement on the Creation of the inter-State Economic Committee of the Economic Union of 21 October 1994 were classified as contrary to the object and purposes of the said Agreement, and to the Memorandum of the Council of the Heads of States of the Commonwealth of Independent States 'Basic Orientations of the Integration

[1] The Law of Ukraine of 10 December 1991 On the Operation of International Treaties on the Territory of Ukraine.

Development of the Commonwealth of Independent States' of 21 October 1994 – as not falling under the operation of the Vienna Convention inasmuch as the said act is not a treaty'.[2]

In summarizing the above, the Economic Court considers it necessary to note the following.

Inasmuch as the absolute majority of agreements analysed relate to open treaties, the reservations to them do not require special acceptance by the States-Participants of the Agreements (Article 20, Vienna Convention). The reservations are an exception of:

Ukraine to the Agreement on Joint Activity Relating to Research and Use of Outer Space of 30 December 1991,

Republic Armenia, Republic Moldova, and *Turkmenistan* to the Agreement on the Principles of Customs Policy of 13 March 1992,

Turkmenistan and *Ukraine* to the Agreement on the Creation of a Unified System of Anti-Aircraft Defence of States-Participants of the Commonwealth of Independent States of 10 February 1995, –

which needed acceptance by all States-Participants by virtue of the fact that the said Agreements are closed treaties. The absence of statements of objection within a year against the reservations enables us to consider them to be accepted by tacit consent, and the States which made the reservation, – to be participants of the respective agreements (Article 20, Vienna Convention).

The Vienna Convention (Article 21(1)[a] and [b]) regulates the legal consequences of lawful reservations. According to this international legal document, in the event of the acceptance of a reservation of a State by other participants of the treaty, the said State becomes a participant of the treaty and all of the provisions thereof extend to it except those to which the reservation was made. Such provisions do not apply in the mutual relations of the State which made the reservation with the other participants of the treaty.

If a State objects to the reservation of another State, then it may make a statement concerning the impossibility of accepting the treaty as a

[2] However, one cannot concur with the reference of the depositary to Article 27 of the Vienna Convention as the grounds for the unlawfulness of the reservation to the Convention on Ensuring the Rights of Persons Belonging to National Minorities of 21 October 1994. The said Article denies the possibility to refer to the provisions of internal law as justification for failure to fulfil the treaty. The Azerbaidzhan Republic when acceding to the Convention on Ensuring the Rights of Persons Belonging to National Minorities made a reservation concerning the priority of national legislation. The reservation might be deemed to be lawful if the supremacy of the Constitution and laws of the Republic were recognized in the Constitution of the Azerbaidzhan Republic.

whole with respect to the State which made the reservation. If it does not make such a statement, then the treaty will not be applied between the said States only with respect to the article to which the reservation was made and against which there is an objection (Article 21(3), Vienna Convention).

Although the Vienna Convention does not contain provisions concerning the unlawfulness of reservations, it seems a logical conclusion that violations of procedural norms affecting the forms of declaring a reservation do not make such a reservation invalid.

If a reservation does not correspond to material norms, then the States-Participants of the Treaty may by means of an objection against such a reservation deprive a State of the possibility of becoming a participant to the Treaty. Illustrative in this respect is the objection of the Republic Armenia to a reservation made by the Azerbaidzhan Republic to the Convention on Ensuring the Rights of Persons Belonging to National Minorities of 21 October 1994, which not only classified it as incompatible with the principles of international law but also opposed the accession of the Azerbaidzhan Republic to the said Convention (Note of 1 November 1995). In order to become a participant of the Treaty, a State may in accordance with the Vienna Convention (Article 23[4]) at any time remove the reservation, and likewise another State – remove the objection. The absence of objections to an unlawful reservation makes the State a participant of a treaty with the ensuing of those consequences with respect to the operation of the treaty as in the event of lawful reservations. The practice of the operation of unlawful norms is permitted by international law on condition of compliance with them by States but they may not be referred to when settling disputes in international agencies.

Having regard to the foregoing, the **Economic Court considers it advisable to make the following recommendations:**

1. Reservations (or dissenting opinion, remark, statement reservation) may be made by the State-Participant of a treaty and by an acceding State when signing, ratifying, and confirming a treaty.

2. A reservation made by a State when signing a treaty should, in the event of the entry thereof into force from the moment of signature, be formalized as an individual official document appended to the treaty. If at the moment of signature of the treaty the State is not ready to formulate and formalize duly the reservation, it may send a document containing the reservation to the depositary of the treaty within three months.

3. If under the conditions of the treaty or according to a municipal procedure a treaty is subject to ratification, then a reservation made when signing the treaty must be reflected in the instrument of ratification of

the State or in a protocol concerning the exchange or handing over for keeping of the instruments of ratification, or in both the said documents. Otherwise, the reservation is considered to be not declared.

4. A reservation may be formulated by a State only with respect to those articles of a treaty which are not essential for its content and must not violate the integrity of the treaty and present the fulfilment thereof by other participants.

5. If a treaty contains provisions prohibiting reservations to be made or limited the possibility of declaring them with respect to specific articles, a State may formulate reservations to the articles authorized in the treaty.

6. The depositary must in circulating copies of the treaty with reservations to States-Participants inform them about the right to declare objections against reservations.

7. If the depositary considers that reservations made by a State-Participant or acceding State are incompatible with the object and purposes of the treaty or are not permitted by the treaty, it must notify the unlawfulness of the reservations to the declarant-State. The depositary shall inform all other participants of the treaty that they not only may object to the reservation, but also declare the termination of the operation of the treaty between themselves and the State which made the reservation.

If a treaty to which a reservation has been made is closed, then the depositary must, when circulating a copy of the treaty to participants, inform them about the need to recognize such reservation by all participants of the treaty within a year.

In the absence of declarations concerning the recognition of or objection against a reservation within the said period, the depositary shall deem such reservation to be accepted by the States-Participants by means of tacit consent.

Acting Chairman **Kh. Tolibov**

15 May 1996

Decision of Economic Court of the Commonwealth of Independent States [on the Interpretation of Certain Agreements and CIS Decisions]

[No. 01-1/1-98, 22 June 1998. *Решения Экономического суда Содружества Независимых Государств (1997–1998 гг.)* (Minsk, 1999), pp. 77–94]

City of Minsk

The Economic Court of the Commonwealth of Independent States composed of:

presiding – Chairman of the Economic Court, A. B. Kazhenov,

judges of the Economic Court, D. D. Apostol, I. K. Vylkov, L. Sh. Makhmudova, V. I. Miroshnik, A. O. Sarsenbaev, and Kh. Tolibov,

secretary, S. I. Bystrova,

with the participation of General Counsellor of the Economic Court, M. N. Pronina,

having considered in open judicial session the case at the request of the Executive Secretariat of the CIS on interpreting reservations to treaties,

HAS ESTABLISHED

The Executive Secretariat of the Commonwealth of Independent States has applied to the Economic Court with a request concerning the interpretation of:

the Agreement on Cooperation in the Dissemination of Knowledge and Adult Education of 17 January 1997;

the Agreement on Provision with Dwelling Premises of Military Servicemen, Citizens Discharged from Military Service, and Members of Their Families in States-Participants of the Commonwealth of Independent States of 28 March 1997;

the Decision of the Council of the Heads of States of 19 January 1996 concerning extension of the period of operation of the Decision of

States-Participants of the Commonwealth of Independent States on Measures Relating to Stabilization of the Situation in the Sector of the State Boundary of the Republic Tadzhikistan with Afghanistan of 22 January 1993;

the Decision on the Procedure for the Training and Education of Military and Civilian Personnel of States-Participants of the Commonwealth of Independent States Allotted to the Collective Forces for the Maintenance of Peace of 8 October 1996;

the Decision on Urgent Measures for the Development of the inter-State Teleradion Company 'Mir' of 17 January 1997;

the Decision on the draft Conception of Economic Integration Development of the Commonwealth of Independent States of 27 March 1997;

the Decision on the Mechanism for Realization of the Conception of Economic Integration Development of the Commonwealth of Independent States of 9 October 1997

on the subject of determining their objects and purposes and the compatibility with them of reservations formulated by States when signing the said documents.

The Executive Secretariat in so doing requests questions to be answered: who and by what means may one determine that the reservations formulated by States are incompatible with the objects and purposes of the document, what may be the further fate of reservations formulated to the said documents.

Having heard the judge-rapporteur A. O. Sarsenbaev, the representative of the Executive Secretariat of the Commonwealth, M. M. Tyshkevich, having analysed the opinion of the General Counsellor of the Economic Court, M. G. Pronina, and having investigated and evaluated the materials of the case, the Economic Court has come to the following conclusions.

In accordance with Rule 19(2) of the Rules of Procedure of the Council of Heads of States and the Council of Heads of Governments confirmed by Decision of the Council of Heads of States of 17 May 1996, the applicable law in the process of interpreting inter-State and inter-governmental agreements is the 1969 Vienna Convention on the Law of Treaties.

Article 19 of the Convention provides for the right of States when signing, ratifying, adopting, or acceding to a treaty to formulate a reservation except for those instances when:

(a) the reservation is prohibited by the treaty;
(b) the treaty provides that only certain reservations may be made, among which the particular reservation does not fall, or

(c) in instances not falling under points (a) and (b), the reservation is incompatible with the object and purposes of the treaty.

A study, taking into account the rules set out in Article 19 of the Convention, of the Agreement on Cooperation in the Domain of the Dissemination of Knowledge and Adult Education of 17 January 1997 and the Agreement on the Provision of Dwelling Premises to Military Servicemen, Citizens Discharged from Military Service, and Members of Their Families in States-Participants of the Commonwealth of Independent States of 28 March 1997 being interpreted has shown that they do not contain a prohibition against formulating a reservation and do not determine to which provision of the agreements they may be made. Consequently, the admissability of reservations to the said agreements formulated by States must be assessed from the position of their compatibility with the object and purposes of the agreements.

The Agreement on Cooperation in the Domain of the Dissemination of Knowledge and Adult Education of 17 January 1997 was signed by the Azerbaidzhan Republic, Republic Armenia, Republic Belarus, Republic Kazakhstan, Kyrgyz Republic, Republic Moldova, Russian Federation, and Republic Tadzhikistan. The Agreement was not signed by Georgia, Turkmenistan, Republic Uzbekistan, and Ukraine.

When signing the Agreement, the Azerbaidzhan Republic formulated the reservation: 'with the exception of Article 9'. The said Article provides that in order to realize the Agreement the Parties shall create the inter-State Committee for the Dissemination of Knowledge and Adult Education, which shall effectuate its activity in accordance with the Statute thereon, being an integral part of the Agreement. The Economic Court considers that this reservation is incompatible with the object and purposes of the Agreement. The purposes of the Agreement being interpreted have been determined in its Preamble. There, in particular, are indicated the need to create an inter-State system of uninterrupted education for the adult population and the creation of a mechanism for the realization of cooperation of the Parties in effectuating joint programmes and projects in the sphere of disseminating knowledge and educating adults.

Proceeding from the said purposes as the object of the Agreement, as is clear from the content thereof, are the actions of the Parties (obligations) to be realized both at the national and the inter-State levels. This also is the creation of favourable conditions for the dissemination on their territories of information in the domain of science, technology, and education, and also cooperation in this domain, assistance in working out and effectuating national programmes in the sphere of cooperation determined by the Agreement, the effectuation of systematic consultations relating to determining priority orientations in this sphere, conducting joint scientific–practical conferences, symposiums, and the like. The practical fulfilment of obligations of the Parties formulated in the Agreement and above all on the inter-State level, presuppose the creation of an organizational mechanism called upon to ensure the development of integration processes and international contacts in the sphere of cooperation.

Such a mechanism has been provided for by Article 9 of the Agreement, affecting the creation of the inter-State Committee, the basic orientations of activity, functions, and powers of which have been determined by the respective Statute, which is an integral part of the Agreement.

It is evident that without the creation of such an organizational mechanism the realization of the Agreement, and above all the part concerning inter-State measures, would in practice become impossible.

The Republic Armenia signed the Agreement on Cooperation in the Domain of the Dissemination of Knowledge and Adult Education of 17 January 1997 with a reservation concerning a change of the version of Article 14. The last provided for the entry of the Agreement into force from the date of its signature. The version of this Article proposed by the Republic Armenia said: 'The present Agreement shall enter into force from the day of handing over for keeping to the depositary of the third notice concerning the fulfilment of the municipal procedures by the States which have signed it that are necessary for the entry into force thereof. For Parties who have fulfilled the necessary procedures later, it shall enter into force on the day of handing over the respective documents to the depositary.'

The said reservation, as is evident from the text thereof, concerns all participants of the Agreement and is contrary to the concept of a reservation given in Article 2 of the Vienna Convention on the Law of Treaties as a unilateral statement made by a State by means of which it wishes to exclude or change the legal operation of determined provision of a treaty in their application to the particular State. In accordance with the Vienna Convention on the Law of Treaties, the consent of a State to the obligatoriness of a treaty for it is expressed by ratification, adoption, or confirmation if the representative of the State signed the treaty on condition of ratification, adoption, or confirmation (Article 17). Consequently, the representative of the Republic Armenia has the right by means of a reservation to provide for the fulfilment of municipal procedures as a means of expressing consent to the obligatoriness of the Agreement with respect to his State. According to information of the depositary, notification has not been received about fulfilment of municipal procedures by the Republic Armenia.

According to the depositary, notifications have not been received from States-Participants of the Agreement on Cooperation in the Domain of the Dissemination of Knowledge and Adult Education of 17 January 1997 concerning objections against the reservation formulated by the Azerbaidzhan Republic as incompatible with the object and purposes of the Agreement, and also against the reservation of the Republic Armenia.

The Agreement on the Provision of Dwelling Premises to Military Servicemen, Citizens Discharged from Military Service, and Members of Their Families in States-Participants of the Commonwealth of Independent States of 28 March 1997 was signed by the: Republic Armenia, Republic Belarus, Republic Kazakhstan, Kyrgyz Republic, Russian Federation, and Republic Tadzhikistan.

The Agreement was not signed by the Azerbaidzhan Republic, Georgia, Republic Moldova, Turkmenistan, Republic Uzbekistan, and Ukraine.

When signing the Agreement, a reservation was formulated by the Republic Armenia affecting a change of Article 3, paragraph 1, and excluding paragraphs 2 and 3 of the same Article, and also a change of Article 4, paragraph 1.

Article 3 established:

Citizens discharged from military service and members of their families shall when moving to a permanent place of residence from the territory of one to the territory of another State-Participant, be provided at the chosen place of residence with dwelling premises according to the norms established for citizens of the State on whose territory they arrived.

A State-Participant in the armed forces and other military formations in which the citizens specified in the present Article have undergone military service shall acquire in good time dwelling premises for them at the permanent place of residence chosen by them on the territory of the other State-Participant on condition of the handing over of the dwelling premises occupied by these citizens at the former place of service (or residence) or if the dwelling premises at the former place of service (or residence) were not granted to them.

The procedure and periods for the acquisition of the said dwelling premises shall be determined by the governments of the States-Participants on a bilateral basis.

The Republic Armenia formulated a reservation affecting Article 3 of the Agreement of the following content:

(1) in place of the word combination 'according to norms established for citizens of the State on whose territory they arrived', enter 'according to legislation of the country-place of sojourn';
(2) exclude paragraphs 2 and 3 from Article 3.

The operation of paragraphs 2 and 3 of the said Article were excluded with respect to themselves by means of a respective reservation by the Republic Belarus.

The Economic Court considers that the reservations formulated by the Republic Armenia and the Republic Belarus are incompatible with the object and purposes of the Agreement.

As is evident from the Preamble and Article 1 of the Agreement, the purpose of the conclusion of such an Agreement was the taking by the States-Participants of agreed measures when deciding questions of guaranteed provision with dwelling premises of the following categories of citizens who are foreign with respect to the State of their sojourn or who have the right to acquire citizenship of the State-Participant on whose territory the permanent place of residence has been chosen:

(1) military servicemen (except military servicemen on active duty) undergoing military service in the armed forces and other military formations of States-Participants of the Commonwealth of Independent States who were previously on military service in the Armed Forces and other military formations of the former USSR, Unified Armed Forces of the Commonwealth of Independent States (hereinafter: military servicemen), and members of their families;

(2) citizens from among the aforesaid military servicemen discharged from military service after 31 December 1991 and members of their families.

In so doing the procedure for the provision by States-Participants of the Agreement of a dwelling premise to military servicemen and members of their families in the event of transfer or their being sent to undergo military service on the territory of another State is regulated by Article 2 of the Agreement, and citizens discharged from military service and members of their families, by Article 3 of the Agreement.

Article 3, paragraph 1, establishes merely a norm of dwelling space with which citizens discharged from military service and members of their families must be provided. As regards the procedure for provision, including the question of on whom lies this duty, it was provided for by paragraphs 2 and 3 of the Article being analysed.

Therefore the reservation of the Republic Armenia affecting a change of the version of paragraph 1 and the exclusion of paragraphs 2 and 3 of Article 3 means a change in essence of the procedure for the provision of dwelling space to citizens discharged from military service and members of their families.

The reservation made by the Republic Armenia changes the provisions of Article of the Agreement in its relations with all other participants of the Agreement. It changes in the same measure the provisions of Article 3 for all other participants in their relations with the Republic Armenia. In particular, they remove from States-Participants of the Agreement the duty to acquire for citizens who underwent service in their armed forces or other military formations dwelling premises in the Republic Armenia if it was elected by these citizens as the place of permanent residence. The Republic Armenia does not bear such a duty with respect to citizens who underwent service in its Armed Forces and other military formations and chose another State-Participant of the Agreement as their permanent place of residence.

The provision in the said instances of a dwelling premise to citizens discharged from military service and members of their families shall be done in the procedure established by legislation of the State at the place of residence chosen.

The legal regime established by the reservation of the Republic Armenia, despite the purposes of the Agreement, does not create guarantees of the timely provision of dwelling premises to citizens discharged from military service and members of their families. Therefore the reservation of the Republic Armenia should be deemed to be incompatible with the purpose of the Agreement – the taking of agreed measures to decide questions of the provision with dwelling premises the citizens specified in Article 3 and the object of this Article, that is, the character of the actions which have been determined in it.

Proceeding from the foregoing, the reservation formulated by the Republic Belarus concerning the exclusion with respect to it of Article 3, paragraphs 2 and 3, of the Agreement also is deemed to be incompatible with the object and purposes of the Agreement.

The reservation formulated by the Republic Armenia concerns Article 4, paragraph 1, of the Agreement establishing the right of all citizens to which its operation extends when departing for a permanent place of residence from the territory of one to the territory of another State-Participant to exchange the dwelling premises occupied by them for permanent residence irrespective of their departmental affiliation with citizens of another State-Participant, and also the sale of dwelling premises privatized by them irrespective of the period of privatization. The formulation of Article 4 of the Agreement proposed by the Republic Armenia consolidates the right to exchange by citizens to whom the operation of the Agreement extends only certain types of dwelling premises as an additional means of resolving the housing problem for the citizens specified in the Agreement and should be deemed to be admissible.

According to the information of the depositary, the Agreement on the Provision of Dwelling Premises to Military Servicemen, Citizens Discharged from Military Service, and Members of Their Families in

States-Participants of the Commonwealth of Independent States of 28 March 1997 has not entered into force since the condition provided for in Article 9 of the Agreement has not been fulfilled – receipt by the depositary of the third notification concerning the fulfilment by States-Participants of municipal procedures for the entry thereof into force.

As of 22 June 1998 such notifications had been received only from two States – the Republic Belarus (with the reservation made to Article 3) and the Republic Tadzhikistan. No objections had been received from States-Participants of the Commonwealth of Independent States which signed the Agreement against the reservations formulated by the Republic Armenia and Republic Belarus at the depositary.

In accordance with Article 19 of the 1969 Vienna Convention on the Law of Treaties, a State may not formulate a reservation incompatible with the object and purposes of the Agreement, that is, affecting the essence thereof. However, the Vienna Convention does not determine the legal consequences of such reservations.

Article 20 of the Vienna Convention regulates the acceptance of lawful reservations (in the terminology of the Convention, 'permitted by the treaty') and objections against them, and Article 21 of the Convention, the legal consequences of such reservations and objections to them.

The provision that Article 21 of the Vienna Convention regulates the legal consequences of lawful reservations is confirmed, in the view of the Economic Court, by the following considerations.

Article 21(1) of the Convention speaks of reservations operating with respect to another participant in accordance with Articles 19, 20, and 23 of the Convention. In establishing legal consequences for reservations operating with respect to another State, Article 21(1) of the Convention refers to Articles 19, 20, and 23 of the Convention. However, Article 19 consolidates in substance two provisions:

(1) the right of a State when signing, ratifying, adopting or confirming a treaty or acceding thereto to formulate a reservation;
(2) instances when a State does not have such a right (exceptions from the general rule concerning the possibility of formulating a reservation). Therefore the reference to Article 19 of the Convention means that it is speaking of the consequences of reservations formulated in accordance with the right of a State to make such reservations consolidated therein. The legal consequences provided for by Article 21 of the Convention may not extend to exceptions from the said general rule. The Economic Court considers that inasmuch as in accordance with Article 19 of the Vienna Convention a State does not have the right to formulate a reservation incompatible with the object and purposes of the treaty, then States-Participants of the treaty must

determine the consequences of such a reservation for the purpose of eliminating the incompatibility.

When reservations are formulated by States, the depositary in accordance with the functions placed on it and in accordance with Article 23 of the Vienna Convention brings to the information of States-Participants of the Agreement the text thereof with the reservations formulated when signing it or confirming the obligatoriness of the Agreement for it. In so doing it has the right to draw the attention of States to reservations incompatible with the object and purposes of the Agreement. The final decision on this question is adopted by the States-Participants of the Agreement. They determine too the consequences of such reservations by proceeding from the possibility of terminating the operation of the treaty with the State which made the reservation, revocation of the reservation by the State which formulated it, or the making of changes therein.

The Rules of Procedure of the Council of Heads of States and the Council of Heads of Governments of the Commonwealth of Independent States, including the documents to be adopted at sessions of the highest organs of the Commonwealth in addition to treaties, also specify decisions. With regard to what questions are decisions adopted, the Rules of Procedure do not establish. In accordance with Rule 19(2) of the Rules of Procedure, decisions are adopted by consensus, except for decisions on procedural questions.

Consensus is defined as the absence of an official objection by even one of the States-Participants put forward by it as representing an obstacle to the adoption of the decision with regard to the question being considered (Rule 20[1]). A decision so adopted is binding upon the States-Participants who participated in the adoption thereof (Rule 20[1], paragraph 2). The Rules of Procedure do not provide for the formulation by a State participating in the adoption of a decision of reservations. At the same time, Rule 20[2] establishes that any State-Participant may declare its noninterest in a particular question, which does not prevent the adoption of a decision. Inasmuch as the Rules of Procedure do not determine nor limit in any way the group of such questions, but use the general formulation 'a particular question', the Economic Court considers that this may be the entire group of questions with regard to which a decision is adopted or individual questions consolidated in a particular provision (or point, article) of a decision. The Rules of Procedure, regrettably, do not regulate the form in which a State-Participant of a session may declare its noninterest in a particular question. Evidently this is why many decisions adopted by the Councils of the Heads of States and Heads of Governments are formalized as treaties – that is, signed by the heads of States or heads of Governments and specify therein which States have not signed this decision or formulated reservations and the essence thereof.

The Economic Court considers that such a procedure is applicable only to those decisions which are in essence an international treaty.

The Economic Court in its Advisory Opinion of 15 May 1996 at the request of the Inter-State Economic Committee of the Economic Union well-foundedly pointed out that the decisions of the councils of the heads of States and governments approving draft agreements and annexes thereto are relegated to international agreements. In addition, the Economic Court considers that decisions of the councils of heads of States and governments containing mutually binding and normative provisions are international agreements with regard to the substance of international relations (or questions) which are of general interest being regulated and having the attributes of international agreements or decisions concerning the making of amendments to agreements.

Thus, the study of decisions specified in the request of the Executive Secretariat showed that certain of them are in essence international agreements. Thus on 9 October 1992 the States of the CIS signed the Agreement on the Cooperation of States-Participants of the Commonwealth With Regard to Ensuring a Stable Situation on Their Foreign Boundaries. The said Agreement was signed by all the States-Participants of the CIS, except for the Republic Moldova, Turkmenistan, and Ukraine. Being guided by this Agreement and proceeding from the necessity of taking additional measures with regard to stabilization of the situation on the Tadzhik–Afghan sector of the boundary, States-Participants of the Commonwealth of Independent States on 22 January 1993 adopted the Decision concerning measures relating to stabilization of the situation in the sector of the State Boundary of the Republic Tadzhikistan with Afghanistan, point 1 of which provided for reinforcing the Group of Border Forces of the Russian Federation in the Republic Tadzhikistan by one battalion from among the Armed Forces of the Republic Kazakhstan, Kyrgyz Republic, Russian Federation, Republic Uzbekistan, and other States-members of the Council of Collective Security and a number of other obligations. The operation of the Decision was determined before the end of 1993. Only one State did not sign it – Ukraine.

On 19 January 1996 a Decision was adopted by the Council of the Heads of States to extend the period of operation of the Decision of States-Participants of the Commonwealth concerning measures relating to stabilization of the situation on the sector of the State Boundary of the Republic Tadzhikistan with Afghanistan from 1 January to 31 December 1996. The Republic Belarus when signing on 19 January 1996 the Decision concerning extension of the period of operation of the Decision of 22 January 1993 made a reservation: 'point 1 of the Decision of 22 January 1993, except for the Republic Belarus'. The said reservation affects the essence of the Agreement and therefore must be deemed to be incompatible with the purposes and object of the Agreement. One should take into account that the operation of the Decision of 19 January 1996, just as the Agreement of 9 October 1992, was terminated in connection with the expiry of the period.

On 19 January 1996 the States-Participants signed the Agreement on the Training and Instruction of Military and Civilian Personnel of States-Participants of the Commonwealth of Independent States for participation in operations relating to the maintenance of peace. In Article 2 of the said Agreement it was established that centres for training peacekeeping forces, the quantity and periods of their readiness for work, and also the procedure for training personnel therein to be allocated to the Collective Forces for the Maintenance of Peace in the Commonwealth of Independent States, is determined by the Council of Heads of Governments of the Commonwealth. By Decision of 18 October 1996 the Council of the Heads of Governments confirmed the List of centres for training peacekeeping forces of the States-Participants of the Commonwealth of Independent States and the Procedure for Training and Instruction of Military and Civilian Personnel allocated to the Collective Forces for the Maintenance of Peace. Taking into account the interlinkage of the aforesaid documents (the Decision of 18 October 1996 was adopted on the basis of and in execution of the Agreement and augments it), the Economic Court came to the conclusion that the Decision also is an international agreement which determines the law applicable when interpreting it. Consequently, in this instance when determining the rights of States to formulate reservations and to determine their consequences it is necessary to be guided by the Vienna Convention on the Law of Treaties.

Both when signing the Agreement of 19 January 1996 and the Decision of 18 October 1996 the Republic Belarus formulated the reservation: 'Belarus shall not send military contingents to the peacekeeping forces.' However, it should be taken into account that the express purpose of both the Agreement of 19 January 1996 and the Decision of 18 October 1996 was to raise the quality of training of military and civilian personnel for participation in operations relating to the maintenance of peace. Therefore, the object of the international Agreement is questions of organizing the instruction and training, material–technical provision, and financing of the centres for training peacekeeping forces.

Taking into account what has been said, the reservation formulated by the Republic Belarus is in essence not such because it is not directed towards a change or revocation of the operation with respect to the Republic Belarus of a particular provision of the Agreement. And although the Agreement decides questions of the training of military and civilian personnel allocated by States of the Commonwealth to the Collective Forces for the Maintenance of Peace in the Commonwealth of Independent States, it does not decide questions of such allocation. Therefore the provision formulated by the Republic Belarus that it shall not send military contingents to the peacekeeping forces means merely the statement of a State made when signing the Agreement and is not a reservation.

The Council of Heads of Governments by its Decision of 27 March 1997 approved the draft Conception of Economic Integration Development of the Commonwealth of Independent States.

The said Decision was signed by Georgia with the reservation: 'Georgia shall take part in the realization of those provisions of the Conception which are not contrary to prevailing national legislation, State interests, and also obligations to other States and international organizations.'

This same Decision was signed by the Republic Uzbekistan with the reservation: 'In accordance with legislation of the Republic Uzbekistan and its economic interest.'

Ukraine signed the Decision with the reservation: 'Except for provisions relative to Payments, Currency, and Customs unions, single information space, and also other provisions which are contrary to the Constitution and legislation of Ukraine.'

The Decision concerning the draft Conception of Economic Integration Development of the Commonwealth of Independent States is not an international treaty since it does not formulate specific obligations of its participants. It, as was said in the introduction to the Conception, represents a system of views mutually agreed by States-Participants of the Commonwealth on purposes and priorities of socio-economic development common to them under conditions of a deepening of inter-State economic relations, paths, mechanisms, and stages of their practical effectuation. The content of the Conception is testimony to this.

By virtue of the foregoing, the law applicable to this Decision, which regulates in particular the procedure for its adoption, is the Rules of Procedure of the Council of Heads of States and the Council of Heads of Governments of the Commonwealth of Independent States of 17 May 1996. As already pointed out, the Rules of Procedure do not provide for the formulation of reservations of States to decisions adopted by consensus. Therefore, the aforementioned texts of provisions formulated by Georgia, Republic Uzbekistan, and Ukraine when signing the Decision cannot be deemed to be reservations. Nor are they such by their content.

The said provisions are of a general character and express a general position of the State with regard to problems of economic integration as a whole or to certain forms thereof.

In the provision formulated by Georgia it is well-foundedly indicated that it will take part in the realization of those provisions of the Conception which are not contrary to State interests, and also obligations to other States and international organizations. The same should be said about the reference of the Republic Uzbekistan to its economic interests.

The statement formulated by Ukraine when signing the Decision: 'Except for provisions relative to Payments, Currency, and Customs unions, single information space...' should be regarded as an expression of its noninterest in the Decision concerning those forms of integration.

However, the statements of States (Georgia, Republic Uzbekistan, Ukraine) that their participation in the realization of the Conception is conditioned by its conformity to national legislation or the constitution of the State without regard to the specific provisions of the Conception may be construed only as the absence of the intention of the States to promote the achievement of the purpose of economic integration.

It should be noted that the Council of Heads of States of the Commonwealth of Independent States by a Decision of 28 March 1997 basically approved the Conception of Economic Integration Development, having granted the right to governments of the States-Participants of the Commonwealth when realizing the Conception to make necessary clarifications and changes at the regular session of the Council of Heads of States of the Commonwealth. The Decision was adopted by consensus and signed by the Chairman of the Council of the Heads of States.

On 9 October 1997 the Council of Heads of Governments of the Commonwealth adopted the Decision on the mechanism for the realization of the Conception of Economic Integration Development of the Commonwealth of Independent States. The said Decision established the procedure for working out, agreeing, and effectuating joint integration measures. This procedure presupposed the working out by States-Participants of the Commonwealth proposals relating to participation in the realization of the basic provisions of the Conception during the period before 2005, which include specific measures directed towards the creation of conditions facilitating the deepening and expansion of international economic cooperation and integrating into the world economic community.

The Decision contains also commissions to respective organs of the Commonwealth with regard to working out their proposals, and also working out on the basis of the proposals of States and organs of the Commonwealth Programmes for joint actions of governments and Basic

Measures for economic integration development of States-Participants of the Commonwealth of Independent States. The said Programme and Basic Measures are subject to confirmation respectively by the Council of Heads of Governments and the Council of Heads of States of the Commonwealth.

The Decision of 9 October 1997 was signed by Georgia with the reservation: 'Georgia will take part in the effectuation of the Decision concerning the mechanism of realization of the Conception of Economic Integration Development of the Commonwealth of Independent States in that part of the Conception to which there are no comments at the session of the Council of the Heads of Governments of the Commonwealth of Independent States of 27 March 1997. As regards the remaining part of the Conception, Georgia will take part with the reservation and position expressed on 27 March 1997 at the session of the Council of Heads of Governments of the Commonwealth of Independent States with regard to the draft Conception of Economic Integration Development of the Commonwealth of Independent States.' The said Decision was signed by Ukraine with the reservation: 'Taking into account national legislation.'

Proceeding from the foregoing, the provisions formulated by Georgia and Ukraine are not reservations. The position expressed in the statements made may be realized by them when working out proposals regarding the composition of integration measures which are mentioned in the Decision. Moreover, it was noted in the said Decision that States-Participants of the Commonwealth autonomously determine the procedure for the working out, adoption, and realization of the measures. As experience shows, in particular the working out of the Basic Measures of Integration Development of States-Participants of the Commonwealth of Independent States in 1997 (approved by Decision of the Council of Heads of States on 28 March 1997), measures are provided therein for the realization of agreements and decisions previously adopted, the preparation of new draft agreements, and the like, and consequently, such acts are not a treaty.

The same should be said about the statement formulated by the Azerbaidzhan Republic when signing the Decision on urgent measures relating to the development of the inter-State Teleradio Company 'Mir' of 17 January 1997, the provisions of which basically are in the nature of commissions and, in the view of the Economic Court, an act of internal law of the Commonwealth. In signing this Decision, the Azerbaidzhan Republic indicated: 'Taking into account national legislation.'

The dissenting opinion expressed by the Republic Armenia when signing the aforementioned Decision also is not a reservation, but testifies to the position of the Republic Armenia on the question of the development of inter-State telecommunications links.

In the Preamble to the Decision its purpose was fixed – the need to expand the volumes of inter-State radio and television broadcasting and telecommunications links, and point 1 speaks of the need to work out the draft Statute on the Status of Radio, Television, and Telecommunications Channels of inter-State communion of the Commonwealth. The Republic Armenia in its dissenting opinion pointed to the exclusion from the text of the Preamble and point 1 the word combination 'telecommunications links' and 'telecommunications' (channel). In addition, the Republic Armenia changes the version of point 3 of the Decision. As a result the position was created whereby the inter-State Teleradio Company 'Mir' is granted the right to use and develop telecommunications networks on a contractual basis with international operators operating in States (point 1 provides for granting to Teleradio Company 'Mir' the possibility on a licence basis the use and development of telecommunications networks of all types on conditions established for budget organizations).

The Economic Court considers that the aforesaid situation with the reservations formulated to decisions of the Council of Heads of States and the Council of Heads of Governments is to be explained, in particular, by the inadequate working out of the legal base for the adoption of such documents of the Commonwealth as decisions.

On the basis of the foregoing and being guided by points 5 and 16 of the Statute on the Economic Court of the Commonwealth of Independent States and by points 143 and 148 of the Reglament of the Economic Court of the Commonwealth of Independent States, the Economic Court has decided:

1. To deem that the reservations formulated by the:

Republic Azerbaidzhan concerning the exclusion with respect to it of the operation of Article 9 of the Agreement on Cooperation in the Domain of the Dissemination of Knowledge and Adult Education of 17 January 1997;

Republic Armenia on changing the version of Article 3, paragraph 1, and on excluding with respect to it the operation of Article 3, paragraphs 2 and 3, of the Agreement on the Provision of Dwelling Premises to Military Servicemen, Citizens Discharged from Military Service, and Members of Their Families in States-Participants of the Commonwealth of Independent States of 28 March 1997;

Republic Belarus on excluding with respect to it the operation of Article 3, paragraphs 2 and 3, of the Agreement on the Provision of Dwelling Premises to Military Servicemen, Citizens Discharged from Military

Service, and Members of Their Families in States-Participants of the Commonwealth of Independent States of 28 March 1997

are incompatible with the objects and purposes of the said international arrangements.

2. Statements containing general references to national legislation formulated by:

Georgia, Republic Uzbekistan, and Ukraine when signing the Decision concerning the draft Conception of Economic Integration Development of the Commonwealth of Independent States of 27 March 1997;

Georgia and Ukraine when signing the Decision on the mechanism for the realization of the Conception of Economic Integration Development of the Commonwealth of Independent States of 27 March 1997;

the Azerbaidzhan Republic when signing the Decision on urgent measures relating to the development of the inter-State Teleradio Company 'Mir' of 17 January 1997

are not reservations.

3. States-Participants of the Agreement, and also the Executive Secretariat, may in fulfilling the functions of depositary, apply to the Economic Court of the Commonwealth of Independent States with a request to interpret an Agreement on the subject of the determination of its purposes and object and compatibility therewith of reservations formulated.

4. The legal consequences of reservations incompatible with the purposes and object of an Agreement shall be determined by States-Participants in the event of the adoption by them or autonomous decision concerning the incompatibility of reservations to the purposes and object of the Agreement, or on the basis of the respective decision of the Economic Court.

5. To deem advisable the reworking of Rules 20 and 21 of the Rules of Procedure of the Council of Heads of States and Council of Heads of Governments of the Commonwealth of Independent States, confirmed by Decision of the Council of Heads of States on 17 May 1996, for a view to determining the list of questions with regard to which decisions may be adopted, the possibility of formulating reservations when adopting them, and determination of the form of an expression of noninterest of States in a particular question.

6. To recommend to States-Participants of the Commonwealth of Independent States when formulating reservations to use the Advisory Opinion of the Economic Court of 15 May 1996 at the request of the inter-State Economic Committee of the Economic Union on the conformity of certain agreements adopted within the framework of the Commonwealth to which reservations were made to the provisions of the 1969 Vienna Convention on the Law of Treaties.

7. To send a copy of the Decision to the Executive Secretariat of the Commonwealth of Independent States and to States-Participants of the Commonwealth of Independent States.

8. The present Decision shall be final.

9. The Decision shall be subject to publication in the publications of the Commonwealth and the mass media of States-Participants of the Agreement on the Status of the Economic Court of the Commonwealth of Independent States.

CIS Parties to 1969 Vienna Convention on Law of Treaties

[Adopted at Vienna, 22 May 1969.
Opened for signature at Vienna, 23 May 1969.
Entered into force, 27 January 1980.
Registered: 27 January 1980, No. 18232.
Published: *UNTS*, vol. 1155, 331]

Armenia: acceded 23 October 1996
Azerbaidzhan: has not acceded
Belarus: acceded 1 May 1986
Georgia: acceded 8 June 1995
Kazakhstan: acceded 5 January 1994
Kyrgyzstan: acceded 10 June 1999
Moldova: acceded 26 January 1993
Russian Federation: acceded 29 April 1986 (as legal-continuer of USSR)[3]
Tadzhikistan: acceded 6 May 1996
Turkmenistan: acceded 4 January 1996[4]
Ukraine: acceded 14 May 1986
Uzbekistan: acceded 12 July 1995

[3] The Edict of the Presidium of the Supreme Soviet of the USSR concerning the Accession of the Union of Soviet Socialist Republics to the Vienna Convention on the Law of Treaties was adopted 4 April 1986 and appears in *Ведомости Верховного Совета СССР* (1986), no. 16, item 263. It contains the official text of the reservations made by the USSR to the 1969 Vienna Convention. Pursuant to Article 84(2) of the 1969 Vienna Convention, it entered into force for the USSR on 29 May 1986. The Russian Federation has not withdrawn the reservations made by the USSR.

[4] The Decree of the Medzhlis of Turkmenistan was adopted 24 November 1995. See *Ведомости Меджлиса Туркменистана* (1995), no. 3, item 48.

Draft Subject Classification of Multilateral Treaties and Other International Legal Documents

V. D. Bordunov[5]

Russia is a party to more than 20,000 multilateral and bilateral treaties and other international legal documents which are the legacy of Tsarist Russia and the Soviet Union and also those concluded after the demise of the USSR by Russia with other States. This enormous morass of treaties is not easy to use by practitioners, scholars, teachers, students, and postgraduates unless it is properly systematized and classified. This task may be resolved through the information processing of the entire block of Russian treaties in accordance with certain rules and methods and the creation of a subject classification offering a clear view as to which domain of international law they appertain and which questions they address.

Various methods exist for resolving this problem. One is to place them in chronological order by the precise date on which they were concluded. But this method does not record the specific nature of the subject of an individual treaty and without this it is unrealistic to classify and systematize Russian treaties. It is another matter when the chronological approach is used in combination with a subject classification. In this event the corpus of treaties is distributed amongst discrete groups and ultimately placed in order. In other words, the classification is a method and simultaneously a means of transforming primary information concerning international treaties into processed and classified data. It is precisely this methodology of classification that has been used with respect to the treaties of Russia so as to present them not merely in chronological sequence but also linking them with specific branches and institutes of international law.

The subject of the subject classification is not only multilateral treaties but also declarations, amendments to international conventions, acts of the ECSC, and the like. This circumstance explains the use in the title

[5] Reprinted from *Sudebnik*, II (1997), 640–7, © by V. D. Bordunov; translation © by William E. Butler.

above of the term 'international legal documents'. The subject classification takes into account the structure of the textbook *Международное право* edited by Iu. M. Kolosov and V. I. Kuznetsova and the three-volume set of collected documents *Действующее международное право* [Prevailing International Law] edited by Iu. M. Kolosov and E. S. Krivchikova. The documents would be placed, as a rule, alphabetically within the branches and institutes or individual topics.

This is the first attempt to develop a subject classification of Russian treaties.

Subject Classification Scheme

1 **Principles of International Law**
2 **Subjects of International Law**
3 **Territory**
  3.1 Legal Regime of Spitzbergen Archipelago
  3.2 International Rivers
  3.3 Frontier Questions
4 **Population**
  4.1 International Legal Questions of Citizenship
  4.2 Refugees
5 **Law of International Treaties**
6 **Legal Succession**
7 **Diplomatic and Consular Law**
8 **International Organizations**
  8.1 United Nations
  8.2 Privileges and Immunities of United Nations and Specialized Agencies of United Nations, Legal Status of Representations of States Attached to International Organizations of Universal Character
  8.3 Specialized Agencies of United Nations
    8.3.1 World Meteorological Organization
    8.3.2 World Health Organization
      8.3.2.1 International Sanitary Rules
    8.3.3 World Intellectual Property Organization
    8.3.4 Universal Postal Union
    8.3.5 International Atomic Energy Agency
    8.3.6 International Development Organization
    8.3.7 International Bank for Reconstruction and Development

13 Armed Conflicts and International Law

13.1 Laws and Customs of Land Warfare
13.2 Prohibition of Means and Methods of Waging Military Actions
13.3 Protection of Cultural Valuables in Event of Armed Conflict
13.4 Protection of Rights of Person During Armed Conflicts
13.5 Commencement of War
13.6 Neutrality During War
13.7 Ending of Military Actions and State of War
13.8 Means and Methods of Waging Naval Warfare

14 International Struggle Against Criminality

14.1 Struggle Against Illegal Acts Directed Against Safety of Civil Aviation, Maritime Navigation, and Stationary Marine Objects
14.2 Struggle Against Seizure of Hostages
14.3 Struggle Against Illegal Turnover of Narcotics
14.4 Struggle Against Forgery of Monetary Notes
14.5 Struggle Against Slave Trade
14.6 Struggle Against Dissemination of Pornographic Publications
14.7 Struggle Against Trade in Women and Children
14.8 International Police Organization (Interpol)
14.9 Prevention and Punishment of Crimes Against Persons Enjoying International Protection
14.10 Transfer of Persons Sentenced to Deprivation of Freedom
14.11 Physical Protection of Nuclear Material

15 International Economic Law

15.1 International Trade
  15.1.1 Settlements, Payments. Purchase–Sale Contract
  15.1.2 Trademarks
  15.1.3 Trade in Foodstuffs
15.2 International Banks
15.3 International Exhibitions
15.4 Cooperation on Questions of Taxation

16 International Legal Regulation of Scientific–Technical Cooperation

16.1 International Scientific–Technical Organizations
  16.1.1 International Agency for Cancer Research

17.17 International Maritime Organizations of Special Competence
- 17.17.1 International Hydrographic Organization
- 17.17.2 International Council for Marine Research
- 17.17.3 International Fund for Compensation of Damage from Pollution by Oil

18 International Air Law
- 18.1 Struggle Against Illegal Interference in Activity of Civil Aviation
- 18.2 International Carriage by Air
- 18.3 International Civil Aviation and International Civil Aviation Organization
- 18.4 Joint Financing of Air Navigation Servicing
- 18.5 Compensation of Damage Caused by Foreign Aircraft to Third Persons on Land

19 International Space Law
- 19.1 Principles of Research and Use of Outer Space, Including Moon and Other Celestial Objects
- 19.2 Rescue of Astronauts and Return of Objects Launched into Outer Space
- 19.3 Responsibility for Damage Caused by Space Objects
- 19.4 Registration of Objects Launched into Outer Space
- 19.5 International Maritime Satellite Organization
- 19.6 International Telecommunications Satellite Organization
- 19.7 Space Communications Organization Intersputnik
- 19.8 Agreement on International Programme KOSPAS-SARSAT (1 July 1988)

20 International Legal Regime of Antarctic

21 International Legal Protection of Environment
- 21.1 Protection of Flora and Fauna
- 21.2 Transboundary Pollution of Air, Protection of Ozone Layer, Climate Change
- 21.3 Prevention and Rendering Assistance in Event of Natural and Technological Catastrophes

22 International Customs Law
- 22.1 International Customs Organizations
- 22.2 Cooperation and Mutual Assistance Regarding Customs Questions
- 22.3 Customs Privileges
- 22.4 Carriage of Containers and Cargoes Through Customs. Customs Control

22.5 Prevention and Suppression of Customs Violations

23 International Transport Law

23.1 Motor Vehicle Movement and Carriage

23.2 Road Traffic and Road Signs and Signals

23.3 Road and Container Carriage of Goods

23.4 Railway Transport

23.5 International Carriage on Internal Waterways

Bibliography

This is a rather extensive list of materials for further reading or research, but something less than a proper bibliography of the subject. The materials are ordered according to the Latin alphabet, and not the cyrillic; where entries appear in cyrillic, they are placed as though they were transliterated according to the abbreviated Library of Congress/British Library system.
Only the principal treaty collections have been included; there are many others. Moreover, every general textbook and treatise on public international law contains a chapter on treaties, and only some are listed below. Extensive chronicles of treaty-making are to be found in the Soviet and Russian Yearbooks of international law.

The entries are classified under the following headings:

Bibliographies on the law of treaties
Serials
Indexes of treaties
Treaty collections
Texts
General works
History of treaties
Concept and legal nature of treaties
Codification of law of treaties
Commentary on treaty legislation
Conclusion of treaties
Form, structure, and name of treaties
Ratification of treaties
Parties to treaties
Treaties with international organizations
Subjects and objects of treaties
Operation of treaties
Treaties and third states
Reservations to treaties
Doctrine of changed circumstances
Validity of treaties
Treaties and *jus cogens*
Extinctive prescription and treaties

Interpretation of treaties
Compliance with treaties
Application of treaties in judicial and arbitral proceedings
Language and treaties
Custody of treaties
Termination of treaties
War and treaties
Municipal law and treaties
Treaty of the Union (USSR)
Constitutional treaties of Russian Federation and USSR
Legal assistance treaties
Trade and arbitration agreements
Individual treaties

BIBLIOGRAPHIES ON THE LAW OF TREATIES

Talalaev, A. N. 'Новое в зарубежной литературе по праву международных договоров (Научно-аналитический обзор работ за 1972–1975 гг.)' [New in Foreign Literature on the Law of Treaties (Scientific–Analytical Survey of Works for 1972–1975)], *СЕМП 1975*. M., 1977, pp. 254–82

'Новое в зарубежной литературе по праву международных договоров (Критический-аналитический обзор работ, опубликованных в 1972–1975 гг.)' [New in Foreign Literature on the Law of Treaties (Scientific–Analytical Survey of Works for 1972–1975)], *СЕМП 1976*. M., 1978, pp. 177–95

SERIALS

Бюллетень международных договоров [Bulletin of International Treaties]. M., 1993– .

INDEXES OF TREATIES

Bordunov, V. D. 'Subject Classification of Multilateral Treaties and Other International Legal Documents', *Sudebnik*, II (1997), 640–7

Dobroklonskii, S. *Указатель сношений России с 1462 по 1826 год* [Index of Relations of Russia from 1462 to 1826]. M., 1838, 130 pp.

Ginsburgs, George. *A Calendar of Soviet Treaties 1958–1973*. Alphen aan den Rijn, Sijthoff & Noordhoff, 1981. xx, 908 pp.

Menagios, D. de. *Répertoire des traités, conventions et autres actes principaux de la Russie avec les puissances etrangères depuis 1474 jusqu' à nos jours*. Paris, Amyot, 1874. iv, 72 pp.

Перечень международных договоров Российской Федерации, ратифицированных или денонсированных Российской Федерацией с 1 января 1990 года до 31 августа 1996 года [List of International Treaties of the Russian Federation Ratified or Denounced by the Russian Federation from 1 January 1990–31 August 1996]. M., Изд. Гос. Думы, 1997. 108 pp.

Sabanin, A. V. *Хронологический перечень международных многосторонних договоров, заключенных с 1919 по 1933 г. с кратким изложением их содержания* [Chronological List of International Multilateral Treaties Concluded from 1919 to 1933 with Concise Precis of the Content Thereof]. M., Советское законодательство, 1933

Slusser, Robert M. and Triska, Jan F. *A Calendar of Soviet Treaties 1917–1957*. Stanford, Calif., Stanford University Press, 1959. xiv, 530 pp. (with assistance of George Ginsburgs and Wilfred O. Reiners)

TREATY COLLECTIONS

Adamov, E. A. (ed.). *Сборник договоров России с другими государствами 1856–1917 гг.* [Collection of Treaties of Russia with Other States 1856–1917]. M., Госполитиздат, 1952. 462 pp.

Al'bat, G. P. *Сборник международных конвенций и правительственных распоряжений о военнопленных* [Collection of International Conventions and Governmental Regulations on Prisoners of War]. M., Глав. ком., 1917. 84 pp.

Aleksandrenko, V. N. *Собрание важнейших трактатов и конвенций, заключенных Россией с иностранными державами (1774–1906)* [Collection of Major Treaties and Conventions Concluded by Russia with Foreign Powers (1774–1906)]. Warsaw, Тип. Варшавского учебного округа, 1906. viii, 585, vi pp.

Antonov, K. A. (ed.). *Сборник документов по международной политике и международному праву* [Collection of Documents on International Politics and International Law]. M., 1932–7. 11 vols.

Bakhtov, K. K. (ed.). *Сборник торговых договоров, торговых и платежных соглашений и долгосрочных торговых соглашений СССР с иностранными государствами* [Collection of Trade Treaties, Trade and Payments Agreements and Long-Term Trade Agreements of the USSR with Foreign States]. M., Внешторгиздат, 1961. 624 pp.; 2nd edn., 1965. 886 pp.; Supplement, 1968. 278 pp.

Белорусская ССР в международных отношениях. Международные договоры, конвенции и соглашения Белорусской ССР с иностранными государствами (1944–1959) [Belorussian SSR in International Relations. International Treaties, Conventions, and Agreements of the Belorussian SSR with Foreign States (1944–1959)]. Минск, Изд-во АН БССР, 1960. 1050 pp.

Berezin, Ia. A. (ed.). *Международные отношения в эпоху империализма. Документы из архивов царского и временного правительства* [International Relations in the Epoch of Imperialism. Documents from the Archives of the Tsarist and Provisional Governments]. M., Соцэкгиз, 1934–38. 10 vols. in 13

Боевая солидарность, братская помощь (Сборник важнейших внешнеполитических документов СССР по вьетнамскому вопросу) [Combat Solidarity, Fraternal Assistance (Collection of Major Foreign Policy Documents of the USSR on the Vietnamese Question)]. M., 'Прогресс', 1970. 219 pp.

Deborin, G. A. (ed.). *Международные документы Великой Отечественной войны* [International Documents of the Great Fatherland War]. M., 1943–4. 3 vols.

Декларации, заявления и коммюнике Советского правительства с правительствами иностранных государств 1954–1957 [Declarations, Statements, and Communiqués of the Soviet Government with Governments of Foreign States 1954–1957]. M., Госполитиздат, 1957. 328 pp.

Договоры о нейтралитете, ненападении и согласительной процедуре, заключенных между Союзом ССР и иностранными государствами [Treaties on Neutrality, Nonaggression, and Conciliation Procedure Concluded Between the USSR and Foreign States]. M., 1934. 196 pp. (Наркоминдел)

Документы внешней политики СССР [Documents of Foreign Policy of the USSR]. M., Госполитиздат, 1957– .

Eikhel'man, O. O. *Хрестоматия русского международного права* [Anthology of Russian International Law]. Киев, Унив. тип., 1887–9. 2 vols.

Fituni, L. A. *Межгосударственные торговые договоры и соглашения* [Inter-State Trade Treaties and Agreements]. M., Госюриздат, 1955.

Gratsianskii, I. I. *Собрание ныне действующих торговых трактатов России с иностранними государствами* [Collection of Prevailing Trade Treaties of Russia with Foreign States]. Спб., Хромолит. и тип. В. Грацианский, [1877]. x, 285 pp.

Grimm, E. D. *Сборник договоров и других документов по истории международных отношений на Дальнем Востоке (1842–1925)* [Collection of Treaties and Other Documents With Regard to the History of International Relations in the Far East (1842–1925)]. M., 1927. 218 pp.

Gurevich, B. P. and Moiseev, V. A. (comps.). *Международные отношения в Центральной Азии XVII–XVIII вв. Документы и материалы* [International Relations in Central Asia, XVII–XVIII Centuries. Documents and Materials]. M., 'Наука', 1989. 2 vols.

Iuzefovich, T. *Договоры России с Востоком, политические и торговые* [Treaties of Russia with the East, Political and Trade]. Спб., Тип. О. Бакст, 1869. xxii, 294 pp.

Ivanovskii, I. I. *Собрание действующих договоров, заключенных Россиею с иностранными державами* [Collection of Prevailing Treaties Concluded by Russia with Foreign Powers]. Одесса, Imp. économique, 1889–90. 2 vols. in 3.

Kliuchnikov, Iu. V. and Sabanin, A. V. *Итоги империалистической войны. Серия мирных договоров* [Results of the Imperialist War. Series of Peace Treaties]. M., Литиздат НКИД, 1925–7. 5 vols.

Международная политика новейшего времени в договорах, нотах, декларациях [International Politics of the Modern Era in Treaties, Notes, Declarations]. M., Литиздат НКИД, 1925–9. 3 vols.

Korolev, A. G. and Freifel'd, O. N. *Международные отношения 1870–1918. Сборник документов* [International Relations 1870–1918. Collection of Documents]. Ed. V. M. Khvostov. M., 1940. 407 pp.

Korovin, E. A. *Международные договоры и акты нового времени* [International Treaties and Acts of the Modern Era]. M-Л., Госиздат, 1924. 395 pp.

Martens, F. F. *Собрание трактатов и соглашений, заключенных Россиею с иностранными державами* [Collection of Treaties and Conventions Concluded by Russia with Foreign Powers]. Спб., Тип. Министерство путей сообщения, 1874–1909. 15 vols.

Mertvago, D. F. *Международные договоры, содержащие правила нейтралитета* [International Treaties Containing the Rules of Neutrality]. Одесса, Тип. Киршбаум, 1911. 34 pp.

Международная конвенция о перевозке грузов по железным дорогам и распоряжения и постановления, относящиеся до международных сообщений [International Conventions on the Carriage of Goods by Railway and Regulations and Decrees Relevant up to International Transport]. Спб., Перль, 1901. v, 79, 15 pp.

Международное положение и внешняя политика СССР. Сборник документов и материалов [The International Situation and Foreign Policy of the USSR. Collection of Documents and Materials]. M., Воениздат, 1939. 208 pp.

Международные трактаты и законодательные акты, касаюшиесие вопросу о государственно-правовом отношении Царства Польского и Российской Империи [International Treaties and Legislative Acts Affecting the Question on the State Law Relations of the Kingdom of Poland and the Russian Empire]. [Спб.], Тип. Тренке и Фюсно, [1906]. 60 pp.

Modzhorian, L. A. and Sobakin, V. K. (eds.). *Международное право в избранных документах* [International Law in Selected Documents]. M., 1955–6. 2 vols.

Международное право в избранных документах [International Law in Selected Documents]. Ed. V. N. Durdenevskii. M., 1957–9. 3 vols.

Отношения СССР с ГДР, 1949–1955. Документы и материалы [Relations of the USSR with the GDR, 1949–1955. Documents and Materials]. M., Политиздат, 1974. 727 pp.

Отношения СССР с Народной Кореей, 1945–1980. *Документы и материалы* [Relations of the USSR with People's Korea, 1945–1980. Documents and Materials]. M., Политиздат, 1981. 424 pp.

Ovchinnikov, I. A. *Собрание действующих трактатов, конвенций и других международных актов имеющих отношение к военно-мореплаванию* [Collection of Prevailing Treaties, Conventions, and Other International Acts Relating to Naval Navigation]. Спб., Изд. Морское министерство, 1901. 800 pp.; 2nd edn., 1914. 816 pp.

Политика европейских держав в Юго-Восточной Азии (60-е годы XVIII – 60-е годы XIX в.). Документы и материалы [Policy of European Powers in Southeast Asia. Documents and Materials]. M., Изд-во восточной литературы, 1962. 655 pp.

Политика капиталистических держав и национально-освободительное движение в Юго-Восточной Азии (1871–1917). Документы и материалы [Policy of Capitalist Powers and National-Liberation Movement in Southeast Asia (1871–1917) Documents and Materials]. M., Hayka, 1965–67. 2 vols.

Россия и США: становление отношений 1765–1815. Сборник документов [Russia and the United States: Formation of Relations 1765–1815. Collection of Documents]. M., Hayka, 1980. 752 pp.

Русско-дальневосточные торговые договоры, сохранявшие свою силу до 1917 года [Russian–Far Eastern Trade Treaties Which Retained Force to 1917]. [M., 1926]. 87 pp.

Русско-индийские отношения в XVIII в. Сборник документов [Russian–Indian Relations in the XVIII Century. Collection of Documents]. M., 'Hayka', 1965. 656 pp.

Русско-китайские отношения в XVII в. Материалы и документы [Russo-Chinese Relations in the XVII Century. Materials and Documents]. M., 'Наука', 1969–72. 2 vols.

Русско-китайские отношения в XVII в. Сборник документов [Russo-Chinese Relations in the XVII Century. Collection of Documents]. M., Изд-во восточной литературы, 1958. 455 pp.

Русско-китайские отношения 1689–1916. Официальные документы [Russo-Chinese Relations 1689–1916. Official Documents]. M., Изд-во восточной литературы, 1958. 139 pp.

Русско-монгольсие отношения 1607–1636. Сборник документов [Russian–Mongolian Relations 1607–1636. Collection of Documents]. M., Изд-во восточной литературы, 1959. 352 pp.

Русско-монгольские отношения 1636–1654. Сборник документов [Russian–Mongolian Relations 1636–1654. Collection of Documents]. M., Наука, 1974. 469 pp.

Русско-шведские отношения в XVII веке. Сборник документов [Russian–Swedish Relations in the XVII Century. Collection of Documents]. М-Л., Изд-во АН СССР, 1960. 654 pp.

Sabanin, A. V. (ed.). *Международная политика в 1928* г. *Договоры, декларации и дипломатическая переписка* [*в 1929 г.*], [*в 1930 г.*] [International Politics in 1928. Treaties, Declarations, and Diplomatic Correspondence] {in 1929}{in 1930}]. M., 1929–31. 3 vols.

Samartsev, N. T. (comp.). *Международное право в документах. Сборник важнейших международно-правовых актов* [International Law in Documents. Collection of Major International Legal Acts]. M., 'Международные отношения', 1969. 551 pp.

Сборник грамот и договоров о присоединении царств и областей к государству Российскому в XVII–XIX вв. [Collection of Instruments and Treaties on the Accession of Kingdoms and Regions to the Russian State in the XVII to XIX Centuries]. Comp. A. A. Pazukhin. Петроград, Госиздат, 1922. 742 pp.

Сборник действующих договоров, соглашений и конвенций, заключенных РСФСР с иностранными государствами [Collection of Prevailing Treaties, Agreements, and Conventions Concluded by the RSFSR with Foreign States]. M., НКИД, 1921–3. 5 vols.

Сборник действующих договоров, соглашений и конвенций, заключенных с иностранными государствами [Collection of Prevailing Treaties, Agreements, and Conventions Concluded with Foreign States]. 2nd edn. M., Литиздат НКИД, 1928–36. 4 vols.

Сборник действующих договоров, соглашений и конвенций, заключенных с иностранными государствами [Collection of Prevailing Treaties, Agreements, and Conventions Concluded with Foreign States]. 3rd edn. M., Литиздат НКИД, 1935. 2 vols.

Сборник действующих договоров, соглашений и конвенций, заключенных СССР с иностранными государствами [Collection of Prevailing Treaties, Agreements, and Conventions Concluded by the USSR with Foreign States]. M., Литиздат НКИД, 1924– .

Сборник действующих торговых договоров и иных хозяйственных соглашений СССР, заключенных с иностранными государствами [Collection of

Prevailing Trade Treaties and Other Economic Agreements of the USSR Concluded with Foreign States]. M., Литиздат НКИД, 1935–36. 2 vols.

Сборник действующих трактатов, конвенций и соглашений, заключенных Россией с другими государствами и касающих различных вопросов частного международного права [Collection of Prevailing Treaties, Conventions and Agreements Concluded by Russia with Other States and Concerning Questions of Private International Law]. Спб., Тип. Тренке и Фюсно, 1889–90. 4 vols.

Сборник действующих трактатов, конвенций и соглашений, заключенных Россией с другими государствами [Collection of Prevailing Treaties, Conventions and Agreements Concluded by Russia with Other States]. Спб., Тип. Тренке и Фюсно, 1902–6. 2 vols.

Сборник договоров и дипломатических документов по делам Дальнего Востока, 1895–1905 [Collection of Treaties and Diplomatic Documents on Affairs of the Far East, 1895–1905]. Спб., Изд. МИД, 1906. 763 pp.

Сборник договоров с Китаем, 1689–1881 г. [Collection of Treaties with China, 1689–1881]. Спб., Изд. МИД, 1889. 270 pp.

Сборник конвенций о выдаче преступников, о непосредственных сношениях русских судебных учреждений с таковыми же германскими и австрийскими и о наследствах [Collection of Conventions on Extradition of Criminals, on Direct Relations of Russian Judicial Institutions with Those of Germany and Austria, and on Inheritance]. Спб., Тип. Правительствующего Сената, 1888. 146 pp.

Сборник международных договоров о взаимной правовой помощи по гражданским и уголовным делам [Collection of International Treaties on Mutual Legal Assistance With Regard to Civil and Criminal Cases]. L. V. Efremov (comp.). M., Международные отношения, 1988. 640 pp.

Сборник пограничных договоров, заключенных Россией с соседними государствами. Издан по распоряжению Министра иностранных дел [Collection of Frontier Treaties Concluded by Russia with Neighbouring States. Published by Instruction of the Minister of Foreign Affairs]. Спб., Изд. МИД, 1891. 375 pp.

Сборник секретных дипломитических документов бывшего Министерства иностранных дел [Collection of Secret Diplomatic Documents of the Former Ministry of Foreign Affairs]. M., 1922. 733 pp.

Сборник торговых договоров, конвенции и Соглашении СССР, заключенных с иностранными государствами до 1 января 1941 г. [Collection of Trade Treaties, Conventions and Agreements of the USSR Concluded with Foreign States to 1 January 1941]. Ed. D. Mishustin. M., 'Международная книга', 1941. 408 pp.

Shtein, B. E. (ed.). *Локарнские соглашения* [The Locarno Agreements]. M., Литиздат НКИД, 1925. 39 pp.

Sobakin, V. K. (comp.). *Современное международное право. Сборник документов* [Contemporary International Law. Collection of Documents]. M., 'Международные отношения', 1964. 666 pp.

Собрание государственных грамот и договоров, хранящихся в Государственной коллегии иностранных дел [Collection of State Instruments and

Treaties Kept in the State College of Foreign Affairs]. М., Тип. Н. С. Всеволожского, 1813–28, 1894. 5 vols.

Собрание торговых договоров, заключенных Россиею с иностранными государствами [Collection of Trade Treaties Concluded by Russia with Foreign States]. Спб., Тип. В. Ф. Киршбаум, 1902. 409 pp.

Собрание трактатов, конвенций и других актов, заключенных Россиею с европейскими и азиатскими державами, а также и с Северо-Американскими Соединёнными Штатами [Collection of Treaties, Conventions and Other Acts Concluded by Russia with European and Asian Powers, and also with the United States of America]. Сдб., В Морской тип., 1845; Дополнение (1847); and Прибавление (1858, 1862, 1868, and 1874).

Советский Союз-Народная Польша: 1944–1974: Документы и материалы [Soviet Union–People's Poland: 1944–1974: Documents and Materials]. М., Политиздат, 1974. 664 pp.

Советский Союз-Народная Польша: 1974–1987: Документы и материалы [Soviet Union–People's Poland: 1974–1987: Documents and Materials]. М., Политиздат, 1989. 486 pp.

Советский Союз-Вьетнам: 30 лет отношений 1950–1980: Документы и материалы [Soviet Union–Vietnam: 30 Years of Relations 1950–1980: Documents and Materials]. М., Политиздат, 1982. 655 pp.

Советско-афганские отношения 1919–1969 гг. Документы и материалы [Soviet–Afghan Relations 1919–1969. Documents and Materials]. М., Политиздат, 1971. 439 pp.

Советско-американские отношения 1919–1933 (Сборник документов по международной политике и международному праву) [Soviet–American Relations 1919–1933 (Collection of Documents on International Politics and International Law)]. М., НКИД, 1934. 99 pp.

Советско-американские отношения во время Великой Отечественной войны, 1941–1945. Документы и материалы [Soviet–American Relations During the Great Fatherland War, 1941–1945. Documents and Materials]. М., Политиздат, 1984. 2 vols.

Советско-английские отношения во время Великой Отечественной войны, 1941–1945: Документы и материалы [Soviet–English Relations During the Great Fatherland War, 1941–1945: Documents and Materials]. М., Политиздат, 1983. 2 vols.

Советско-болгарские отношения 1944–1948 гг. Документы и материалы [Soviet–Bulgarian Relations 1944–1948. Documents and Materials]. М., Политиздат, 1969. 508 pp.

Советско-болгарские отношения и связи. Документы и материалы [Soviet–Bulgarian Relations and Links. Documents and Materials]. М., Наука, 1976–87. 3 vols.

Советско-болгарские отношения 1948–1970 гг. Документы и материалы [Soviet–Bulgarian Relations, 1948–1970. Documents and Materials]. М., Политиздат, 1974. 639 pp.

Советско-болгарские отношения 1971–1976 гг. Документы и материалы [Soviet–Bulgarian Relations, 1971–1976. Documents and Materials]. М., Политиздат, 1977. 584 pp.

Советско-болгарские отношения 1977–1982 гг. Документы и материалы [Soviet–Bulgarian Relations, 1977–1982. Documents and Materials] M., Политиздат, 1985. 526 pp.

Советско-болгарские отношения 1983–1986 гг. Документы и материалы [Soviet–Bulgarian Relations, 1983–1986. Documents and Materials] M., Политиздат, 1988. 295 pp.

Советско-чехословацкие отношения во время Великой Отечественной войны 1941–1945 гг. Документы и материалы [Soviet–Czechoslovak Relations During the Great Fatherland War 1941–1945. Documents and Materials]. M., Политиздат, 1960. 291 pp.

Советско-чехословацкие отношения, 1945-1960 гг. Документы и материалы [Soviet–Czechoslovak Relations 1945–1960. Documents and Materials]. M., Политиздат, 1960. 291 pp.

Советско-чехословацкие отношения 1961–1971. Документы и материалы [Soviet–Czechoslovak Relations, 1961–1971. Documents and Materials]. M., Политиздат, 1975. 703 pp.

Советско-чехословацкие отношения 1972–1976. Документы и материалы [Soviet–Czechoslovak Relations, 1972–1976. Documents and Materials]. M., Политиздат, 1977. 455 pp.

Советско-чехословацкие отношения 1977–1982. Документы и материалы [Soviet–Czechoslovak Relations, 1977–1982. Documents and Materials]. M., Политиздат, 1984. 512 pp.

Советско-финляндские отношения, 1948–1983: договор 1948 г. о дружбе, сотрудничестве и взаимной помощи в действии. Документы и материалы [Soviet–Finnish Relations, 1948–1983: Treaty of 1948 on Friendship, Co-operation, and Mutual Assistance in Action. Documents and Materials]. M., Политиздат, 1983. 494 pp.

Советско-французские отношения во время Великой Отечественной войны 1941–1945 гг. Документы и материалы [Soviet–French Relations During the Great Fatherland War 1941–1945. Documents and Materials]. M., Госполитиздат, 1959. 551 pp.

Советско-французские отношения во время Великой Отечественной войны 1941–1945 гг. Документы и материалы [Soviet–French Relations During the Great Fatherland War 1941–1945. Documents and Materials]. M., Политиздат, 1983. 2 vols.

Советско-французские отношения 1965–1976. Документы и материалы [Soviet–French Relations 1965–1976. Documents and Materials]. M., Политиздат, 1976. 255 pp.

Советско-германские отношения от переговоров в Брест-Литовске до подписания Рапальского договора (Сборник документов) [Soviet–German Relations from the Negotiations in Brest-Litovsk to the Signature of the Rapallo Treaty (Collection of Documents)]. M., Политиздат, 1968–71. 2 vols.

Советско-германские отношения, 1922–1925 гг. Документы и материалы [Soviet–German Relations, 1922–1925. Documents and Materials]. M., Политиздат, 1977. 2 vols.

Советско-китайские отношения 1917–1957. Сборник документов [Soviet–Chinese Relations, 1917–1957. Collection of Documents]. M., Изд-во восточной литературы, 1959. 466 pp.

Советско-мексиканские отношения 1917–1980 [Soviet–Mexican Relations (1917–1980)]. M., Политиздат, 1981. 112 pp.

Советско-мексиканские отношения 1968–1980 [Soviet–Mexican Relations, 1968–1980]. M., Политиздат, 1981. 191 pp.

Советско-монгольские отношения, 1921–1966. Сборник документов [Soviet–Mongolian Relations, 1921–1966. Collection of Documents]. M., 'Наука', 1966. 360 pp.

Советско-монгольские отношения, 1921–1974. Документы и материалы [Soviet–Mongolian Relations. 1921–1974. Documents and Materials]. M., 'Международные отношения', 1975–9. 2 vols.

Советско-венгерские отношения 1945–1948 гг. Документы и материалы [Soviet–Hungarian Relations 1945-1948. Documents and Materials]. M. Политиздат, 1969. 356 pp.

Советско-венгерские отношения 1948–1970 гг. Документы и материалы [Soviet–Hungarian Relations 1948–1970. Documents and Materials]. M. Политиздат, 1974. 726 pp.

Советско-венгерские отношения 1971–1976 гг. Документы и материалы [Soviet–Hungarian Relations 1971–1976. Documents and Materials]. M. Политиздат, 1977. 574 pp.

Советско-венгерские отношения 1977–1982 гг. Документы и материалы [Soviet–Hungarian Relations 1977–1982. Documents and Materials]. M. Политиздат, 1984. 422 pp.

СССР-Австрия, 1938–1979 гг. Документы и материалы [USSR–Austria, 1938–1979. Documents and Materials]. M., Политиздат, 1980. 159 pp.

СССР-ГДР, 30 лет отношений, 1949–1979: Документы и материалы [USSR–GDR, 30 Years of Relations, 1949–1979. Documents and Materials]. M., Политиздат, 1981. 755 pp.

СССР и арабские страны, 1917–1960 гг. Документы и материалы [USSR and the Arab Countries, 1917–1960. Documents and Materials]. M. Госполитиздат, 1961. 85 pp.

СССР и страны АФрики, 1946–1962 гг. Документы и материалы [USSR and Countries of Africa, 1946–1962. Documents and Materials]. M. Госполитиздат, 1963. 2 vols.

СССР и страны АФрики, 1963–1970 гг. Документы и материалы [USSR and Countries of Africa, 1963–1970. Documents and Materials]. M., Политиздат, 1982. 2 vols.

СССР и страны АФрики, 1971–1976 гг. Документы и материалы [USSR and Countries of Africa, 1971–1976. Documents and Materials]. M., Политиздат, 1985. 2 vols.

СССР-Италия: Страницы истории, 1917–1984: Документы и материалы [USSR–Italy: Pages of History, 1917–1984. Documents and Materials]. M., Политиздат, 1985. 293 pp.

СССР-Колумбия: 50 лет установления дипломатических отношений, 1935–1985. Документы и материалы [USSR–Colombia: 50 Years of the Establishment of Diplomatic Relations, 1935–1985. Documents and Materials]. M., Политиздат, 1988. 183 pp.

СССР-Куба: Документы дружбы и солидарности [USSR–Cuba: Documents of Friendship and Solidarity]. M., Политиздат, 1985. 63 pp.

СССР-Люксембург: Страницы истории, 1917–1984: Документы и материалы [USSR–Luxembourg: Pages of History, 1917–1984: Documents and Materials]. М., Политиздат, 1985. 271 pp.

СССР (Россия)–Аргентина: Страницы истории, 1885–1986 гг. Документы и материалы [USSR (Russia)–Argentina: Pages of History, 1885–1986. Documents and Materials]. М., Политиздат, 1990. 336 pp.

СССР-Уругвай. 60 лет дипломатических отношений 1926–1986: Документы и материалы [USSR–Uruguay: 60 Years of Diplomatic Relations 1926–1986: Documents and Materials]. М., Международные отношения 1988. 484 pp.

СССР в борьбе против колониализма и неоколониализма, 1960-март 1986 гг. Документы и материалы [USSR in the Struggle Against Colonialism and Neocolonialism, 1960–March 1986]. М., Политиздат, 1986. 2 vols.

СССР в борьбе за безопасность и сотрудничество в Европе, 1964–1987. Сборник документов [USSR in the Struggle for Security and Cooperation in Europe, 1964–1987. Collection of Documents]. М., Международные отношения 1988. 544 pp.

Торговые договоры России с Китаем [Trade Treaties of Russia with China]. Спб., Тип. В. Ф. Киршбаум, 1909. ii, 50 pp.

Трактаты европейских государств с Китаем [Treaties of European States with China]. Кяхта, Кяхтинской общественной тип., 1862. 99 pp.

[Трегубов, С. Н.] *Сборник заключенных Россией, действующих конвенций о выдаче преступников и о непосредственных сношений русских пограничных судебных учреждений с иностранными судебными местами: Особое приложение к настольной книге криминалиста-практика* [Collection of Prevailing Conventions Concluded by Russia on Extradition of Criminals and on Direct Relations of Russian Frontier Judicial Institutions with Foreign Courts: Special Annex to the Table Manual of a Practitioner Criminalist]. Спб., Тип. Родник, 1908. 113 pp.

Troianovskii, K. M. (ed.). *Синяя книга. Сборник тайных документов, извлеченных из архива Министерства иностранных дел* [Blue Book. Collection of Secret Documents Extracted from the Archive of the Ministry of Foreign Affairs]. М., НКИД, 1918. xii, 115 pp.

Украинская ССР на международной арене. Сборник документов и материалов 1944–1961 гг. [Ukrainian SSR in the International Arena. Collection of Documents and Materials 1944–1961]. Киев, Госполитиздат УССР, 1963. 576 pp.

Vashkevich, M. *Сборник действующих трактатов и конвенций, имеющих отношение к военному мореплаванию* [Collection of Prevailing Treaties and Conventions Relating to Naval Navigation]. Спб., Изд. Морское министерство, 1885. 553 pp.

Veniukov, M. I. *Старые и новые договоры России с Китаем* [Old and New Treaties of Russia with China]. 2nd edn. Спб., Тип. В. Безобразов, 1863. iv, 95 pp.

Verkhovskii, N. V. (ed.). *Recueil de traités de commerce et autres arrangements prévus par les dits traités, conclus entre la Russie et les puissances etrangères*. Pg., Imp. W. Kirschbaum, 1915. 695 pp.

Сборник торговых договоров, заключенных Россиею с иностраннымн государствами [Collection of Trade Treaties Concluded by Russia with Foreign States]. Спб., Изд. Министерство торговли и промышленности, 1912. 602 pp.

Внешняя полимика России XIX - начала XX века. Документы Российского министерства иностранных дел. Серии I (1801–1815) *и* II (1815–1830) [Foreign Policy of Russia Nineteenth–Twentieth Centuries. Documents of the Russian Ministry of Foreign Affairs. 1st Series]. М., Госполитиздат, 1960–1995. 16 vols.

Внешняя полимика России: сборник документов [Foreign Policy of Russia: Collection of Documents]. М., 'Международных отношения', 1996– .

Treaties included from 12 June 1990, date of State sovereignty of Russia being proclaimed.

Внешняя политика Советского Союза. Документы и материалы [Foreign Policy of the Soviet Union. Documents and Materials]. М., Госполитиздат, 1949–53. 8 vols.

Внешняя политика Советского Союза в период Отечественной войны. Документы и материалы [Foreign Policy of the Soviet Union During the Fatherland War. Documents and Materials]. М., Госполитиздат, 1946–7. 3 vols.

Внешняя политика Советского Союза и международные отношения. Сборник документов [Foreign Policy of the Soviet Union and International Relations. Collection of Documents]. М., Изд-во ИМО, 1962–85. 23 vols.

Внешняя политика СССР. Сборник документов [Foreign Policy of the USSR. Collection of Documents]. М., 1944–7. 6 vols.

TEXTS

'Венская конвенция о праве международных договоров' [Vienna Convention on the Law of Treaties], *СЕМП 1977*. М., 1979, pp. 396–416

Закон Союза Советских Социалистических Республик о порядке заключения, исполнения и денонсация международных договоров СССР: Принят на девятой сессии Верховного Совета СССР девятого созыва 6 июля 1978 г. [Law of the Union of Soviet Socialist Republics on the Procedure for the Conclusion, Performance, and Denunciation of International Treaties of the USSR: Adopted at the Ninth Session of the USSR Supreme Soviet, Ninth Convocation, 6 July 1978]. М., Известия, 1978. 16 pp.

Also published: *СЕМП 1978*. М., 1980, pp. 435–439

GENERAL WORKS

Alekseev, N. N. and Zaitzeff, L. *Sowjetstaat und Völkerrecht*. Breslau, Kern, 1931

Aust, Anthony. *Modern Treaty Law and Practice*. Cambridge, Cambridge University Press, 2000

Bekiashev, K. A. (ed.). *Международное публичное право* [Public International Law]. М., Проспект, 1998, pp. 159–80

Biriukov, P. N. *Международное право. Учебное пособие* [International Law. Instructional Manual]. М., Юристь, 1998, pp. 112–30

Brownlie, Ian. *Международное право(в двух книгах)* [International Law (in Two Books)], transl. S. N. Andrianov (1977), II, pp. 304–48

Butler, W. E. *Constitutional Foundations of the CIS Countries*. The Hague–London–Boston, Simmonds & Hill Publishing Ltd–Kluwer Law International, 1999a. xxv, 762 pp.

The Russian Law of Treaties. London, Simmonds & Hill Publishing Ltd, 1997. ix, 158 pp.

Russian Law. Oxford, Oxford University Press, 1999b. xlii, 692 pp.

Chernichenko, S. V. *Теория международного права: старые и новые теоретические проблемы* [Theory of International Law: Old and New Theoretical Problems] (M., изд-во НИМП, 1999). 2 vols.

Davydov, A. I. *Лекция на тему 'Международный договор' для студентов ВЮЗИ* [Lecture on Topic 'International Treaty' for Students of VIuZI]. M., 1953. 32 pp.

Durdenevskii, V. N. 'Staatsverträge im Verfassungsrecht der Union der sozialistischen Sowjetrepubliken', *Ostrecht*, no. 1 (1925), pp. 201–17

Esaian, A. A. 'Международная договорная практика Советской Армении' [International Treaty Practice of Soviet Armenia], *Ученые записки Ереванского унив-та, т.* 81, *Серия юридических наук*. Erevan, 1962, II, pp. 3–41

Florinsky, M. T. 'The Soviet Union and International Agreements,' *Political Science Quarterly*, LXI (1946), 61–89

Glebov, I. N. and Zhdanov, Iu. N. *Международное право. Альбом схем* [International Law. Album of Diagrams]. M., МА МВД России Изд-во 'щит-М', 2000, pp. 11–16

Grabar, V. E. 'Договор, международный' [Treaty, International], *Новый энциклопедический словарь*, XVI, cols. 473–479

Ignatenko, G. V. (ed.). *Международное право* [International Law]. 2nd edn. M., 'Высшая школа', 1995, pp. 169–84

Kolchanovskii, N. P. 'Многосторонние международные договоры (Доклад в секции международного права)' [Multilateral International Treaties (Report to the Section on International Law)], *Советское права*, no. 1–2 (1935), pp. 170–3

Kolosov, Iu. M. and Krivchikova, E. S. (eds.). *Международное право* [International Law]. M., Международные отношения, 2000, pp. 177–203

Kolosov, Iu. M. and Kuznetsov, V. I. (eds.). *Международное право. Учебник* [International Law. Textbook]. M., Международные отношения, 1995, pp. 120–40; 2nd edn. 1998, pp. 135–57

Korovin, E. A. 'Soviet Treaties and International Law', *American Journal of International Law*, XXII (1928), 753–63

'Советские договоры и международное право (1917–1927)' [Soviet Treaties and International Law (1917–1927)], *Советское право*, no. 6 (1927), pp. 94–110

Kozhevnikov, F. I. *Международный договор* [International Treaty]. M., 1947. 87 pp. (Military Academy of the Armed Forces of the USSR)

Учебное пособие по международному публичному праву. Вып. 2. Международный договор [Instructional Manual on Public International Law. Vol. 2. International Treaty]. M., Юриздат, 1945. 41 pp.

Lapenna, Ivo. *Conceptions soviétiques de droit international public*. Paris, Editions A. Pedone, 1954, pp. 264–84

Lukashuk, I. I. *Международное право. Общая часть. Учебник для юридических факультетов и вузов* [International Law. General Part. Textbook for Law Faculties and Institutions of Higher Education]. M., изд-во БЕК, 1996. 2nd edn., 2000

'Международные отношения и международный договор' [International Relations and the International Treaty], *Ученые записки Саратовского юридического институтаим. Д. И. Курского*. (Саратов, 1957), VI, pp. 144–83

'Право международных договоров' [Law of International Treaties], *Курс международного права в семи томах* [Course of International Law in Seven Volumes]. M., 1990, IV, pp. 5–90

Role of the Treaty in the Development of International Law. Geneva, Centre Europeen de la Dotation Carnegie, 1965. 9 pp.

'Советский Союз и международные договоры' [Soviet Union and International Treaties], in *Второе ежегодное собрание Советской ассоциации международногоправа. 5–7 февраля 1959 г. Тезисы докладов*. M., 1959, pp. 1–9

'Современное право международных договоров' [Contemporary Law of International Treaties], in *Советская ассоциация международного права. IX ежегодноесобрание. 3–5 февраля 1966 г. Тезисы докладов*. M., 1966, pp. 5–9

'СССР и международные договоры' [USSR and International Treaties], *СЕМП 1959*. M., 1960, pp. 16–43

СССР и международные договоры (некоторые проблемы теории и практики) [USSR and International Treaties (Certain Problems of Theory and Practice)]. M., 1961. 30 pp. (Abstract of докт. дисс., Moscow State Institute of International Relations)

Martens, F. F. *Современное международное право цивилизованных народов* [Contemporary International Law of Civilized Peoples]. M., изд-во 'Юридический колледж МГУ', 1996. 2 vols.

Mirkine-Guetzevitch, B. S. 'Les traités internationaux de la Russie soviétique', *Revue de droit international*, II (1928), 1012–49

Pashukanis, E. B. 'Договор, международный' [Treaty, international], in *Энциклопедия государства и права*. M., Изд-во Коммунистической академии, 1925, I

Preobrazhenskaia, V. V. *Право международных договоров (Спец. курс): Конспектлекций* [Law of International Treaties (Special Cours): Precis of Lectures]. Львов, Высшая школа, 1974. 36 pp. (in Ukrainian)

Rosenne, Shabtai. *Breach of Treaty*. Cambridge, Grotius Publications Ltd, 1985. xii, 142 pp.

Developments in the Law of Treaties 1945–1986. Cambridge, Cambridge University Press, 1989. xxxv, 535 pp.

Sarsembaev, M. A. *Международное право* [International Law]. Алматы, Жети жаргы, 1996. 448 pp.

Shurshalov, V. M. *Право международных договоров: Учебное пособие* [Law of International Treaties: Instructional Manual]. M., 1979. 82 pp.

Slusser, R. M. and Triska, J. F. 'Professor Krylov and Soviet Treaties', *American Journal of International Law*, LI (1957), 766–73

Talalaev, A. N. *Право международных договоров* [Law of International Treaties]. M., 1980–9. 3 vols.

Vol. 1. *Общие вопросы*. 1980. 312 pp.

Vol. 2. *Действие и применение договоров*. 1985. 294 pp.

Vol. 3. *Договоры с участием международных организаций*. 1989. 271 pp.

Taracouzio, T. A. *The Soviet Union and International Law*. New York, Macmillan, 1935, pp. 235–90

Triska, Jan F. 'The Soviet Law of Treaties', *Proceedings of the American Society of International Law*, LIII (1959), 294–301

and Slusser, Robert M. *The Theory, Law, and Policy of Soviet Treaties*. Stanford, Calif. Stanford University Press, 1962. xiii, 593 pp.

and Slusser, Robert M. 'Treaties and Other Sources of Order in International Relations: The Soviet View', *American Journal of International Law*, LII (1958), 699–722

Tunkin, G. I. (ed.). *Международное право* [International Law]. M., 1994, pp. 142–68

Теория Международного право [Theory of International Law]. [2nd edn.], M., Зерцало, 2000, pp. 75–98

Theory of International Law, transl. W. E. Butler. Cambridge, Mass., Harvard University Press, 1974, pp. 91–112

Ul'ianova, N. N. *Договорные инициативы СССР – важный фактор укрепления мира* [Treaty Initiatives of the USSR – Important Factor for Strengthening Peace]. M., Международные отношения 1983. 72 pp.

'Общие многосторонние договоры в современных международных отношениях' [General Multilateral Treaties in Contemporary International Relations], *Советское право*, no. 6 (1969), pp. 93–8 (in Ukrainian)

Общие многосторонние договоры в современных международных отношениях: некоторые вопросы теории [General Multilateral Treaties in Contemporary International Relations: Certain Questions of Theory]. Киев, Наукова думка, 1981. 259 pp.

Ushakov, N. A. *Международное право* [International Law]. M., Юристь, 2000, pp. 212–21

Общие многосторонние договоры в системе международно-правового регулирования [General Multilateral Treaties in the System of International Legal Regulation]. Киев, 1982. 46 pp. (Abstract for дисс. доктора юридических наук, Ukrainian SSR Academy of Sciences, Institute of State and Law)

Zonnenshtral, A. A. 'Эволюция международных договоров Персии' [Evolution of International Treaties of Persia], *Вопросы торговли*, no. 1 (1927), pp. 73–90

HISTORY OF TREATIES

Andersen, V. 'Неравноправные договоры царской России с Китаем в XIX веке' [Unequal Treaties of Tsarist Russia with China in the XIX Century], *Борьба классов*, no. 9 (1936), pp. 102–12

Andreevskii, I. E. *О договоре Новгорода с немецкими городами и Готландом, заключенном в 1270 г.* [On the Treaty of Novgorod with the German Cities and Gotland Concluded in 1270]. Спб., Тип. Якова Трея, 1855. 106 pp.

Babaev, A. S. *Проблемы международного договора в трудах В. И. Ленина и И. В. Сталина* [Problems of the International Treaty in the Works of V. I. Lenin and I. V. Stalin]. M., Академия общественных наук, 1952

Balkashin, N. N. 'Трактаты России с Китаем' [Treaties of Russia with China]. Омск, тип. Окружного штаба, 1882, pp. 1–176

Barats, G. M. *Критико-сравнительный анализ договоров Руси с Византией: Восстановление текста, перевод, комментарий и сравнение в другими правовыми памятниками, в частности - с Русскою Правдою* [Critical Comparative Analysis of Treaties of Rus with Byzantium: Restoration of Text, Translation, Commentary, and Comparison with Other Legal Monuments, in Particular–with the *Russkaia Pravda*]. Киев, Тип. 1-й Киевской Артели печатного дела, 1910. xii, 265 pp.

Bashmakov, A. A. 'Из истории Адрианопольского трактата' [From the History of the Adrianopol Treaty], *Славянские известия*, no. 8 (1909), pp. 983–1006

Butkov, P. 'Договор о мире, заключенных между Россиею и Швециею у Тявзина 18 мая 1595 года' [Treaty on Peace Concluded Between Russia and Sweden at Tiavzin 18 May 1595], *Журнал Министерства внутренних дел*, no. 9 (1840), pt. 2, pp. 325–78

Chernyshev, V. P. 'Русский-американский торговый договор и новый таможенных тариф С.-А. Соединённых Штатов' [Russo-American Trade Treaty and the New Customs Tariff of the United States], *Русское судоходство*, XXVIII, no. 11 (1913), pp. 8–9

Chernyshevskii, N. G. 'Торговая конвенция с Франциею' [Trade Convention with France], *Современник*, LXV, no. 9 (1857a), otd. 5, pp. 144–5

'Трактат о торговле мореплавании' [Treaty on Merchant Navigation], *Современник*, LXV, no. 9 (1857b), otd. 5, pp. 144–5

Demis, L. N. *Обозрение трактатов о морском торговом нейтралитете* [Survey of Treaties on Maritime Merchant Neutrality]. Спб., Тип. Имп. Академин наук, 1854. 78, 12 pp.

Goriainov, S. M. 'Договор 11/23 сентября 1805 г., заключенный между Россией и Турцией' [Treaty of 11/23 September 1805 Concluded Between Russia and Turkey], *Известия Министерства иностранных дел*, kn. 5 (1912), pp. 529–43

Grabar, V. E. *The History of International Law in Russia 1647–1917. A Bio-Bibliographical Study*, transl. W. E. Butler. Oxford, Clarendon Press, 1990. liii, 760 pp.

Kojk, H. 'Пересмотр эстонско-финского торгового договора в 1930–1931 гг.' [Revision of Estonian–Finnish Trade Treaty in 1930–1931], *Ученые записки Тартуского унив-та*, I (1973), pp. 342–62 (In Estonian)

Lenstrem, K. 'О мирных договорах между Россиею и Швециею в XIV веке' [On Peace Treaties Between Russia and Sweden in the XIV Century], *Ученые записки Казанского унив-та*, kn. 2 (1855), pp. 103–51

Lukashuk, I. I. 'Значение Октябрьской революции и деятельности Советского государства для борьбы народов за демократизм международных договоров' [Significance of October Revolution and

Activity of the Soviet State for the Struggle of Peoples for Democratism of International Treaties], in *Сборник научных работ, посвященных 40-й годовщине Великой Октябрьской социалистической революции* (Саратов, 1958), pp. 51–103

Menshikov, P. 'К русско-китайскому договору' [On the Russian–Chinese Treaty], *Вестник Азии*, no. 8 (1911), pp. 1–44

Muliukin, A. S. 'К вопросу о договорах русских с греками' [On the Question of Russian Treaties with the Greeks], *Журнал Министерства юстиции*, no. 7, pt. 2 (September 1906), pp. 92–104

Ostroukhov, P. A. 'Англо-русский торговый договор 1734 г.: Очерк по истории русской торговой политики (на основании архивных источников)' [Anglo–Russian Trade Treaty of 1734: Essay on the History of Russian Trade Policy (on the Basis of Archival Sources)], *Труды студентов Экономического отделения С.- Петербургского Политехнического Института Императора Петра Великого*, XIII (1914). x, 204 pp.

Pogodin, M. P. О договорах русских князей Олега, Игоря и Святослава, с греками [On Treaties of the Russian Princes Oleg, Igor, and Sviatoslav with the Greeks], *Русский исторический вестник*. М., Унив. тип., 1838, kn. 4, pp. 98–137

Rozenblium, B. D. *Очерки договорного права Китая. Равноправные и неравноправные договоры* [Essays on the Law of Treaties of China. Equal and Unequal Treaties]. Харьков, Юриздат НКЮ УССР, 1928. 100 pp.

Shafirov, P. P. *Discourse on the Reasons for the War Between Sweden and Russia, 1700–1721*, ed. W. E. Butler (Dobbs Ferry, Oceana Publications, 1973)

Shcherba, G. A. 'О буржуазных концепциях неравноправных договоров' [On Bourgeois Conceptions of Unequal Treaties], *СЕМП 1976*. М., 1978, pp. 205–11

Talalaev, A. N. 'В. И. Ленина о международных договорах' [V. I. Lenin on International Treaties], *Советское государство и право*, no. 4 (1958), pp. 23–7

'Право международных договоров: историко-правовой очерк' [Law of International Treaties: Historical–Legal Essay], *СЕМП 1972*. М., 1974, pp. 53–67

Toscano, M. *The History of International Treaties in International Politics* (Baltimore, Johns Hopkins Press, 1966)

CONCEPT AND LEGAL NATURE OF TREATIES

Aleskerov, M. N. 'Некоторые аспекты договоров СССР с независимыми государствами Азии и Африки' [Certain Aspects of Treaties of the USSR with Independent States of Asia and Africa], *СЕМП 1966–1967*. М., 1968, pp. 219–23

'Юридическая природа договорных экономических отношений между СССР и молодыми суверенными государствами Азии и Африки' [Legal Nature of Treaty Economic Relations Between the USSR and Young Sovereign States of Asia and Africa], *Ученые записки Азербайджанского государственного унив-та, Серия юридических наук*, no. 2 (1965), pp. 3–9

'Юридическая природа договоров СССР с развивающимися странами по политическим вопросам' [Legal Nature of Treaties of the USSR with Developing Countries on Political Questions], *Ученые записки Азербайджанского унив-та, Серия Юридические науки*, no. 1 (Баку, 1973), pp. 3–11

'Юридическая природа торговых соглашений СССР с развивающимися странами'[Legal Nature of Trade Agreements of the USSR with Developing Countries], *Ученые записки Азербайджанского государственного унив-та, Серия юридических наук*, no. 2 (1967), pp. 26–32

Andreev, O. 'Международные договорные документы' [International Treaty Documents], *Международная жизнь*, no. 8 (1986), pp. 157–9

Arkhipova, L. B. 'Особенности применения института международных договоров в практике СЭВ' [Peculiarities of Application of the Institute of International Treaties in the Practice of COMECON], *Проблемы совершенствования советского законодательства*, XXII (1981), pp. 188–200

Chalyi, A. A. 'О правовой природе международных межучрежденческих соглашений' [On the Legal Nature of International Inter-Institutional Agreements], *СЕМП 1986*. M., 1987, pp. 315–19

Gervagen, L. L. *Имеют ли международные соглашения свойства права?* [Do International Agreements Have the Properties of Law?]. Пг., Тип. М. А. Александров, 1915. 70 pp.

Gidirim, A. V. 'Понятие международного договора' [Concept of International Treaty], *Научные труды Дипломатической Академии МИД СССР*, VIII (1980), pp. 3–22

Kazanskii, P. E. 'Опыт договорной теории права народов' [Attempt at a Treaty Theory of the Law of Nations], *Журнал Министерства юстиции*, no. 10, pt. 2 (1903), pp. 117–44

Klimenko, B. M. 'Международные договоры как форма реализации межгосударственного сотрудничества' [International Treaties as a Form of Realization of Inter-State Cooperation], in *СССР и проблемы межгосударственного сотрудничества*. M., 1980, pp. 88–108

Kozhevnikov, F. I. 'Некоторые вопросы теории и практики международного договора' [Certain Questions of the Theory and Practice of the International Treaty], *Советское государство и право*, no. 2 (1954), pp. 62–76

Litovchenko, O. I. *Вопросы теории международных договоров в свете практики экономического сотрудничества социалистических государств* [Questions of the Theory of International Treaties in Light of the Practice of Economic Cooperation of Socialist States]. Киев, 1970. 23 pp. (Abstract of канд. дисс., Kiev State University)

Matradze, L. N. *Теоретические вопросы понятия международного договора* [Theoretical Questions of the Concept of an International Treaty]. M., 1972. 14 pp. (Abstract of канд. дисс., Moscow State University, Law Faculty)

Mikhailovskii, G. N. 'Юридическая обязательность международных договоров' [Legal Bindingness of International Treaties], *Известия Министерства иностранных дел*, kn. 5 (1913), pp. 277–311

Shcherbinina, O. E. 'Правовая природа договора на организацию проведение международных торгово-промышленных выставок в

СССР и участие в них' [Legal Nature of Treaty on Organization (or Conducting) of International Trade and Industry Exhibitions in the USSR and Participation Therein], *Правоведение*, no. 2 (1984), pp. 78–82

Shurshalov, V. M. *Основные вопросы теории международного договора* [Principal Questions of the Theory of the International Treaty]. M., 1959. 472 pp. (Institute of State and Law, USSR Academy of Sciences)

Основные вопросы теории международного договора [Principal Questions of the Theory of the International Treaty]. M., 1958. 35 pp. (Abstract of докт. дисс., Institute of State and Law, USSR Academy of Sciences)

Suvorova, V. Ia. 'Роль договорных норм в процессе универсализации международного права' [Role of Treaty Norms in the Process of the Universalization of International Law], *Сборник аспирантских работ*, XVI (Свердловск, 1973), pp. 126–30

Talalaev, A. N. 'Социалистическая экономическая интеграция и вопросы теории права международных договоров' [Socialist Economic Integration and Questions of the Theory of International Treaties], in *Международное научное совещание на тему: 'Межгосударственные связи по линии министерств и ведомств в условии осуществления социалистической экономической интеграции'. Тезисы докладов.* M., Институт государства и права, 1971, pp. 18–22

Юридическая природа международного договора [Legal Nature of International Treaty]. M., Изд-во ИМО, 1963. 263 pp.

Юридическая природа международного договора [Legal Nature of International Treaty]. M., 1967. 26 pp. (Abstract of докт. дисс., Moscow State University, Law Faculty)

Ulianova, N. N. 'Понятие общего многостороннего договора' [Concept of General Multilateral Treaty], *СЕМП 1974*. M., 1976, pp. 90–106

Vasilevskaia, T. Iu. 'Роль международных договоров в прогрессивном развитии международного права' [Role of International Treaties in the Progressive Development of International Law], in *Международно-правовые основы межгосударственного сотрудничества*. M., 1983, pp. 106–12

CODIFICATION OF LAW OF TREATIES

Bakradze, T. V. 'Венская конвенция о праве международных договоров 1969 года' [The 1969 Vienna Convention on the Law of Treaties], *Труды молодых ученых-работников Тбилисского унив-та. Серия гуманитарных и общественных наук*, т. 3/4 (1974), pp. 426–38 (in Georgian language)

Bykov, D. V. 'Венская конференция о праве международных договоров' [Vienna Conference on the Law of Treaties], *СЕМП* 1970. M., 1972, pp. 266–8

Filimonova, M. V. 'Некоторые вопросы развития права договоров в современном международном праве' [Certain Questions of the Development of the Law of Treaties in Contemporary International Law], in *Актуальные вопросы теории современного международного права*. M., 1985, pp. 74–84

Khlestov, O. N. 'Кодификация и прогрессивное развитие права международных договоров' [Codification and Progressive Development of Law of International Treaties], in *Советская ассоциация международного права, XII ежегодное собрание. 30, 31 января и 1 февраля 1969 г. Тезисы докладов.* M., 1969a, pp. 3–8

'Новое в развитии договорного права' [New in the Development of the Law of Treaties], *Советское государство и право*, no. 5 (1970), pp. 54–61

'Право международных договоров (Венская конференция ООН) 1969 г.' [Law of International Treaties (United Nations Vienna Conference) 1969], *Советское государство и право*, no. 12 (1969b), pp. 62–9

Kliuev, V. N. 'Венская конференция по праву договоров и вопросы универсальности' [Vienna Conference on the Law of Treaties and Questions of Universality], *Свердловский юридический институт, Сборник аспирантских* работ (Свердловск, 1970), XI, pp. 94–7

Koretskii, V. M. 'Observations et rapport "Modification et terminaison des traités collectifs"', *in Annuaire de l'Institut de droit international* (Basle, 1967), I, pp. 288–9, 352–8

Korobova, M. A. 'Общий многосторонний договор и буржуазные концепции международного законодательства' [General Multilateral Treaty and Bourgeois Conceptions of International Legislation], *ВМУ. Серия XI. Право*, no. 3 (1983), pp. 48–56

Kozhevnikov, F. I. 'Договорная инициатива в международных отношениях' [Treaty Initiative in International Relations], *Советское государство и право*, no. 12 (1971), pp. 60–67

Lukashuk, I. I. 'Некоторые вопросы кодификации и прогрессивного развития права международных договоров' [Certain Questions of the Codification and Progressive Development of the Law of Treaties], *СЕМП 1966–1967.* M., 1968, pp. 51–71

'Some Problems of Codification and Progressive Development of International Treaties Law', in *The Socialist Concept of International Law* [Dar es Salaam], 1969, pp. 47–50

Makarevich, M. 'Венская конвенция по праву международных договоров' [Vienna Convention on the Law of International Treaties], *Советское право*, no. 11 (1986), pp. 84–93 (in Ukrainian)

'Вторая сессия Конференции ООН по праву международных договоров' [Second Session of the United Nations Conference on the Law of Treaties], *Советское право*, no. 12 (1969), pp. 79–82 (in Ukrainian)

'Первая сессия Конференции ООН по праву международных договоров (Вена, Март-май 1968 г.)' [First Session of the United Nations Conference on the Law of Treaties (Vienna, March–May 1968)], *Советское право*, no. 10 (1968), pp. 93–7 (in Ukrainian); *СЕМП 1969.* M., 1970, pp. 377–80

Nechaev, B. N. *Кодификация права международных договоров* (*Некоторые международно-правовые вопросы теории и практика*) [Codification of the Law of Treaties (Certain International Legal Questions of Theory and Practice)]. M., 1969. 20 pp. (Abstract of канд. дисс., Moscow State Institute of International Relations)

'Право договоров на XV–XVI сессиях Комиссии международного права ООН' [Law of Treaties at the XV–XVI Sessions of the United Nations International Law Commission], *СЕМП 1964–1965.* М., 1966, pp. 398–404

and Vlasova, L. V. 'Венская конференция о праве договоров между государствами и международными организациямн нли между международными организациями 1986 г.' [Vienna Conference on the Law of Treaties Between States and International Organizations or Between International Organizations], *СЕМП 1987.* М., 1988, pp. 274–9

'Право договоров на XVII сессии Комиссии международного права ООН (май-июль 1965 г., январь 1966 г.)' [Law of Treaties at the XVII Session of the United Nations International Law Commission (May–July 1965, January 1966)], *СЕМП 1966–1967.* М., 1968, pp. 279–82

Shibaeva, E. A. 'К вопросу кодификации права договоров с участием международных огранизаций' [On the Question of the Codification of the Law of Treaties with the Participation of International Organizations], *СЕМП 1974.* М., 1976, pp. 170–9

Talalaev, A. N. 'Венская конвенция ООН по праву международных договоров (первая сессия, март-май 1968 г.)' [United Nations Vienna Conference on the Law of Treaties (First Session, March–May 1968)], *Вестник МГУ, Серия XII. Право*, no. 1 (1969), pp. 31–41

Венская конвенция о праве международных договоров. Комментарий. М., изд-во Юридическая литература, 1997

'Вторая сессия Венской конференции ООН по праву международных договоров (апрель-май 1969 г.)' [Second Session of the United Nations Vienna Conference on the Law of Treaties (April–May 1969)], *Вестник МГУ, Серия XII. Право*, no. 3 (1970), pp. 41–8

'Венская конференция ООН по праву договоров 1986 г.' [United Nations Vienna Conference on the Law of Treaties, 1986], *Вестник МГУ, Серия XII. Право*, no. 2 (1987), pp. 59–67

Международные договоры в современном мире: Вопросы права международных договоров в свете работы Венской конференции ООН 1968–1969 гг. [International Treaties in the Contemporary World: Questions of the Law of Treaties in Light of the Work of the United Nations Vienna Conference of 1968–1969]. М., Международные отношений, 1973. 247 pp.

'Некоторые вопросы теории международного договора на Венской конференции ООН' [Certain Questions of the Theory of the International Treaty at the United Nations Vienna Conference], *СЕМП 1970.* М., 1972, pp. 112–27

'О кодификации международного договорного права (обзор некоторых проектов конвенций и кодексов)' [On the Codification of International Treaty Law (Survey of Certain Draft Conventions and Codes)], *СЕМП 1962.* М., 1963, pp. 137–47

Tunkin, G. I. and Nechaev, B. N. 'Право договоров на XIV сессии Комиссии международного права ООН' [Law of Treaties at the XIV Session of the United Nations International Law Commission], *Советское государство и право*, no. 2 (1962), pp. 97–103

Summary: *Staat und Recht*, XII (1963), 1311–12

'Право договоров на XV сессии Комиссии международного права ООН' [Law of Treaties at the XV Session of the United Nations International Law Commission], *Советское государство и право*, no. 2 (1964), pp. 84–92

'Право договоров на XVI сессии Комиссии международного права ООН' [Law of Treaties at the XVI Session of the United Nations International Law Commission], *Советское государство и право*, no. 3 (1965), pp. 70–7

'Право договоров на XVII сессии Комиссии международного права ООН' [Law of Treaties at the XVII Session of the United Nations International Law Commission], *Советское государство и право*, no. 4 (1965), pp. 56–62

Ulianova, N. N. 'Принципы универсальности в международном договоре на Венской конференции ООН' [Principles of Universality in the International Treaty at the United Nations Vienna Conference], *СЕМП 1970*. M., 1972, pp. 128–42

Vasilevskaia, T. Iu. 'Венская конвенция о праве договоров 1969 г. – кодификация права международных договоров' [Vienna Convention on the Law of Treaties 1969 – Codification of the Law of International Treaties], in *Тезисы докладов на теоретической конференции аспирантов Института государства и права АН СССР и юридический факультет МГУ*. M., 1982, pp. 166–8

COMMENTARY ON TREATY LEGISLATION

Babaev, M. 'Советское законодательство о применении международного договора' [Soviet Legislation on the Application of an International Treaty], *Советское право*, no. 10 (1982), pp. 70–3 (in Ukrainian)

Dumina, M. A. 'Советский закон о международных договорах и межведомственные связи стран-членов СЭВ' [Soviet Law on International Treaties and Interdepartmental Links of Member-Countries of COMECON], in *Правовые проблемы экономического сотрудничества социалистических стран*. M., 1983, pp. 98–102

Kozhevnikov, F. I. 'К закону о порядке ратификации и денонсации международных договоров СССР' [On the Law Concerning the Procedure for the Ratification and Denunciation of International Treaties of the USSR], *Проблемы социалистического права*, no. 6 (1938), pp. 66–78

Mironov, N. 'Новое советское законодательство о международных договорах: Закон СССР от 6 июля 1978 г. "О порядке заключения, исполнения и денонсации международных договоров СССР" [New Soviet Legislation on International Treaties: Law of USSR of 6 July 1978, 'On the Procedure for the Conclusion, Performance, and Denunciation of International Treaties'], *Внешняя торговля*, no. 1 (1979), pp. 24–33

Nikolaev, F. 'Закон о договорах' [Law on Treaties], *Международная жизнь*, no. 9 (1979), pp. 97–100

'Закон о договорах' [Law on Treaties], *Человек и закон*, no. 5 (1979), pp. 16–23

Plotkin, M. 'О силе международных обязательств (К изданию нового закона о порядке ратификации и денонсации международных договоров СССР)' [On the Force of International Obligations (On the Publication of the New Law on the Procedure for the Ratification and Denunciation of International Treaties of the USSR)], *Советское государство*, no. 5 (1938), pp. 71–4

'Вопросы международного права на второй сессии Верховного Совета СССР' [Questions of International Law at the Second Session of the USSR Supreme Soviet], *Социалистическая законность*, no. 9 (1938), pp. 71–4

Riiaka, V. A. 'Развитие законодательства СССР о ратнфикации международных договоров' [Development of Legislation of the USSR on the Ratification of International Treaties], in *Проблемы социалистической законности* (Харьков, 1982), IX, pp. 149–56

Shcherbakova, N. V. 'Проблемы применения закона России о международных договорах' [Problems of Applying the Law of Russia on International Treaties], *РЕМП 1998–1999*. Спб., 1999, pp. 349–51

Shmidt, O. Iu. 'Доклад на 2-й сессии Верховного Совета СССР о порядке ратификации и денонсации международных договоров СССР, 20 августа 1938 г.' [Report to Second Session of the Supreme Soviet of the USSR on the Procedure for the Ratification and Denunciation of International Treaties of the USSR, 20 August 1938], *Внешняя торговля*, no. 8 (1938), pp. 8–11

Talalaev, A. N. 'Закон о международных договорах' [Law on International Treaties], *Московский журнал международного права*, no. 2 (1996), pp. 251–57

Закон о международных договорах СССР на службе мира [Law on International Treaties of the USSR in the Service of Peace]. M., Юридическая литература, 1979. 96 pp.

Tunkin, G. I. and Müllerson, R. A. 'Закон о международных договорах СССР', *Советское государство и право*, no. 2 (1979), pp. 22–31

Zvekov, V. P. and Osminin, B. I. (eds.), *Комментарий к федеральному закону 'О международных договорах Российской Федерации'* [Commentary on the Federal Law on International Treaties of the Russian Federation]. M., изд-во Спарк, 1996. 228 pp.

CONCLUSION OF TREATIES

Chalyi, A. A. 'Конституционные основы процедуры заключения международных договоров государств-членов Совета Экономической Взаимопомощи' [Constitutional Foundations of Procedure for Conclusion of International Treaties of States-Members of Council of Mutual Economic Assistance] in *Государственно-правовой механизм осуществления внешней политики в СССР и зарубежных странах*. M., 1981, pp. 68–77

Представительство государства при заключении международных договоров [Representation of State When Concluding International Treaties]. Киев, 1981. 21 pp. (Abstract for дисс. канд. юридических наук, Kiev University)

Druzhkov, M. P. *Заключение международных договоров в рамках и под эгидой международных организаций* [Conclusion of International Treaties Within the Framework of and Under the Aegis of International Organizations]. Киев, 1986

Заключение международных договоров в рамках и под эгидой международных организаций [Conclusion of International Treaties Within the Framework of and Under the Aegis of International Organizations]. Киев, 1982. 22 pp. (Abstract for дисс. канд. юридческих наук, Institute of State and Law, UkSSR Academy of Sciences)

'Некоторые правовые вопросы процесса заключения многосторонних договоров в рамках и под эгидой ООН' [Some Legal Questions of the Process of Concluding Multilateral Treaties Within the Framework and Under the Aegis of the United Nations], *Вестник Киевского унив-та. Серия: Международные отношения и международное право*, XIII (1981), pp. 88–93

Dzhantaev, Kh. M. 'Процедура заключения международных договоров международными организациями (По материалам Комиссии международного права ООН)' [Procedure for Conclusion of International Treaties by International Organizations (According to Materials of the United Nations International Law Commission)], *Тезисы докладов на теорет. конференции аспирантов Института государства и права АН СССР и юридический факультет МГУ*. M., 1983, pp. 148–9

Fabrikov, E. M. *Международный договор (его подготовки и оформление)* [International Treaty (Preparation and Formalization Thereof)]. M., 1957. 57 pp. (Moscow State University)

Filimonova, M. V. 'Вступление в силу универсального кодифицирующего договора' [Entry into Force of Universal Codifying Treaty], *Правоведение*, no. 3 (1973), pp. 84–8

Ivanov, S. N. 'Вступление международного договора в силу' [Entry of International Treaty into Force], in *Развитие социальной деятльности Советского государства и права*. (Свердловск, 1980), pp. 32–6

'Вступление международных договоров в силу' [Entry of International Treaties into Force], *Правоведение*, no. 5 (1981), pp. 75–80

Karpenko, I. N. 'Некоторые вопросы участия государств в заключении международных договоров' [Certain Questions of the Participation of States in the Conclusion of International Treaties], in *Проблемы государства и права на современном этапе*. M., 1970, II, pp. 310–21

Kuznetsov, I. N. *Порядок заключения, ратификация и денонсации международных договоров* [Procedure for Conclusion, Ratification, and Denunciation of International Treaties]. M., 1976. 45 pp.

Lukashuk, I. I. *Органы, представляющие государство при заключения международных договоров* [Agencies Representing the State When Concluding International Treaties]. Киев, 1965. 93 pp.

Reprinted in 1966 without change.

'Разработка проекта международного договора' [Working Out a Draft International Treaty], *Научные труды Саратовского юридического института. Саратов*, 1957, I, pp. 3–136

Mironov, N. V. 'Заключение, исполнение и денонсация международных договоров в СССР (Новое законодательство и некоторые проблемы теории договоров)' [Conclusion, Performance, and Denunciation of International Treaties in the USSR (New Legislation and Certain Problems of the Theory of Treaties)], *СЕМП 1978*. M., 1980, pp. 13–40

Международные договоры СССР (Порядок заключения, исполнение и денонсация договоров) [International Treaties of the USSR (Procedure for Conclusion, Performance, and Denunciation of Treaties)]. M., Знание, 1980. 63 pp.

Nyporko, Iu. 'Договоры и исполнительные соглашения США' [Treaties and Executive Agreements of the United States], *Советское право*, no. 12 (1973), pp. 80–3 (in Ukrainian)

Orlova, T. O. 'Юридическая техника в международных договорах Российской Федерации' [Legal Technique in International Treaties of the Russian Federation], in V. M. Baranov (ed.). *Проблемы юридической техники: сборник статей*. Нижний Новгород, 2000, pp. 195–204

'Legal Technique in International Treaties of the Russian Federation', *Sudebnik*, V (2000), 127–38

Tiunov, O. I. 'Об основании юридической силы международного договора' [On the Grounds for the Legal Force of an International Treaty], *Ученые записки Пермского унив-та*, no. 284. *Государство, право, законность*, no. 4 (1973), pp. 175–95

FORM, STRUCTURE, AND NAME OF TREATIES

Belonogov, A. M. 'Исполнительное соглашение как форма международных обязательств США' [Executive Agreement as Form of International Obligations of the USA], *США*, no. 6 (1973), pp. 8–9

Durdenevskii, V. N. 'Международные "исполнительные соглашения" президента США' [International 'Executive Agreements' of the President of the United States], *Советское государство и право*, no. 1 (1946), pp. 55–61

Liashchenko, V. I. 'Структурные особенности текстов двусторонних политических договоров и коммюнике' [Structural Peculiarities of Texts of Bilateral Political Treaties and Communiqués], *Вестник Киевского унив-та. Серия: Международные отношения и международное право*, III (1976), pp. 45–53

Lukashuk, I. I. 'К вопросу о соглашениях, подобных международным договорам' [On the Question of Agreements Similar to International Treaties], *Советское государство и право*, no. 12 (1960), pp. 91–6

'О значении формы международных договоров' [On Significance of the Form of International Treaties], *Правоведение*, no. 3 (1958), pp. 87–94

'О наименованиях международных договоров' [On the Names of International Treaties], in *Вопросы теории и практики современного международного права* M., 1960, pp. 68–87

'Преамбула международных договоров' [Preamble of International Treaties], in *Научная конференция по итогам научно-исследовательской работы за 1958 год*. Saratov, 1959, pp. 42–6

'Приложения к международным договорам' [Annexes to International Treaties], *Правоведение*, no. 3 (1959), pp. 134–6

'*Структура и форма международных договоров*' [Structure and Form of International Treaties]. Саратов, 1960. 131 pp.

Mataradze, L. N. *Форма международного договора* [Form of International Treaty]. Тбилиси, 'Мецниераба', 1971. 59 pp.

RATIFICATION OF TREATIES

Aleksandrenko, V. N. 'Порядок заключении и утверждении трактатов в Северо-Американских Соединённых Штатах' [Procedure for Conclusion and Confirmation of Treaties in the United States of America], *Журнал Министерства юстиции*, no. 7, pt. 2 (September 1906), pp. 64–91

Ametistov, E. M. 'Юридическая природа акта ратификации международных договоров' [Legal Nature of Act of Ratification of International Treaties], *Советское государство и право*, no. 5 (1983), pp. 85–92

Belonogov, A. M. *Белый дом и Капитолий – партнеры и соперники: Принятие США международных обязательств* [The White House and Capital Hill – Partners and Rivals: Acceptance by the USA of International Obligations]. M., Международные отношения, 1974. 199 pp.

Международные договоры США и американский конгресс [International Treaties of the United States and the American Congress]. M., 1974. 26 pp. (Abstract for канд. юридических наук, MGIMO)

'Об особенностях ратификации договоров в Соединенных Штатах Америки' [On the Peculiarities of the Ratification of Treaties in the United States of America], *Советское государство и право*, no. 7 (1973), pp. 107–12

Grinberg, A. I. 'Вопросы ратификации в договорной практике Италии' [Questions of Ratification in the Treaty Practice of Italy], *Научные труды МГИМО*, V (1976), pp. 165–80

Kulakov, R. 'В интересах народов: К ратификации Президиумом Верховного Совета СССР пактов о правах человека' [In the Interests of Peoples: On the Ratification by the Presidium of the Supreme Soviet of the USSR of the Covenants on Human Rights], *Советы депутатов трудящихся*, no. 11 (1973), pp. 99–104

Lazarevskii, N. I. 'Международные договоры и народное представительство' [International Treaties and Popular Representation], *Право*, no. 50 (1907), cols. 3207–3217

Litovchenko, O. I. 'Ратификация международных договоров' [Ratification of International Treaties], *Ученые записки Саратовского юридического института* (Саратов, 1970), XIX, pp. 83–91

Nefedov, B. I. 'О юридической природе актов ратификации международных договоров' [On the Legal Nature of Acts of Ratification of International Treaties], in *Международное и внутригосударственное право: проблемы сравнительного правоведения*. Свердловск, 1984, pp. 115–17

Nolde, B. E. 'Законодательная санкция международных договоров в России' [Legislative Sanction of International Treaties in Russia], *Право*, no. 46 (1906), cols. 3561–3573

Polents, O. E. *Ратификация международных договоров* [Ratification of International Treaties]. M.-Л , 1950. 62 pp. (АН СССР. Институт права)

'Порядок ратификации договоров США' [Procedure for Ratification of Treaties of the USA], *Международная жизнь*, no. 9 (1963), pp. 155–6

'Ратификация международных договоров (Защита канд. дисс. О. Э. Поленц в Институте права Академии наук СССР) [Ratification of International Treaties (Defence of Kandidat Dissertation of O. E. Polents at the Institute of Law of the USSR Academy of Sciences)], *Известия АН СССР. Отделение экономики и права*, no. 4 (1948), pp. 283–86; *Советское государство и право*, no. 6 (1948), pp. 98–9

Riiaka, V. A. *Ратификация международных договоров* [Ratification of International Treaties]. Киев, 1983. 25 pp. (Abstract for дисс. канд. юридических наук, Kiev University)

Serbin, Iu. 'Ратификация международных договоров' [Ratification of International Treaties], *Международная жизнь*, no. 5 (1976), pp. 159–60

Sintsova, T. A. 'Деятельность Президиума Верховного Совета СССР по ратификации международных договоров (1957–1967 гг.)' [Activity of the Presidium of the Supreme Soviet of the USSR With Regard to Ratification of International Treaties (1957–1967)], *Вестник ЛГУ*, no. 23. *Экономика, философия, право*, no. 4 (1969), pp. 110–17

Talalaev, A. N. 'Действует ли нератифицированный договор?' [Does an Unratified Treaty Operate?], *Международное право*, no. 1(1) (1998), pp. 207–10; English text: pp. 211–13

Triska, Jan F. and Slusser, R. M. 'Ratification of Treaties in Soviet Theory, Practice and Policy', *British Yearbook of International Law*, XXXIV (1959), 312–33

PARTIES TO TREATIES

Alieva, Z. A. 'Договоры универсального характера и современное право международных договоров' [Treaties of a Universal Character and the Contemporary Law of International Treaties], in *Актуальные проблемы современного международного права*. Баку, 1984, pp. 66–73

Barchukova, N. K. 'Договорно-правовое регулирование партнерство и сотрудничество между Европейским союзом и Российской Федерации' [Treaty-Law Regulation of Partnership and Cooperation Between the European Union and Russian Federation], *Московский журнал международного права*, no. 1(29) (1998), pp. 61–79

Kheine, M. 'Значение многостороннего договора универсального характера для мира, безопасности и разоружения' [Significance of the Multilateral Treaty of a Universal Character for Peace, Security, and Disarmament], *Вестник Киевского унив-та Серия*: *Международные отношения и международное право*, XXIV (1987), pp. 55–8

Kliuev, V. N. 'К вопросу об участии в общих международных договорах: соотношение права и обязанности' [On the Question of Participation in General International Treaties: Correlation of Rights and Duties], in *Вопросы универсальности и эффективности международного права*. Свердловск, 1981, pp. 66–74

Lukashuk, I. I. 'Опыт классификации потенциальных участников международного договора' [Experiment at Classifying Potential Participants of International Treaty], *Научная конференция по итогам научно-исследовательской работы за 1957 год. Тезисы докладов*. Саратов, 1958, pp. 10–13

'Право на участие в международных договорах' [Right to Participate in International Treaties], *Советское государство и право*, no. 4 (1985), pp. 94–100

Стороны в международных договорах [Parties to International Treaties]. M., Юридическая литература, 1966. 151 pp.

Ul'ianova, N. N. 'Многосторонний договор в системе международно-правового регулирование' [Multilateral Treaty in the System of International Legal Regulation], in *Идеи мира и сотрудничество в современном международном праве*. Киев, 1990, pp. 108–24

Общие многосторонние договоры в современных международных отношениях [General Multilateral Treaties in Contemporary International Relations]. Киев, 1981

Vysotskii, A. F. 'К вопросу о содержании понятия регионального соглашения в свете расширяющегося регионального сотрудничества государств' [On the Question of the Content of the Concept of a Regional Agreement in Light of Expanding Regional Cooperation of States], *Вестник Киевского унив-та. Серия: Международные отношения и международное право*, XXIV (1987), pp. 58–62

TREATIES WITH INTERNATIONAL ORGANIZATIONS

Arkhipova, L. B. 'Принцип уважения государственного суверенитета в практике заключения договоров международными организациями социалистических стран' [Principle of Respect for State Sovereignty in the Practice of Conclusion of Treaties by International Organizations of Socialist Countries], in *Социалистическая экономическая интеграция и государственный суверенитет (Правовые аспекты)*. M., 1987, pp. 93–100

Druzhkov, M. P. *Заключение многосторонних договоров в рамках и под эгидой международных организаций* [Conclusion of Multilateral Treaties Within the Framework and Under the Aegis of International Organizations]. Киев, Наукова думка, 1986. 104 pp.

Dzhantaev, Kh. M. 'Некоторые вопросы права договоров с участием международных организаций' [Certain Questions of the Law of Treaties with the Participation of International Organizations], *Тезисы докладов на теорет. конференции аспирантов Института государства и права АН СССР и юридический факультет МГУ*. M., 1982, pp. 168–9

Khaled, Khussein. *Договоры между государствами и международными организациями или международными организациями* [Treaties Between States and International Organizations or Between International Organizations]. Киев, 1985. 21 pp. (Abstract for дисс. канд. юридических наук, Kiev University)

Lukashuk, I. I. 'Международная организация как сторона в международных договорах' [International Organization as a Party to International Treaties], *СЕМП 1960*. M., 1961, pp. 144–54

Magar, S. I. *Международные договоры с участием международных организаций* [International Treaties with the Participation of International Organizations]. M., 1973. 15 pp. (Abstract for дисс. канд. юридических наук, Moscow University)

Malinin, S. A., Kovaleva, T. M. 'Договорная правоспособность международных организаций' [Treaty Legal Capacity of International Organizations], *Правоведение*, no. 4 (1988)

Sardar, Kusein Assad. *Право договоров международных организаций* [Law of Treaties of International Organizations]. M., 1987. 16 pp. (Abstract for дисс. канд. юридических наук, Faculty of Laws, People's Friendship University)

Stepanov, V. P. 'Договоры международных организаций социалистических стран' [Treaties of International Organizations of Socialist Countries], in *Проблемы правоведения* (Киев, 1974), XXVIII, pp. 78–87 (in Ukrainian)

'О праве международной организации на участие в многосторонних международных договорах' [On the Right of an International Organization to Participate in Multilateral International Treaties], *Советское право*, no. 12 (1971), pp. 77–81 (in Ukrainian)

Соглашения с участием международных организаций: их правовая природа и тенденции развития [Agreements with the Participation of International Organizations: Their Legal Nature and Trends of Development]. Киев, 1973. 17 pp. (Abstract for канд. дисс. юридических наук, Unified Council of Institute of Philosophy and Institute of State and Law, Ukrainian SSR Academy of Sciences)

SUBJECTS AND OBJECTS OF TREATIES

Doporov, Iu. 'О роли договоров в международных отношениях' [On the Role of Treaties in International Relations], *Международная жизнь*, no. 10 (1984), pp. 58–65

Fogels, A. G. 'Объект международного договора о взаимной помощи' [Object of International Treaty on Mutual Assistance], *Правоведение*, no. 4 (1966), pp. 146–53

Khvatov, V. Ia. 'К вопросу о субъекте и объекте международного договора о научном сотрудничестве' [On the Question of the Subject and Object of an International Treaty on Scientific Cooperation], *СЕМП 1969*. 1970, pp. 215–31

'Об объекте международного договора' [On the Object of an International Treaty], *Правоведение*, no. 4 (1968), pp. 84–92

Litovchenko, O. I. 'О методе определения целей действенного международного договора' [On the Method of Determining the Purposes of a True International Treaty], in *Тезисы докладов научной конференции молодых ученых 24–25 января 1966 г.* (Киев, 1966), pp. 9–10 (in Ukrainian)

'Экономические отношения социалистических государств и проблемы объектов международных договоров' [Economic Relations of Socialist States and Problems of Objects of International Treaties], in *Сборник работ аспирантов* (Саратов, 1968), I, pp. 67–84 (Saratov Juridical Institute)

Lukashuk, I. I. 'О главных факторах, определяющих основное содержание международного договора' [On the Principal Factors Determining the Basic Content of an International Treaty], *Ученые записки Саратовского юридического института им. Д. И. Курского* (Саратов, 1957), V, pp. 26–38

Mataradze, L. N. 'Об объекте международного договора' [On the Object of the International Treaty], *Советское государство и право*, no. 7 (1972), pp. 114–18

Talalaev, A. N. 'Объекты международного договора' [Objects of an International Treaty], Ученые записки Пермского государственного университета им. А. М. Горького, XIV, *Юридические науки*, no. 4 (1960), pp. 53–64

OPERATION OF TREATIES

Blishchenko, I. P. 'Двусторонние договоры и европейская безопасность' [Bilateral Treaties and European Security], in *Проблемы современной Европы.* M., 1974, pp. 145–59

'Действие международного договора на территории СССР' [Operation of International Treaty on the Territory of the USSR], *Правоведение*, no. 6 (1968), pp. 105–13

'Многосторонние договоры и их значение в укреплении европейской безопасности' [Multilateral Treaties and Their Significance in Strengthening European Security], in *Проблемы современной Европы.* M., 1974, pp. 159–61

'Communication du gouvernement soviétique au sujet de l'attitude prisé par la Russie Soviétique vis-à-vis des traités conclus par les gouvernements russes précédents', *Bulletin de l'Institut Intermédiaire International*, XI (1925), 154–5

Farkhutdinov, I. Z. 'Действие международных договоров в сфере иностранных инвестиций' [Operation of International Treaties in Sphere of Foreign Investments], *Труды Московской государственной юридической академии*, no. 5 (1999), pp. 135–40

Ivanov, S. N. *Действие во времени международных договоров и договорных норм* [Operation in Time of International Treaties and Treaty Norms]. Свердловск, 1982. 16 pp. (Abstract for дисс. канд. юридических наук, Sverdlovsk Juridical Institute)

'Деиствие договорных норм вне пределов срока действия договора' [Operation of Treaty Norms Beyond Limits of Period of Operation of Treaty], in *Вопросы универсальности и эффективности международного права.* Свердловск, 1981, pp. 75–7

'Проблема временного применения международных договоров' [Problem of Provisional Application of International Treaties], in *Вопросы совершенствования социального и правового регулирования.* Свердловск, 1981, pp. 22–6

Kalamkarian, R. A. *Фактор времени в праве международных договоров* [The Factor of Time in the Law of International Treaties]. M., Наука, 1989. 175 pp.

Korobova, M. A. *Расширение сферы действия норм общего многостороннего договора* [Expansion of the Sphere of Operation of the Norms of a General Multilateral Treaty]. M., Изд-во Московского университета, 1983. 114 pp.

Manasuev, A. V. 'Действие и применение международных договоров' [Operation and Application of International Treaties], *Московский журнал международного права*, no. 4(32) (1998), pp. 94–124

TREATIES AND THIRD STATES

Boiarshinov, V. G. and Abragina, Z. K. 'О военных обязательствах СССР по двусторонним международным договорам СССР с другими странами' [On Military Obligations of the USSR Under Bilateral Treaties of the USSR with Other Countries], *СЕМП 1983*. M., 1984, pp. 244–6

Karpenko, I. N. *Международный договор и третьи государства* [International Treaty and Third States]. M., 1972. 24 pp. (Abstract to канд. дисс., Institute of State and Law, USSR Academy of Sciences)

'Понятие 'третьего государства' в международном праве' [Concept of 'Third State' in International Law], in *Проблемы государства и права на современном этапе*. M., 1971, III, pp. 205–12

Korobova, M. A. *Общий многосторонний договор и неучаствующие государства* [General Multilateral Treaty and Non-Participating States]. M., 1979. 21 pp. (Abstract for дисс. канд. юридческих наук, Moscow University)

'Общий многосторонний договор, международный обычай и не участвующие в договоре государства' [General Multilateral Treaty, International Custom, and States Not Participating in the Treaty], *СЕМП 1981*. M., 1982, pp. 93–109

'Понятие третьего государства в праве международных договоров' [Concept of Third State in the Law of International Treaties], *Вестник МГУ. Право*, no. 5 (1969), pp. 68–77

'Принцип нераспространения действия международного договора на третьи государства (pacta tertia nec nocent nec prosunt)' [Principle of Not Extending Operation of International Treaty to Third States], in *Сборник аспирантских статей 'Актуальные проблемы правовой науки'*. M., 1970, pp. 89–110

'Юридические основания прав и обязанностей государств, не участвующих в общем многостороннем договоре' [Legal Grounds for Rights and Duties of States Not Participating in General Multilateral Treaty], in *Международное право и современность*. Тбилиси, 1984, pp. 152–67

Pereterskii, I. S. 'Значение международного договора для третьего (не заключившего этот договор) государства' [Significance of International Treaty for Third State (Which Has Not Concluded this Treaty)], *Советское государство и право*, no. 4 (1957), pp. 71–80

Transl.: *Revista espanola de derecho internacional*, no. 3 (1957), pp. 642–8

Rozenblium, B. D. 'О распространении действия международных договоров, заключенных Союзом ССР и отдельными республиками, на вновь вступающие в СССР республики' [On Extending the Operation of

International Treaties Concluded by the USSR and Individual Republics to Republics Newly Entering the USSR], *Советское право*, no. 5 (1927), pp. 98–107

Volosov, M. E. 'К вопросу об отказе от прав и выгод, представляемых государствами, не участвующими в международных договорах' [On the Question of Renunciation of Rights and Advantages Granted to States Not Participating in International Treaties], *Сборник аспирантских работ.* Свердловск, 1969, VIII, pp. 64–70

RESERVATIONS TO TREATIES

Borisov, C. [Krylov, S. B.], 'Суверенное право государств-участников многосторонних договоров заявлять оговорки' [Sovereign Right of States-Participants of Multilateral Treaties to Declare Reservations], *Советское государство и право*, no. 4 (1952), pp. 54–69

Durdenevskii, V. N. 'К вопросу об оговорках в международных договорах' [On the Question of Reservations to International Treaties], *Советское государство и право*, no. 4 (1956), pp. 97–100

Transl.: *Rechtswissenschaftlicher Informationsdienst,* no. 6 (1957), pp. 163–6

'Согласие сторон при оговорках в международных договорах' [Consent of Parties in Event of Reservations to International Treaties], *Вестник МГУ, Серия общественных наук*, no. 4 (1951), pp. 93–102

Transl.: *Soviet Press*, no. 3 (1951), pp. 3–4, 45

Filippov, S. V. *Оговорки в теории и практике международного договора* [Reservations in the Theory and Practice of the International Treaty]. M., 1958. 102 pp.

Оговорки в теории и практике международного договора [Reservations in the Theory and Practice of the International Treaty]. M., 1959. 15 pp. (Abstract of канд. днсс., Moscow State Institute of International Relations, Chair of International Law)

'Возникновение и развитие института оговорок к многосторонним договорам [Arising and Development of Institution of Reservations to Multilateral Treaties], *СЕМП 1960.* M., 1961, pp. 232–40

'Институт оговорок к многосторонним договорам в практике Советского государства' [Institution of Reservations to Multilateral Treaties in the Practice of the Soviet State], *Вестник МГУ, серия X. Право*, no. 3 (1960), pp. 58–72

'Оговорка в международном праве' [Reservation in International Law], *Правоведение*, no. 5 (1972), pp. 84–92

'Оговорки к многосторонним договорам в практике развивающихся стран'[Reservations to Multilateral Treaties in the Practice of Developing Countries], *Труды ун-та Дружбы народов им. Патриса Лумумбы, т. 20. Экономика и право.* M., 1967, II, pp. 85–106

Оговорки к многосторонним международным договорам [Reservations to Multilateral International Treaties]. M., 1963. 15 pp. (Abstract of канд. дисс., Moscow State University, Law Faculty)

'Советский Союз и оговорки к многосторонним договорам' [The Soviet Union and Reservations to Multilateral Treaties], *СЕМП 1959*. M., 1960, pp. 126–41

Meleshnikov, A. V. 'Оговорки и отсылки международного права и российского законодательства' [Reservations and References to International Law and Russian Legislation], in V. M. Baranov (ed.), *Проблемы юридической техники: сборник статей*. Нижний Новгород, 2000, pp. 425–39

Mukhammed, Kasem Bulad. *Теория и практика применения института оговорки к международным договорам* [Theory and Practice of Institution of Reservations to International Treaties]. M., 1987. 15 pp. (Abstract for дисс. канд. юридических наук, People's Friendship University)

Shutak, I. D. *Правовые оговорки в доктрине международного права* [Legal Reservations in the Doctrine of International Law]. Spb., Алетея, 1999. 251 pp.

Spivakova, T. I. 'Оговорки и заявления в договорной практике Российской Федерации' [Reservations and Statements in the Treaty Practice of the Russian Federation], *Московский журнал международного права*, no. 3(31) (1998), pp. 137–47

Tsaga, Z. 'Правовое значение оговорок к многосторонным договорам и возражений' [Legal Significance of Reservations to Multilateral Treaties and Objections], in G. I. Tunkin (ed.), *Проблемы международного права*. M., 1961

Zharskii, A. V. 'Reservations to International Treaties in CIS Practice', *Sudebnik*, IV (1999), 519–603

DOCTRINE OF CHANGED CIRCUMSTANCES

Baikov, A. L. *Правовое значение оговорки rebus sic stantibus в международных отношениях* [Legal Significance of the Reservation *rebus sic stantibus* in International Relations]. M., Типо-лит. В. Ф. Рихтер, 1916. 91 pp.

Bonucci, A. 'Оговорка 'rebus sic stantibus' в международном праве' [Reservation 'rebus sic stantibus' in International Law], *Журнал Министерства юстиции*, no. 10, pt. 2 (December 1910), pp. 234–41

Chekharin, Iu. E. 'К вопросу о коренном изменении обстоятельств в праве международных договоров' [On the Question of a Fundamental Change of Circumstances in the Law of International Treaties], *Научные труды Дипломатической Академии МИД СССР*, VI (1980), pp. 152–8

Karaulov, L. 'Принцип неизменности обстоятельств в межгосударственной практике' [Principle of Immutability of Circumstances in Inter-State Practice], in *Общественно-политические проблемы развивающихся стран*. M., 1975, pp. 8–11

Korovin, E. A. 'Оговорка rebus sic stantibus в международной практике РСФСР' [Reservation rebus sic stantibus in the International Practice of the RSFSR], *Советское право*, no. 3 (1923), pp. 53–7

Kovalev, F. N. 'Коренное изменение обстоятельств (Доктрина и практика)' [Fundamental Change of Circumstances (Doctrine and Practice)], *Советское государство и право*, no. 3 (1970), pp. 66–74

Ladyzhenskii, A. M. 'Международные договоры и оговорка относительно 'rebus sic stantibus' [International Treaties and the Clause relating to 'rebus sic stantibus'], *Юридический вестник*, no. 10(2) (1915), pp. 34–58

'Оговорка об изменившихся обстоятельствах в советском праве' [Reservation Concerning Changed Circumstances in Soviet Law], *Право и жизнь*, no. 2–3 (1925), pp. 11–20

Tiunov, O. I. 'Взгляды русских юристов на истоки обязательности международных договоров и основания оговорки rebus sic stantibus' [View of Russian Jurists on the Sources of the Obligatoriness of International Treaties and the Grounds for the Reservation rebus sic stantibus], *Ученые записки Пермского гос. унив-та*, no. 264 (1972), pp. 173–87

Zeits, A. G. Влияние изменившихся обстоятельств на силу договора [Influence of Changed Circumstances on the Force of a Treaty]. *Иркутск, Изд. 'Власть труда'*, 1928

VALIDITY OF TREATIES

Aleksandrov, R. 'Ничтожность международного договора' [Nullity of International Treaty], *Международная жизнь*, no. 3 (1974), pp. 153–4

On the 1938 Munich Agreement.

Anisimov, L. N. and Mazurov, V. K. 'Недействительность (ничтожность) Мюнхенского соглашения' [Invalidity (Nullity) of the Munich Agreement], *Правоведение*, no. 5 (1975), pp. 80–6

Kais, Adnan Abdel-Karim. *Международная противоправность Кэмп-Дэвидских соглашений* [International Unlawfulness of Camp-David Agreements]. Киев, 1985. 23 pp. (Abstract for дисс. канд. юридических наук, Kiev University)

Lazarev, M. I. 'Признание недействительными империалистических договоров в международной практике СССР' [Deeming Invalid Imperialist Treaties in the International Practice of the USSR], *Ученые записки Института международных отношений*, II (M., 1958), pp. 122–42

'Признание недействительными империалистических противоправных договоров' [Deeming Invalid Imperialist Unlawful Treaties], *Труды Института права АН СССР* (M., 1952), I, pp. 42–77

Shatrov, V. P. 'Борьба африканских государств против неравноправных договоров за упрочение международной законности' [Struggle of African States Against Unequal Treaties for the Stability of International Legality], in *Международно-правовые проблемы стран Африки*. M., 1989, pp. 12–45

and Shiltakh, V. Kh. *Неправомерные договоры и международное право: Учебное пособие* [Unlawful Treaties and International Law: Instructional Manual]. M., Изд-во УДН, 1986. 59 pp.

Shcherba, G. A. 'Делимость положений международного договора в случае его недействительности' [Separability of Provisions of International Treaty in Event of Invalidity Thereof], *СЕМП 1977*. M., 1979, pp. 252–60

Shurshalov, V. M. *Основания действительности международных договоров* [Grounds for the Validity of International Treaties]. M., 1957. 230 pp. (USSR Academy of Sciences, Institute of State and Law)

Taksher, I. 'Признание договоров недействтельными' [Deeming Treaties to be Invalid], *Советское право*, no. 4 (1960), pp. 87–91 (in Ukrainian)

Talalaev, A. N. 'Ничтожность тайн (к 10-летию объявления недействительными Съездом народных депутатов СССР секретных протоколов с Германией)' [Nullity of Secrecy (On the Tenth Anniversary of Declaring Invalid by the Congress of People's Deputies of the USSR the Secret Protocols with Germany)], *Московский журнал международного права*, no. 4(36) (1999), pp. 119–26

'О действительности международных договоров' [On the Validity of International Treaties], *Советское государство и право*, no. 6 (1960), pp. 114–19

TREATIES AND *JUS COGENS*

Karpenko, I. N. 'Императивные нормы (jus cogens) и их воплощение в международных договорах' [Imperative Norms (jus cogens) and Their Embodiment in International Treaties], *СЕМП 1970*. M., 1972, pp. 204–10

Litovchenko, O. I. 'Единство воли и императивность основных принципов в международных договорах социалистических государств' [Unity of Will and Imperativeness of Basic Principles in International Treaties of Socialist States], *Ученые записки Саратовского юридического института* (Киев, 1966), XIV, pp. 130–7

EXTINCTIVE PRESCRIPTION AND TREATIES

Esaian, A. A. 'К проблеме давности в международном праве' [On the Problem of Limitations in International Law], *Вестник Ереванского унив-та. Общественные науки*, no. 2 (1968), pp. 19–35

Piradov, A. S. *Сроки, предусмотренные в мирных договорах 1947 г. с Италией, Румынией, Болгарией, Венгрией и Финляндией* [Periods Provided for in Peace Treaties of 1947 with Italy, Romania, Bulgaria, Hungary, and Finland]. M., 1947. 20 pp.

INTERPRETATION OF TREATIES

Evintov, V. I. 'Некоторые вопросы толкования многоязычных международных договоров' [Certain Questions of Interpretation of Multilingual International Treaties], *Советское государство и право*, no. 1 (1978), pp. 109–15

Fogels, A. G. 'Различие идеологий и некоторые вопросы толкования в международном праве' [Difference of Ideologies and Certain Questions of Interpretation in International Law], in *Социалистическая революция и правовая идеология*. Рига, 1977, pp. 130–45

Lukashuk, I. I. 'О задачах толкования норм современного международного права' [On the Tasks of Interpreting Norms of Contemporary International Law], *Вестник Киевского унив-та. Серия: Международные отношения и Международное право*, X (1980), pp. 78–81

'О толковании норм международного права международными организациями' [On the Interpretation of Norms of International Law by International Organizations], *Вестник Киевского унив-та. Серия: Международные отношения и международное право*, XV (1982), pp. 47–53

'Толкование международных договоров как средства внешней политики' [Interpretation of International Treaties as Instrument of Foreign Policy], *Советское право*, no. 10 (1979), pp. 77–8 (in Ukrainian)

Толкование норм международного права [Interpretation of Norms of International Law]. Киев, 1980. 20 pp. (Abstract for дисс. канд. юридических наук, Institute of State and Law, UkSSR Academy of Sciences)

and Maksimov, S. E. 'Использование структурно-семантического анализа при толковании англоязычного текста международного договора' [Use of Structural-Semantic Analysis When Interpreting an English-Language Text of International Treaty], *Вестник Киевского унив-та. Серия: Международные отношения и международное право*, XX (1985), pp. 44–7

Pereterskii, I. S. *Толкование международных договоров* [Interpretation of Treaties]. M., Госюриздат, 1959. 172 pp.

COMPLIANCE WITH TREATIES

Abarenkov, V. P. 'Кто не соблюдает заключенные соглашения' [Who Does Not Comply with Agreements Concluded], *США*, no. 6 (1984), pp. 59–63

Ametistov, E. M. 'Актуальные задачи развития советского законодательства о порядке исполнении международных договоров СССР' [Urgent Tasks of Developing Soviet Legislation on the Procedure for the Performance of International Treaties of the USSR], *Вестник Киевского унив-та. Серия: Международные отношения и международное право*, XXVIII (1989), pp. 75–82

Butkevich, V. G. 'Вопросы применения международных договоров в советских судах (Исторический очерк)' [Questions of Application of International Treaties in Soviet Courts (Historical Survey)], *Вестник Киевского унив-та. Серия: Международные отношения и международное право*, IV (1977), pp. 77–87

'Исполнение международных договоров' [Performance of International Treaties], in *Проблемы реализации норм международного права*. Свердловск, 1989, pp. 12–25

Durdenevskii, V. N. and Krylov, S. B. 'Нарушение империалистическими государствами принципа соблюдения международных договоров' [Violation by Imperialist States of Principles of Compliance with International Treaties], *Международная жизнь*, no. 2(1955), pp. 64–71

Dzhebrin, D. 'Конституционные гарантии исполнения международных договоров' [Constitutional Guarantees of Performance of International Treaties], *Вестник Киевского унив-та Серия: Международные отношения и международное право*, XVIII (1984), pp. 54–7

Ignatenko, G. V. 'Акты о порядке исполнения международных договоров СССР в механизме реализации международно-правовых норм' [Acts on the Procedure for the Performance of International Treaties of the USSR in the Mechanism of the Realization of International Legal Norms], in *Проблемы реализации норм международного права*. Свердловск, 1989, pp. 12–25

'XXVII Съезд КРСС и актуальные вопросы исполнения международных договоров СССР' [XXVII Congress of the CPSU and Urgent Questions of the Performance of International Treaties of the USSR], in *Исполнение международных договоров в СССР: Вопросы теории и практики. Межвузовский сборник научных трудов*. Свердловск, 1986, pp. 4–11

Kasenova, M. B. *Исполнение международно-правовых договорных норм в СССР* [Performance of International Legal Treaty Norms in the USSR]. M., 1987. 25 pp. (Abstract for дисс. канд. юридических наук, Institute of State and Law, USSR Academy of Sciences)

'Некоторые вопросы внутригосударственного механизма исполнения норм международных договоров СССР' [Certain Questions of the Intra-State Mechanism for the Performance of Norms of International Treaties of the USSR], in *Тезисы докладов на теорет. конференции аспирантов Института государства и права АН СССР*. M., 1985, pp. 22–5

Kliuchnikov, Iu. V. 'Проблема гарантии' [Problem of Guarantee], *Международная летопись*, no. 10-11 (1925), pp. 34–95

Kliuev, V. N. 'Договоры по вопросам международной безопасности: меры, содействующие их реализации' [Treaties with Regard to Questions of International Security: Measures Facilitating Realization Thereof], in *Проблемы реализации норм международного права*. Свердловск, 1989, pp. 62–9

Kotliarov, I. I. 'Правовые вопросы контроля за соблюдением международных обязательств' [Legal Questions of Control Over Compliance with International Obligations], *Международное сотрудничество и международное право*. M., 1977, pp. 40–9

Kurdiukov, G. I. 'О целях и интересах государств при исполнении норм международных договоров' [On the Purposes and Interests of States When Performing Norms of International Treaties], in *Исполнение международных договоров в СССР: Вопросы теории и практики. Межвузовский сборник научных трудов*. Свердловск, 1986, pp. 27–36

Marochkin, S. Iu. 'Применение в СССР норм международного договоров (К разработке проблем)' [Application in the USSR of Norms of International Treaties (Towards Working Out the Problems)], in *Проблемы реализации норм международного права*. Свердловск, 1989a, pp. 4–11

'Юридические основания и практика применения судами международных договоров при разрешения гражданских дел' [Legal Grounds and Practice of Application by Courts of International Treaties When Settling Civil Cases], in *Проблемы реализации норм международного права*. Свердловск, 1989b, pp. 99–108

Mironov, N. V. 'Институт исполнения международных договоров в советском праве' [Institution of Performance of International Treaties in

Soviet Law], in *Исполнение международных договоров в СССР: Вопросы теории и практики. Межвузовский сборник научных трудов*. Свердловск, 1986, pp. 12–22

'Правовая система внутригосударственного обеспечения исполнения международных договоров в СССР' [Legal System of Internal Provision for Performance of International Treaties in the USSR], *Научные труды Дипломатической академии МИД СССР*, VIII (1980), pp. 23–41

Pereterskii, I. S. 'Понятие гарантии в международном праве' [Concept of Guarantee in International Law], *Советское государство и право*, no. 9 (1956), pp. 45–54

Rubanov, A. A. 'Теоретические аспекты исполнения международных договоров СССР, влияющих на советскую правовую систему' [Theoretical Aspects of Performance of International Treaties of the USSR Influencing the Soviet Legal System], in *Исполнение международных договоров в СССР: Вопросы теории и практики. Межвузовский сборник научных трудов*. Свердловск, 1986, pp. 22–7

Rykov, V. E. 'Роль правительства Индии в исполнении международных договоров' [Role of the Government of India in the Performance of International Treaties], in *Проблемы реализации норм международного права*. Свердловск, 1989, pp. 135–42

Shtein, B. E. 'Гарантийный договор' [Guarantee Treaty], *Большевик*, no. 13-14 (1925), pp. 85–96

Shurshalov, V. M. 'Юридическое содержание принципа pacta sunt servanda и его реализация в международных отношениях' [Legal Content of Principle pacta sunt servanda and Realization Thereof in International Relations], *СЕМП 1958*. M., 1959, pp. 150–63

Sokolov, V. A. 'О контроле выполнения взаимных обязательств в двусторонних соглашениях СССР с иностранными государствами' [On Control of the Fulfilment of Mutual Obligations in Bilateral Agreements of the USSR with Foreign States], *СЕМП 1968*. M., *1969*, pp. 343–5

Stepanenko, V. I. 'Влияние международных договоров на расширение сферы уголовной юрисдикции' [Influence of International Treaties on Expansion of Sphere of Criminal Jurisdiction], in *Проблемы реализации норм международного права*. Свердловск, 1989, pp. 99–108

Suvorova, V. Ia. 'Применение мер в случае нарушения международного договора СССР другими его участниками (теоретический аспект)' [Application of Measures in Event of Violation of International Treaty of USSR by Other Participants Thereof (Theoretical Aspects)], in *Исполнение международных договоров в СССР: Вопросы теории и практики. Межвузовский сборник научных трудов*. Свердловск, 1986, pp. 44–51

Talalaev, A. N. 'Незыблемость международных обязательств' [Immutability of International Obligations], *Международная жизнь*, no. 4 (1981), pp. 127–32

Tiunov, O. I. 'Значение средств обеспечения международных договоров в создании безопасного мира' [Significance of Means for Securing

International Treaties in Creation of Safe World], in *Всеобъемлющая система международной безопасности и международное право*. M., 1987, pp. 87–90

'Международно-правовые средства реализации международных договоров' [International Legal Means of Realization of International Treaties], in *Вопросы универсальности и эффективности международного права*. Свердловск, 1981, pp. 27–37

'О несостоятельности буржуазных концепций об основании обязательной силы международных договоров и нормы pacta sunt servanda' [On the Unfoundedness of Bourgeois Conceptions on the Grounds for the Obligatory Force of International Treaties and the Norms pacta sunt servanda], *Ученые записки Пермского унив-та*, т. 300, no. 5 (1974), pp. 106–37

Принцип соблюдения договоров в международном праве [The Principle of Compliance with Treaties in International Law]. Пермь, 1976

'Понятие и классификация средств обеспечения международных договоров' [Concept and Classification of Means of Securing International Treaties], in *Теоретические вопросы советского строительства*. Пермь, 1985, pp. 70–82

СССР и обеспечение международных договоров. Учебное пособие по спец. курсу [USSR and Ensuring International Treaties. Instructional Manual for a Special Course]. Perm, 1986. 88 pp.

СССР и обеспечение международных договоров. Учебное пособие [USSR and Ensuring International Treaties. Instructional Manual]. Иркутск, 1989. 148 pp.

'Средства обеспечения международных договоров (понятие и классификация)' [Means of Ensuring International Treaties (Concept and Classification)], in *Исполнение международных договоров в СССР: Вопросы теории и практики. Межвузовский сборник научных трудов*. Свердловск, 1986, pp. 37–44

Tunkin, G. I. 'Беззастенчивое нарушение международных соглашений и норм международного права' [Brazen Violation of International Agreements and Norms of International Law], *Советское государство и право*, no. 9 (1951), pp. 49–61

Zakharova, N. V. *Выполнение обязательств, вытекающих из международного договора* [Fulfilment of Obligations Arising from International Treaty]. M., Наука, 1987. 140 pp.

APPLICATION OF TREATIES IN JUDICIAL AND ARBITRAL PROCEEDINGS

Galenskaia, L. N. 'Применение международных договоров в арбитражной практике' [Application of International Treaties in Arbitrazh Practice], *Журнал частного международного права*, no. 3(17) (1997), pp. 3–9 (English text: pp. 10–16)

Rozenberg, M. G. (comp.). *Арбитражная практика за 1996–1997 гг.* [Arbitration Practice for 1996–1997]. M., Статут, 1998. 280 pp.

Арбитражная практика за 1998 гг. [Arbitration Practice for 1998]. M., Статут, 1999. 272 pp.

Международный договор и иностранное право в практике Международного коммерческого арбитражного суда [International Treaty and Foreign Law in the Practice of the International Commercial Arbitration Court]. 2nd edn. M., Статут, 2000. 304 pp.

LANGUAGE AND TREATIES

Evintov, V. I. Многоязычные договоры в современном международном праве [Multilingual Treaties in Contemporary International Law]. Киев, Наукова думка, 1981. 134 pp.

Многоязычные договоры в современном международном праве: Особенности подготовки и толкования [Multilingual Treaties in Contemporary International Law: Peculiarities of Preparation and Interpretation]. Киев, 1979. 31 pp. (Abstract for дисс. канд. юридических наук, Institute of State and Law, UkSSR Academy of Sciences)

'Особенности составления разноязычных текстов современных международных договоров' [Peculiarities of Drawing Up Variant Language Texts of Contemporary International Treaties], *СЕМП 1979*. M., 1980, pp. 161–70

Проблема многоязычия в праве международных договоров' [Problem of Multilingualness in Law of International Treaties], *СЕМП 1975*. M., 1977, pp. 123–33

Laptev, P. A. 'Проблемы перевода международно-правовых актов и новые технико-юридических процедуры их имплементации в правовую систему Российской Федерации' [Problems of Translation of International Legal Acts and New Legal Technique Procedures of Implementation Thereof into the Legal System of the Russian Federation], in V. M. Baranov (ed.). *Проблемы юридической техники: сборник статей*. Нижний Новгород, 2000, pp. 142–61

Liashchenko, V. I., Shvets, A. V. 'К вопросу о средствах связи между предложениями о структурных единицах текстов двусторонних политических договоров и коммюнике' [On the Question of Means of Linkage Between Sentences Concerning Structural Units of Texts of Bilateral Political Treaties and Communiques], *Вестник Киевского унив-та. Серия: международные отношения и международное право*, IV (1977), pp. 40–8

Lukashuk, I. I. 'Язык международных договоров' [Language of International Treaties], *РЕМП 1992*. спб., 1993, pp. 174–85

Maksimov, S. E. *Прагматические и структурно-семантические особенности текста международного договора: На материале английского языка* [Pragmatic and Structural–Semantic Peculiarities of Text of International Treaty: For English-Language Materials]. Киев, 1984. 23 pp. (Abstract for дисс. канд. филологических наук, Kiev Pedagogical Institute of Foreign Languages)

'Проблема аутентичности текстов многоязычных международных договоров в свете прагматических особенностей договорного текста'

[Problem of Authenticity of Texts of Multilingual International Treaties in Light of Pragmatic Peculiarities of Treaty Text], *Вестник Киевского унив-та. Серия: Международные отношения и международное право*, XVIII (1984), pp. 57–60

Timoshenko, N. L. *Лексика советских политических договоров 1917–1985 гг.: функциально-стилистический анализ* (На материале имен. лексики) [Lexicon of Soviet Political Treaties 1917–1985 (On the Material of Nominative Lexicon)]. Киев, 1987. 14 pp. (Abstract for канд. филологических наук, Kiev University)

'Советские политические договоры периода Великой Отечественной войны (Характеристика лекс. особенности)' [Soviet Political Treaties of the Period of the Great Fatherland War (Characteristics of Lexical Peculiarities)], *Вестник Киевского унив-та. Серия: Международные отношения и международное право*, XXVII (1988), pp. 14–19

'Советские политические договоры с развивающимися странами (лингвистические описание)' [Soviet Political Treaties with Developing Countries (Linguistic Description)], *Вестник Киевского унив-та. Серия: Международные отношения и международное право*, XXIX (1989), pp. 71–5

CUSTODY OF TREATIES

Aiueva, T. N. 'Значение института регистрации международных договоров для прогрессивного развития международного права' [Significance of the Institution of Registration of International Treaties for the Progressive Development of International Law], in *Международное сотрудничество и международное право*. M., 1977, pp. 130–5

Регистрация международных договоров [Registration of International Treaties]. Киев, 1978. 23 pp. (Abstract for дисс. канд. юридических наук, Kiev University)

'Регистрация международных договоров в международных огранизациях' [Registration of International Treaties in International Organizations], *Правоведение*, no. 1 (1977), pp. 105–9

'Юридическая природа регистрации международных договоров' [Legal Nature of Registration of International Treaties], *Известия Северо-Кавказского научного центра высшей школы. Общественные науки*, no. 3, (Ростов н/Дон, 1976), pp. 89–93

Aliev, N. I. 'Регистрация международных договоров непризнанных государств' [Registration of International Treaties of Unrecognized States], *СЕМП 1974*. M., 1976, pp. 254–7

Kliuev, V. N. 'К вопросу о депозитариях многосторонних договоров всеобщего характера' [On the Question Concerning Depositaries of Multilateral Treaties of a Universal Character], *СЕМП 1971*. M., 1973, pp. 266–71

Serbin, Iu. 'Депозитарий международного договора' [Depositary of International Treaty], *Международная жизнь*, no. 9 (1976), pp. 159–60

Ulianova, N. N. 'Депозитарий многостороннего договора' [Depositary of Multilateral Treaty], *СЕМП 1964–1965*. M., 1966, pp. 335–46

TERMINATION OF TREATIES

Iosifova, S. *Вопросы денонсации международных договоров* [Questions of Denunciation of International Treaties]. M., 1990. 21 pp. (Abstract for дисс. канд. юридических наук, Moscow University)

Kozhevnikov, F. I. 'Советское государство и международные договоры' [The Soviet State and International Treaties], *Ученые записки Академии общественных наук при ЦК ВКП(б)*, I (M., 1947), pp. 80–112

Talalaev, A. N. 'Прекращение международных договоров в истории и практике Советского государства' [Termination of International Treaties in the History and Practice of the Soviet State], *СЕМП 1959*. M., 1960, pp. 144–55

'Прекращение международных договоров в практике Советского государства' [Termination of International Treaties in the Practice of the Soviet State], in *Отчетная научная конференция. Тезисы докладов юридического факультета* (Perm, 1958), pp. 11–12

Volosov, M. E. 'Критерии правомерности прекращения действия международных договоров' [Criteria for Lawfulness of Termination of Operation of International Treaties], *Правоведение*, no. 4 (1969), pp. 111–15

Прекращение действия международных договоров и договорных обязательств [Termination of Operation of International Treaties and Treaty Obligations]. M., 1969. 17 pp. (Abstract of канд. дисс., Institute of State and Law, USSR Academy of Sciences)

Zakharova, N. V. 'Отказ Советского государства от договоров, нарушавших права восточных стран' [Renunciation by Soviet State of Treaties Violating the Rights of Oriental Countries], *СЕМП 1962*. M., 1963, pp. 126–34

Zuev, V. I. 'Законные права египтского народа (К вопросу о денонсировании Египтом неравноправного договора с Англией 1936 г.)' [Legal Rights of the Egyptian People (On the Question Concerning the Denunciation by Egypt of the Unequal Treaty with England of 1936)], *Советское государство и право*, no. 2 (1952), pp. 60–4

WAR AND TREATIES

Durdenevskii, V. N. 'Довоенные договоры после войны' [Prewar Treaties After the War], *Советское государство и право*, no. 1 (1947), pp. 30–42

Fogels, A. G. 'К вопросу о содержании casus foederis в договорах о взаимопомощи, заключенных Советским Союзом' [On the Question of the Content of casus foederis in Treaties on Mutual Assistance Concluded by the Soviet Union], *Вестник ЛГУ*, no. 23, *Серия экономики, философии и права*, no. 4, (1966), pp. 134–8

Khrenov, V. M. *Влияние войны на международные договоры* [Influence of War on International Treaties]. M., 1952. 21 pp. (Abstract of канд. дисс., Moscow State Institute of International Relations, Chair of International Law)

L-ev, S. 'К вопросу о влиянии войны на силу международных и частноправовых договоров' [On the Question of the Influence of War on the Force of International Treaties and Private-Law Contracts], *Вестник Красного Креста*, no. 1 (1915), pp. 88–100

MUNICIPAL LAW AND TREATIES

Bakhin, S. V. 'О правовой природе норм, унифицированных посредством международного договора' [On the Legal Nature of Norms Unified by Means of an International Treaty], *РЕМП 1998–1999*. Спб., 1999, pp. 45–65

Bartsits, I. N. 'Международное право и правовая система России' [International Law and the Legal System of Russia]', *Журнал российского права*, no. 2 (2001), pp. 61–70

Правовое пространство России: вопросы конституционной теории и практики [Legal Space of Russia: Questions of Constitutional Theory and Practice]. M. (2000), pp. 201–14

Batyr, V. A. 'Актуальные проблемы имплементации норм МГП в законодательстве Российской Федерации'[Urgent Problems of the Implementation of Norms of International Humanitarian Law in Legislation of the Russian Federation], *Московский журнал международного права* (December 1999), pp. 193–209

Blishchenko, I. P. *Международное и внутригосударственное право* [International and Municipal Law]. M., 1960

Butkevich, V. G. *Советская конституция и международные договоры* [The Soviet Constitution and International Treaties]. Киев, 1972. 16 pp. (Abstract for канд. дисс., Kiev State University)

Chalyi, A. A. 'К вопросу о классификации международных договоров в законодательстве Союза ССР'[On the Question of the Classification of International Treaties in Legislation of the USSR], *Вестник Киевского университета Серия: Международ-ые отношения и международное право* (Киев, 1980), X, pp. 64–8

Danilenko, G. M. 'The New Russian Constitution and International Law', *American Journal of International Law*, LXXXVIII (1994), 77–87

'Применение международного права во внутренней правовой системе России: практика Конституционного суда'[The Application of International Law in the Internal Legal System of Russia: Practice of the Constitutional Court], *Государство и право*, no. 11 (1995), pp. 115–25

Durdenevskii, V. N. 'Международные договоры в конституционном праве СССР'[International Treaties in the Constitutional Law of the USSR], *Советское государство и право*, no. 4 (1925), pp. 16–30

Freund, H. *Les rapports des traités russo-allemands et l'application du droit soviétique en Allemagne*. Paris, Marchal & Billard, 1925

Gavrilin, D. A. 'Теории соотношения международного и внутригосударственного права и их отражение в практике государств'[Theory of Correlation of International and Municipal Law and Reflection Thereof in the Practice of States], *РЕМП 1998–1999*. Спб., 1999, pp. 130–40

Grevtsova, T. P. 'Международный договор в системе источников советского внутригосударственного права'[International Treaty in the System of Sources of Soviet Municipal Law], *СЕМП 1963*. M., 1965, pp. 171–9

Henderson, J. 'Reference to International Law in Decided Cases of the First Russian Constitutional Court', in R. A. Müllerson, M. Andenas, and M. Fitzmaurice (eds.), *Constitutional Reforms in Central and Eastern Europe and Russia and International Law* (The Hague, Kluwer, 1998)

Lazarev, M. I. 'О соотношении норм государственного закона и международного договора'[On the Correlation of Norms of a State Law and International Treaty], *Общественные науки в Узбекистане*, no. 5 (1966), pp. 14–19

Lebedev, M. A. 'Международные договоры СССР межведомственного характера'[International Treaties of the USSR of an Interdepartmental Character], *Советское государство и право*, no. 7 (1982), pp. 88–92

Lukashuk, I. I. 'Конституция России и международное право'[The Constitution of Russia and International Law], *Московский журнал международного права*, no. 2 (1995), pp. 29–41

Нормы международного права в правовой системе России: Учебно-практическое пособие [Norms of International Law in the Legal System of Russia: Instructional–Practical Manual]. M., Спарк, 1997. 90 pp.

Makovskii, A. L. (ed.). *Государственно-правовые институты в международных договорах, относящиеся к внутреннему законодательству* [State Law Institutes in International Treaties Relating to Internal Legislation]. M., 1994. 53 pp.

'Осуществление международно-правовых норм во внутригосударственном праве'[Effectuation of International Legal Norms in Municipal Law], in M. M. Boguslavskii, *Международное частное право. Современные проблемы*. M., 1994, pp. 104–12

Margolis, E. 'Soviet Views on the Relationship Between National and International Law', *International and Comparative Law Quarterly*, IV (1955), 116–28

Marochkin, S. Iu. *Действие норм международного права в правовой системе Российкой Федерации* [Operation of Norms of International Law in the Legal System of the Russian Federation] (Тюмень, изд-во Тюменского унив-та, 1998). 200 pp.

Meshera, V. F. 'О международном договоре как источнике советского права' [On the International Treaty as a Source of Soviet Law], *Правоведение*, no. 1 (1963), pp. 124–6.

Mironov, N. V. Иерархия норм международных договоров при их применении во внутригосударственном праве СССР'[Hierarchy of Norms of International Treaties in Event of their Application in Municipal Law of the USSR], *Ученые записки ВНИИСЗ советското законодательства* (M., 1970), XXII, pp. 118–30

Соотношение международного договора и внутригосударственного закона'[Correlation of International Treaty and Municipal Law], *СЕМП* 1963. M., 1965, pp. 150–70

Morozova, L. A. (ed). 'Российская правовая система и международное право: современные проблемы взаимодействие' [The Russian Legal System and

International Law: Contemporary Problems of Interaction], *Государство и право* no. 2 (1996), pp. 3–28; no. 3 (1996), pp. 8–32; no. 4 (1996), pp. 36–47

Müllerson, R. A. 'Националъно-правовая имплементация международных договоров'[National Legal Implementation of International Contracts], *СЕМП 1978*. M., 1980, pp. 125–40

and Chalyi, A. A. 'Проблемы действителъности международного договора, заключенного в нарушение норм внутреннего права' [Problem of Validity of International Treaty Concluded in Violation of Norms of Internal Law], *СЕМП 1982*. M., 1983, pp. 171–88

Neshataeva, T. N. 'К вопросу о правовых системах, регулирующих международные отношения' [On the Question of the Legal Systems Regulating International Relations], *РЕМП 1993–1994*. 1995, pp. 47–63

Pavlova, L. V. 'Международное право в правовой системе Республики Беларусь' [International Law in the Legal System of the Republic Belarus], *РЕМП 1998–1999*. Спб., 1999, pp. 342–7

Petrova, G. V. 'О приведении норм российского финансового законодательства в соответствии с международно-правовыми нормами' [On Bringing Norms of Russian Financial Legislation into Conformity with International Legal Norms], *Журнал российского права*, no. 12 (2000), pp. 86–96

Pshenichnov, M. A. 'Юридико-технические средства обеспечения соответствия российского законодательства международному праву' [Legal Technique Means of Ensuring the Conformity of Russian Legislation to International Law], in V. M. Baranov (ed.). *Проблемы юридической техники: сборник: статей*. Нижний Новгород, 2000, pp. 179–94

Shestakov, L. N. 'Заключение международных договоров, содержащих отличные от национального законодательства правила' [Conclusion of International Treaties Containing Rules Differing from National Legislation], *Вестник московского унив-та. Серия Право*, no. 6 (1983), pp. 36–44

Tikhomirov, Iu. A. 'Реализация международно-правовых актов в российской правовой систем' [Realization of International Legal Acts in the Russian Legal System], *Журнал российского права*, no. 3/4 (1999), pp. 87–8

Tolstik, V. A. *Иерархия российского и международного права* [Hierarchy of Russian and International Law]. Нижний Новгород, Нижегородская академия МВД РФ, 2001. 128 pp.

Usenko, E. T. 'Соотношение и взаимодействие международного и националъного права и Российская Конституция' [The Correlation and Interaction of International and National Law and the Russian Constitution], *Московский журнал международного права*, no. 2 (1995), pp. 13–28

Vasilev, A. M. 'О системах советского и международного права, [On the Systems of Soviet and International Law], *Советское государство и право* no. 1 (1985), pp. 69

Volzhenkina, V. M. *Нормы международного права в российском уголовном процессе* [Norms of International Law in Russian Criminal Procedure] (Spb., Iuridicheskii tsentr press, 2001). 359 pp.

Zimnenko, B. L. 'Международное право и Российское право: их соотношение' [International Law and Russian Law: Correlation Thereof]. *Московский журнал международного права*, no. 3(39) (2000), pp. 162–8

'Согласование норм внутригосударственного и международного права в правовой системе России' [Agreeing Norms of Municipal and International Law in the Legal System of Russia], *Московский журнал международного права*, no. 4(40) (2000), pp. 94–103

Zybailo, A. I. 'Актуальные проблемы применения норм международного права в Республике Беларусь' [Urgent Problems of Applying Norms of International Law in the Republic Belarus], *РЕМП 1998–1999*. Спб., 1999, pp. 308–14

TREATY OF THE UNION (USSR)

Brovka, Iu. P. 'К вопросу о соотношении юридической силы обязательств по международным договорам Союза ССР и Белорусской ССР' [On the Question of the Correlation of Legal Force of Obligations of International Treaties of the USSR and Belorussian SSR], in *Тезисы докладов на научной конференции юридического факультета*. Минск, 1966, pp. 183–5

Lukashuk, I. I. 'Советские союзные республики – полноправные стороны в международных договорах' [Soviet Union Republics – Full-Fledged Parties to International Treaties], in *Научная конференция Саратовского юридического института им. Д. И. Курского по итогам научно-исследовательской работы за 1956 год*. Саратов, 1957, pp. 9–14

Союз ССР и советские союзные республики как стороны в международных договорах [The USSR and Union Republics as Parties to International Treaties]. Киев, 1969. 29 pp.

Nechaev, B. N. 'Советский Союз и международные договоры' [The Soviet Union and International Treaties], in *Международное значения образования СССР и актуальные проблемы права*. М., 1983, pp. 37–44

CONSTITUTIONAL TREATIES OF RUSSIAN FEDERATION AND USSR

Abdulatipov, R. G. (ed.). *Федеративный договор: Документы, комментарий* [Treaty of the Federation: Documents, Commentary]. М., Республика, 1992. 79 pp.

Ignatenko, G. V. 'Международно-правовой статус субъектов Российской Федерации' [International Legal Status of Subjects of the Russian Federation], *Российский юридический журнал*, no. 1 (1995), pp. 6

Kolpakova, T. P. 'Конституционно-договорные основы международных и внешнеэкономических связей субъектов Российской Федерации' [Constitutional–Treaty Foundations of International and Foreign Economic Links of Subjects of the Russian Federation], *Журнал российского права*, no. 6 (2001), pp. 80–7

Lukashuk, I. I. 'Об участии совстских союзных республик в международных договорах' [On the Participation of Soviet Union Republics in International Treaties], *СЕМП 1958*. М., 1959, pp. 506–13

Pustogarov, V. V. 'Международная деятельность субъектов федерации' [International Activity of Subjects of the Federation], *Московский журнал международного права*, no. 2 (1992), pp. 12–5

LEGAL ASSISTANCE TREATIES

Bastrykin, A. I. 'Вызов свидетелей, экспертов и вручение документов по уголовным делам по договорам о правовой помощи с социалистическими странами' [Summons of Witnesses, Experts, and Handing Over of Documents With Regard to Criminal Cases Under Treaties on Legal Assistance with Socialist Countries], *Правоведение*, no. 2 (1988), pp. 65–9

'Исполнение договоров о правовой помощи, заключенных СССР с другими социалистическими государствами (Уголовно–процессуальные проблемы)' [Performance of Treaties on Legal Assistance Concluded by the USSR with Other Socialist States (Criminal Procedure Problems)], in *Исполнение международных договоров СССР: Вопросы теории и практики.* Свердловск, 1986, pp. 109–18

'Применение процессуальных норм при оказании правовой помощи по международным договорам' [Application of Procedural Norms When Rendering Legal Assistance Under International Treaties], *Ученые записки Тартуского унив-та*, no. 849 (1989), pp. 17–26

Biriukov, P. N. 'Выдача преступников: международные договоры и законодательство Российской Федерации' [Extradition of Criminals: International Treaties and Legislation of the Russian Federation], *РЕМП 1998–1999.* Спб., 1999

Butler, W. E. 'Recognition and Enforcement of Russian Judicial Decisions: A New Treaty', *Sudebnik*, III (1998), 303–17

'Draft Convention Between the Russian Federation and the United Kingdom of Great Britain and Northern Ireland on the Mutual Recognition and Execution of Judicial Decisions Regarding Civil and Trade Cases', *Sudebnik*, I (1996), 299–330

Prepared by W. E. Butler, J. Carver, L. Collins, V. Lowe, A. L. Makovskii, N. I. Marysheva, and A. A. Rubanov

Marysheva, N. I. 'Международная правовая помощь и ее виды' [International Legal Assistance and the Types Thereof], in N. I. Marysheva (ed.). *Проблемы международного частного права (сборник статей)*. M., 2000, pp. 190–205

'Новое законодательство о выполнении договоров СССР о правовой помощи' [New Legislation on the Fulfilment of Treaties of the USSR on Legal Assistance], *Социалистическая законность*, no. 10 (1988), pp. 45–8

'Правовая помощь по договорам России с иностранными государствами и тенденции ее развития' [Legal Assistance Under Treaties of Russia with Foreign States and Trends of Development Thereof], *РЕМП 1996–1997.* Спб., 1998b, pp. 148–60

'Правовая помощь по уголовным делам(Международный аспект)' [Legal Assistance With Regard to Criminal Cases (International Aspect)], in *Проблемы совершенствования советского законодательства* (1989), XLIV, pp. 135–81

Международно-правовые аспекты экстрадиции. Сборник документов [International Legal Aspects of Extradition. Collection of Documents]. M., Юридическая литература, 2000. 320 pp.

Nefedov, B. I. 'Необходимость изменения советского законодательства в связи с заключением договоров о правовой помощи' [Necessity of Changing Soviet Legislation in Connection with Conclusion of Treaties on Legal Assistance], in *XXVII Съезд КПСС и вопросы совершенствования правовых мер борьбы с преступностью*, Омск, 1987, pp. 208–15

'Новый институт уголовного права' [New Institution of Criminal Law], *Вестник Киевского унив-та. Серия: Международные отношения и международное право*, XXVII (1986), pp. 58–63 (in Ukrainian)

On transferring prisoners to serve punishment in home country

Pavlyk, L. 'Договоры о правовой помощи – надежный способ защиты интересов и прав граждан' [Treaties on Legal Assistance – Reliable Means of Defence of Interests and Rights of Citizens], *Советское право*, no. 3 (1990), pp. 71–3

'Подписание договора о правовой помощи между СССР и Финляндией' [Signature of Treaty on Legal Assistance Between the USSR and Finland], *Человек и закон*, no. 12 (1978), pp. 34–5

Razdobarin, S. 'Совершенствование деятельности народных судов республики по выполнению договоров с иностраннымн государствами по оказанию правовой помощи' [Improvement of Activity of People's Courts of Republic With Regard to Fulfilment of Treaties with Foreign States With Regard to Rendering Legal Assistance], *Советское право*, no. 6 (1988), pp. 42–5 (in Ukrainian)

Shostak, E. Ia. *О выдаче преступников по договорам России с иностранными державами* [On the Extradition of Criminals Under Treaties of Russia with Foreign Powers]. Киев, Унив. тип., 1882. 50 pp.

Volozhanin, V. P. 'Исполнение договоров о правовой помощи при оформлении документов на основании решений иностранных судов' [Performance of Treaties on Legal Assistance When Formalizing Documents on Basis of Decisions of Foreign Courts], in *Исполнение международных договоров СССР: Вопросы теории и практики*. Свердловск, 1986, pp. 95–8

TRADE AND ARBITRATION AGREEMENTS

'Anglo-Soviet Trade Pact', *Great Britain and the East*, LIII (1939), p. 347

Bakhtov, K. K. 'Торговые договоры и соглашения СССР с иностранными государствами' [Trade Treaties and Agreements of the USSR with Foreign States], in G. E. Koftov, D. F. Ramzaitsev, and V. B. Spandarian (eds.), *Справочник по внешней торговле СССР*. M., Внешторгиздат, 1958

Benjamin, Peter. 'Soviet Treaty Practice on Commercial Arbitration Since 1940', *American Journal of International Law*, LIII (1959), 882–9

Bogaevskii, P. M. 'Торговые трактаты' [Trade Treaties], *Sudebnik*, II (1997), 871–924

First publication in printed form of the Kiev (1914) edition of author's lectures at the Kiev Commercial Institute.

Butler, W. E. 'Bogaevskii's "Trade Treaties"', *Sudebnik*, II (1997), 869–70

Cheklin, N., Korolenko, A. 'Торгово-экономические договоры и соглашении СССР с народно-демократическимн странами' [Trade and Economic Treaties and Agreements of the USSR with People's-Democratic Countries], *Внешняя торговля*, no. 11 (1951), pp. 14–23

Fituni, L. A. 'О научной классификации и систематике межгосударственных торговых и соглашений' [On a Scientific Classification and System of Inter-State Trade Treaties and Agreements], in *Научные записки*. Moscow, Институт внешней торговли, 1955

Ganetskii, Ia. *Советско-германский торговый договор* [Soviet–German Trade Treaty]. М-Л., Госиздат, 1926

Gefting, V. F. *Новый торговый договор с Германией* [New Trade Treaty with Germany]. М., Г. А. Леман и С. И. Сахаров, 1918

Genin, I. 'Договор о торговле и мореплавании между СССР и Турцией' [Treaty on Trade and Navigation Between the USSR and Turkey], *Советская торговля*, no. 26 (1927), pp. 10–12

'Торговый договор с Турцией' [Trade Treaty with Turkey], *Торговля СССР с Востоком*, no. 3–4 (1934), pp. 3–10

Glanz, R. (ed.). *Deutsch-russisches Vertragswerk vom 12. Oktober 1925*. Berlin, R. v. Decker, 1926

Goikhbarg, A. G. 'Монополия внешней торговли в торговых договорах с иностранными государствами' [Monopoly of Foreign Trade in Trade Treaties with Foreign States], *Внешняя торговля*, no. 8 (1933), pp. 12–14

Grabar, V. E. 'Советско-Германский договор12 октября 1925 года' [Soviet–German Treaty of 12 October 1925], *Вестник финансов*, no. 3 (1926), pp. 99–111

Ivaniukov, I. 'Торговый договор с Германией 1904 г.' [Trade Treaty with Germany of 1904], *Юридический вестник*, CXXXIX (February 1915), pp. 517–32

Kantorovich, A. 'Торговые договоры РСФСР' [Trade Treaties of the RSFSR], *Экономическое строительство*, no. 2 (1923), pp. 76–95

Kaufman, M. 'Торговый договор с Турцией' [Trade Treaty with Turkey], *Советская торговля*, no. 11 (1927), pp. 1–2

Korolenko, A. S. 'Торговые договоры СССР' [Trade Treaties of the USSR], *Внешняя торговля*, no. 4 (1948), pp. 8–14

Lokot, T. V. *К русско-германскому торговому договору* [On the Russo-German Trade Treaty]. Спб., Тип. М. Ф. Александров, 1915. 37 pp.

Mousset, Albert. 'L'accord commercial franco-soviétique', *L'Europe nouvelle*, no. 831 (January 1934), pp. 27–8

Nikolskii, P. A. 'О русском-германском торговом договоре' [On the Russo-German Trade Treaty], *Народное хозяйство*, III, kn. 4 (April 1902), pp. 1–43

Poznanskii, I. S. *О русско-германском торговом договоре* [On the Russo-German Trade Treaty]. Спб., 'Биржевые Ведомости', 1881. 10 pp.

Sobolev, M. N. *История русско-германского торгового договора* [History of the Russo-German Trade Treaty]. Пг., Министерство финансов, 1915. 202 pp.

Znavich, I. 'Англо-советское торговое соглашение' [Anglo-Soviet Trade Agreement], *Вопросы торговли*, no. 5 (1930), pp. 25–38

INDIVIDUAL TREATIES

Adamov, E. 'Брест-Литовский мир и претензии держав Антанты к России' [Brest-Litovsk Peace and Claims of the Entente Powers Against Russia], *Международная жизнь*, no. 6 (1922), pp. 13–17

'Agreement with Sweden', *Russian Information and Review*, II, no. 15 (1 May 1922), pp. 355–6

Batueva, T. M. 'Прохождение договора о покупке Аляски в контрессе США в 1867–1868 гг.' [Passage of Treaty on Purchase of Alaska in the United States Congress in 1867–1868], *Новая и новейшая история*, no. 4 (1971), pp. 117–24

Beletskii, V. N., Boltin, E. A. 'Политические основы советско-чехословацкого договора 1970 года' [Political Foundations of Soviet–Czechoslovak Treaty of 1970], *СССР-ЧССР: Сотрудничество и сближение*. M., Прага, 1980, pp. 81–98

Diko, N. S. 'Межамериканский договор о взаимной помощи: (Пакт Рио-де-Жанейро 1947 г.)' [Inter-American Treaty on Mutual Assistance (Rio de Janeiro Pact of 1947)], *Дипломатический вестник*, 1983 год. M., 1984, pp. 231–3

Gotov, D. 'Договор братства и дружбы' [Treaty of Fraternity and Friendship], *Проблемы ДальнегоВостока*, no. 1 (1981), pp. 13–18
On the 1936 Mongolian–USSR Treaty.

Ioffe, A. 'Советско-Британские договоры' [Soviet–British Treaties], *Большевик*, no. 14 (1924), pp. 68–77

Kafarov, Z. M. 'Международно-правовое значение договора о дружбе между РСФСР и Афганистаном' [International Legal Significance of Treaty on Friendship Between the RSFSR and Afghanistan], *СЕМП* 1982. M., 1983a, pp. 302–7

Принцип суверенного равенства государств в договорных отношениях СССР со странами Среднего Востока (Афганистан, Иран, Турция) [Principle of Sovereign Equality of States in Treaty Relations of the USSR with Countries of the Middle East (Afghanistan, Iran, Turkey)]. M., 1983b. 25 pp. (Abstract for канд. дисс. юридических наук, UDN)

Kalamkarian, R. A. 'Некоторые аспекты международных договоров между СССР и развивающихся странами' [Certain Aspects of International Treaties Between the USSR and Developing Countries], in *Проблемы развивающихся стран Азии, Африки и Латинской Америки*. M., 1974, pp. 13–16

Kamenev, L. B. *Англо-Советский договор и СССР* [Anglo-Soviet Treaty and the USSR]. M., 1925

Khamidullin, R. 'Советско-вьетнамский договор в действии' [Soviet–Vietnamese Treaty in Operation], *Агитатор*, no. 22 (1979), pp. 40–50

Khvatov, V. Ia. *Борьба СССР за обеспечение мира и международного сотрудничества в послевоенных международных договорах* [Struggle of the USSR for Ensuring Peace and International Cooperation in Postwar

International Treaties]. Leningrad, 1955. 15 pp. (Abstract of канд. дисс., Leningrad State University)

Kochanovskii, O. 'К 20-летию договора между СССР и КНДР' [Towards the 20th Anniversary of the Treaty Between the USSR and Korean People's Democratic Republic], *Международная жизнь*, no. 7 (1981), pp. 129–30

Korn, Walter. *Der deutsch-russische Konsular-Vertrag*. Munich, Schnitzler & Co., 1927

Korobovskii, Iu. 'Новые договоры в области международного гуманитарного права' [New Treaties in the Domain of International Humanitarian Law], *Московский журнал международного права* (December 1999), pp. 139–58

Lebedev, M. A. 'Международно-правовое значение договорных взаимоотношений СССР с развивающимися странами в политической области' [International Legal Significance of Treaty Relations of USSR with Developing Countries in the Political Domain], in *Актуальные проблемы современного международного права*, VI (M., 1976), pp. 82–99

Marbor, P. 'Правовые нормы в конвенции об основных принципах взаимоотношений между СССР и Японией' [Legal Norms in the Convention on Basic Principles of Mutual Relations between the USSR and Japan], *Вестник советской юстиции*, no. 15–16 (1925), pp. 594–6

'Правовые нормы в соглашениях между СССР и Китаем' [Legal Norms in Agreement Between the USSR and China], *Вестник советской юстиции*, no. 18 (1925), pp. 704–5

'Правовые нормы в соглашениях между СССР и Германией от 12 октября 1925 г.' [Legal Norms in Agreements Between the USSR and Germany of 12 October 1925], *Революционная законность*, no. 1–2 (1926), pp. 63–5

'Советско-английские договоры 1924 г.' [Soviet–English Treaties of 1924], *Международная жизнь*, no. 9–10 (1929), pp. 62–76

Martius, Georg. 'Die rechtlichen Grundzuge der deutsch-russischen Vertrage vom 12. Oktober 1925', *Osteuropa*, I (1925–26), 443–53

Mazov, V. A. 'Международно-правовое значение договоров СССР и ПНР с ФРГ' [International Legal Significance of Treaties of the USSR and Polish People's Republic with the FRG], *Труды МГИМО: Актуальные проблемы современного международного права*, no. 4 (1973), pp. 71–8

Mersmann-Soest, O., Wohl, P. *Die deutsch-russischen Vertrage vom 12. Oktober 1925*. Berlin, F. Vahlen, 1926

Nekrasova, G. A. 'Новые договоры ГДР с социалистическими странами – важный вклад в европейскую безопасность' [New Treaties of the GDR with Socialist Countries–Important Contribution to European Security], *Советское государство и право*, no. 7 (1968), pp. 117–21

'Первый международный договор между ГДР и ФРГ' [First International Treaty Between the GDR and FRG], in *Проблемы государства и права на современном этапе*, VIII (M., 1974), pp. 323–8

Nikolaev, N. N. 'К 20-летию подписания совместной советско-японской декларации' [On the Twentieth Anniversary of the Signature of the Joint Soviet–Japanese Declaration], *Проблемы Дальнего Востока*, no. 3 (1976), pp. 47–58

Ogryzko, V. S. 'О некоторых аспектах политики ФРГ в отношениях с ГДР после подписания договора об основах отношений между ФРГ и ГДР' [On Certain Aspects of FRG Policy in Relations with the GDR After Signature of the Treaty on Basic Relations Between the FRG and GDR], *Вестник Киевского унив-та. Серия: Международные отношения и международное право* (1984), XIX, pp. 68–71

Rapoport, M. 'Брестский мир и его международно-правовое значения' [The Brest Peace and Its International Legal Significance], *Проблемы социалистического права*, no. 2 (1939), pp. 27–40

Sabanin, A. V. 'Советско-германские договоры от 12 октября 1925 года' [Soviet–German Treaties of 12 October 1925], *Еженедельник советской юстиции*, no. 1 (1926), pp. 7–11

Saltanov, V. S. 'Договоры СССР, ПНР и ГДР с ФРГ и европейская безопасность', [Treaties of the USSR, Polish People's Republic, and German Democratic Republic with the Federal Republic of Germany and European Security], *Ученые записки Азербайджанского унив-та. Серия истории и философии*, no. 3 (1973), pp. 41–5

'Двусторонние договоры социалистических государств о дружбе, сотрудничестве и взаимной помощи и их международно-правовое значение' [Bilateral Treaties of Socialist States on Friendship, Cooperation and Mutual Assistance and Their International Legal Significance], *СЕМП 1971*. M., 1973, pp. 80–95

Pustogarov, V. V. 'Реваншистские притязания Бонна и международное право' [Revanchist Claims of Bonn and International Law], *Советское государство и право*, no. 10 (1985), pp. 90–7

Potomov, Iu. 'Мирный договор или военный пакт?' [Peace Treaty or Military Pact?], *Новое время*, no. 14 (1979), pp. 4–5

Radovich, Iu. V. 'Значение Договора о дружбе, сотрудничестве и взаимной помощи между СССР и ГДР от 7 октября 1975 г. для обеспечения европейской безопасности и сотрудничества в Европе' [Significance of the Treaty on Friendship, Cooperation, and Mutual Assistance Between the USSR and GDR of 7 October 1975 for Ensuring European Security and Cooperation], in *Проблемы безопасности и сотрудничества в Европе*. M., 1979, pp. 79–98

Tarshilov, A. N. 'Договор о дружбе, сотрудничестве и взаимной помощи между СССР и ГДР от 7октября 1975 г.и его значение для дальнейшего сближения двух стран' [Treaty on Friendship, Cooperation and Mutual Assistance Between the USSR and GDR of 7 October 1975 and its Significance for Further Rapprochement of the Two Countries], in *Из истории социалистического и коммунистического строительства в СССР*, I. M., 1978, pp. 91–100

Tavrov, G. [Tunkin, G. I.] 'Атлантический договор и возрождение германского империализма' [The Atlantic Treaty and Renaissance of German Imperialism], *Правда*, 20 September 1954, pp. 3

'Договор подготовки войны' [Treaty for the Preparation of War], *Советское государство и право*, no. 2 (1952), pp. 41–51

Европейские проблемы и Парижские соглашения' [European Problems and the Paris Agreements], *Новое время*, no. 44 (1955), pp. 6–9

Translated: 'The Paris Agreements and European Problems', *New Times*, no. 44 (1955), pp. 6–8

'Общеевропейский договор и международное право' [General European Treaty and International Law], *Правда*, 10 April 1954, pp. 3

Tunkin, G. I. 'Международнонправовые аспекты заключения германского мирного договора' [International Legal Aspects of Concluding the German Peace Treaty], *Советское государство и право*, no. 10 (1961), pp. 179–92

Summary: *Staat und Recht*, XI (1962), 384–87

'О некоторых вопросах международного договора в связи с Варшавским договором' [On Certain Questions of the International Treaty in Connection with the Warsaw Pact], *Советское государство и право*, no. 1 (1956), pp. 98–104

'Парижские соглашения и международное право' [The Paris Agreements and International Law], *Советское государство и право*, no. 2 (1955), pp. 13–22

Ulianova, N. N. 'Международные договоры Советской Украины' [International Treaties of Soviet Ukraine], *Советское право*, no. 11 (1966), pp. 88–92 (in Ukranian)

'Совместное участие Белорусской и Украинской Советских Социалистических Республик в международных договорах в 1921–1923 гг.' [Joint Participation of Belorussian and Ukrainian Soviet Socialist Republics in International Treaties in 1921–1923], in *Проблемы совершенствования советского законодательства и деятельности государственных органов*. Минск, 1969, pp. 26–8

Urtimtsev, N. 'Попытки ревизии договоров: Панама-США' [Attempts to Revise Treaties: Panama–USA], *Международная жизнь*, no. 3 (1980), pp. 116–17

Uryson, I. 'Статьи Версальского договора, относящихся к России' [Articles of the Versailles Treaty Relating to Russia], *Материалы Народного комиссариата юстиции*, no. 15 (1922)

Zakharov, Iu. 'СССР-ФРГ: Пять лет Московскому договору' [USSR – FRG: Five Years of the Moscow Treaty], *Международная жизнь*, no. 8 (1975), pp. 31–40

Zatulovskii, I. Ia. 'Межправительственные соглашения между СССР и НРБ – правовая основа развития и углубления сотрудничества обеих стран' [Intergovernmental Agreements Between the USSR and People's Republic of Bulgaria – Legal Foundation for the Development and Deepening of Cooperation of Both Countries], in *Братская дружба, всестороннее сотрудничество*. Сывтывкар, 1980, pp. 99–106

Index

9 780521 816069